The Streaming of *Hill House*

ALSO BY KEVIN J. WETMORE, JR.,
AND FROM MCFARLAND

The Theology of Battlestar Galactica: American Christianity in the 2004–2009 Television Series (2012)

Back from the Dead: Remakes of the Romero Zombie Films as Markers of Their Times (2011)

The Empire Triumphant: Race, Religion and Rebellion in the Star Wars Films (2005)

Black Dionysus: Greek Tragedy and African American Theatre (2003)

The Athenian Sun in an African Sky: Modern African Adaptations of Classical Greek Tragedy (2002)

EDITED BY KEVIN J. WETMORE, JR.,
AND FROM MCFARLAND

Uncovering Stranger Things: Essays on Eighties Nostalgia, Cynicism and Innocence in the Series (2018)

The Oberammergau Passion Play: Essays on the 2010 Performance and the Centuries-Long Tradition (2017)

Catholic Theatre and Drama: Critical Essays (2010)

Portrayals of Americans on the World Stage: Critical Essays (2009)

The Streaming of *Hill House*
Essays on the Haunting Netflix Adaption

Edited by KEVIN J. WETMORE, JR.

McFarland & Company, Inc., Publishers
Jefferson, North Carolina

LIBRARY OF CONGRESS CATALOGUING-IN-PUBLICATION DATA

Names: Wetmore, Kevin J., Jr., 1969– editor.
Title: The streaming of Hill House : essays on the haunting Netflix adaption / edited by Kevin J. Wetmore, Jr.
Description: Jefferson : McFarland & Company, Inc., Publishers, 2020. | Includes bibliographical references and index.
Identifiers: LCCN 2020008065 | ISBN 9781476678658 (paperback : acid free paper) ∞
    ISBN 9781476638836 (ebook)
Subjects: LCSH: Haunting of Hill House (Television program : 2018–) | Jackson, Shirley, 1916–1965—Film adaptations. | Netflix (Firm) | Streaming video.
Classification: LCC PN1992.77.H348 S77 2020 | DDC 791.45/75—dc23
LC record available at https://lccn.loc.gov/2020008065

BRITISH LIBRARY CATALOGUING DATA ARE AVAILABLE

ISBN (print) 978-1-4766-7865-8
ISBN (ebook) 978-1-4766-3883-6

© 2020 Kevin J. Wetmore, Jr. All rights reserved

No part of this book may be reproduced or transmitted in any form or by any means, electronic or mechanical, including photocopying or recording, or by any information storage and retrieval system, without permission in writing from the publisher.

Front cover image © 2020 Shutterstock

Printed in the United States of America

McFarland & Company, Inc., Publishers
  Box 611, Jefferson, North Carolina 28640
  www.mcfarlandpub.com

To the women who write
(and write about) horror,
first and foremost, Shirley Jackson
and those who followed her.

Acknowledgments

The editor first and foremost wishes to thank the contributors, without whom there would be no book. Their work is insightful and inspiring.

Thanks to McFarland, especially assistant editor Dylan Lightfoot.

Thanks to Loyola Marymount University, especially the William H. Hannon Library and its wonderful staff.

Thanks are due to Lacy, who watched them all multiple times with me. Thanks to Kevin III and Cordelia for giving up some time with daddy so he could finish this project.

Thanks are due to Nicholas Diak, herald of horror scholarship, for spreading the world, and to Ian McDonald, my brother in the dark arts. Thanks to the members of the Horror Writers Association, especially the Los Angeles Chapter.

Lastly, Caveat Lector! Spoilers, like ghosts, exist on every page.

Table of Contents

Acknowledgments — vi

Introduction—Holding Darkness Within: Welcome to Hill House
    KEVIN J. WETMORE, JR. — 1

I. Jackson and Flanagan

The Hunters and the Haunted: The Changing Role of Supernatural Investigation
    STEVE MARSDEN — 15

Hijacking Jackson: Adapting Mike Flanagan's *Oculus*
    FERNANDO GABRIEL PAGNONI BERNS — 27

II. The House

It's Coming from Inside the House: Houses as Bodies Without Organs
    MATT BERNICO — 39

A House Without Kindness: Hill House and the Phenomenology of Horrific Space
    ZACHARY SHELDON — 50

III. The Trauma

Some Things Can't Be Told: Gothic Trauma
    JEANETTE A. LAREDO — 63

Recovery from Trauma in Post-9/11 Horror/Terror of Mike Flanagan's Oeuvre
    AARON K.H. HO — 74

Education, Praxis and Healing
 ELIZABETH LAURA YOMANTAS 85

"A House Is Like a Body": Processes of Grief and Trauma
 DANA JEANNE KELLER 95

IV. The Haunted

Mike Flanagan's Mold-Centric *The Haunting of Hill House*
 DAWN KEETLEY 107

Where the Heart Is
 ALEX LINK 118

The Future Isn't What It Used to Be: Hauntology, Grief and Lost Futures
 MELISSA A. KAUFLER 128

Ghosts of Future Past: Spatial and Temporal Intersections
 ADAM DANIEL 142

V. Gender and Queering

Red Room, Red Womb: Phantom Feminism
 ELSA M. CARRUTHERS 155

The Horrific Feminine: Terrifying Women
 CAMILLE S. ALEXANDER 166

Haunted Families, Queer Temporalities and the Horrors of Normativity
 EMILY E. ROACH 176

VI. Comparative Hauntings

"Came Back Haunted": International Horror Film Conventions
 THOMAS BRITT 189

The Beloved Haunting of Hill House: An Examination of Monstrous Motherhood
 RHONDA JACKSON JOSEPH 200

The Madwoman in the Parlor: Motherhood and the Ghost of Mental Disorder in *Hill House* and *Hereditary*
 MARIA GIAKANIKI 211

Family Remains: Family Bonds Against the Paranormal
in *The Haunting of Hill House* and *Supernatural*
    Melania Paszek   222

"They Never Believe Me": Discourses of Belief in *Hill House*
and #Me Too
    Brandon R. Grafius   233

VII. Horror Makers on *The Haunting of Hill House*

A Ghost Is a Wish Your Heart Makes
    Christa Carmen   245

The Screaming Meemies Resurrected
    Angie Martin   248

What Really Walks There?
    Tim Waggoner   251

Spirits and Mediums: Adapting Jackson
    Kevin J. Wetmore, Jr.   253

Gothic Storytelling
    John Palisano   258

About the Contributors   267

Index   271

Introduction

Holding Darkness Within: Welcome to Hill House

Kevin J. Wetmore, Jr.

Hill House—Then

The consensus appears to be that Shirley Jackson's *The Haunting of Hill House* (1959) is one of the greatest, if not the greatest, novels about hauntings in English. It was a finalist for the National Book Award, has made numerous best ten horror novels of all-time lists, and singled out for praise by Stephen King as one of the finest novels, period. Indeed, on *Paste Magazine*'s "Best 50 Horror Novels of All Time" list *The Haunting of Hill House* is ranked number one as, "the best—and best-written—horror novel of all time."[1] Its influence has been profound and it is held up as a model for aspiring writers of the weird and eerie. I was once part of a workshop of four professional horror writers each teaching the attendees one aspect of writing horror: plot, character, setting and mood. All four of us, unbeknownst to each other, selected text from *The Haunting of Hill House* to use as an exemplary version of each of those aspects.

The book has produced a great deal of scholarship as well. Richard Pascal summarizes the critical consensus: "The familiar view that the psychological drama of *The Haunting of Hill House* traces the ultimately unsuccessful struggle of Eleanor, the focal character, to construct a unified adult personality in defiance of a voracious mothering force embodied by Hill House is compelling."[2] Yet, as Pascal also reminds us, the house is also haunted by "a sex crazed patriarch who had fashioned himself in the image of his omnipotent, possessive and inscrutably willful God": Hugh Crain.[3] Crain built the house, saw a succession of wives die in it, compiled a graphic scrapbook for his daughter Sophie warning her to be subservient to her parents and avoid "lusts and ingratitudes," lest her "soul burn forever, in fire a thousandfold more keen."[4] Crain's absent presence in the house as a distant, judgmental father haunts the novel as much as mothers. Pascal's point is that the house is more than a monstrous mother—it is a monstrous family. The other aspect of the novel that receives critical acclaim is the ambiguity of the haunting. It is never clear if Hill House is actually haunted—the possibility remains that it is all the product of the disturbed mind of Eleanor Vance, the protagonist.

At heart it is a simple tale. Dr. John Montague, a paranormal investigator, rents the legendary Hill House in order to discover if it is actually haunted. He invites a number of allegedly psychically gifted individuals, only two of whom accept the invitation: Eleanor Vance, a sensitive and sheltered young woman who was the long-time caregiver to her dying and demanding mother, and Theodora, a young bohemian and clairvoyant who is indicated to also be a lesbian currently fleeing an argument with her "roommate." Joining them is Luke Sanderson, the nephew of the woman who owns the house. Strange things happen to all four. They see, hear and feel seemingly inexplicable phenomena, much of which seems centered around Eleanor. The Dudleys, a married couple who are the house's caretaker and housekeeper who refuse to be in the house when it is dark, tend to their needs, and warn them about the house. Mrs. Montague, the professor's wife, arrives with her associate Arthur Parker. They hold a séance, yet experience nothing supernatural. Eventually, the other three believe the house exerts a profound negative influence on Eleanor and insist she leave. As she drives down the winding drive, she apparently intentionally drives her car into a large oak tree, killing herself. The novel remains ambiguous as to if her death was due to her own emotional instability, a supernatural influence from the house, or a combination of the two.

MGM purchased the rights to the novel and Robert Wise directed an acclaimed film version in 1963. Jan de Bont directed a widely panned film adaptation in 1999.[5] The story has also been adapted for stage and radio. Enter Mike Flanagan, writer/director of effective, well-received horror films such as *Oculus*, *Hush*, *Ouija: Origin of Evil*, and Netflix's adaptation of Stephen King's *Gerald's Game*. He created *The Haunting of Hill House*, a ten-episode series for Netflix that dropped on October 12, 2018. Netflix referred to it as a "reimagining" of Jackson's novel. Jen Chaney of *Vulture* refers to it as "a non-literal adaptation of its source material."[6] Holly Green of *Paste Magazine* refers to it as "less an adaptation and more of a gutting, all but looting the original book for its setting and character names and leaving the rest for dead."[7] In a review entitled "How Netflix's *The Haunting of Hill House* Betrays Shirley Jackson," Green heaps contempt on the series, referring to it as a "ransacking" of the novel, and the adaptation "egregious and disrespectful," concluding "The Haunting of Hill House was never 'just' a ghost story, but this series is definitely 'just a TV show.'"[8]

A number of critics hated it for its treatment of Jackson's material. Indeed, when I approached horror writers about writing short pieces on their take for this book, several refused and when I explained that even negative evaluations were welcome, they still could not bring themselves to write about the show, so much did they dislike it. An equal if not greater number, however, loved it. Many had complex reactions, loving how the show "remixed" Jackson but finding specific elements highly problematic. Virtually every critic and author loathes the final words of the series and find them to be the closest the series comes to "betraying" Jackson.[9]

That line and Green notwithstanding, critical response was mostly positive, if not glowing. Indeed, Green's final salvo is countered by many critics. *GQ*'s television critic Tom Philip called the series "the first great horror TV show."[10] On *Ars Technica*, Jennifer Ouellette called it "the best by far" of all adaptations of the novel, believing, "even though it veers sharply from the original storyline, there are sufficient nods to the novel throughout to keep the staunchest fan happy" (Green would disagree).[11] Lindsey Romain, writing for *Nerdist*, gushed, "Shirley Jackson is my favorite writer of all time, the book is my favorite horror story of all time, and I still fell absolutely in love with this new version."[12] Romain argues that the show's family drama is "brutally resonate [sic]," "genuinely terrifying," well-acted, and "never feels like a betrayal" of Jackson because of the feminist heart of the series and the quirkiness of the female characters.[13] She also singles out "Two Storms" as a "stunning hour of television (many critics single that episode out as the height of the series for its technical beauty that reinforces the terror and emotion of the episode)."[14]

The series features profound changes from the novel, and unexpected echoes in other directions.[15] Some strike people as more egregious than others. For example, Steve Crain, the oldest son of the family in the series (named after Stephen King, as the character Shirley is named after Shirley Jackson), authored a book entitled *The Haunting of Hill House* about his family's time in the house, from which he reads aloud and the words are Jackson's. In other words, Jackson is erased and her masterpiece is assigned to a male author. Indeed, much of the criticism of the show concerns the fact that even though women are the "heart of the series,"[16] the narrative refocuses and even privileges the male characters. As Jeanette A. Laredo writes in her essay of this volume, "Flanagan's male-centered adaptation of *Hill House* is a stark reversal from Shirley' Jackson's female Gothic novel."[17]

Yet Flanagan does not claim to deliver the definitive version of Jackson's novel. Instead he offers a "remix" that phantasmagorically blends elements of Jackson's novel with a larger narrative about the things that haunt us, in every sense of the word. The show is, in Flanagan's words:

> about life after a haunting, what happens after the credits roll.... When you talk about being haunted or wrestling demons, that is a rich metaphor. We came into this with the philosophy that there is nothing more boring than a normal "ghost." For us, the ghosts that were the most interesting were the ones we create ourselves throughout our lives.[18]

In other words, the "now" of the series is the adult phase of the children's lives, and the series then flashes back to the events of their occupancy that have shaped the time they were first haunted and their mother mysteriously died. This serves as a pretext to explore addiction, depression, family dynamics, infidelity, suicide, mental illness, trauma and loss. It also concerns how we survive individually and collectively after all that. The people we would usually lean upon are also the very people who keep the trauma alive, or as the critic in the *Los Angeles Times* noted: "Each member of the family becomes a living, breathing reminder of the worst time in their lives."[19]

Hill House—Now

The volume is divided into seven sections. The divisions are somewhat arbitrary. Jeanette A. Laredo's essay concerns trauma but deals a great deal with gender. Similarly, the essays by Brandon R. Grafius and Maria Giakaniki both compare *Hill House* to other narratives and engage in discussions of gender, horror and the house itself. John Palisano, in the final section, writes from the perspective of a horror writer himself, but his analysis of Flanagan's adaptation of Jackson's novel belongs equally in the first section. I have grouped the essays by affinity and theme as closely as possible, but the entire book, truth be told, forms a series of intertexts with each other, perhaps more than in most of the collections I have edited.

The first section, "Jackson and Flanagan," considers the relationship between the novel and the Netflix adaptation, among others. In "The Hunters and the Haunted: The Changing Role of Supernatural Investigation," Steve Marsden suggests Jackson's original novel and the filmed adaptations of it all "employ popular fictional and non-fictional discourses around the methodology of paranormal investigation," advancing the idea that the investigations all demonstrate the ironic failing of the ghost hunt, albeit in different ways. Considering the epiphenomena and paratextual elements of film such as advertising, Marsden conjectures a relationship between the text and the context of ghost hunting in period, seeing each adaptation as a reflection of how the culture that produced it regards hauntings and their investigations. Fernando Gabriel Pagnoni Berns sees a confluence of influences and echoes in Flanagan's *The Haunting of Hill House* from his previous film *Oculus*. *Oculus* also focuses on a family, in this case siblings and their dead parents, whose lives were devastated by a haunting in the children's youth. Pagnoni Berns argues, convincingly so, that the Netflix series is an adaptation of Jackson's novel, but also a transposition of *Oculus*, as well as Flanagan's other films.

The second section considers and conceptualizes Hill House itself. Building on the work of Gilles Deleuze and Félix Guattari, Matt Bernico sees Hill House as a "body without organs," producing "fascist and paranoid desire in order to devour those who live within it," and ultimately requires the viewer to question the relationship between reality and imagination. Zachary Sheldon begins with the idea that horror narratives are often occupied with spatiality as a source of fear. Grounding his analysis in the work of phenomenologist Gaston Bachelard and studying the architectural features of the home such as the secret cellar, the foyer, the walls and the Red Room, Sheldon sees in the series violations of traditional senses of space that make Hill House "not sane."

The four essays in section three all consider the way in which the series engages, depicts and processes trauma. First up, Jeanette A. Laredo examines *The Haunting of Hill House* through the lens of modern trauma theory and critique the implications of "fixing" trauma that the series presents with its ending. In "Some Things Can't be Told: Gothic Trauma," Laredo argues the series uses Gothic tropes such as traumatic repetition, fractured storylines, and unexplained gaps in time to represent the psychological trauma of the Crains. "Fixing" trauma, however, comes at a cost, both to the characters but also to the story itself, in which the effects of trauma can be blunted, and are by the rather impossible "happy ending" of the series.

The experience of 9/11 profoundly changed horror cinema, and films post–9/11 reflect the sociophobics of a terrified/terrorized nation as well as become a means by which the 9/11 experience may be recapitulated in a controlled medium, allowing audiences to process the experience.[20] Aaron K.H. Ho surveys scholarly theories of post–9/11 horror cinema, noting conversely that these theories ignore the "optimism and recovery from trauma" present in a number of horror films. Ho then considers how the experience of 9/11 as cultural trauma is reflected in Flanagan's series, and finding an odd stir of echoes with the film *Die Hard*.

Elizabeth Laura Yomantas begins her essay with "Education is the vehicle for praxis and healing in *The Haunting of Hill House*," noting that the three older siblings, having already begun primary education when they arrive at Hill House, can cope, whereas the twins, of pre-school age upon arrival, are unable to process the trauma after they leave Hill House. Using education theory and studying the pedagogy of Olivia, the children's seeming chief educator, Yomantas argues the formative education Olivia provided Steven, Shirley and Theo not only shaped their choices of career but also gave them the skills to process the trauma of the haunting in a manner Eleanor and Luke could not.

Starting with the idea that the haunting itself is symbiotic, in which the Crain family shapes the experience as much as the house itself does, Dana Jeanne Keller's "'A House Is Like a Body': Processes of Grief and Trauma" argues the "Red Room" in Hill House is heart and stomach, as Nell calls it ("Silence Lay Steadily"), but also womb in order to understand "the haunted house as vital matter which affects and is affected by the psychological processes—particularly the grief and trauma—of all beings (alive and dead) residing within its walls." Keller also uses the Kübler-Ross stages of death to examine how the characters process grief and trauma.

The next four essays in the section entitled "The Haunted" explore the way in which Hill House haunts and the Crain family is haunted. The section begins with Dawn Keetley's fascinating "Mike Flanagan's Mold-Centric *The Haunting of Hill House*," a "weird reading" of the "mute matter" of Hill House—the importance of black mold and other decaying elements to the world of the series. Grounding her work in research that mold and other environmental contaminants might give rise to "hauntings," Keetley considers forms of "non-human" life in the house and how they share space with human lives.

Temporality and spatiality inform Alex Link's essay, "Where the Heart Is." Time and space are unstable, proximity and distance interchangeable (or at least not indicative of the relationship between family members) as are inside and outside. Link also cannily observes the series' connection between commerce and hauntings—Olivia and Hugh flipping a haunted house to make money, Shirley fixes dead bodies for money, and Steven makes his living writing books about hauntings. In the end, however, temporality is a "digestive process"—ultimately we are all consumed by time.

Unstable temporality also informs the next essay. Under Derrida's conception of hauntology, ghosts are neither present nor absent and thus both absent and present, just like time. The past and future are both present and absent in the present moment, memories of the former and the promise of and plans for the latter shape how we experience the now. As John Connolly observes, hauntology "connects to nostalgia at the point where the yearning is neither for the past nor the future, but for past versions of the future."[21] Melissa A. Kaufler, using the central figure of the Bent-Neck Lady, explores how "time is out of joint," to quote Shakespeare, in and after Hill House. Nell exists simultaneously in the past, present and future—she haunts herself. Following the late Mark Fisher, Kaufler argues that the series demonstrates how under late capitalism we grieve for lost futures that have never occurred and will never occur. She posits, convincingly, that "Flanagan's *Haunting* utilizes hauntological concepts to demonstrate the loss of future and the expansive range of grief that goes along with it."

Adam Daniel is also concerned with temporal instability and dislocation, investigating "how the series dissolves some conventional boundaries in televisual representations of time and space" in order to convey a haunting, which in and of itself is unstable with multiple definitions. Gillian Beer notes that ghosts are concerned with the insurrection, not the resurrection, of the dead, and that the ghost is an incursion of the past into the present.[22] Daniel demonstrates the incursion of "non-representational ghosts" from the past into the present.

Gender and sexual orientation are the subject of the fifth section, in which three essays consider feminism, the horrific feminine and the queering of Hill House. Elsa M. Carruthers reminds us that Jackson's house was "born bad," but Flanagan's house grew up to become bad, raised, as it were, by William and Poppy Hill. Poppy, like Olivia, is a tragic mother figure, one who is victimized by "The Cult of True Womanhood and Domesticity," the Victorian conception of how women in general and mothers in particular should conduct their lives and run the domestic sphere. On a meta level, Carruthers notes that the Netflix series does to Jackson's feminism and themes what the house does to the mothers in it—make them phantoms, ghosts and shadows of that which was once living.

Camille S. Alexander, alternately, finds much positive in the representation of women in the series. Rather than being the victims, sexual objects or final girls of more traditional horror films and shows, the women of *The Haunting of Hill House* have depth and complexity. "Female characters," she notes, "are elegant and beautiful with somewhat terrifying appearances, casting them as horrific feminine characters," especially in the form of Olivia Crain and the Bent-Neck Lady.

On the other hand, Emily E. Roach in "Haunted Families, Queer Temporalities and the Horrors of Normativity" finds the seeming queer-positive construction of Theo actually is undercut by the erasure of Nell's queer desire from the novel as well as the series positing "the heteronormative model of marriage and childbearing" as the saving grace within the house. Roach conjectures that such a solution problematizes the series' presentation of queerness, as the series is a "representation of middle-class American normativity that is a site of violence for queer people, and one which is literally and metaphorically broken." What is a terrifying phantasm for the straight characters is everyday reality for queer people.

In the sixth section, "Comparative Hauntings," the authors put Netflix's *The Haunting of Hill House* into conversation with a variety of other texts, from international horror cinema through the television show *Supernatural* to Toni Morrison's novel *Beloved*, among others. Thomas Britt posits that Flanagan's series is not just an adaptation of Jackson's novel but "a product of a related, more recent set of influences, which are international genre films about domestic horrors, dreams, and the afterlife," finding the influence of such films as *Kwaidan*, *Kairo*, *El Orfanato*, and *Inception* in the Netflix series.

The next two essays form a fascinating intertext with each other. Rhonda Jackson Joseph compares Flanagan's Olivia Crain with Sethe Suggs from Toni Morrison's *Beloved* (herself based on the historic figure of Margaret Garner, the African American slave woman who killed her children rather than allow them to be returned to slavery). In this fascinating contrast, Joseph considers why mothers are driven to kill their own children, how murdered children return as supernatural entities, and the haunted domestic sphere as the home of the monstrous mother who but for society would not have been monstrous.

Ari Aster's 2018 film *Hereditary* has been hailed as a primary example of what is being called "elevated horror" (a controversial term, as it seeks to define films and television out of the very genre by distinguishing them from "regular horror," which is to be critically looked down upon). *The Haunting of Hill House* is often cited as another example of elevated horror. Maria Giakaniki returns us to the themes of motherhood and mental disorder, in this case to compare their representation in *Hill House* and *Hereditary*. Much like in Joseph's essay, the two narratives present portrayals of motherhood in crisis and allow the creators to use the uncanny to explore the relationship between trauma and mental disorder, particularly as it relates to motherhood.

Melania Paszek compares the series to another television program: the long-running *Supernatural*, seeing in both shows certain affinities centered around an exploration of how encounters with the uncanny and knowledge of a larger paranormal reality affect the family dynamic. She observes that both narratives demonstrate the paradoxical result of the family both growing stronger and more divided as a result of their experiences with the supernatural.

Brandon R. Grafius considers the discourses of belief in *The Haunting of Hill House* in light of the #MeToo movement. The movement demands a shift from how we have decided (and who decides) which stories are credible and whether or not to believe someone's narrated experience. Aligning the series alongside the testimonies of Anita Hill, the victims of Harvey Weinstein, and Dr. Christine Blasey Ford, Grafius finds a patriarchy—one which has set itself up as the ultimate arbiter of what is true—under assault but still dominant, especially within horror narratives. Nell and Luke most assuredly see real ghosts as children, and their parents do not believe them. Steve sets himself up as the authority of the unreality of ghosts, mansplaining to his family what they "actually" experienced instead of accepting the reality of their explanations of their experiences. The essay demonstrates the social context out of which the series has emerged, and how that series comments on that context.

In the final section, I invited several fellow horror authors who had commented on the series on social media to explore their thoughts on the series. In "A Ghost Is a Wish Your Heart Makes," Christa Carmen, whose collection *Something Borrowed, Something Bloodsoaked* features several ruminations on addiction as haunting, considers the nature of ghosts in the series, and how they often reflect the guilt of the individual characters. Award-winning author Angie Martin offers a personal, positive assessment of the Netflix series, discussing the effect of fear and terror it created in her, reminiscent of childhood scary movies and ghost stories. Prolific Bram Stoker Award–winning writer Tim Waggoner discusses "What Really Walks There?," and why, for him, the series is successful at telling a ghost story for people who don't like ghost stories. The editor then joins the discussion to consider Flanagan's series in the context of other adaptations of Jackson's novel, including the two film versions, a radio abridgement, and especially three stage versions, arguing that the medium determines whether or not one remains faithful to the spirit of Jackson's work. Lastly, Horror Writers Association President John Palisano considers the novel and the series as modern embodiments of gothic storytelling.

Jackson described the eponymous dwelling as:

> a house without kindness, never meant to be lived in, not a fit place for people or for love or for hope. Exorcism cannot alter the countenance of a house; Hill House would stay as it was until it was destroyed.[23]

Note that the house was "never meant to be lived in," and it is "not a fit place for people or for love or hope." Jackson goes out of her way to assure the reader that the house is a bad place. Even if not actually haunted by ghosts, Hill House serves as a place of negative energy at which one is left prey to one's own fears, despair and depression. Except according to both the Netflix series and Jackson herself, the house is actually haunted.

The ambiguity found in the novel is nowhere in the series, except perhaps in Steven's denial of ghosts. The series shows again and again real ghosts—not just in the house but the presence of Nell at her own wake and in the car as Shirley and Theo drive to Hill House to save Luke. The episode entitled "Steven Sees a Ghost" ends with skeptic Steven seeing his dead sister Nell in his apartment and wondering (and asking her) why she is there, until she is revealed to be a ghost. The ghosts that haunt Luke and Nell, the Bowler Hat Man and the Bent Neck Lady, are just as real. Sometimes visible only to them, but nonetheless real for it.

The reality of the ghosts leads us to two conclusions. First, that the story itself, as Jackson writes in the opening lines of the novel, is really about the nature of reality. Jackson herself wrote, "No one can get into a novel about a haunted house without hitting on the subject of reality head-on, either I have to believe in ghosts, *which I do*, or I have to write another kind of novel entirely" (emphasis mine).[24] Jackson's novel may be ambiguous, but Jackson herself is not. In her notes while writing the novel she jotted down, "The house *is* the haunting (can never be un-haunted)" (emphasis hers).[25] Hill House is a genuinely haunted house, regardless of whether Steven Crain or the critics think so. The ghosts are both metaphoric, but also real in and of themselves, which makes the series work on multiple levels, as explored in this volume. We live in a reality in which the supernatural is a presence with efficacy in our lives in this novel and in this series.

The second conclusion we must reach then, proceeding from the first, is a disturbing one that Michael T. Wilson identifies in the novel: "The keen irony here is that the house, through its haunting, seems to indicate that death is not the end—the end is actually something worse..."[26] The series shows, terrifyingly, that death is not the end. Terrified of the Bent-Neck Lady since she lived in Hill House, Nell is tricked by the house into killing herself by hanging and learning at the moment of her death that *she* is the Bent-Neck Lady. She relives every appearance of the apparition backwards, this time from the ghost's perspective, and realizes she has been terrifying herself. She spends the rest of the series haunting her family. Like Eleanor Vance, Nell Crain has in a sense always been a ghost.

The series thus terrifies not just on a "just horror" level, with jump scares, music creating tension, use of gore and makeup. The series terrifies on an existential level, on the level of true terror. The show is about how scary reality truly is. The authors in this volume look at the series and, through different prisms, view how it terrifies—usually by what it has to say about our lives today. We are a haunted people. Mike Flanagan has given us not the Hill House purists may want, but he has given us the Hill House America in 2018 deserves.

A Note on Episode Citation for the Netflix Series

Episodes are cited in text by individual episode titles in order to help the reader identify the narrative.

Episode 1 "Steven Sees a Ghost"
Episode 2 "Open Casket"
Episode 3 "Touch"

Episode 4 "Twin Thing"
Episode 5 "The Bent-Neck Lady"
Episode 6 "Two Storms"
Episode 7 "Eulogy"
Episode 8 "Witness Marks"
Episode 9 "Screaming Meemies"
Episode 10 "Silence Lay Steadily"

All other citations are via endnotes.

Notes

1. Steve Foxe and the Paste Staff, "The 50 Best Horror Novels of All Time," Paste Magazine.com (August 30, 2018) https://www.pastemagazine.com/articles/2018/08/the-best-horror-novels-of-all-time.html?p=2. Accessed October 22, 2018.
2. Richard Pascal, Walking Alone Together: Family Monsters in 'The Haunting of Hill House.'" *Studies in the Novel* 46.4 (2014): 469.
3. Pascal, 470–471.
4. Shirley Jackson, *The Haunting of Hill House* (New York: Penguin, 1984), 169.
5. See Steve Marsden's and Kevin Wetmore's chapters in this volume for details on the film adaptations of Jackson's novel.
6. Jen Cheney, "*The Haunting of Hill House* Is Scary but Slow," *Vulture* (October 11, 2018) http://www.vulture.com/2018/10/the-haunting-of-hill-house-netflix-review.html. Accessed October 22, 2018.
7. Holly Green, "How Netflix's *The Haunting of Hill House* Betrays Shirley Jackson" Paste Magazine.com (October 18, 2018) https://www.pastemagazine.com/articles/2018/10/how-netflixs-the-haunting-of-hill-house-betrays-sh.html. Accessed October 22, 2019.
8. Ibid.
9. "Whatever walked there, walked together" is how the series ends. Jackson's famous line is "and whatever walked there, walked alone" (Jackson, 2). Ruth Franklin, who wrote the award-winning recent definitive biography on Jackson wrote of this moment in the series: "When I heard the way the show's ending alters that line, the words 'Are you fucking kidding me?' escaped my lips. The show stares all the bleakness of death right in the face and then pulls back." (Ruth Franklin, "The Haunting of Hill House Finale Recap: Ghosts in the Machine." *Vulture*. October 18, 2018. http://www.vulture.com/2018/10/the-haunting-of-hill-house-recap-season-1-episode-10.html. Accessed October 22, 2018.
10. Tom Philip, "The Haunting of Hill House Is the First Great Horror TV Series," GQ.com (September 25, 2018). https://www.gq.com/story/the-haunting-of-hill-house-is-the-first-great-horror-tv-series. Accessed October 22, 2019.
11. Jennifer Ouellette, "Latest Adaptation of *Haunting of Hill House* Will Haunt Your Dreams." *Arstechnica* (October 22, 2018). https://arstechnica.com/gaming/2018/10/haunting-of-hill-house-offers-chills-aplenty-but-also-tugs-at-the-heart/. Accessed October 22, 2018.
12. Lindsey Romain, "Why You Should Watch *The Haunting of Hill House*" Nerdist (October 2, 2018). https://nerdist.com/why-you-should-watch-the-haunting-of-hill-house/. Accessed October 22, 2018.
13. Ibid.
14. Ibid.
15. For a list of key differences, see Jacob Shelton, "The Book That Inspired 'The Haunting of Hill House' Is Way Darker Than the Show." Ranker.com (October 31, 2018). https://www.ranker.com/list/hill-house-book-versus-tv-show/jacob-shelton. Accessed November 10, 2018.
16. Romain.
17. See Laredo's chapter in this book.
18. Quoted in Ouellette.

19. Libby Hill, "These Houses Are Haunted by Families," *Los Angeles Times* (October 23, 2018): E2.
20. Kevin J. Wetmore, Jr., *Post-9/11 Horror in American Cinema* (New York: Continuum, 2012), 1–7.
21. John Connolly, *Horror Express* (Hornsea: PS Publishing, 2018), 25.
22. Gillian Beer, "Ghosts" *Essays in Criticism* 28 (July 1978): 260.
23. Jackson, 35.
24. Quoted in Judy Oppenheimer, *Private Demons: The Life of Shirley Jackson* (New York: G.P. Putnam's Sons, 1988), 226.
25. Ruth Franklin, *Shirley Jackson: A Rather Haunted Life* (New York: Liveright Publishing, 2016), 415.
26. Michael T. Wilson, "'Absolute Reality' and the Role of the Ineffable in Shirley Jackson's *The Haunting of Hill House*." *The Journal of Popular Culture* 48. 1 (2015): 116.

I

Jackson and Flanagan

The Hunters and the Haunted

The Changing Role of Supernatural Investigation

STEVE MARSDEN

From the beginning, folk accounts of hauntings, reports of supernatural investigation, and their fictional representations have had a complex intertextual relationship. A boom of recent criticism has shown us just how fictions are enhanced by being framed by non-fictional references and conventions, putatively true experiences become fictionalized or gain emotional believability by borrowing narrative devices from fiction, and fictional stories and visual media help structure the public's expectations and individuals' experiences of the paranormal.[1]

Shirley Jackson's *The Haunting of Hill House* and its three filmed adaptations, Robert Wise's *The Haunting*, Jan de Bont's *The Haunting*, and Mike Flanagan's *The Haunting of Hill House*, each employ popular fictional and non-fictional discourses around the methodology of paranormal investigation.[2] Each version parodies the limited views and techniques of researchers (paranormal or psychological), and emphasizes how narrow approaches, narrative presumptions, and preconceived views ultimately fail to capture the complexities required to understand hauntings and their entanglements with family, folklore, history, and psychology. The written outcomes of the studies in each version fail to reflect the complexity of their subjects. Though each focuses on the ironic failures of ghost-hunting, each has been released in a web of intertextual and paratextual relationships that frame its reception in terms of putatively non-fictional paranormal accounts.[3]

Jackson's novel uses and parodies nineteenth century and contemporary supernatural investigation, but her essays on the book's composition and influences act as paratexts that frame it in terms of nonfiction haunting accounts—including her own. The influences, both of non-fictional ghost-hunting accounts and of her own uncanny experiences (seeing a seemingly haunting burned building from a train, and an apparent experience of sleep-writing) enumerated in "Experience and Fiction" have been explored by Melanie Anderson and Jackson's most recent biographer, Ruth Franklin.[4] The recent publication of Jackson's "The Ghosts of Loiret" provides additional framing, offering a non-fiction encounter with an apparently haunted photograph. It also offers new possible non-fictional sources. In *Gothic Realities*, Andrew Cooper argues that non-fictional and fictional accounts of ghostly encounters share devices and techniques in a symbiotic way, in order to gain the status of "'realistic' or 'real'" for their readers.[5] Jackson's essays provide authenticity for her fictional account (haunting the composition of her novel), and show her playful awareness of the line between story and domestic experience. In "Loiret," Jackson, after hearing the first words of a ghost story at a party, sees several changes occur to an old photograph: figures that weren't there appear and disappear. Her husband immediately blames contamination from M.R. James' haunted engraving story "The Mezzotint."[6] Eventually, the phenomenon spreads to other photos, including the illustrations from her non-fictional books of ghosts: "a nun kept looking out the window at Ballechin House," and she could see into the window of a photo postcard depicting Borley Rectory, the site of another famous haunting.[7] Finally, after other uncanny goings-on around the house, she puts her photographs away. She frames her own haunting not with the fiction as her husband suggests, but by reading about "the mystery of Glamis castle" and Borley Rectory and a story about a skull on a mantel, in another gift from her husband, "A book called *Some Haunted Houses of England & Wales*," mentioned three times in the essay.[8]

Elliott O'Donnell, prolific writer of supernatural fiction and nonfiction, was the first self-styled "ghost hunter"[9] He collected these "well-authenticated" ghost stories "taken from the lips of eye-witnesses and transferred to manuscript in as nearly as possible the narrator's own language" in which can be found "Harley House, Portishead: The Black Antennae," notes "from the diary of a gentleman—since deceased" of a poltergeist experience that begins with mysterious violent knocking in the room in which the mother of a family had died after a protracted illness.[10] Among things that cannot be found in that volume are an account of Borley Rectory or Glamis Castle, or a story of a cursed skull. Treatments of both Glamis Castle and the Screaming Skull of Bettiscombe, on the other hand, *can* be found together in *Haunted Houses: Tales of the Supernatural*, which also contains an account of the haunting at Ballechin House and a reference to its report.[11]

Melanie Anderson has explored parallels between *HoHH* and *The Alleged Haunting of B— House* (1899), by Ada Goodrich-Freer (pseudonymously as "Miss X"), a report of a country-house ghost hunt conducted by some persons involved with the Society for Psychical Research, between February and May of 1897.[12] Jackson wrote in "Experience and Fiction": "[t]hey thought that they were being terribly scientific and proving all kinds of things, and yet the story that kept coming through their dry reports was not at all the story of a haunted house, it was the story of several earnest, I believe misguided, certainly determined people, with their differing motivations and backgrounds."[13] While parallels to the *events* reported in *B— House* to those of *HoHH* have been noted, the reasons for their methods and "dry reports" may bear further scrutiny.

B— House is the end of an intertextual debate that began in *The Times*, when an anonymous correspondent accused the investigators of bad practice, alleging that their "experiences" had been caused by narrative contamination, suggestion, fear, priming, and hallucinations.[14] Some investigators "sat up all night with loaded guns in a condition of abject fright; others, there is reason to suspect, manufactured phenomena for themselves, and nearly all seem to have begun by assuming supernatural interference instead of leaving it for the final explanation of whatever might be … otherwise inexplicable." He charges her with suggesting the haunting by telling the history of the house: "in the drawing room after dinner we listened to our hostess, who is an excellent narrator, expounding the story of the wicked major." To Goodrich-Freer's reports of "subjective" visions of two spectral nuns, he noted, "Any investigator, however honest, is tremendously handicapped by this liability to manufacture the very phenomena under investigation." Jackson's investigators mirror Goodrich-Freer's methodological flaws, while her storytelling technique attempts to overcome what makes *The Alleged Haunting of B— House* a failed attempt to tell the story of whatever happened there (and makes, presumably, Dr. Montague's own article a failure).

Goodrich-Freer claims she attempted to limit suggestion by avoiding discussing the house's history or the haunting "with newcomers," a rule which she apparently broke with the *Times* correspondent.[15] Montague also claims to be "most unwilling now to influence" his party's "minds with its complete history."[16] He tries to prevent narrative contamination. They "ought not to be affected, perhaps even warped, by half-remembered spooky stories which belong more properly to a—let me see—a marshmallow roast."[17] However, eager to "see that they were all amused" he does exactly that. Montague's desire to assume the role of father giving a "bedtime story" or professor assuming a "an unmistakable classroom pose" likewise overcomes him, and he begins to shape the romantic storytelling the group's playful banter had begun, leading with a theory of haunting, then telling local folk stories and scandal. The actual "experiences" in the house will take place between ghost story and Montague's "one unshakable solidity in a world of fog": "notes."[18]

As Anderson has pointed out, the party's methods cannot capture the inner reality of the haunting.[19]

Goodrich-Freer preferred something similar for documentation of both subjective and shared experiences and to avoid spreading rumors and planting suggestion: "If anyone had an 'experience' to relate," she preferred investigators not gossip, instead telling her directly, or "still better," she preferred "not to hear it at all, but to receive it in writing."[20]

Montague's wife, a spiritualist and automatic-writer, seems even more closed off from the nuance of experience, her planchette producing mostly gothic fantasies, echoing her feelings about her marriage, perhaps echoing Goodrich-Freer's distrust mediums and "induced phenomena" like automatic writing that offers as much of the normal as subconscious psychology.[21] Still, a legitimate message involving Eleanor sneaks through.

When Luke and Eleanor speculate about Montague's book they wonder if Mrs. Montague, Arthur, and Mrs. Dudley will make it in. Eleanor hopes "he doesn't reduce us to figures on a graph." A glance at the "Conspectus of Audile Phenomena" in the appendix of *B— House* will show the results of precisely this approach.[22]

The group's skepticism about Montague's book might well reflect Jackson's understanding of Goodrich-Freer's exclusions. *B— House* is a dry but densely intertextual bricolage of journals, notes, letters, charts, timetables, spiteful and ironical interjections, and most amusingly, allusions to letters, conversations, and diaries she cannot or will not include, including the details of "induced experiences" of a visiting medium. Written in the context of an English market of personal reputation and standing, and with a pseudo-medical desire to leave specific places and names out, the book is notable for exclusions and suppressions. It would be sixty or more years before most of the blanks could be somewhat reasonably filled in.[23] Fewer people have names than pseudonyms, including its author, "Miss X," herself.

A more modern method of framing the haunting is suggested by a source Jackson does not include by name in her paratextual essays. According to Ruth Franklin, Jackson was reading newspaper reports of the James Hermann teenage poltergeist case.[24] Her reading led her to ghost hunter and psychoanalyst Nandor Fodor's assertion that "Without discovering the sign language of the poltergeist, we can never understand it. The poltergeist is not a ghost. It is a bundle of projected repressions. No psychoanalyst could dream of a more glorious opportunity for the study of psychic mechanisms than that offered by the bedlam in a poltergeist-haunted house."[25] When Fodor wrote Jackson, she acknowledged the influence.[26]

By the time Robert Wise and screenwriter Nelson Eddings adapted the novel, the spiritualism of (now Dr. Markham)'s wife and her hyper-masculine assistant were less in fashion. He is removed and she is made into a skeptic, simplifying a new love-triangle plot, removing comic relief, and allowing a "conversion narrative" of skeptic to believer, common to supernatural fiction and factual accounts alike..[27] It also, through its endorsement of the Fodor hypothesis, makes Eleanor's repression and jealousy more obvious for a moviegoing audience. The film, lacking the failed final report, makes it clear that Markway (who seems even more boyishly thrilled by the idea of a haunting at the beginning) does not finally understand how Eleanor's inner life made her vulnerable. Characters' notes wouldn't reflect Jackson's subjective explorations: likewise, because Markway is unable to hear Eleanor's subjective voiceover, he cannot interpret the haunting as well as the film's audience.

The press kit released to theaters showing the 1963 film helped viewers frame the movie in terms of current supernatural studies. The national publicity campaign requested true accounts of supernatural experiences, to be sent to MGM.[28] In the same document, Nandor Fodor, who had inspired Jackson, endorsed the film, claiming, "Haunted Houses do exist, and the unknown forces and powers contained within these so-called 'Evil Places' are often activated by the human passions of people who come in contact with them." He goes on, "in these days of increasing parapsychological interest. 'The Haunting' is a picture to see and reflect upon."

This endorsement is just one way that it encourages the theater owner to "activate" the audience's "interest" in the supernatural. An article run in many papers details the real hauntings that, it asserts, happened (elsewhere) co-incidentally during filming. Local experts on the supernatural or "reputable mediums," it suggests, might be placed in the theater lobby. Psychic tests might be run before the film. It also lists current non-fictional books on psychic phenomena and psychical research, including those produced by the Duke Parapsychology Lab as recommended reading for the audience.

By 1999, when *The Haunting* was adapted by Jan de Bont, parapsychological studies were less academically credible, and psychic detective narratives were more popular. Duke's Parapsychology Lab, featured in earlier versions, had been removed from campus. Shari Hodges Holt has explored how both Markway and his wife are conflated into an Eleanor who acts as an "assertive psychic detective, who exposes the truth of the haunted house through her empathy with the dispossessed," she gives less attention to the parody of academic psychology that is left over.[29]

Instead of Montague or Markway, whose over-credulous telling of ghost stories to the suggestible was a methodological failing, skeptical Doctor Marrow's narrative contamination of his subjects is part of an unethical psychological experiment. His plot arc is a skeptic conversion narrative. De Bont's film has a complex production history: two available scripts, differ significantly from each other and the finished film, particularly in their treatment of the experiment being conducted by Dr. Marrow and its results.[30] The first, dated July 30, 1998, was written by David Self. The second, dated November 11, 1998, contains significant revisions by Michael Tolkin. The film omits much of interest, leaving only suggestive ghosts of the sub-plot.

Self's script focuses on the ethics of psychological testing: James Marrow is a researcher at Amherst, whose proposed study of "how non-factual ideas take hold and spread among people, and how those ideas grow and change" or "Modelling small-group dynamics in the formation of narrative hallucinations" is considered too flamboyant and not "neutral-seeming" enough by an older colleague.[31] Though the colleague is less concerned with ethics than experimental design, photos in Marrow's lab of suffering subjects in Stanley Milgram's obedience study and Phillip Zimbardo's Stanford Prison experiments, juxtaposed with photos pictures of Hitler in front of crowds and people killed in soccer riots imply that the real horror will be human suggestibility.

Marrow tells his subjects (not selected for any paranormal backgrounds) that he is studying "perception and cognitive style."[32] The fireside ghost story is part of the experiment: we hear later as he coldly relays to his recorder that he has given them "the history of the house ... per local legend."[33] Luke Sanderson, a veteran test subject, begins to suspect the experiment is not what it seems, but only once an agitated Nell has found out the history of the house through various portraits and documents does Marrow explain. The study is practically an inversion of Goodrich-Freer's, Montague's and Markway's. "I've given you a powerful suggestion that you're in a haunted house," he says, "I picked Hill House because it fits expectations of what a haunted house should be. And then I spun you this story about Hugh Crain."[34] The study is a study precisely of how telling a [putatively] fictional story leads to the audience becoming participants and how one's "interpretation of the environment" affects the others.[35] Marrow is focusing on the tendency for story to bleed into perception in small groups. Nell's seeing ghosts and her elaboration of the story are proof of his thesis. He will later say he "made up the story ... for all practical purposes": he extracted it "out of a sociology paper on folklore."[36] If Goodrich-Freer and Montague/Markway may be reading local gossip too suggestively, Marrow's overly skeptical reading has led him to believe that he's telling a fiction. Montague and Markway were both blinded by their initial assumptions about the house and limited by their bumbling methodologies: Self's Marrow is a narrow-minded skeptic unethically exploiting what are not now his houseguests or his research assistants, but the subjects of his experiment.

Self's script comments ironically on Marrow's academic pursuits. Instead of the chill reception of Montague's out-of-fashion article, Marrow, though a chastened, mutilated believer, has apparently produced the "sexy" study initially planned, accepting an important award for revealing "the keys of mass delusional behavior": for this hypocrisy, he achieved not only tenure, but a named chair.³⁷ We see his "sick look. Sick at the jaded irony of it all." Marrow's earns success from suffering of others presented as spectacle, disguised as objective science that conceals both the individual experiences of his subjects, and the history of Hill House.

Michael Tolkin's revisions maintain the focus on research ethics. Instead of a study in the psychology of narrative, his Marrow is studying fear and performance. Marrow's current experiment, studying the effect of random versus predictable electric shocks on task performance, is under ethics review. However, he wants to expand the study to "how fear works in a group."³⁸ The cover story, a sleep study of insomniacs, is never clearly explained. His chair has some misgivings.

One misgiving is due to the involvement of Mary Lambretta who, chafing at the restraints of academic inquiry like Montague, was "thrown out of the department for trying to get a Ph.D. in psychic studies." Lambretta adds a dynamic of traditionally gendered belief and disbelief lacking in Self's script, promising an inverted *X-Files* dynamic. While Marrow "doesn't believe in the paranormal," it's implied he'll exploit Lambretta's belief to spread fear during the study. Marrow implies that her apparent precognition is due to sensory contamination: "You hear the vibrations in the [telephone] wire." Marrow mocks her about her "*intuition*," but he lets her select his test subjects on its basis.

Lambretta acts mostly to allow a paranormal frame to be adopted by the audience earlier. Before being injured by a harp string, she implies something special about Nell, seems to be sensing more than the other characters, and, after hearing Marrow's story, hints that there is more to it. Immediately before the harp blinds her, she offers to relay her impressions non-discursively, to "play" the house's "music."

Other changes abound. Notably Marrow is considerably more redeemed, with a less ironic ending. After being questioned by Mr. Dudley, "You find out what you wanted to know, mister?" the scene transitions with a sound bridge of applause, but instead of winning an award, his book, *Fear and Performance*, is being printed. It's dedicated to the people killed in the house, "They'll be happy to see this. Their names in a book, it kind of makes them immortal, doesn't it?" It is hard to imagine what could have been reported on such a topic from the Spielberg-esque funhouse ride of the events in the house.

De Bont's final cut has lost several markers that would have made it make a coherent argument about the relationship between study, narrative, and haunting. Speeches about experimental ethics, the Zimbardo and Stanford experiments, and the like, are elided. Mary Lambretta is left with a suggestively vestigial role: her psychic background on the cutting room floor. Mr. Dudley's final question "Did you find out what you wanted to know, doctor?" is answered only by an exhausted look on Marrow's face.

Like the 1963 release, promotional and paratextual elements (a DVD special feature) ask the viewer to consider the movie within nonfictional (though much less academic) frames. A summer-program professor tells of the rumored haunting of Harlaxton Manor, the site of exterior shooting. The manager of a nearby hotel, provides a haunted room story, and then spins into a more elaborate experience he had at another hotel. A walk-through of the Winchester Mystery House (a source for Jackson's novel and later interpretations) leads into what seems to be a promotional narration, accompanied by sepia dramatic re-enactment by English actor Roy Dotrice of his entry in the then-newly released *Ghostly Encounters* by Astrid St. Aubyn, a collection of the ghost stories of the famous. The principal actors are interviewed about their supernatural belief and experiences, using their skepticism or belief as a way to frame the authenticity of their performances.

In Mike Flanagan's 2018 miniseries re-configuration, *The Haunting of Hill House*, Dr. Montague is reconfigured as Nell's dangerously ineffectual therapist. The most literal ghost-hunter (Steven Crain) has lost the trappings of scholarly inquiry, now a part of the ghost-tourist industry that produces haunting non-fiction read by people who want to believe (and vicariously experience).[39] The interpenetration of investigator, skeptic, author, and exploiter of ghost stories is made clear in the only formal investigation we watch Crain conduct. After listening to a woman deliver a heartfelt and particularly gruesome story of her husband's apparition, Crain outlines a plan familiar to viewers of modern ghost-hunting media: he will set up some electronic equipment, then sleep in the haunted room. Crain notices a shelf full of his previous efforts: *The Haunting of Hill House* is the first in a series of ten *Haunting of* books, all the others about famous haunted places consumers of non-fictional haunting media (and ghost tourists) would recognize. The woman and her dead husband were fans and believers. After Crain explains away the ghost as a leaky roof, car horns, and "the grieving mind," he signs a copy of his first book, then explains that he will write the supernatural version of the apparition ("Steven Sees a Ghost"). He has conducted research of the house's history as a hospice beforehand, just for such a purpose: narrative framing by "historical deathlore" is common in modern ghost-hunting practice.[40] Of course, he explains, he will have to take "certain liberties" with the story. Crain is not a believer, but a fictionalizer of "other people's stories," putting them into convincing prose and giving them "the right voice," which, to judge by the excerpt from the in-world *HoHH*, identical with Jackson's first lines, is the highly wrought and ominous language of fiction ("Steven Sees a Ghost"). Crain is familiar to a genre audience as an allusion to the skeptical but exploitative ghost investigator and popularizer already parodied in Mikael Håfström's 2009 adaptation of Stephen King's *1408*. Mike Enslin, a failed novelist, turns to "true ghost" accounts in the wake of a family tragedy, understanding their place in the ghost-tourist industry, and gets his comeuppance (and a spousal reconciliation) when he encounters a very bad place.[41]

Ironies multiply in Flanagan's treatment: Crain has written his own family's ghost story, including the accounts of his father and younger siblings, cynically cashing in after a failed fiction-writing career. He believes that the hauntings stem from mental illness, suggestion, and mass delusion, but sensationalizes his family's stories. Thanks to Flanagan's shifting narrative focalization in each episode, the audience comes to realize, as they share each family member's subjective experiences, that what Steven writes off as mental illness has been the truth all along. Crain, despite being the expert ghost-hunter, understands the real and metaphoric hauntings that directly concern him no better. His debunking habit and his appropriation of others' stories have ruined many family relationships, preventing him from believing Nell and Luke, and even from taking his sighting of Nell's apparition seriously. Unlike the written reports mentioned in the other versions, however, Steven's *The Haunting of Hill House* is contradicted, and elements of his reporting and interpretation questioned, by Theo, Nell, and most notably by Hugh in "Witness Marks," where he reveals that Steven had seen a ghost as a child, and had miscategorized the experience.

Despite Steven's account and habits of mind being called into question, his blinkered view and tendency to remain at a skeptical and authorial distance enables the forces within the Red Room to trap him. In the Red Room, he finds himself composing a complex metanarrative that suggests the plot of *1408* and uses the recontextualized and sometimes modified words of Jackson's novel: only direct contact with an undeniable ghost allows him to return from his trapping fabulation, and accept the idea that "Some things can't be told. They have to be lived" ("Silence Lay Steadily"). Meanwhile, the reader is left with a wealth of more or less seriously interrogated fictional and nonfictional frames for haunting to choose from, of which traditional ghost-hunting is one of the less-important.

Whereas the de Bont versions put the burden of investigation into the house's past into Nell's hands, her investigatory zeal paralleling and related to her family trauma, Flanagan's miniseries notably lacks any substantial, organized on-screen investigation of the house's history or the hauntings. Instead, it focuses on the family dynamics and subjective limitations that prevent such an investigation. While each of the members of the family stumble on clues about the house's past, their communication and trust problems mean that the evidence is seldom compiled or compared, and while multiple family members see apparitions while they live in the house, they are unwilling to believe one another, framing of one another's experience and their own dismissively. Steven's off-screen compilation of the accounts in his *The Haunting of Hill House* is mentioned only in passing: any assertions of "deathlore" or the history of the house that book might contain is omitted as irrelevant. As in *The Haunting of B— House*, where Goodrich-Freer purports to offer the record of experience alone, saying, "The editors offer no conclusions," and in Jackson's novel and the Wise film, the audience is expected to do much of the interpretation, as we are the only survivors to have access to all of the evidence together.[42] Flanagan, by providing many subjectively focused narrative threads, can more explicitly guide viewers to weigh the evidence. We are often presented with multiple refocalizations of significant events as we put together the contrasting experiences of the family. As the family members slowly come to question their own interpretations and explanatory frameworks, we are offered an unprecedented number of tools to understand how individual assumptions, mindsets, relationships, past experiences and stories, as well as degrees of "sensitivity" all work together to color reactions both to trauma and to the paranormal.

If the audience is asked to do a good deal of the work of sorting out the status of different apparitions, it is as a broader and more interlinked community itself. In a major streaming release, paratexts are more diffuse and less controlled by the releasing studio: elaborate making-of videos work along with independently and user-generated content: YouTube videos, Twitter threads, fan-compiled wikis, lists of Easter eggs, and keys to references and sources, including lists of "real life" hauntings inspiring the series (and previous incarnations). Reality ghost-hunting and paranormal shows are ubiquitous on Netflix and other streaming services.

The miniseries and its bloom of inter-and-paratexts help the audience understand how stories haunt each other and us. Jackson wrote that *The Haunting of B— House* was "not at all the story of a haunted house, it was the story of several earnest, I believe misguided, certainly determined people, with their differing motivations and backgrounds."[43] Each adaptation of her story uses the heightened skepticism around subjective paranormal experience and our changing cultural attitudes towards it to show how people absorb, negotiate, create, and communicate or fail to communicate the stories that haunt us.

Notes

1. L. Andrew Cooper, *Gothic Realities: The Impact of Horror Fiction on Modern Culture* (Jefferson, NC: McFarland, 2014) argues the entanglement and mutual enhancement of fictional and non-fictional discourses about ghosts. Susan Owens, *The Ghost: A Cultural History* (Tate: London, 2017) and Owen Davis, *The Haunted, a Social History of Ghosts* (New York: Palgrave Macmillan, 2007) are broad popular overviews of cultural trends on the subject.

2. Robert Wise, dir. *The Haunting*, Warner Bros., 1968 Jan de Bont, dir. *The Haunting*. Paramount, 1999.

3. For a study of how paratexts work to inflect or shift the interpretive frame for film, Jonathan Gray, *Show Sold Separately: Promos, Spoilers, and Other Media Paratexts* (New York: NYU Press, 2010).

4. See particularly Ruth Franklin, *Shirley Jackson: A Rather Haunted Life*, New York:

Liveright, 2016, 401–427 and Melanie R. Anderson, "Perception, Supernatural Detection, and Gender," in *The Haunting of Hill House*. In *Shirley Jackson, Influences and Confluences*: New York: Routledge, 2016.

    5. Cooper, *Haunting Realities*, 246.
    6. Shirley Jackson, "The Ghosts of Loiret," in *Let Me Tell You: New Stories, Essays and Other Writings* (New York: Random House, 2016) 244.
    7. *Ibid.*, 248, 249. She also sees motion in a photo of "The Priory," the site of a murder that influenced her *We Have Always Lived in the Castle*.
    8. Jackson, "Loiret," 247.
    9. Davies, 95.
    10. Elliott O'Donnell, *Some Haunted Houses of England & Wales* (London: Eveleigh Nash, 1908), v, 160–166. O'Donnell notes "An attempt to solve the mystery surrounding these hauntings will appear in a subsequent volume."
    11. Charles G. Harper, *Haunted Houses: Tales of the Supernatural with Some Account of Hereditary Curses and Family Legends* (London: Chapman & Hall, 1907). There is no picture of Borley Rectory in the book, though there is one of Barnack Rectory.
    12. Anderson, "Perception." Ada Goodrich-Freer and John, Marquess of Bute, eds. *The Alleged Haunting of B— House* (London: George Redway, 1899).
    13. Shirley Jackson, "Experience and Fiction," *Come Along with Me: Classic Short Stories and an Unfinished Novel* (New York: Penguin, 1995).
    14. "A Correspondent" [J. Callendar Ross], "On the Trail of a Ghost" *The Times* (8 June 1897): 10.
    15. Goodrich-Freer, *B— House*, 86.
    16. Jackson, *THoHH*, 288.
    17. *Ibid.*, 289.
    18. *Ibid.*, 281.
    19. Anderson, 25.
    20. Ada Goodrich-Freer (Miss X), "Psychical Research and an Alleged 'Haunted' House," *The Nineteenth Century* 42 (Aug. 1897), 217–234.
    21. Goodrich-Freer, *B— House*, 103.
    22. *Ibid.*, 245–249.
    23. John Campbell and Trevor H. Hall. *Strange Things: The Story of Fr Allan McDonald, Ada Goodrich-Freer, and the Society for Psychical Research's Enquiry into Highland Second Sight*. (London: Routledge & Kegan Paul Ltd., 1968). Susan Zeiger, "Miss X, Telepathy, and Affect at Fin De Siècle," *Victorian Language and Culture* 46 (2018): 347–364, offers more sympathetic insight.
    24. Franklin, *A Rather Haunted Life*, 405–406.
    25. Nandor Fodor and Hereward Carrington, *Haunted People: Story of the Poltergeist Down the Centuries* (New York: Signet Mystic, 1968), 100.
    26. Franklin, *A Rather Haunted Life*, 405–406.
    27. Shari Hodges Holt, "The Tower or the Nursery: Paternal and Maternal Revisions of Hill House on Film," in *Shirley Jackson: Influences and Confluences*, edited by Melanie R. Anderson and Lisa Kroger (New York: Routledge, 2016) is the best general treatment of the adaptation. See Cooper, *Gothic Realities*, 148 for his treatment of conversion narratives.
    28. "The Haunting—Pressbook," TCM *Archives*, http://www.tcm.com/tcmdb/title/1560/The-Haunting/tcm-archives.html#tcmarcp-121024.
    29. Holt, "Hill House on Film," 173.
    30. A consideration particularly of Self's original script is undertaken in Darryl Hattenhauer, "Steven Spielberg's *The Haunting*: A Reconsideration of David Self's Script," in *Shirley Jackson: Essays on the Literary Legacy*, ed. Berenice M. Murphy (Jefferson, North Carolina: McFarland, 2005), 251–266.
    31. David Self, *The Haunting* (script, July 30, 1998), 79–80, 6–7.
    32. *Ibid.*, 31.
    33. *Ibid.*, 38.
    34. *Ibid.*, 79.
    35. *Ibid.*, 80.

36. *Ibid.*, 82.
37. *Ibid.*, 123.
38. Michael Tolkin, and David Self, *The Haunting of Hill House* (script, November 10, 1998), unpaginated.
39. An introduction to the practice may be found in Annette Hill, "Psychic Tourists" in *Paranormal Media: Audiences, Spirits and Magic in Popular Culture* (New York: Routledge, 2011), 89–107.
40. Christopher D. Bader, Joseph O. Baker, and F. Carson Mencken, *Paranormal America* (New York: NYU Press, 2017), 101.
41. Mikael Håfström, dir., *1408* (The Weinstein Company, 2009).
42. Goodrich-Freer, *B— House*, 235.
43. Shirley Jackson, "Experience and Fiction," *Come Along with Me: Classic Short Stories and an Unfinished Novel* (New York: Penguin, 1995).

Hijacking Jackson
Adapting Mike Flanagan's Oculus

FERNANDO GABRIEL PAGNONI BERNS

Arguing that the TV series *The Haunting of Hill House* is an adaptation seems to be a truism. After all, Mike Flanagan's work is an adaptation of Shirley Jackson's famous novel of the same title. There is, however, another source of inspiration behind the TV hit: Flanagan's own film *Oculus* (2013).

Oculus revolves around a pair of siblings, Tim (Brenton Thwaites) and Kaylie Russell (Karen Gillian). Tim has recently been released from a mental institution where he had spent most of his youth after he and his sister witnessed their father brutally killing their mother and subsequently committing suicide. Kaylie is adamant in her conviction that an antique mirror displayed at the Russell home was the cause of their violent childhood, as the old piece of furniture—she argues—exerted an evil influence on both of their parents. As an adult, Kaylie solicits Tim's help in an attempt to destroy the antique source of evil which, according to her, "feeds on people."

From the brief synopsis sketched above it is easy to observe that *Oculus* shares many elements in common with Flanagan's TV series. There are siblings in both the stories who spent their youth trying to repair familial trauma. At the end, the siblings unite in an attempt to destroy the antique source of evil. In the TV show, the house is the foundation of horror, the antique which, like the mirror, "feeds on people." In both the film and the TV series, the past still haunts the present, as young people are incapable of moving on with the weight of what went before resting on their shoulders.

Both Jackson and Flanagan share a preoccupation with the role that family occupies in society: the statement that "Jackson's characters dream of belonging in one big happy family" and the "irreconcilable conflict" between these desires and "the family's failure in their lives"[1] are also applicable to

Flanagan's work. A traumatic past still oozing pain, however, is a topic to which Flanagan has returned repeatedly through his career.

The serialized version of The *Haunting of Hill House* is a rewrite of both Jackson's novel and Flanagan's previous film. In fact, it can be argued that Flanagan *hijacked* Jackson's novel and turned it into the framework for his own authorial obsessions on familial horror and trauma. This shift from literature to film as sources imbricates together politics of adaptation and politics of auteur. The concept of the author is further diluted since this particular case ("a Netflix series") involves a postmodern movement enhancing, fragmenting and diminishing "authorial authority."[2]

In this essay, I will analyze the ways in which the concepts of auteur-oriented cinematic practices and film adaptation blend together through the hijacking of literary sources. I argue that *The Haunting of Hill House* is more indebted to Mike Flanagan's body of work than it is to Shirley Jackson's novel of haunted families.

Issues of Adaptation

Adaptation theory is one of the oldest areas in film studies and, as such, it has changed considerably through the years. Presently, adaptation has opened its scope to encompass not just the study of literary works and how they were brought to the big screen, but also the interconnection of other mediums as well. Thus, the source for adaptation can be found now in comic books, short films, TV series, web series, graphic novels and even journalistic news.[3] Further, the phenomenon of the transposition has suffered a process of inversion in the last years: there are many examples of feature films brought to the small screen as a TV series, as happened with Michael Crichton's *Westworld*; born as a novel, it was further adapted by Crichton to film in 1973 and turned later, twice, into a TV series.[4] The phenomenon of TV revivals and remakes such as *The Chilling Adventures of Sabrina* (first a comic book which evoked the popular character through the lens of horror fiction) further added complexity to the previously "simple" passage from literature to film.[5]

The most basic and commonplace focus in evaluating adaptations was, historically, the issue of *fidelity*. The different levels of "faithfulness" were taken as measures of evaluation, usually leading to hierarchies: the film, according to this view, was just an "illustration," a passive audiovisual "reflection" of the literary work, and as such, a "minor" work. It was "good" only if the film closely followed the main narrative of the adapted literary work.

After the 1970s, fortunately, academia slowly gave space to other approaches, in which film holds merits of its own. Rather than being just an adaptation, a movie was not second to the literary work but a completely brand-new work; a cultural production with merits all of its own.

In this framework, there were not "original sources" anymore but just interpretations. In his text *Nietzsche, Freud, Marx* (1990), Michel Foucault describes these philosophers as "masters of suspicion." He argued that they all approach cultural discourse with suspicion, viewing it as distorted by a concealed motive: the "will to power" (Nietzsche), sexual desire (Freud), and class interest (Marx). Foucault builds on this premise, arguing that "language does not say exactly what it means. The meaning that one grasps ... is perhaps in reality only a lesser meaning that shields ... the meaning underneath it."[6] This idea became central to adaptation studies.

Interpretation becomes an infinite hermeneutical job, never able to access a real point of origin; as Foucault explains, "the further one goes in interpretation, the closer one approaches at the same time an absolutely dangerous region where interpretation is not only going to find its point of no return but where it is going to disappear itself as interpretation."[7] In other words, there is *no original source*, but just interpretation of other interpretations (i.e., other texts). Even the primary text, what is commonly defined as "original source," is in turn related in different ways to previous texts that precede it chronologically. Thus, when a given text is interpreted/analyzed, what the interpreter finds under it is just another interpretation. In other words, the "source" is just another adaptation within the chain of adaptations of previous texts. Jackson's *The Haunting of Hill House* was not born in a vacuum, but it connects, in themes and narrative devices, with other texts dealing with haunted houses, the supernatural and, even, writing records about psychic researchers.[8] In fact, *The Haunting of Hill House* is a *gothic* novel revolving around the "perceptions of reality,"[9] a topic that can be traced to the genre's roots.

As a result interpretation is infinite. There is no original meaning; there is nothing to interpret but interpretations. The premise of adaptation "is one of ceaseless interpretation, in which the reader has to complete a meaning that the text leaves underdetermined."[10] Jackson's *The Haunting of Hill House*, for example, is the author's own interpretation of other texts on haunted houses. In this scenario, each artistic work answers to the politics of readership, interpretation and authorship, mediated, in turn, by social and cultural contexts. In other words, a movie based on a previous work is a rewriting that speaks about itself and the society and the auteur that produced it rather than solely of the work on which it is based. Rather than the fixed dyad of original and illustration, there is an infinite semiosis in which each text is connected to others in some way. Thus, each film should be analyzed following its internal logic rather than in a vis-à-vis scheme with the novel.

In this scenario, Flanagan's *The Haunting of Hill House* is both an adaptation of Jackson's novel and a transposition of the director's previous films, especially *Oculus*. This particular film was a work of adaptation itself, as it was a transposition of Flanagan's own short *Oculus: Chapter 3—The Man with the Plan* (2005), where a young woman (Karen Gillian) is convinced that an old mirror is responsible for the horrors that her family suffered in the past.[11] Flanagan admitted that he struggled with the adaptation of his short film to full length, as he felt challenged with what could be done with a simple premise like that taking place in the short film. As a way to expand the story, Flanagan created two separate storylines, one set in the past and one in the present, both intertwining through the narrative to create a disorienting effect "that would be similar for the viewer as it was for Tim and Kaylie [the film's two main siblings] in the room."[12] This is the same approach that Flanagan will take when helming the adaptation of Jackson's novel. The trauma of child abandonment so strong in Jackson's novel[13] nicely fits Flanagan's interests in the horrors of family disintegration and mental illnesses.

How trauma still haunts the present is, arguably, *Oculus*' main theme. The horrors of familiar disintegration persists and gives shape to the lives of both Tim and Kaylie right up to the point that they find themselves trapped into acts of repetition and/or denial.[14] In this sense, it can be argued that the main outline of Jackson's novel was attractive for Flanagan as his own fictional universe was informed by traumatic experiences filtered through the tropes of horror fiction.

It is possible to argue that Mike Flanagan, even with a still brief body of work, can be labeled as an *auteur*. Auteur theory means that some directors are elevated to the category of *auteurs* if they have a distinctive voice running through their entire output, thus creating personal, distinctive, and "authored" films. Narrative strategies, *mise-en-scène* and a very particular philosophy are all elements that compose the authorial voice, reappearing again and again through an auteur's work.

Jackson's novel is an excuse that allowed Flanagan to return to his beloved ideas on trauma and temporal fragmentation as essayed in *Oculus*. Further, *Gerald's Game* (2016) and *Before I Wake* (2016), two films directed by Flanagan, also revolve around the theme of personal trauma; sexual abuse in the former and the loss of a child in the latter. Furthermore, *Gerald's Game*, like *The Haunting of Hill House*, is told through discontinued times that zigzag between the past and the present.

In essence, Netflix's *The Haunting of Hill House* is equally an adaptation of Jackson's work and Flanagan's previous films, uniting in a unique work themes and narratives that seamlessly blend together authorial voices. This authorship does not belong solely to Jackson or Flanagan, but Netflix Originals as well, as the streaming service "possess an authorial authenticity rather than being wholly data-driven and computationally composited."[15] Three auteurs unite, then, to make a truly interesting adaptation of Shirley Jackson's *The Haunting of Hill House*. In the next section, I will discuss how Flanagan hijacked Jackson's novel to create a transposition of his own universe.

Oculus *in Serialized Form*

The serial format allows "complex plotlines and more in-depth character studies across a broader storytelling canvas"[16] as the viewer of TV series is able to empathize with each of the different characters, investing in their different adventures and the decisions they must take as the series progresses. In fact, each of the first five chapters of *The Haunting of Hill House* centers on one of the five siblings, so audiences have the chance to know all them better.

Both the film and the TV series engage with a night of horrors and its traumatic aftermath. *Oculus* begins with Kaylie and Tim, as kids (Annalise Basso and Garrett Ryan Ewald, respectively), running away from the familiar home after an unseen horrible event. As audiences will learn later, their father Alan (Rory Cochrane) killed his wife (and Kaylie and Tim's mother) after weeks of increasingly erratic behavior. In fact, *both* parents were behaving increasingly aggressively to each other and their children. Police, doctors and Tim believed that Alan somehow lost his mind under the effects of a high concentration of stress. Kaylie, however, is adamant in her beliefs: their parents were slowly possessed by the evil influence of an evil, antique mirror residing in the house.

The male breadwinner losing his mind right up to the point of attacking and murdering his own family is an echo of previous texts revolving around haunted houses, most famously *The Amityville Horror* (Stuart Rosenberg, 1979), while the haunted mirror as a filmic motif can be traced back to *Mirror, Mirror* (Marina Sargenti, 1990) and, especially, *The Boogey Man* (Uli Lommel, 1980), the latter telling the story of a brother and a sister who are traumatized by witnessing a murder that happened during their childhood. This murder happens in front of a mirror and the killed man's soul haunts the siblings until adulthood. The ideas behind these films allegorize the horror of intrafamiliar violence and mental health deterioration that haunts many real families. Interpersonal violence—subjects exposed to verbal and physical abuse or a violent crime—within the core of the family and the household is one of the most recurrent foundations for trauma[17] and its legacies of repetition and antisocial attitudes.

Besides intrafamiliar trauma, mental illness is the other theme running through the stories. Through supernatural possession, these stories of men and women haunted by evil forces reenact the trauma of watching the ways in which a beloved person starts to become an Other, a foreign person occupying a familiar body. "One of the most traumatic experiences for both parents and children can be the feeling of total helplessness in the face of obvious physical or mental deterioration"[18] as the possessions taking the parents' bodies and personalities may be read as an extreme case of alteration of normal behavior as illustrated by symptoms of schizophrenia or Alzheimer's.

Like *Oculus*, the first episode of *The Haunting of Hill House* ("Steven Sees a Ghost") also starts with a "then," a flashback to the times when the main characters were little children. Like the film, the episode starts with a brother (Steven) protecting his sister (Nellie) from unseen horrors "like a good brother does." *Oculus*, in turn, begins with Tim protecting his sister from their deranged father, who is at the brink of killing the little girl. This parallel situation creates a sense of strong bond between brothers and sisters that must unite together against the horrors of the house, being a cursed home or mirror or domestic abuse.

In the middle of the night, Hugh Crain (Henry Thomas) wakes up all his kids—Shirley, Theo, Nell, Steven and Luke—and carries them out of the house. They do so, leaving Hugh's wife Olivia (Carla Cugino) and mother of the children behind. As in *Oculus*, the exact nature of what had transpired is left in darkness, but audiences knows that the mother is dead, presumably killed. Before that night, the kids were witnesses of the (supposedly) mental deterioration of her mother, whose behavior becomes increasingly unpredictable (starting with painful migraines in "Open Casket") and aggressive (like punching a mirror in front of one of her kids in "Witness Marks").

The series begins with an episode revolving primarily around Steven (Michiel Huisman), the most skeptic of the siblings as he was the only one who, as a child, did not experience in a direct way any supernatural phenomena. Steven is a version of Tim, the brother of *Oculus*. As the film starts, Tim—now a young man—is discharged after spending his childhood in a mental institution. Together with his sister, he survived the brutal attack of both his mother and father, a situation that marked him with PTSD. Like Steven, Tim has grown up strongly believing that the horrors he experienced as a kid were all products of a mental illness assaulting his parents. Tim explains to Kaylie: "Look, Kaylie, we were just kids. We made up a scary story so we wouldn't have to accept the fact that our father was a murderer. He was... He was a sick man who tortured and killed our..." In *The Haunting of Hill House*, Steven explains the past events still haunting the family in similar terms: "Our family has a disease that's never been treated, because it was easier to listen to your [his father] crazy stories about an evil house" ("Witness Marks").

Both the TV series and the film establish that the kids and the parents love each other right up to the point that mental deterioration starts to assault the family. Thus, both texts take their time to narrate how good the parents were before the mental/supernatural breakdown. In *Oculus*, Alan and his wife Marie (Katee Sackhoff) are devoted to each other, the two of them always blended in an embrace and laughing at any silly thing or joke. Alan is not even bothered when Kaylie and Tim disturb him at his office to play with toy pistols. As a serial narrative, *The Haunting of Hill House* has more time and space to narrate its story, with many scenes of Olivia and Hugh taking good care of their children. Hugh is depicted as a good father, calming the nocturnal fears of his daughter. Olivia in turn, stays with Nellie until she falls asleep at night. Both parents allow the children to play freely within the ample corridors of the manor and even with the antiques scattered through the place. The scenes of loving parenthood heavily contrast with the subsequent images of parents scaring and/or chastising their children; while in *Oculus* this shift from love to hate is almost abrupt (there are only two scenes of parents-as-loving-persons in the entire film), the series can play more widely with ambiguity. Audiences are in the dark about the reasons behind Hugh's hasty fleeing from his home in the middle of the night. Has he hurt his wife? Is Olivia planning hurting the kids? The only thing viewers know until the last episode is that the children are in danger and that the parents are somehow responsible for this situation. The supernatural manifestations, from the point of view of children, seem to be a fitting form of explaining the abrupt changes overtaking loving parents.

Against a world of adults crumbling down in mental illness or supernatural possession, brothers and sisters must unite together to survive. The relationship between the siblings, however, is an uneasy blend of love and resentment. In the series, Shirley (Elizabeth Reaser) feels frustrated by the fact that her pragmatic approach to problems has turned her into the one in charge of fixing all the troubles within the family, while Steven is less than enthusiastic with the grudges that his success as a writer of real supernatural phenomena has awakened in his siblings. Further, everyone is tired of coping with the problems of substance abuse consuming Luke's (Oliver Jackson-Cohen) life and the emotional rollercoaster that Nell (Victoria Pedretti), the most traumatized of the siblings, is. Still, the siblings clearly love each other. Even if Theo (Kate Siegel) is not talking to Nell, or Shirley scares Luke away from Nell's wedding, the different flashbacks display many scenes of brotherly love. In *Oculus*, it is clear that Kaylie has taken care of her younger brother—and paid for his welfare—since the death of their parents. All the problems of communication between brothers and sisters seem to come from their traumatic past, not from a lack of mutual affection.

Kaylie and Tim are condensations of the five siblings of *The Haunting of Hill House*. Kaylie is pragmatic and strong-willed, a successful businesswoman just like Shirley is (an antiques dealer the former, the director of a funerary parlor the latter). Unlike Shirley, however, Kaylie is the one who strongly believes in the supernatural as a cause for the horrors of her infancy, just as Nell does in the series. Further, Kaylie is emotionally detached as consequence of her trauma right up to the point of keeping his partner at a distance just as Theo does with her girlfriend Trish (Levy Tan). In turn, Tim embodies Nell's vulnerability together with Luke's dependence on psychiatric care: both men lived part of their lives as inmates in hospitals. The serialized form allowed Flanagan to unpack the many characteristics of Tim and Kaylie in more characters, each one marked by a distinctive issue working as a traumatic emotional scar.

After an initial flashback, *Oculus* starts with Tim being released, after careful medical consideration, from the mental hospital. The young man is ready to go on with his life, but Kaylie asks for his help in a plan that she has concocted. She has bought the evil mirror and now she wants to gather evidence that could be declared as proof of its supernatural nature. Like Nell (and, in a lesser degree, Hugh) in the series, Kaylie's insistence in the supernatural keeps the wounds open. Both Tim (*Oculus*) and Steven (*The Haunting of Hill House*) bear a grudge towards their sisters and their inability to cope in a healthy way with their shared traumas. In the first episodes of the series, Shirley, Steven and Theo ignore Nell's calls, as they know what their sister stands for: the belief in the supernatural after years of the family assuming that everything that happened in the house can be logically explained. In *Oculus*, Tim's happiness of being released from the hospital turns into bitterness after learning that his sister wants his help in her plans to destroy the haunted mirror.

There are three familiar images that both the film and the series share. First, the image of a haunted house. Even if an evil mirror is the source of horrors in the film, the entire house seems affected by its presence. The plants of the house die off even if sitting far away from the mirror, a dog goes missing, and even the telephones are affected by its presence, emitting distorted voices from the past rather than connecting the siblings with the exterior world. After an initial fight, Tim calls his sister to make amends. She accepts and asks him to reunite with her at the house. Tim asks for the address, but she states clearly that she refers to "the house." Tim knows what she means: the house where they both lived as children with their parents. *The house* becomes an ominous image, a blueprint for the manor of *The Haunting of Hill House*.

Second, both *The Haunting of Hill House* and *Oculus* share a climax where all the ghosts inhabiting the house or the mirror come out to scare the siblings. During a flashback taking place at the film's climax, a young Kaylie and Tim run away from various ghostly apparitions, including a dark-haired woman wearing a white dress who looks like the Bent-Neck Lady haunting Nell. In the film, those who have been killed within the house remain in the place, forever trapped in the realm that the building offers. The last shot of the film displays the ghostly images of Kaylie—who has been murdered by the mirror in the previous scene—and Alan and Marie observing how the police take Tim again to a mental institution. In the series finale ("Silence Lay Steadily"), the house does not turn out to be so as evil as it initially seems. The house draws people in and eats them, but it also can offer a happy ending, a reunion of living people with those deceased. As in *Oculus*, all those trapped within the house come out for the last time. Unlike the bleak ending of the film, however, Flanagan seems more inclined to offer some kind of hope at the end here.

The ghosts themselves are the third point shared by the film and the series. Visually, the ghosts of both stories look completely alike. When Steven sees Nell's ghost in the first episode, she is a gray skinned woman with blank eyes and a mouth that she can open to extreme lengths to let out a scream of horror. The ghosts haunting *Oculus* are strikingly similar: pale skinned with huge mouths which emit cries of agony.

Ghosts can visually look as any creator wants them to look. Since Mike Flanagan choose to make his ghosts look *exactly alike*, it can be argued that he wanted to highlight the fact that his *The Haunting of Hill House* is barely an adaptation of Jackson's novel. He is, in fact, adapting his own *Oculus*, his own world of trauma and family disintegration. Both the ghosts and the haunted house are the visual bridges between Flanagan's creations, shaping a corpus representing a personal vision of death and trauma.

Many found that the series finale unraveled in its horrors to avoid the bleak end proposed by Jackson. From this point of view, Jackson has been, certainly, erased from the story,[19] turned victim of authorial treachery.[20] In fact, *Oculus*' end seems to fit better Jackson's bleak finale (the impossibility of really coming home and find peace); thus, Flanagan gives his series a different end, one charged with hope. It is not treason if we keep in mind that Flanagan is adapting his own film rather than Shirley Jackson's novel. It can be argued that the literary work is, here, another specter haunting this new iteration on haunted houses. There is no more "original source" in adaptation, but just specters. Thus, *The Haunting of Hill House* is, certainly, a work on hauntology.

Notes

1. Tricia Lootens, "Whose Hand Was I Holding? Familial and Sexual Politics in Shirley Jackson's the Haunting of Hill House," in *Shirley Jackson: Essays on the Literary Legacy*, ed. Bernice Murphy (Jefferson, NC: McFarland, 2005), p. 157.

2. Kamilla Elliot, "Screened Writers," in *A Companion to Literature, Film, and Adaptation*, ed. Deborah Cartmell (Malden, MA: Blackwell, 2012), 189.

3. For example, Sofia Coppola's *The Bling Ring* (2013) is based on the *Vanity Fair* article "The Suspects Wore Louboutins," by Nancy Jo Sales (2010). The resulting film is strongly faithful to the article.

4. The first series was *Beyond Westworld* (CBS, 1976), which was quickly cancelled after only three episodes.

5. Further, the popular TV show *Mystery Science Theater 3000* has been adapted to comic book format by Dark Horse publishers.

6. Michel Foucault, "Nietzsche, Freud, Marx," in *Transforming the Hermeneutic Context: From Nietzsche to Nancy*, ed. Gayle Ormiston and Alan Schrift (SUNY Press, 1990), 59.

7. Foucault, "Nietzsche, Freud, Marx," 63.

8. Shirley Jackson, *Come Along with Me: Classic Short Stories and an Unfinished Novel* (New York: Penguin Books, 2012), 200–1.

9. Jodey Castricano, "Shirley Jackson," in *The Handbook of the Gothic*, ed. Marie Mulvey-Roberts (New York: Palgrave Macmillan, 2016), 42.

10. Colin MacCabe, *Perpetual Carnival: Essays on Film and Literature* (Oxford: Oxford UP, 2017), 2.

11. The film, in turn, has a third adaptation with *Dobaara: See Your Evil* (Prawaal Raman, 2017), a Hindi film to which Flanagan served as executive producer.

12. "Director Mike Flanagan Interview, Oculus," *MoviesOnLine*, 2014.

13. Mark Jancovich, *Rational Fears: American Horror in the 1950s* (Manchester: Manchester University Press, 1996), 285.

14. Especially with Kaylie's insistence to return to the family's previous home to reenact the night her parents die. Further, Kaylie reproaches Tim for "forgetting" (a form of denial) what happened to both of them in their childhood.

15. Matt Hills, "Black Mirror as a Netflix Original: Program Brand 'Overflow' and the Multidiscursive Forms of Transatlantic TV Fandom," in *Transatlantic Television Drama: Industries, Programs and Fans*, ed. Matt Hills, Michele Hilmes and Roberta Pearson (Oxford; Oxford University Press, 2019), 234.

16. Yvonne Griggs, *Adaptable TV: Rewiring the Text* (New York. Palgrave Macmillan, 2018), 73.

17. Priscilla Dass-Brailsford, *A Practical Approach to Trauma: Empowering Interventions* (Los Angeles: SAGE, 2007), 215; Claire Renzetti and Jeffrey Edleson (Eds.), *Encyclopedia of Interpersonal Violence*, Vol. 1 (Los Angeles: SAGE, 2008), 522.

18. Barbara Draimin, Carol Levine and Lockhart McKelvy, "AIDS and Its Traumatic Effect in Families," in *International Handbook of Multigenerational Legacies of Trauma*, ed. Yael Danieli (New York: Plenum Press, 1998), 594.

19. https://www.nytimes.com/2018/10/11/arts/television/netflix-the-haunting-of-hill-house-review.html.

20. https://www.pastemagazine.com/articles/2018/10/how-netflixs-the-haunting-of-hill-house-betrays-sh.html.

II
The House

It's Coming from Inside the House

Houses as Bodies Without Organs

Matt Bernico

Life requires an abode—a fixed space from which we live, move, and have our being. Before nearly any other facts can be established about one's place in the world, one's body comes to rest somewhere.[1] "Before he is 'cast into the world,'" writes Gaston Bachelard, "... man is laid in the cradle of the house."[2] The house, in Bachelard's view, is not simply the place one inhabits, but also a space that grips one's memory, desire, and even one's material being. Bachelard describes houses as assemblages that protect their inhabitants so that they can "dream in peace."[3] There is certainly something to Bachelard's phenomenology of houses as places that shape and hold life. However, what about houses that are disordered, unstable, places of trauma, full of neglect and violence? What if the house that encloses upon one's life has sinister intentions or produces harmful desires? It is from this perspective, a phenomenology of malignant and haunted houses, that this essay will consider Hill House.

While Bachelard provides some framework for understanding the connections between memory, desire, and houses, it is beyond the capacity of his project to talk about a house that is haunted—especially one like Hill House. Riffing off of Bachelard's thoughts on houses, this project will turn to two other philosophers who have found a way to speak about desire and its production: Gilles Deleuze and Félix Guattari. The goal of this project is to read Hill House as what Deleuze and Guattari call a Body without Organs (BwO)—here, an unstable entity that lets the dead live and beckons the living to die through inscription of its trauma on the Crain family. Bringing Bachelard, Deleuze, and Guattari together will shed light on a common thought between this constellation of theorists, namely how "imagination augments the values of reality."[4] To perform this reading, this essay will begin with a Bachelardian reading of Hill House that then gives way to a description of the house as a Body without Organs. Then, gathering these threads together, this project will draw out some observations on how Hill House, a specific instantiation of the haunted house topos, acts as an invitation to think through the relationship between imagination and reality.

Inscription

Bachelard's book, *The Poetics of Space*, begins with an in-depth explanation of the house as a grounding point for the life worlds of everyday people. Bachelard writes that "our house is our corner of the world. As has often been said, it is our first universe, a real cosmos in every sense of the word."[5] One's first dwellings, whether it is actually a house, or instead an apartment, are—barring one's own physical bodies—the first discernable physical limits one might encounter. For example, during childhood, there are parts of the house that may be off limits, parents set up gates that curb their toddler's urges to run everywhere. It may even be considered a milestone for a child's first steps up the stairs or navigating a tricky bit of architecture for the unsteady legs and ambitious eyes of a two-year-old.

Though, these limits of the house may also be found in the very architecture and design of the house. Each stubbed toe signals the blueprints of the house being inscribed upon one's body. Bachelard explains that

> the house we were born in is physically inscribed in us.... After twenty years, in spite of all the other anonymous stairways; we would recapture the reflexes of the "first stairway," we would not stumble on that rather high step ... we would push the door that creaks with the same gesture, we would find our way in the dark to the distant attic. The feel of the tiniest latch has remained in our hands.[6]

The sedimentation of years of mindless habits like opening doors, using the stairs, or avoiding a creaky floorboard become part of who one is. Only when one moves to a new space are those idiosyncrasies explicated from their everyday practice.

Even more, it is from these spaces of creaky doors, latches, and stairs that individuals think and dream—one is always within the house and the house is within them.[7] The inscription of houses on bodies goes even deeper to what Bachelard calls the oneiric level. While perhaps the physical traces may fade over time, there is also the house as it lives in one's memories. The house crystalizes in one's memory as something that is more or less than it really was—the totality of the house eludes one's recollection yet one may often find themselves thinking back to that childhood bedroom or particularly frightening basement.

From this brief introduction to Bachelard's phenomenological approach to architecture and space, one can see some initial evidence for the house as a "psychological diagram" for the inhabitant.[8] These initial insights lead Bachelard toward his own specific analysis of houses where he attempts to "read a house."[9] By "reading a house" he intends to analyze the imagined connotations that undergird one's experience and expectations of a space. To read a house, Bachelard begins with two general principles:

> (1) A house is imagined as a vertical being. It rises upward. It differentiates itself in terms of its verticality… (2) A house is imagined as a concentrated being. It appeals to our consciousness of centrality.[10]

The verticality of a house situates it as a space between two poles: the attic and the cellar.[11] The attic and the roof are the rational and protective pole whereas the cellar is the "dark entity" of the house, carrying with it notions of a subterranean irrationality akin to Poe's *Cask of the Amontillado*—a trope reborn in *The Haunting of Hill House*. Bachelard's second point on centrality is about the way houses become places of refuge for their inhabitants.[12]

These orienting ideas reveal a great deal about the ways Bachelard thinks about houses and, in turn, domestic life. Houses, in his view, are sheltering and overwhelmingly positive spaces that inform one's body and imagination. It is easy to see how all of this comes off a bit too positive—Bachelard's thoughts on houses presume the family situations within them as happy. House as refuge is a far cry from the house as site of the contentious domestic labor, abusive relationships, and neoliberal foreclosure that many experience today. As an intervention into Bachelard's positivity, while still keeping his analytic framework intact, this project will move to read Hill House from *The Haunting of Hill House*.

Hill House is the oneiric house *par excellence*—since its initial dreaming up in Shirley Jackson's *The Haunting of Hill House* in 1959, Hill House is a literary house that has occupied the minds of fans, directors, television producers. While the cinematic adaptations of Jackson's work in *The Haunting* (1963) and again in *The Haunting* (1999) offer a ready-made mythology of Hill House, the House's most recent recasting in *The Haunting of Hill House* (2018) affords the most fitting opportunity to think through Bachelard's *The Poetics of Space* because only this adaptation features the house contextualized by family life.

Externally, Hill House, as it appears in its 2018 iteration, is the Bisham Manor in LaGrange, Georgia.[13] The structure itself is a 1920s era Tudor mansion, though Mike Flanagan, the director of *The Haunting of Hill House*, goes on to explain,

> It's one of the strangest buildings I've ever seen.... You look at it from one angle and it looks Victorian, very angular and clean. From another angle it looks medieval—it has these stone turrets that don't make any sense![14]

The nonsensical feeling that Flanagan cites is a contributor to the overall vibe of the house: many families before the Crain family have lived, renovated, added to, and died in Hill House. It's not the cursed project of one builder as noted in *The Haunting* (1999), but instead is what Flanagan and Hugh Crain alike describes as "schizophrenic."[15]

The interior, filmed in studio, carries on this disorienting vibe with a backdrop of statues and gothic ornamentation reminiscent of, yet more subdued than, the many cherubic faces littering the set of *The Haunting* (1999).[16] The set design itself is beautifully haunting, inset with eerie and intense detail. Flanagan notes,

> We wanted the house to be full of implied or explicit faces that were always staring at the characters—or the audience.... Almost all our wallpaper has different facial patterns inside it. They're in the doorknobs too—some are animals, some human. Then there's the placement of windows in relation to fireplaces: we laid out eyes and an open mouth in all the rooms. It's a subconscious thing, but it creates this sense of unease.[17]

Hill House's set design echoes the initial thoughts of Eleanor Lance in *The Haunting* (1963), "It's staring at me."[18] The house is, just as much as the Crain family, a character in its own right. Though, Hill House is the home of many ghosts, there's something about the house itself that seems to have its own agenda to hold and keep all who enter its doors. Channeling Jackson's original text, Eleanor in the 1963 iteration gets it right again. "I'm like a small creature swallowed whole by a monster and the monster feels my tiny movements inside."[19] Hill House is certainly haunted, but to simply call it a haunted house would be missing the point. Hill House is itself an entity that seeks to consume its visitors and trap them within its walls. *The Haunting of Hill House* is not just a ghost story, but the story of a sentient house that seeks to possess and perversely protect its inhabitants for all time.

Houses Without Organs

Clearly, Hill House is something outside of what Bachelard might imagine. Yet at the same time, as Bachelard describes, Hill House inscribes its own logics on its victims. Following Bachelard's thoughts on imagination and reality in the context of a house, it is helpful to backup Bachelard with Gilles Deleuze and Félix Guattari's work on inscription and bodies. While Bachelard offers a way to talk about houses, Deleuze and Guattari can add some helpful provisions on the ways bodies can become disordered, allowing for destructive desires to flow through them.

Deleuze and Guattari's *Anti-Oedipus* and *A Thousand Plateaus* are expansive works that are impossible to give a suitable overview of in this format. Talking about Deleuze and Guattari is doubly difficult because to be accurate in one's summary requires the use of a great deal of abstruse vocabulary. In light of this, I'll do my best to explain my terms in a way that they become usable rather than obstructive.

In Deleuze and Guattari's *A Thousand Plateaus*, the entire concept of the self or individual is displaced as merely a way of speaking about the consistencies of multiplicities in the world. Beginning their text, Deleuze and Guattari give the provision that while their names show up on the cover of their books, they themselves are multiple. To refer to oneself as something stable and nameable is like saying "the sun rises, when everybody knows it's only a manner of speaking." It is simply a social convention to "talk like everybody else."[20] Instead of singular entities, individuals are better thought of as the locations where the concatenation of actors coincide and flow. One says "I" to refer to not only the thing that appears, but also the histories and inscriptions that the "I" carries with it. The point is that humans are not individuated discrete beings, but instead messy consistencies of connections.

From this perspective, then, one may begin asking about the production of one's own desires or how the "I" became what it is. In an attempt to "talk like everybody else," the point of Deleuze and Guattari's analysis is to find a way to speak about why bodies work the way they do and how they come to desire. In Deleuze and Guattari's *Anti-Oedipus*, they use the term "desiring-production" to talk about the blueprint of the body and what other actors are at work in the "I."[21] Desiring-production is the way Deleuze and Guattari think through the minutiae of how desire is produced in a body. What is plugged into the body to produce desire X?

Desiring-production is a blueprint to desire in the body, but the specific layout of that blueprint is important and value laden. The mouth is connected to the stomach, but how? Which is primary in this relationship? To get at how desire is produced through the arrangement of desiring-production, Deleuze and Guattari turn to another term: "Body without Organs" or BwO. The BwO in Deleuze and Guattari's own words:

> is the field of immanence of desire, the plane of consistency specific to desire (with desire defined as a process of production without reference to any exterior agency, whether it me a lack that hollows it out or a pleasure that fills it.[22]

Then, the BwO is a way to think about the body which does not hierarchize, judge, and organize its functions. From the perspective of the BwO, one sees how the body may be malleable, shaped, or transformed toward other organizations of self and desire. Body as BwO inquires into the organization of the body. In a series of rather evocative images, Deleuze and Guattari ask when it comes to breathing, why bother with the nose or the mouth? Why not just have an opening directly into the lungs?[23] While not actually suggesting this, these provocations serve to ask questions about the largely unidentified bodily techniques one uses unconsciously on the body.

The BwO is a way one negotiates the body between organizing strata and experimentation.[24] Said in a slightly different register, Vilém Flusser, a media philosopher, asks whether speech comes from the body's specific physiognomy, from the development of speech centers of the brain, or from the development of historical technical practice of speech?[25] Flusser leaves the question open, but still the same logic prevails. Human speech is a particular technique, developed through particular assignments and stratification of human anatomy and cultural values. Speech is the stratification of the human utterance.

So far, the BwO may seem like a way to speak about the body and its possible transformations. Though, in the instance of architecture and houses it is important to assert that the BwO is not just a mythology that one might lend to understand the production of desire or the performance of bodily technique. Rather, the BwO is comprised of real entities which connect and influence other actors within a plane of consistency. For example, in the opening pages of *Anti-Oedipus*, Deleuze and Guattari write,

> Capital is indeed the body without organs of the capitalist, or rather of the capitalist being ... it produces surplus value, just as the body without organs reproduces itself, puts forth shoots, and branches out to the farthest corners of the universe.[26]

In this sense, the BwO becomes a way to understand the ways systems reproduce themselves and overcome supposed barriers. The example of capital as BwO of the capitalist lends a fluidity to understanding complex systems. Capital as BwO explains the mystification of labor in capitalism. Because Capital inscribes itself on the BwO of workers, it appears as if Capitalism is the cause for their labor. In support of this observation, Deleuze and Guattari cite Marx's explanation in *Capital*, "Capital thus becomes a very mystic being since all of labour's social productive forces appear to be due to capital, rather than labour as such..."[27] The point is that capital as a BwO of capitalists creates a mechanism through which capitalism is reproduced as central to the production of capitalist desire.

Deleuze and Guattari's BwO, like Bachelard's topoanalysis of houses, is a way to talk about the connection between the imaginary and the real. However, Deleuze and Guattari would disagree with Bachelard over those exact terms—Deleuze and Guattari's metaphysics are quite more sophisticated than that of Bachelard. Regardless, these theories both try to make sense of the ways bodies are inscribed upon by a multiplicity of other actors. Making a full comparative philosophy between Deleuze and Guattari and Bachelard needs much more space than is possible here. Despite this, there are some clear resonances between these modes of thinking about the construction of the self.

In Bachelard's view, houses inscribe themselves physically on the bodies of their inhabitants in both their waking and dreaming lives. The same could be said from the view of Deleuze and Guattari. Houses, like humans or capitalism, have a BwO that give rise to virtual horizons. What is gained from Deleuze and Guattari's view, however, is how the house as BwO might add negative virtualities to the spectrum of BwO. The BwO is an experimental space for understanding what one's body might be capable of. When it comes to experimenting, Deleuze and Guattari recommend caution with regard to the BwO,

> If you free it with too violent an action, if you blow apart the strata without taking precautions, then instead of drawing the plane you will be killed, plunged into a black hole, or even dragged toward catastrophe.[28]

If one's experiments take them too far too quickly, one could end up with a monstrous result. Deleuze and Guattari take time to list out a number of "botched" BwO which end in the introduction to troubling desires.[29]

Deleuze and Guattari lay out the hypochondriac body, the paranoid body, the schizo body, and the drugged body as examples of the ways bodies come to pass intensities which are bad or harmful. These botched BwO come through numerous types of experimentation and destratification. One avenue of destratification that Deleuze and Guattari do not mention, however, is the one which Bachelard emphasizes entirely: houses. If the subject is considered not a singular entity, but the contribution of and construction by a multiplicity of factors, then the houses and architecture one lives in and around certainly can be counted among the machinery that inscribes upon one's body.

Not a Heart, but a Stomach

Looking at a set of blueprints pictorializing the layout of Hill House with her daughter, Shirley, Olivia Crain explains, "Every house needs a heart ... a house is like a person's body: The walls are like bones, the pipes are veins, It needs to breathe, It needs light and flow. It all works together to keep us safe and healthy inside" ("Open Casket"). In Bachelard's view, this all seems right—houses protect their inhabitants. Yet this is not the case for Hill House. Hill House is a home turned on its head: unfixed from time and the constraints of mortality, Hill House protects its inhabitants with a smothering kind of love: it entraps its inhabitants with eternal life, but under glass. As it's revealed in the final episode of season one, if one dies in Hill House, their soul remains trapped within the house. Based on the explication of Hill House's specific mechanics, through the lens of both Bachelard and Deleuze and Guattari, one can begin to see the ways physical space merges with imaginary space. Hill House, like all houses, inscribes desire onto its inhabitants and functions as a BwO.

In the closing moments of episode ten, "*Silence Lay Steadily,*" there are two explanations of how Hill House actually works. Through the juxtaposition of conversations between Hugh and Olivia alongside a disjointed and nonlinear monologue from Nell, one gets both an idea of how the house works and how it has shaped the expression of motherhood and desire in the Crain family. These two explanations give one a glimpse into how the House itself has produced and organized desire for the Crain family.

The specific supernatural mechanics of the house are expressed most lucidly through Nell. Each of the Crain family are led back to Hill House after Nell's funeral. After unveiling the true events of the night Olivia died, each of the Crain family is drawn into Hill House's center, the Red Room. The house draws the Crains individually into delusions specifically tailored to, at first, relieve their own particular pains and then acutely twists those reliefs into a unique tableau of horror ("Steven Sees a Ghost"). Though their recently deceased sister, Nell, is able to find her siblings and free them from Hill House's grasp.

At first speaking nonlinearly, but then finding the right order of words, Nell reflects on the moment between Shirley and Olivia in episode 2, elaborating on the specific nature of Hill House.

> Mom says that a house is like a body and that every house has eyes, and bones, and skin, and a face. This room [the Red Room] is like the heart of the house—No not a heart, a stomach ["Open Casket"].

Nell's elaboration on what it is that Hill House is doing exactly reveals the end game of the house. What's terrifying about Hill House isn't that it contains ghosts, but rather it's the house itself. It's a point that echo's Shirley Jackson's original sentiments about Hill House, that Hill House, for whatever reason, was "born bad."[30] Rather than keeping its inhabitants safe and healthy inside, Hill House slowly digests its inhabitants. Where its heart should be is instead a stomach. Hill House consumes its victims until they're nothing but spirit—and even then it can't bear to let them go. Hill house even reuses the remains of its inhabitants to draw in more victims.

Nell explains how the house works, but in the back and forth between Hugh and Olivia, the effects of Hill House become apparent. Hugh is the only member of the Hill House not drawn into the Red Room. Instead, the house stops him in the hallway where he encounters Poppy Hill. As Nell saves her siblings from Hill House's nightmares, Olivia saves Hugh from Poppy. Forcing Poppy to back off, Olivia and Hugh hammer out the wreckage of their family.

Olivia and Hugh's differences quickly come to a head—Olivia rejoices at her family's return to Hill House, while Hugh explains that he's been "holding a door closed ... because I knew there were monster on the other side that wanted what was left of our family" ("Silence Lay Steadity"). In this conversation, the tension quickly emerges. Olivia understands Hill House as a place of refuge from the horrors of everyday life, whereas Hugh recognizes the refuge that Hill House offers is one that stamps out life in trade for safety. Olivia relates her post-death experience to Hugh as something positive and something that she wants for the rest of her family. Olivia is willing to trade her family's human lives for an eternal ghostly existence within the walls of Hill House. There is an interesting tension in the way Olivia talks about her family's safety and future in Hill House. It's clear that she has different intentions from some of the other inhabitants walking the halls. Olivia clearly loves her family so much that she wants them to be safe with her, but the way Olivia articulates "safety" is a particularly perverse and gendered expression of overbearing motherly love. In Olivia's first meeting with Poppy Hill in episode nine, Poppy convinces Olivia that to truly protect her family, she needs to "wake them up" from the nightmare of pain, struggle, and loss. This is the exploitation and subversion of a parental desire that recasts safety as a safety from life, rather than from harm.

Following this logic, *The Haunting of Hill House* concludes by deconstructing the logic of the Bachelardian house for a house which alters the desire of its inhabitants. *The Haunting of Hill House* makes audiences confront the place where safety and shelter double back on themselves and open up plateau where being safe means either safety from the monsters or safety *as* monsters. Out of this doubling back, emerges two types of familial desire with regard to safety. On the one hand, Hugh recognizes that pain and trauma are a part of life, that can be lessened through parental protection. On the other, Olivia expresses a safety founded in a separation from life.

It is important to note that this is a desire produced in Olivia by Hill House and not of her own volition. Even before Poppy gives Olivia the language of "safety as waking up." Hill House had a firm grasp on Olivia's imagination. In episode seven, "Eulogy," Olivia hands Hugh the master blueprints for Hill House. Troubled by what he's received, Hugh notices the repetition of a shape scrawled across the blueprints. "I didn't know what this was. It looked familiar. You used the same shape dozens of times—over and over. It's the footprint of our house. Our forever house" ("Eulogy"). The Crains' "forever house" was the house that they'd build after they made enough money from flipping houses, which was what brought them to Hill House in the first place. The "forever house" is an expression of the desire to provide fixity and safety for the Crain children, though the repetition of the "forever house" within the blueprints for Hill House demonstrates that Hill House has consumed their dreams and has already marked the Crain family for life.

Beyond just Olivia and Hugh, the Crain children are altered by Hill House as well. Hill House has a lasting impact on each of the children, but it is particularly visible in the ways it has etched a type of paranoia into Steve. Steve processes his past trauma through writing and publishing stories of hauntings. The show itself attributes some of Jackson's original lines specifically to Steve's exaggerated retelling of his family's story. Despite having this outlet, Steve is convinced that his mother's suicide could be attributed to some kind of genetic disorder. The genetic explanation gives Steve some kind of solace, yet at the same time it pushes him get a vasectomy straight out of college as to not pass whatever this genetic issue is down to future children ("Witness Marks").

Deleuze and Guattari might diagnose Steve's pattern of behavior with what they call the paranoid BwO. Across both *Anti-Oedipus* and *A Thousand Plateaus*, Deleuze and Guattari spend a lot of time working out paranoia. Deleuze and Guattari pick up on paranoia from one of Freud's classic cases with Daniel Paul Schreiber. For Freud, paranoia stems from the oedipal arrangement where one believes that they're always being watched.[31] Paranoia plays a big part in the organization of the BwO. The production of paranoid desire the BwO means that it feels like it's always under the gaze or attack from another power. Steve's experience in Hill House inscribes this type of desire into his own life. Hill House forces Steve to come to terms with what he sees the night of his mother's suicide. Out of this trauma, he reasons that it must be something genetic. In Steve's perspective, it's his own body that is under attack and, as a result, he literally re-organizes the arrangement of his own organs in the shape of a secret vasectomy. Not only does he regiment his own body under his own paranoid gaze, but he keeps it a secret—not unlike the way Hugh, his father, keeps the monsters behind the door at a safe distance.

Hill House becomes a part of the production of desire in the Crain family. The House itself is responsible for the destruction of its own inhabitants through the inscription of itself on their bodies. Rather than a house that protects, that is a house with a heart, Hill House has arranged itself into a machine that produces fascist and paranoid desire in order to devour those who live within it. As Bachelard points out, we carry our houses with us as psychological diagrams of our memory, but as *The Haunting of Hill House* reminds us, houses can turn into places of trauma and entrapment—places that produce mangled BwO.

Notes

1. Special thanks to Emma Canady and Shannan Bernico for their editorial assistance on this chapter.
2. Gaston Bachelard. *Poetics of Space*. Boston, MA: Beacon Press, 1994, 7.
3. *Ibid.*, 6.
4. Bachelard, 3.
5. *Ibid.*, 4.
6. *Ibid.*, 14.
7. *Ibid.*, 13.
8. *Ibid.*, 39.
9. *Ibid.*, 14.
10. *Ibid.*, 17.
11. *Ibid.*, 17.
12. *Ibid.*, 31.
13. Alicia Hill. "Series Filmed in LaGrange Receiving Lots of National Attention." *LaGrange Daily News*. October 19, 2018. Accessed March 26, 2019. https://www.lagrangenews.com/2018/10/18/series-filmed-in-lagrange-receiving-lots-of-national-attention/.
14. Ian Berriman and Sfx. "The Haunting of Hill House Showrunner on Turning the Classic Ghost Story Into a Netflix Original." *Gamesradar*. October 13, 2018. Accessed March 26, 2019. https://www.gamesradar.com/the-haunting-of-hill-house-showrunner-on-turning-the-classic-ghost-story-into-a-netflix-original/.
15. *Ibid.*
16. *The Haunting*. Directed by Jan de Bont. Performed by Liam Neeson, Catherine Zeta-Jones, Owen Wilson. USA: DreamWorks Home Entertainment, 1999. DVD.
17. Berriman.
18. *The Haunting*. Directed by Robert Wise. Performed by Julie Harris, Claire Bloom, Richard Johnson. MGM/Argyle, 1963. Amazon Video.
19. *Ibid.*
20. Gilles Deleuze and Félix Guattari. *A Thousand Plateaus: Capitalism and Schizophrenia*. Translated by Brian Massumi, Minneapolis: University of Minnesota Press, 1987, 3.
21. Gilles Deleuze and Félix Guattari. *Anti-Oedipus: Capitalism and Schizophrenia*. Minneapolis: University of Minnesota Press, 1983, 1.
22. *Ibid.*, 154.
23. *Ibid.*, 150.
24. *Ibid.*, 159.
25. Vilém Flusser, *Gestures*. Translated by Nancy Ann Roth, Minneapolis: University of Minnesota Press, 2014, 27.
26. Gilles Deleuze and Félix Guattari, *Anti-Oedipus: Capitalism and Schizophrenia*. Minneapolis: University of Minnesota Press, 1983, 10.
27. Karl Marx, *Capital*, Translated by Ernest Untermann, New York: International Publishers, 1967, Vol 3, 827.
28. Deleuze and Guattari, *A Thousand Plateaus*, 161.
29. *Ibid.*, 150–151.
30. Shirley Jackson, *The Haunting of HIll House*, epub, pg. 104.
31. Freud, Sigmund. *On Metapsychology—The Theory of Psychoanalysis: "Beyond the Pleasure Principle," "The Ego and the Id" and Other Works*. Harmondsworth: Penguin Books, 1991, 90.

A House Without Kindness
Hill House and the Phenomenology of Horrific Space

ZACHARY SHELDON

While Netflix's *The Haunting of Hill House* is a captivating psychological drama that showcases the far-reaching consequences of childhood trauma, mental illness, and secret-keeping, at its core is Hill House. And Hill House is no mere house. As experienced through the memories and descriptions of each of the Crains, Hill House is brought to life as the epicenter of mystery and an enduring terror that altered the lives of this family forever. And while the show's plot is mainly dedicated to unraveling the specific mystery and resulting fallout of what happened there one fateful night in 1992, Hill House itself looms large in the background. The house becomes more than just a setting for the drama to unfold as the show invites viewers to consider the house as a pervasive and malevolent force.

Shirley Jackson's original descriptions of Hill House are amongst the most famous in contemporary fiction, and the force of her poetic prose is evocative throughout her short novel. Hill House, we learn, is "not sane," but is "a place of despair" and "a house without kindness" that "seemed awake" and was "not a fit place for people or for love or for hope."[1] The suggestive nature of Jackson's language means that adapting such prose into cinematic form is an exercise in turning the imaginative space of the novel's Hill House into a visually represented physical space that tangibly evokes the same peculiar sense of discord that Jackson so lucidly creates.

Noteworthy here is how the horror genre has often been concerned with using spatiality as an element in provoking tension and fear. Specifically, violating the sanctity of spaces that are otherwise considered "safe" or "comforting" is a common horror theme, particularly in relation to domestic locations like the home. Stephen King names this particular horror archetype that of the "Bad Place," and uses Shirley Jackson's novel as an exemplar to illustrate its tendencies.[2] That such archetypes have lasting cultural resonance suggests a universal quality to the human experience of domestic, lived spaces.

In *The Poetics of Space*, phenomenologist Gaston Bachelard looks to poetry and other artistic expressions as a way of understanding this relationship between human beings and physical space. With particular deference for the qualities that define a "home," Bachelard's analysis sees clues in the poetry and art of a variety of cultures that imply certain universal insights into how human beings navigate and experience physical spaces, especially houses. Bachelard's analysis is often warmly cheerful, even nostalgic in places as it describes the comfort and creative atmosphere that a home and its various elements provide, which is intriguingly juxtaposed with how horror stories, and horror films in particular, often subvert and transform the relationship between their characters and their homes into one of terror.

Looking to Mike Flanagan's *The Haunting of Hill House* provides a chance to see these subversive strategies in action. Though Hill House may seem merely a backdrop to the story's main dramatic action, the series' use of its space is nonetheless deliberate and significant for its influence on the show's characters. Moreover, the show's presentation of this space offers an opportunity for juxtaposing specific features of Flanagan's Hill House—namely the house's dumbwaiter and secret cellar, moldering walls, main foyer space, and the Red Room—with Bachelard's imaginative phenomenology of the home. This, in turn, offers a unique perspective for examining the phenomenon of horrific spaces. By way of beginning, let us turn to phenomenology generally, and Bachelard specifically.

Phenomenology, Poetry and the Space of the Home

Phenomenology as a branch of philosophy is chiefly concerned with how human beings derive meaning from experience. This entails recognizing that as human beings we are *embodied* and so each individual relates to what phenomenologists refer to as the "Lifeworld" through the data we receive through our senses. Recognizing the inherent "Being-in-the-world" that characterizes every individual's experience brings with it questions about how knowledge and experience are constructed, and what essential qualities exist in particular experiences that define them as *those* specific experiences. But rather than being a tacit endorsement of subjectivism, phenomenology instead has a somewhat transcendentalist underpinning in that the discipline aims to explore what is true about experiences, and thus knowledge, for *all* people.

Given phenomenology's emphasis on embodiment, it is no surprise that examinations of space and place are fairly common in the field. As Dylan Trigg acknowledges, "being-in-the-world means being *placed*. At all times, we find ourselves located in a particular place, specific to the bodily subject experiencing that place. We are forever in the *here*, and it is from that *here* that our experiences take place."[3] Places wield tremendous influence over the shape and tenor of other experiences, often determining what kinds of events, experiences, or things can happen in particular spaces. While other sensory data and phenomena may be of greater importance to certain experiences, space and place are factors that are not easily forgotten or ignored.

The process of *doing* phenomenology entails developing a particular skill of attending to one's senses in a reflexive and bounded manner. This entails engaging in an experience with intentionality, apprehending and assessing experience to determine what is most essential and defining about that experience. A phenomenologist works to "bracket" preconceived notions and preoccupations in order to more carefully attend to the phenomena that they are experiencing *as* they are experiencing it, a process otherwise known as the phenomenological reduction or *epoché*. But the resulting analysis of these experiences is not merely a report on what was seen or felt. Instead, phenomenological research aims to be evocative, even artistic in its reportage. There is no sense in merely talking about the essential facets of an experience—the aim is instead to reproduce or evoke that same kind of feeling in the reader. Phenomenological scholarship is thus an intentionally creative, artistic act. One phenomenologist, Max van Manen, even labels a chapter in his book on phenomenological pedagogy, "The Research Is the Writing."[4] Phenomenology recognizes the power of language not as a descriptive tool but as one that can create resonant images and senses through poetic turns of phrase and careful crafting of prose. Such writing can "strike a chord" or "ring true" with readers in a way that a plain description or philosophical argument simply cannot.

To this end, phenomenology has a particular affinity for the arts in general, recognizing in many of them a tendency towards the same distillation and focus of experience. In fields as diverse as painting, poetry, and film, oftentimes the artist concentrates on what in film theory is called "defamiliarization." That entails depicting and describing a familiar phenomenon in such a way that it is experienced anew, illuminated in some resonant, transcendent fashion that imbues the experience with new significance, showcasing the essential, particular qualities that made it that uniquely special experience in the first place. Also worth noting is that some theorists have described film as being one of the most phenomenological of the arts, in that choices in shot composition and editing direct the audience's attentions in particular ways, effectively performing the *epoché* for them.[5]

Poetry is one particularly salient expression of this ideal, with its attendance to an incredibly deliberate use of language in an evocative fashion. And so, it is to poetry that Gaston Bachelard turns in *The Poetics of Space*, noting specifically that "the reader of poems is asked to consider an image not as an object and even less as the substitute for an object, but to seize its specific reality."[6] Bachelard's project is to examine how poets and writers have described and characterized the physical spaces of the home, aiming to understand what universal, transcendent qualities exist in the spaces that humans inhabit, and that in turn determine how human beings exist in those spaces. While acknowledging that the home is materially constructed as a geometric object, Bachelard argues that "a house that has been experienced is not an inert box. Inhabited space transcends geometrical space."[7] How inhabitance transforms geometry, and vice versa, is one of his major concerns.

The chief substance by which the home's geometry is transformed is the imagination. He argues that the main benefit of the house is that "the house shelters daydreaming, the house protects the dreamer, the house allows one to dream in peace."[8] This perspective brings out two qualities of Bachelard's work that are of particular interest in connecting it to *Hill House*. First, it demonstrates that at times Bachelard's outlook towards the home and its influence is one tinged with warmth and nostalgia. "Daydreaming" is discussed at length in *The Poetics of Space* but "nightmares" are never mentioned at all. And while Bachelard acknowledges that there are spaces that evoke dark feelings and fear (such as basements, to be explored below), his analysis tends to avoid fear and the darker sides of the imagination altogether. Second, the mention of daydreaming and dreaming generally acknowledges that the boundaries of the house are not actually set in stone, but rather are fluid, limited only by the imaginer him- or herself. A home's "verticality," how it stretches beyond the immediately visible through its basement and reaches into the stars in attic spaces, connects the home to a "cosmicity" beyond the physical realm.[9]

This cosmic sense of the home, I believe, is the opening through which horrors may rear their ugly heads. Though Bachelard may not acknowledge them, nightmares flourish in the home just as much as dreams. What Bachelard's observations do provide, though, is a foil through which the depiction and use of the home in *The Haunting of Hill House* may be more fully examined. In doing so, we can come to understand just how traditional conceptions of space and place are effectively violated in the name of the horrific.

The Dumbwaiter and the Secret Cellar

When Luke crawls into the kitchen's dumbwaiter and asks Theo to help him take a ride in the "perfect kid-sized elevator" he has no idea what a ride he is in for as he ultimately descends to a secret basement, sees the arm of a ghoul, and is then released back into his father's arms at the seeming will of Hill House itself ("Eulogy"). Several visual and spatial elements stand out for their contribution to the horror of Luke's ordeal. First, of course, is the image of the trapped child. Related to this is the specificity of where he is trapped: in a confining space that descends into darkness. This descent is crucial, as is the basement setting. That all of this is uncontrolled by any human actor in the situation is the icing on the cake.

I begin with this scene because it is the one which most comfortably fits in Bachelard's established taxonomy of the house and its various effects, though it too offers some amendments to Bachelard's rosy take on the home. First, though the poets that Bachelard examines and takes his insights from are not children, there is a consistent trend in his work towards consideration of the childhood home, rather than the home in general. The childhood home, he asserts, is the one in which our imagination takes root, in effect acting as the ideal home that we return to in our later conceptions of idealized spaces and places.[10] The imaginative access of a child is just the sort of defamiliarization that phenomenology aims for, such that Luke's presence as a child in the midst of this horror is prescient and noteworthy: his is the age and kind of imagination that is most open to influence.

The small space that Luke crawls into and the ensuing horrific encounter evoke what Bachelard terms "Intimate Immensity." Any notion of "immensity" inherently begins in the imagination, as "immense" does not exist as an object but only as a concept of scale that we assign to objects based on imaginative categories. Imaginative immensity is thus as intimate a feeling as can perhaps be experienced, emerging purely from within us. And small spaces not only denote a "need for secrecy,"[11] but inspire the consideration of immensity: "Large issues from small ... thanks to a liberation from all obligations of dimensions, a liberation that is a special characteristic of the activity of the imagination."[12] Later, Bachelard makes the case that poetic space is one of expansion, which "goes from deep intimacy to infinite extent" and brings about a sense of "grandeur" for the imagining subject.[13] We can see at least the beginning aspect of this in Luke's experience, as the tight confines of the dumbwaiter give way to the immense darkness of the cellar in which anything might dwell. The grandeur that he experiences in this expansion is not, however, the peaceful grandeur that Bachelard evokes, but one of incipient dread.

Luke's descent into the space of a cellar is significant, to Bachelard's thinking. Bachelard's ideal home is three levels—basement, main floor, and attic—with the basement and attic levels enacting a dialectic of house and universe that is conducive to daydreaming. The verticality of the house suggested by the descending basement and ascending attic provoke "cosmicity" to our imaginings: the basement enables us to envision and imagine subterranean elements, connecting us to the earth's depths; the attic prompts us to look to the sky, allowing our imaginings to expand in the other direction.[14] Cellars, he acknowledges in line with psychoanalysis, are the "*dark entity* of the house" where "we are in harmony with the irrationality of the depths.... In the cellar, darkness prevails both day and night, and even when we are carrying a lighted candle, we see shadows dancing on the dark walls."[15] Bachelard's concern with the cellar is fleeting, and he quickly moves on to connecting the significance of the cellar to its staircase, which leads us up and out of the darkness and into the light of the main floor and, eventually, the daydream-supporting attic.

But I would like to linger briefly on the cellar as shown in Luke's ordeal because I believe it suggests more than the mere possibility of depthless horror. Specifically, there are several shots in the cellar looking *back* towards Luke as his flashlight penetrates flickers in the dark. Though brief, these shots are crucial for extending the notion that there *is* a rationality to the darkness, not merely a sense of cosmic irrationality provoked by the seeming boundlessness of the darkness that provokes the imagination when confronted with immensity contrasting with the intimacy of a space. While the ghoul that crawls from behind the beer barrel is presented from Luke's perspective, these few quick shots, coupled with what can only be seen as Hill House's decision to bring Luke down to the depths, suggest a different sense of horror than that which Bachelard connects to the cellar trope. Rather than irrationality or unknown depths, this depiction of the basement implies a horror that is frightening in its ability to be perfectly understood: Hill House is rational in its methods and in its targeting, and that this rationality may not be understood to those subjected to its torture is the real horror that is revealed here. This is not a rationality beyond human reckoning but is instead a rationality that we *could* understand if given the chance. That we have no access to understand is where the nightmare seeps in.

The Walls of Hill House

In Jackson's novel, the walls and floors of Hill House are intimated to be canted and filled with gaps and fissures that allow at least some visitors to rationalize the house's odd breezes or the tendency for its doors to shut of their own accord. But Flanagan's adaptation, which puts Hugh and Olivia's efforts at renovation near the center of the plot, does not suffer such imperfections. For the most part, instead, the house is precise in its construction. The central hallway where the family's bedrooms are—and where viewers spend a fair amount of time throughout the series—seems instead nearly perfect in its angles and construction. Nothing to fear there, or so it seems. The interior of the walls is where the real damage purports to be, with moisture and mold constantly plaguing Hugh's efforts to finish the house and leading both to the injury of his hand and the discovery of William Hill's body ("Eulogy").

It is easy to psychologize Hill House's mold and decay as pointing to the inner state of the house or its occupants, or to see the moldering walls of the house's lower levels as symbolic of Olivia's spreading madness. I will leave such explications to others. What interests me, primarily, is the pin-straight level of the upstairs walls, the seeming perfection with which they come together to form the central hallway and structure of the house. Bachelard asserts that the small spaces of corners, the meeting places of walls and floor and ceiling, are special in that they are "the germ of a room, or of a house," a special place where the imagination can flourish, and anything can grow out of such a small starting point.[16] Even more poignant, however, are cracks and gaps in the walls, which is where the imagination can truly flourish and the poet may create a new universe in which to live.[17]

What I would like to suggest is that Flanagan's neat, square, ordered presentation of most of Hill House's halls and walls is actually what makes them so frightening. Though Jackson herself, in line with Bachelard, makes the case that it is the house's gaps and canted angles that give it the uncanny, skewed look that many visitors find within it and which seemingly open the imagination to exploring its horrors, I argue that Flanagan's more trim presentation actually reinforces the notion of Hill House's insanity under "conditions of absolute reality."[18] Where gaps may have offered some imaginative explanation for the appearance of the Bowler Hat Man or the slamming and pounding of doors, the lack of such fissures deny the rationalization of these horrors and provoke a much more frightening line of thinking: that they are entirely real. The perfection of the walls is maddening in that it leaves no gap for the imagination to exploit, making the irrational sights the walls contain that much more affecting.

The Foyer

Hill House's main entryway and staircase are the epitome of the house's Gothic style, inviting visitors in and yet diminishing them and their presence in the house. Like so many other elements in Hill House, the architectural features of the foyer evoke possibility—both positively and negatively. Three elements from Bachelard stand out in examining the foyer: the imaginative depths of closed things; the evocative possibilities of doors; and the shifts in imagination that accompany staircases. Flanagan's portrayal of the foyer supports Bachelard's descriptions in the first two cases and modifies the assertions of the third.

With regard to closed things and doors, Bachelard emphasizes evocative possibility. In a discussion of chests and drawers, Bachelard makes the case that "there will always be more things in a closed, than in an open, box," continuing to say that "to verify images kills them, and it is always more enriching to *imagine* than to *experience*."[19] This assertion works for both dreams and nightmares. A gift is never quite as good as the anticipation of the gift; and the more we know about the monster lurking in the dark the less scary they are. But in not knowing we imagine far better or worse than what may actually exist, such that a simple door "can give images of hesitation, temptation, desire, security, welcome and respect."[20] Closed things, openings into new areas, are alive with possibility. The foyer of Hill House, with its many visible doors and halls leading to unexplored, hinted at areas of the house—simultaneously begs to be explored and fills the visitor with a dread of the unknown. Who knows what may be lurking in those unknown spaces, behind closed doors and around dark corners?

Staircases, for Bachelard, are typically fixed in our imaginations in relation to their destination. Cellar stairs are always imagined in relation to the descent into darkness that they provoke—we see ourselves at the top of them, looking down into the abyss; in contrast, stairs to the attic evince notions of "ascension to a more tranquil solitude."[21] The exception is stairs between a main floor and a "bedchamber" which are traversed often in both directions; the oneiric memory associated with such stairs, Bachelard asserts, is the joy accompanying a child's growth and the ability to take more than one stair at a time, developing long, leaping strides.[22]

But the stairs of Hill House are never so simply known. Throughout the series they may be seen to exemplify only two of Bachelard's oneiric patterns of movement. They are briefly shown as a space for children to traverse, explore, and play when the Crain family first moves in. In the remainder of the series, however, the stairs lead only to misery, no matter whether one is ascending or descending. Even in the escape to safety as Steve clings to Hugh and the pair descend together, they are only leaving one horror for another— abandoning Olivia in her madness for the broken family life to follow.

How the foyer stairs break Bachelard's mold, and how the elements of closed things and doors are used to the horrific advantage of the series is best exemplified in the sixth episode, "Two Storms." Here the series engages in its most imaginative uses and transformation of spaces as Hugh and various other characters traverse Shirley's funeral home only to find themselves standing in the halls and foyer of Hill House, tangibly depicting and exploring their memory. Flanagan's camera is mobile throughout all of this, whirling and gliding around his characters to showcase the melding of the past and present as they transition between the two spaces, blurring the lines between real and imagined. This visual exploration of the foyer, its alcoves, and the staircase presents Hill House as omnipotent and omnipresent, with no boundaries or limits to its influence. Indeed, the house's reach is demonstrated time and time again throughout the series to transcend limits on space, with ghosts appearing often far from the house's decaying walls. In this specific episode, the stairs lead Hugh from one tangible element of chaos and fear—the broken chandelier in the foyer—to other manifestations of the house's supernatural power—the hail, broken windows, and damaging influx of water. In other episodes, the staircase leads to the rooms where ghosts appear and chaos reigns. Ascending brings no relief to the imagination, and certainly no tranquility.

The foyer itself serves as the setting for Nell becoming lost in plain sight, disappearing into the dark fabric of the house as the others search for her even as she calls and reaches for them right before her eyes. In this sense the entryway to the house may be looked at as the entryway to its horrors. In Nell's case, even the foyer's open space become emblematic of the closed spaces and evocative doors of Bachelard, to the extent that the whole space of the house seems closed to her, an inaccessible reality that she can imagine but not touch.

Of note in all of this is that this visual presentation of Hill House and its exploration by Flanagan's roaming camera does not *emphasize* the house and its features. Never is the house's design or architecture caricatured or cast in stark, horrific relief. Instead, it is almost maliciously presented as a background element, acting merely as the space in which this family drama takes place. But it is through this ostensible disregard for the atmosphere of Hill House the camera is able to use the space to build a more pronounced, pervasive sense of dread. If the camera in this episode and its long sequences adopts the remembered perspective of Hugh and the Crain children, it betrays the dark influence of the house on their minds and memories. Especially as the camera circles and hovers throughout the family's activities during the storm, it is oppressive in its closeness, restless and relentless in its pursuit of their minds. Bachelard says that "when we recall the old house in its longitudinal detail, everything that ascends and descends comes to life again dynamically."[23] The dynamics that Flanagan emphasizes are probably not those which Bachelard would have seen as possible in such a space, but a clear dynamic relationship between ascent and descent is clearly present nonetheless.

The Red Room

Hill House's most evocative and enduring mystery is, of course, the Red Room, which acts as the centerpiece for how Flanagan subverts the expectations of space that Bachelard constructs. The room plays with elements of imaginative space that have already been mentioned, but also displays a logic of its own that disrupts attempts to explain the room through human rationality.

First, the room showcases a particular kind of intimate immensity for each of its varied inhabitants. By taking the form of a safe space for each, this one small room in the larger mansion takes on qualities that are useful and comforting for each family member. In this the room both calls out for the secrecy that Bachelard points to but invites imaginative contemplation for each of the Crains by being a safe haven where they can let down their guard—which is in turn what the house seems to feed upon.

Additionally, the room evokes the verticality that Bachelard so often emphasizes but complicates his assessment of the warmth and safety an attic or attic-like space provides. The vertiginous staircase leading to the Red Room first requires one to ascend to reach the house's ultimate horror. And though attic-like in its location, and even in some of its manifestations, there is no tranquility there save for the mad peace of Olivia's ostensible insanity. As has already been mentioned, the imagination here is inspired to the ultimate detriment of the inhabitant.

Most interesting, however, is the room's subversive mystery as the core of the house and its atmosphere, providing an altogether different explanation for why viewers and inhabitants should be afraid of Hill House. Recall Bachelard's assertions that a simple door "can give images of hesitation, temptation, desire, security, welcome and respect," and that "there will always be more things in a closed, than in an open, box."[24] In a viewer's initial assessment, the lacquered red door is a perfect fit for such descriptors and is thus rife with the imaginative possibilities of the unknown that exist beyond that liminal threshold. But in the end, Bachelard's belief that "to verify images kills them," and that "it is always more enriching to *imagine* than to *experience*" is subverted by the revelation of what the Red Room actually is. When we learn that we have actually seen inside the Red Room in nearly every episode, we realize that the horror of the house is not the mystery of what it could potentially contains. Instead, the horror is encapsulated in the Red Room's fluidity, how it exemplifies that Hill House follows a logic innate to the house, yet impossible for the Crains to comprehend.

Conclusion

Space does not permit a full exploration of the remainder of Hill House, and so unfortunately my closing observations must be brief. Many of the visual elements of *Hill House* complicate Bachelard's imaginative assessment

60　II. The House

of the home and call into question the nature of what "horrific space" is. Ultimately, film is a powerful tool of defamiliarization and offers a diversity of avenues for phenomenological exploration and insight. My hope is that I have not set Bachelard up as a straw man. Rather, I hope that this simple and preliminary demonstration of how *The Haunting of Hill House* uses space in defying Bachelard's assertions provokes further analysis and reflection on how the cinematic art uses its tools to play on and violate expectations of comfort and space in the horror genre.

Notes

1. Shirley Jackson, *The Haunting of Hill House* (New York: Penguin, 1959/2006), 1, 30.
2. Stephen King, *Danse Macabre*, Reprint edition (New York: Gallery Books, 2010), 278, 282–84.
3. Dylan Trigg, *The Memory of Place: A Phenomenology of the Uncanny* (Athens, OH: Ohio University Press, 2013), 4. Emphasis his.
4. Max Van Manen, *Phenomenology of Practice: Meaning-Giving Methods in Phenomenological Research and Writing* (Walnut Creek, California: Left Coast Press, 2014), 389.
5. Vivian Sobchack, *The Address of the Eye: A Phenomenology of Film Experience* (Princeton, NJ: Princeton University Press, 1992), 91.
6. Gaston Bachelard, *The Poetics of Space*, trans. Maria Jolas (Boston: Beacon Press, 1964/1994), xix.
7. Bachelard, 47.
8. Bachelard, 6.
9. Bachelard, 23–25.
10. Bachelard, *The Poetics of Space*, 56.
11. Bachelard, 81.
12. Bachelard, 154–55.
13. Bachelard, 201, 202.
14. Bachelard, 23–29.
15. Bachelard, 18, 19. Emphasis his.
16. Bachelard, *The Poetics of Space*, 136.
17. Bachelard, 144.
18. Jackson, *The Haunting of Hill House*, 1.
19. Bachelard, *The Poetics of Space*, 88. Emphasis his.
20. Bachelard, 224.
21. Bachelard, 25–26.
22. Bachelard, 26.
23. Bachelard, *The Poetics of Space*, 26.
24. Bachelard, 88, 224.

III
The Trauma

Some Things Can't Be Told
Gothic Trauma

Jeanette A. Laredo

The Netflix adaptation of Shirley Jackson's novel *The Haunting of Hill House* has been hugely popular, not for its jump scares or special effects, but for how it portrays the psychological trauma of the Crain family. The Crains are haunted by the ghosts of Hill House and the loss of their mother which causes the disintegration of their family. Crain parents Olivia and Hugh move into the infamous Hill House with their children Steven, Shirley, Theo, Nell and Luke only to experience a series of disturbing paranormal events that climax in the trauma of Olivia's death. According to modern theories of trauma, psychological trauma results in a split between the conscious self and the traumatized Other that does not allow trauma to be accessed by the conscious self. This split creates gaps in memory that frustrate the survivor's ability to construct a coherent narrative of their trauma. Because the survivor's trauma cannot be integrated into linear reality it tends to return and repeat itself. Olivia Crain's mysterious death presents a traumatic absence that fragments the narrative of *Hill House*. Past and present merge as the Crain siblings struggle with their incomplete impressions of the night their mother died and are confronted with the repetition of that trauma in the death of their sister Nell. This essay will examine Netflix's *The Haunting of Hill House* through the lens of modern trauma theory and critique the implications of "fixing" trauma that the series presents with its ending.

Gothic Trauma

The word trauma comes from the Greek "ραῦμα" meaning a physical wound, but psychoanalysis expands the term to include "psychic injury" caused by "emotional shock."[1] Throughout this essay trauma will refer to psychological trauma which is the result of an overwhelming experience that compromises one's ability to cope with the emotions that arise from that experience. In the case of the Crain family, each member experiences the dual traumas of losing a loved one and living in a haunted house. According to Shoshana Felman's and Dori Laub's *Testimony: Crisis of Witnessing in Literature, Psychoanalysis and History* (1992) and Cathy Caruth's *Unclaimed Experience: Trauma, Narrative and History* (1996), trauma results in a split between the conscious self and the traumatized Other that does not allow trauma to be accessed by the conscious self. This split creates gaps in memory that frustrate the survivor's ability to construct a coherent narrative of their trauma. These gaps are the result of trauma's "paradoxical temporality" since trauma is an event that happens "too soon, too unexpectedly, to be fully known" or to be integrated into linear reality.[2] Because of this, trauma can return in the form of unconscious repetition, becoming an event that "in effect, does not end."[3] Trauma can also result in a crisis of witnessing if outside witnesses fail to testify to the trauma of the Other.

Since the publication of Horace Walpole's seminal novel *The Castle of Otranto* (1764), the Gothic genre has been thematically concerned with trauma. In Walpole's novel, the young and vulnerable Isabella flees through underground tunnels and decrepit churches after her fiancé is crushed to death by a giant helmet to escape the lecherous advances of her would-be father in law Lord Manfred. Walpole's novel established many of the stock elements the genre: repressed family secrets, haunted castles, and the intrusion of the supernatural. Taking a cue from its Gothic source material, Netflix's *Haunting of Hill House* incorporates these elements to create a sense of gnawing unease in the viewer with one critic calling it a "modern Gothic masterpiece."[4] In addition to these plot elements, *Haunting* also borrows the disjointed narrative structure common to Gothic works that represents the fragmenting experience of trauma. *Otranto* established "the pattern for later writers, who work with techniques of interruption, deferral, ellipsis, framing, to splice stories into bits and pieces and disrupt superficial narrative unity or linearity," to produce texts that are "fragmented, interrupted, unreadable, or presented through multiple framings and narrators."[5]

The conventions of the Gothic genre mirror these characteristics of trauma—traumatic repetition, fractured storylines, and unexplained gaps in time—and the Netflix series uses these Gothic tropes to represent the psychological trauma of the Crains. The series specifically uses the phenomenon of a haunting as a powerful metaphor for the traumatic experience where an event does not end and continues to return. In fiction most ghosts haunt the place of their sudden death, but *Haunting* follows the current trend of films like *Insidious* (2010) where it is the person instead of the place that is haunted.

As a result, Nell's ghost appears in the house, Steven's apartment, Shirley's funeral home, and in Theo's car. Her ability to appear anywhere recreates the tendency of trauma to transcend time and place, staying with the traumatized individual instead of at the site where the trauma occurred.

A Ghost Is Just an Absence: Traumatic Gaps and Fragmentation

In the opening episode of the series Steven Crain has debunked the haunting of a fan, Mrs. Walker, by her dead husband, telling her "Ghosts are guilt. Ghosts are secrets. Ghosts are regrets and failings. But most times, most times … a ghost is a wish" ("Steven Sees a Ghost"). We can also add to this list that ghosts are absences. Because trauma happens too soon to be incorporated into linear time it creates an absence in experience that can fragment the survivor's narrative. The absence that plagues *Haunting* is the mysterious death of Olivia Crain. Olivia embodies the gaps left by trauma because as a ghost she is present yet absent, evoking Derrida's concept of the trace. Drawing on Levinas's idea of the Other, Derrida defines the trace as "a sign (signifier and signified) derives its meaning from its difference from other signs (e.g., black is not white, up is not down)." Thus, a sign always contains a trace of "what it absolutely is not."[6] The trace as a "mark of the absence of a presence, an always already absent present" resembles absences left by trauma.[7] Olivia's ghost is a specter of the Crain's traumatic past, an "already absent present" that haunts them in the present.

Olivia's death/absence fragments her family's subsequent narratives. The result is a kaleidoscope of perspectives which the series achieves by telling each episode from the subjective viewpoint of one of the five Crain siblings in order from oldest to youngest: Steven, Shirley, Theo, Luke and Nell. Their memories of the last night in the house are incomplete shards that don't fit neatly together to form a narrative whole. Despite writing a book on Hill House, Steven has the most fragmented picture of that night. Awakened by his father, Steven must promise to "keep [his] eyes closed no matter what [he hears]" while his father carries him to the car ("Two Storms"). Steven of course opens them and sees a shadowy figure with long flowing hair and streaming white robes, the quintessential female ghost. By telling his son to close his eyes, Hugh acts as Steven's rational consciousness, denying him the full knowledge of his trauma. Carrying him to the car like a child, Hugh infantilizes Steven by not trusting him with the truth of what is happening. Also Hugh telling Steven that the figure he saw is "not mom" leaves Steven unsure about whether what he has really seen is a ghost or his mother, or both ("Two Storms").

This is a role Hugh will play through the series as he paternally reassures his distraught children that the supernatural chaos around them has a perfectly rational explanation. When Luke tells his father about the man he saw in the basement Hugh responds that once Luke can acknowledge the difference between "what's real and what's imaginary" he can have a have the "big boy [bowler] hat" he covets ("Twin Thing"). Hugh's insistence that Luke grow up is a male rejection of the paranormal as feminine and irrational. By denying the truth of the supernatural and the trauma it represents, Hugh only further splinters his family's narrative and allows it to return with a vengeance.

"I Felt Nothing": Trauma and Dissociation

Confronted with the trauma of their mother's death, the Crain siblings experience varying levels of dissociation. Dissociation is a common response to the traumatic experience which "produces an overwhelming need to escape what is, in reality, inescapable."[8] Freud theorized that dissociation occurs when the ego "actively represses memories of the traumatic event to protect itself from experiencing the painful affect associated with them."[9] Dissociation can result in the survivor feeling disconnected from their body and emotions as their "awareness becomes fragmented."[10]

Steven attempts to solve this fragmentation by writing an authoritative account of the Crain family haunting. Steven's book masquerades as the official narrative of the haunting at Hill House, but it does not fully capture the disjointed, jarring, and incomplete nature of the family's traumatic experience. Steven fills in the gaps and simplifies his family's trauma for the sake of narrative cohesion. Instead of a literal haunting, Steven writes the story of a family haunted by mental illness, preferring to blame a natural cause instead of a supernatural one for his mother's death. It's a successful formula that Steven uses to create a whole *Haunting* franchise and he tells Mrs. Walker that he'll still write a story about her "haunting" even though it isn't true ("Steven Sees a Ghost"). Her experience has all the makings of a good ghost story: a traumatic loss, a deeply loving relationship between husband and wife, and a "haunted" home that served as a hospice in the 1960s. Steven explains that "I'll need to take some liberties. I always do," describing how he'll weave the truth into a good ghost story ("Steven Sees a Ghost"). Like his planned account of Mrs. Walker's haunting, Steven's novelization of his family's trauma may be a good ghost story, but it comes at a terrible cost. Shirley accuses him of "raping the family" because his account is a violation and a denial of the very real trauma they have experienced ("Steven Sees a Ghost"). In writing this authoritative account of his family's haunting Steven denies the rest of his siblings a voice. This is perfectly dramatized when Nell confronts her brother at book reading for his latest work *The Haunting of Alcatraz*:

> Now, you stand there, and you talk about ghosts and spirits … and yet you don't believe in any of it. And you tell me I'm crazy and that Mom was crazy, and Luke's crazy, and we're all just nuts, and then you tell *our* stories, *my* stories, the same stories you told me were just *dreams or delusions* ["The Bent-Neck Lady," emphasis added].

Here Nell represents Steven's traumatized Other, crying out to him with the knowledge of the repressed trauma that has been denied by his authoritative account. Steven must silence Nell's narrative and co-opt her stories because he must deny the existence of ghosts. Acknowledging them would mean admitting that he has been a victim of trauma, a truth that would engulf and destroy his sanity. Ironically, or perhaps fittingly, it is this denial of his trauma that creates a ghost in his sister Nell. By denying the truth of her experience and failing to witness her trauma Steven pushes her towards Hill House and her death. His denial is so complete that he cannot even recognize her ghost when he sees it at the end of episode one ("Steven Sees a Ghost").

Like her older brother Steven, Shirley also suppresses her traumatic experiences with the supernatural and believes that a mental illness killed her mother instead of a haunting. Shirley's way of dissociating from her trauma is to erase all evidence that it ever happened. Inspired by the funeral director who "fixed" her mother for viewing after her violent death, Shirley likewise "fixes" the dead loved ones of her clients as the director and embalmer of a funeral home. The term "fix" has a dual meaning that is relevant here: "to mend or repair" and "to make fast or permanent."[11] Shirley repairs the bodies of dead people by cleaning them, filling their wounds with modeling material, dressing them and applying makeup. By repairing them she attempts to "fix" the trauma by returning the dead person to a time before they were dead. This activity represents Shirley's attempt to resolve her own trauma by going back to a time before it happened. But Shirley's attempts to surpass the source of trauma only fail to "uncover the lost truth of some ideal past" she can never get back to.[12] Instead, Shirley misses "both the abyssal logic and the paradoxical temporality of the [traumatic] experience" since by fixing these people she cannot return them to life, and can only make their condition more permanent or "fixed."[13] This instead leads to a proliferation of trauma. When Shirley is preparing her sister for burial a carrion beetle erupts from between Nell's lips, breaking the illusion of life that Shirley has tried to create ("Open Casket"). The beetle is an echo of the Shirley's past trauma with a dead kitten who had an identical insect emerge from its mouth. In this moment, Shirley's past and present trauma merge as the ghost of her mother appears on the table next to Nell. Bruised, torn, and hollow-eyed,

Olivia is not the "fixed" version of herself that Shirley saw at the funeral viewing as a child. She holds the box that served as the kitten's coffin and an unearthly screech comes from inside. The moment is a compounding of Shirley's traumas that are a terrifying reminder of what she cannot repair or escape.

As the middle child, Theo is predictably torn between her older siblings who rationalize their mother's haunting as mental illness and the younger twins who acknowledge the supernatural as the source of their trauma. Theo believes the twins because she has the ability to sense people's emotions and experiences through touch. This is yet another example of how the series codes the supernatural as feminine. From Theo's grandmother Mary who was "always bundled up" against a chill no one else could feel, to Olivia whose "color storm" headaches show her visions of the house's past inhabitants, to Shirley who says strange things in her sleep and Nell who describes Hill House as "loud," the Crain women all possess a sensitivity to the supernatural ("Touch"). Theo's "sensitive" nature does not allow her to deny that the supernatural exists, so instead she dissociates by building walls to isolate herself physically, by wearing gloves, and emotionally by keeping people at arm's length. Theo describes how, as a child, she would imagine "building a big wall all around [herself] made of the strongest bricks in the whole world" and she would add bricks "until that wall was so thick and so strong [she] knew [she'd] be safe in there forever" ("Touch"). Theo's extreme boundaries may protect her from experiencing the trauma of loss, but they also prevent her from witnessing the trauma of her sister Nell.

In yet another example of "the twin thing" Luke and Nell both experience dissociation in a way that mimics death. Traumatized by his encounter with ghosts and nearly being killed by his own mother, Luke dissociates by abusing drugs. This is not surprising since multiple studies examining people who abuse drugs or alcohol have found between 36 percent and 50 percent have a lifetime prevalence of posttraumatic stress disorder.[14] Luke starts using when "the things from when [he] was a kid ... [come] back," namely the ghost of the tall man in the bowler hat. The tall man's haunting of Luke as an adult resembles the symptoms of substance withdrawal. Luke has been sober for 90 days, but he still experiences chills, sweating and a stiffening of his limbs. These symptoms, while common to drug withdrawal, are also evocative of rigor mortis. Rigor mortis is the stiffening of the joints and muscles of a dead body that begins few hours after death and can last anywhere from one to four days. Luke's dissociation is death-like because dissociation entails the separation of victim from their body and emotions, "on an experiential level ... [it] feels like a partial death" and "people facing extreme traumatic situations may feel they are about to die or are dying."[15] Nell experiences a similar death-like dissociation in the form of sleep-paralysis. Sleep paralysis occurs when a person wakes up before finishing their REM (Rapid Eye Movement) cycle of sleep. During the REM cycle, the brain switches off the body's muscles to prevent a person from acting out the vivid dreams that occur during this stage of sleep. People experiencing sleep paralysis are unable to move or speak and report terrifying hallucinations. The cause of Nell's sleep paralysis is no hallucination, but the ghost of the Bent-Neck Lady who has haunted her since childhood. Instead of fighting or fleeing this supernatural threat, Nell's dissociative coping mechanism is to literally "play dead" as sleep paralysis keeps her in a corpse-like state.

"The Bent-Neck Lady... She's back": Traumatic Repetition and Ghost as Traumatized "Other"

Since trauma cannot be fully absorbed the moment it occurs, it and can return in the form of unconscious repetition. One example given by Felman and Laub is the experience of Holocaust survivor Martin Gray. Gray watched his entire family burn in the crematoriums of Treblinka and Warsaw. Years later he married and moved to France only to lose his family again in the flames of a forest fire. Gray recounts that this second loss of his family was "just like Warsaw" with "the crackling of the fire" and "for the second time I remained alone with nothing but my life."[16] *Haunting* is full of these traumatic repetitions and the series uses ghosts as a fruitful metaphor for trauma that continues to return and repeat. There is the death of Shirley's kittens that foreshadows the death of her mother, and the death of Arthur during a visitation from the Bent-Neck Lady, but traumatic repetition is most apparent in the death of Nell. Nell's death is uncannily similar to her mother's: she dresses in her mother's clothes and falls from the same spiral staircase. Nell's death represents a traumatic repetition for her siblings because they were unable to process the original traumatic event of Olivia's death. Their unresolved trauma was not validated by witnesses and as a result they failed to witness Nell's trauma, causing trauma to return and repeat itself.

Trauma returns because of the split between the conscious self and the traumatized Other and this phenomenon is best represented in *Haunting* by Nell and the Bent-Neck Lady. The double wounding of trauma results in a doubling of the self, as trauma creates a split between the conscious self and what Caruth calls the traumatized Other. Emmanuel Levinas defines "the Other [as] what I myself am not. The Other is this, not because of the Other's character, or physiognomy, or psychology, but because of the Other's very alterity."[17] Caruth conceives the traumatic Other as an internal rather than an external other, defining it as "the other within the self that retains the memory of the 'unwitting' traumatic events of one's past" (Caruth 1996). The specter of the Bent-Neck Lady represents Nell's traumatized Other and she cries out with the hidden knowledge of the trauma Nell has yet to experience. Hovering above a paralyzed young Nell, all she can whisper is "no no no no no" in an urgent denial of what she is seeing and despair that it cannot be prevented ("The Bent-Neck Lady"). Young Nell is unable to recognize herself as the traumatized Other, because the Other is fundamentally changed by trauma and is no longer recognizable by the conscious self. This lack of recognition traps Nell in an endless loop of trauma past, present and yet to be experienced.

"A little spill": Traumatic Time in Hill House

When Nell wakes screaming after a visit from the Bent-Neck Lady, Hugh comforts her by telling her that a child's dreams can sometimes "spill out" into wakefulness ("Steven Sees a Ghost"). Hugh's description of the Bent-Neck Lady as a "a little spill" resembles the phenomenon of traumatic time, a moment that is too full and unable to hold the excess of temporality trauma creates. Writing about Holocaust survivors, Lawrence Langer calls this phenomenon durational time. Unlike linear time, durational time "exists this side of the forgotten, not to be dredged from memory because it is always, has always been there ... [a] constantly re-experienced time, [that] threatens the chronology of experienced time ... [that] leaps out of the chronology, establishing its own momentum, or fixation."[18] This spilling out of time occurs when Nell realizes she *is* the Bent-Neck Lady. Past and present collapse as hanging in her noose she drops into the past during key moments when the Bent-Neck Lady appeared to Nell: at the motel, when Nell is driving Luke to rehab, on the night Arthur dies all the way back to young Nell's first encounter with the apparition. This convergence of past and present represents the experience of Nell's trauma as one that is outside the bounds of linear time ("The Bent-Neck Lady").

The series recreates parts of the temporal and emotional experience of trauma with its format. Available on demand in ten binge-able episodes, the series entices viewers to watch in one or two sittings. Dr. John Mayer explains how binging "can work like a steel door that blocks our brains from thinking about those constant stressors that force themselves into our thoughts," and many binge viewers find themselves disconnected from the present as they watch hours of their favorite show.[19] Binging also releases the pleasure chemical dopamine causing a "drug-like high" which can soon turn into situational depression when the show ends.[20] In a University of Toledo study, "142 out of 408 participants[who] identified themselves as binge-watchers ... reported higher levels of stress, anxiety and depression" than those who did not binge.[21]

As a result, binging *Hill House* is a pale echo of the anxiety-inducing experience of trauma as one outside of linear time for victims.

Whatever Walked There Walked ... Together? The Cost of "Fixing" Trauma

After nine episodes of soul-wrenching terror, most viewers were happy to see a positive ending for the Crains, but some fans questioned if this uneasy peace was too good to be true. The final episode of the series shows the Crain siblings gathered around Luke, who is celebrating two years of sobriety by cutting into a cake with red frosting. This detail is chilling because it suggests the Crains never escaped the Red Room at Hill House. Oliver Jackson-Cohen, the actor who plays Luke, explains "For Luke, when Luke gets taken to the hotel room, he's worn Converse [sneakers] throughout the show, and all of a sudden his Converse are red" and "Steven is wearing a red jumper [in his Red Room delusion.]"[22] While show creator Mike Flanagan has put to rest any doubts that the ending is as it appears, he admits there was a debate about whether to save or damn the Crains: "We talked for a very, very long time about putting the Red Room window, that weird vertical window, in the background of this shot. And I ultimately decided not to. It was too cruel."[23]

It may be less cruel, but Flanagan's "good" ending is completely at odds with the phenomenon of trauma. Throughout the series the house has been depicted as the site of trauma and narrative rupture. Hugh fails to "fix" both the house and his children's trauma by staying silent and keeping the secret of the night their mother died. Instead of preventing trauma, his silence only prevents him from witnessing the trauma of his children. This leads to the repetition of that experience that drives them back to the very site of trauma: Hill House. The series repeatedly illustrates how efforts to fix trauma by locating its source or returning to a time before will inevitably fail and that witnessing the trauma of others is the only way to begin healing.

Instead, Flanagan chooses to make the Crain men the arbiters of trauma. In Steven's final conversation with his father he says:

> STEVEN: I wish you would have told me.
> HUGH: You didn't tell your *sisters* what you saw. Why not? Some things can't be told. You live them or you don't. But they can't be told. I'm sorry.
> STEVEN: No. I'm sorry, Dad ["Silence Lay Steadily," emphasis added].

On the surface, Hugh's reply gestures to the narrative impossibility of representing trauma, but the meaning of his words takes a turn when Steven does get to experience his father's trauma via an extended flashback. It seems that the knowledge of trauma is reserved for the Crain men as Steven vows to keep the house and its ghosts. Flanagan chooses this "good" ending to present the idea that trauma is fixable through the sacrifice of a patriarchal figure, explaining: "If they're still in the Red Room, it robs Hugh's sacrifice [and the show itself] of any meaning."[24]

Flanagan's male-centered adaptation of *Hill House* is a stark reversal from Shirley' Jackson's female Gothic novel. Jackson crafts a story that is "a careful representation of female experience in a world as claustrophobic as the bad angles of Hill House."[25] Her open-ended narrative uses narrative ruptures and the supernatural to represent the confusion and terror women experience when they are trapped in domestic roles by a patriarchal society. Much like Hugh, Flanagan moves into the house that Jackson built and attempts to "fix" these narrative defects by tying up loose ends and firmly shutting doors to create a narrative that contains the supernatural and makes rational sense. This is most apparent in Flanagan's revision of the final line of Jackson's book from "whatever walked there walked *alone*," to "whatever walked there walked *together*." ("Silence Lay Steadily"). This changes Jackson's message of fragmentation and loneliness to one of unity and communion, effectively reducing "the ungraspable terrors" of the supernatural to "mere 'issues,' as if evil were just another trauma to be confronted, then resolved."[26] In the same way that Steven chooses to smooth out the fragmented, disjointed and terrifying edges of his family's trauma to tell a good ghost story, Flanagan blunts the impact of a series that has authentically represented trauma at a cost more terrible than any of the specters haunting Hill House.

Notes

1. Felman, Shoshana, and Dori Laub. *Testimony: Crises of Witnessing in Literature, Psychoanalysis, and History* (New York: Routledge, 1991), 67.
2. Belau, Linda. "Trauma and the Material Signifier." *Postmodern Culture: An Electronic Journal of Interdisciplinary Criticism* 11, 2 (2001). http://muse.jhu.edu/article/27729; Caruth, Cathy. *Unclaimed Experience: Trauma, Narrative, and History* (Baltimore: Johns Hopkins University Press, 1996), 3–4.
3. Felman and Laub, *Testimony*, 67.
4. Rodriguez, Alfonzo. "The Haunting of Hill House: A Modern Gothic Masterpiece." *The Carolinian*. October 31, 2018, https://carolinianuncg.com/2018/10/31/the-haunting-of-hill-house-a-modern-gothic-masterpiece. See also John Palisano's essay in this volume.
5. Grove, Allen W. "To Make a Long Story Short: Gothic Fragments and the Gender Politics of Incompleteness." *Studies in Short Fiction* 34,1 (1997): 2; Kilgour, Maggie and Molson Kilgour. *The Rise of the Gothic Novel*. (Routledge, 2013), 6.
6. Derrida, Jacques. *Writing and Difference* (Chicago: University of Chicago Press, 1978), 394.
7. Derrida, Jacques. *Of Grammatology* (Baltimore: Johns Hopkins University Press, 1976), xvii.
8. Elizabeth A. Waites, *Trauma and Survival: Post-Traumatic and Dissociative Disorders in Women* (New York: Norton, 1993), 14. (Waites 1993).
9. Bremner, J. Douglas, and Charles R. Marmar. *Trauma, Memory, and Dissociation*. (American Psychiatric Press, 2002), 11.
10. Lanius, Ulrich F., Sandra L. Paulsen, and Frank M. Corrigan, eds. *Neurobiology and*

Treatment of Traumatic Dissociation: Towards an Embodied Self. (Springer Publishing Company, 2014), 52.
 11. "fix, V." OED Online. June 2019. Oxford University Press. https://www.oed.com/view/Entry/70815?rskey=P7qiTw&result=3 (accessed June 06, 2019).
 12. Belau, Maternal Signifier, http://muse.jhu.edu/article/27729.
 13. *Ibid.*, http://muse.jhu.edu/article/27729.
 14. Jacobsen, L.K., S.M. Southwick, and T.R. Kosten. "Substance Use Disorders in Patients with Posttraumatic Stress Disorder: A Review of the Literature." *The American Journal of Psychiatry* 158, 8 (2001): 206. doi:10.1176/appi.ajp.158.8.1184.
 15. Frankel, Jay. "Identification and 'Traumatic Aloneness': Reply to Commentaries by Berman and Bonomi." *Psychoanalytic Dialogues* 12, 1 (2002): 167.
 16. Felman and Laub, *Testimony*, 66.
 17. Emmanuel Lévinas, *Time and the Other and Additional Essays* (Pittsburgh, Pennsylvania: Duquesne University Press, 1987), 83.
 18. Otto, "Disoriented, Twice Removed from the Real, Racked by Passion in Walpole's Protean Theatres of Sensation," 693.
 19. Page, Danielle. "What Happens to Your Brain When You Binge-Watch a TV Series." NBC News. October 4, 2017. https://www.nbcnews.com/better/health/what-happens-your-brain-when-you-binge-watch-tv-series-ncna816991.
 20. *Ibid.*
 21. *Ibid.*
 22. Maas, Jennifer. "'Haunting of Hill House': Oliver Jackson-Cohen Points to Red Room Clue That Hints Crains Never Made It Out." *The Wrap*. November 12, 2018. https://www.thewrap.com/haunting-of-hill-house-red-room-ending-luke-oliver-jackson-cohen.
 23. Vineyard, Jennifer. "Haunting of Hill House Ending, Explained: Mike Flanagan Talks Easter Eggs." *Thrillist*. October 15, 2018. https://www.thrillist.com/entertainment/nation/haunting-of-hill-house-ending-explained-mike-flanagan-interview.
 24. Maas, Jennifer. "'Haunting of Hill House' Creator Shuts Down Red Room Theories." *The Wrap*. November 27, 2018. https://www.thewrap.com/haunting-of-hill-house-ending-red-room-luke-cake-theory-face-value-mike-flanagan.
 25. Mandelo, Brit. "Whatever Walked There, Walked Alone: Revisiting Shirley Jackson's the Haunting of Hill House." *TOR*. October 12, 2018. https://www.tor.com/2018/10/12/whatever-walked-there-walked-alone-revisiting-shirley-jacksons-the-haunting-of-hill-house/.
 26. Nussbaum, Emily. "Netflix's Soul-Dead Version of 'The Haunting of Hill House.'" *The New Yorker*. November 2, 2018. https://www.newyorker.com/magazine/2018/11/12/netflixs-soul-dead-version-of-the-haunting-of-hill-house.

Recovery from Trauma in Post-9/11 Horror/Terror of Mike Flanagan's Oeuvre

Aaron K.H. Ho

> One never inherits without coming to terms with some specter, and therefore with more than one specter.
> —Jacques Derrida

A crumbling building consumes lives of citizens who spend productive hours within. Windows burst and shatter violently (as if) upon an ungovernable impact beyond imagination, a monument destroyed by supernatural power. Some die of asphyxiation, some from leaping off a great height (who can unsee the controversial and extremely disturbing photograph, *The Falling Man*, by Richard Drew?); and others from imbibing poisonous substances. An authoritative, protective (paternal?) figure keeps returning to the building to extricate the people trapped inside although many have already died, and in the process, he sacrifices himself. The tragedy reaches such a mythic status that books are written on it. Survivors suffer from post-traumatic stress disorders and return to the site to make sense of the senseless tragedy. The above-mentioned scenario describes the events of 9/11 and *The Haunting of Hill House* (henceforth, *The Haunting*).

There is a long history of genre films representing obliquely and commenting indirectly on real-world events. As early as 1967, in "The Imagination of Disaster," Susan Sontag argues that sci-fi movies function as allegories of fears about communism and the threats of nuclear war in avoidance of direct confrontation of trauma which may lead to pathology and panic. The association of media representations with, as Noam Chomsky notes, the first attack on American soil since the 1812 war is, therefore, hardly surprising or new. Paul A. Cantor argues that *"after 9/11, American popular culture would never be the same again."*[1] By extension, it is generally assumed by academics and scholars that "American horror films must, first and foremost, be seen in the context of American culture, politics, and history."[2] As a result, much has been written to link American horror films with 9/11. However, *The Haunting* contributes to the post–9/11 conversations not merely in terms of content but also ideas; while other representations focus mainly on fear and zombies, as we shall see later, Mike Flanagan's television series on specters negotiates and navigates the trauma surrounding 9/11, reaching a rapprochement, an optimism rarely seen in his previous or other filmmakers' productions. Catharsis, as originally used by Aristotle, purges pity and fear through tragedy (and possibly comedy), but Flanagan employs horror as a therapeutic method to recover from the national trauma of 9/11, as exemplified in the happy ending of the television series.

Post–9/11 Horror

Among the first to note the possibility of post–9/11 horror, John S. Nelson argues that before we could assimilate our traumatic experiences into our cultural memory, elements of the event have to be broken down and reconfigured into digestible morsels; and horror offers a "safe" way to encode the elements in the process of cinematic assimilation and to subconsciously resolve the anxieties and trauma. Then-president George W. Bush denounced 9/11 and all acts of terrorism as "evil" and Nelson observes the potentiality of horror films as representations of evils in the post–9/11 era. Furthermore, at the root of the horror genre is the intense effect of fear of the unknown, as terrorists are often seen as the "Other." As Adam Lowenstein points out, "the modern horror film may well be the genre of our time that registers most brutally the legacies of historical trauma."[3] Post–9/11 horror then simultaneously draws attention to and disguises the terror.

In terms of sub-genres of horror, scholars have discussed the allegorical possibility of 9/11 in films, a process whereby viewer, history, and representation negotiate and produce cultural meanings. Kyle Bishop traces the renaissance of zombies in popular media, a trend that was dying in the '90s to be revived by 9/11: "it does not take much of a stretch to see the parallel between zombies and anonymous terrorists who seek to convert others within society to their deadly cause."[4] Following Bishop, Terence McSweeney (2010), Anna Froula (2010), and Nicole Birch-Bayley (2012) dissect various zombie films and television series in reference to 9/11. Beth A. Kattelman (2009), Marita Gronnvoll (2010), Reynold Humphries (2010), Guy Westwell (2014), and Aaron Michael Kerner (2015) draw parallels between the inhumane interrogation tactics at Guantanamo Bay and the rise of "torture porn" productions such as *Saw*. Christina Wilkins (2018) discusses the post–9/11 vampires. In general, most essays on post–9/11 horror representations on terrorism posit a bleak future for humankind, exemplified by the recent television series *The Passage* (2019), which ends with vampires terrorizing humans and taking over the world. Missing in the critical analysis of post–9/11 horror is the optimism and recovery from trauma found in Flanagan's television series on ghosts.

Mike Flanagan and Post-9/11 Horror

Flanagan confided in an interview that one of his greatest influences when preparing for *Ouija: Origin of Evil* (2016) was *Die Hard*.[5] On the surface, a horror film may share limited commonalities with an action flick but in both movies as well as most of Flanagan's other productions (*Oculus, Before I Wake, Gerald's Game,* and *The Haunting*), citizens are trapped or tormented or killed in a building by an evil force. Flanagan's constant return to the same theme—people haunted, dying in a house—mirrors the trauma theory of Freud and, later Cathy Caruth, who both state that when trauma is unassimilated, it "returns to haunt the survivor later on."[6] In order to retroactively overcome the trauma by filling in narrative gaps to grasp the incompressibility of the event, this haunting recurs as flashbacks, hallucinations, and dreams—all narrative techniques that Flanagan utilizes in *The Haunting*.

The impact of *Die Hard* as an action thriller on Flanagan goes beyond coincidental narratives. When 9/11 first happened, pundits and the Bush administration often called the horrific event "unimaginable." Yet, Jean Baudrillard (2003), Robert Altman (2002), Norman Mailer (2004), and Slavoj Žižek (2002) took the unpopular and controversial but ultimately convincing opinion that Western apocalyptic and action productions presaged and even constructed the events of 9/11. Žižek writes, "for us, corrupted by Hollywood, the landscape and the shots of the collapsing towers could not but be reminiscent of the most breathtaking scenes in big catastrophe productions."[7] Following Žižek et al, Geoff King perceives the similarities between the collapse of the Twin Towers and action movies such as *Independence Day, Armageddon* and—*Die Hard*. As a film about a group of former terrorists holding a building of citizens hostage in Los Angeles and blowing up part of the building, *Die Hard* provides Flanagan a framework to incorporate real-life situations into his oeuvre.

In an interview regarding *The Haunting*, he said:

> what makes scariest work is when you can ground it in the world. If you're grounded in real-life horror, in the darkness that we all really have to deal with, then the genre,

as an allegory, really starts to work.... The heavier ideas that I wanted to talk about in the show, we get this chance to deal with them, allegorically and metaphorically.... We get to deal with real, authentic, dark human stuff, but we get a pass and we get to deal with it in different ways because it's a genre show.... [W]hat I love the most about the genre [is] a chance to really look at the real darkness that we all have, in a safe and metaphorical space.[8]

If we read his statement and his film influences—as advised through his insistence on the allegory—with reference to 9/11, the one common and most traumatizing "real-life horror ... *we* all really have to deal with" (my emphasis) is our shared cultural memory of terrorists' driving planes into the buildings. As Flanagan explained in another interview, "when you talk about a person being haunted, a ghost is boring unless it's directly tied to an experience, emotion or something that's intrinsic to a character. We're all haunted as people."[9] His statement on haunting mirrors Freud's ideas of trauma in "Remembering, Repeating and Working Through" (1914) and "Mourning and Melancholia" (1917), in which the ego, in a refusal to separate itself from the object of loss, enters a pathological state where the self replays the trauma inwardly and torments itself. Flanagan could have easily said, "We're all haunted as *a* people" by our common experience and feelings of horror at the events of 9/11.

Haunting Trauma

Productions about zombies and vampires offer bleak metaphors of the future fearful of terrorists preying on human civilization, but Flanagan, by grounding his work in reality, deals with the real-life aftermath of trauma after being terrorized. "Terrorism," Behzad Hassani writes, "erodes both the individual and the community level, the sense of security and safety of the daily life. It defies our natural need to conceptualize life on earth as predictable, orderly, logical, and controllable,"[10] just as horror is irrational and uncontrollable. This trauma affects the entire community including survivors, witnesses, and people watching the attacks on television. While there were about 15,552 people at World Trade Center on the day of the attack,[11] the repercussions spread far and wide throughout the USA. Three months after the attack, 71 percent of all Americans experienced depressed feelings[12]; 44 percent had at least one of the five post-traumatic stress disorder symptoms.[13] Three years after the attack, E. Alison Holman et al. reported that the "53% increased incidence of cardiovascular ailments" was linked to watching the attacks on television.[14] These researchers' findings, that many Americans could suffer long-term trauma vicariously through televised images of the collapse of the Twin Towers, are supported by numerous other studies.[15] Judith

78   III. The Trauma

Herman's influential study on *Trauma and Recovery* defines psychological trauma as "an affliction of the powerless. At the moment of trauma, the victim is rendered helpless by overwhelming force."[16] Quoting the *Comprehensive Textbook of Psychiatry*, Herman elaborates that "the common denominator of psychological trauma is a feeling of 'intense fear, helplessness, loss of control, and the threat of annihilation.'"[17] All these feelings of trauma align with those evoke by horror and Flanagan transposes these traumatic feelings into horror. Talking about movies in general, Carl Plantinga argues that films generate and reconfigure negative emotions as a form of "working through."[18] Films' therapeutic function to address traumatic memory, supported by research by Barbara Klinger (2006) and Stefan Schulenberg (2003), is employed by Flanagan's compulsive return to horror throughout his career.

Jeffrey C. Alexander explains that cultural trauma "occurs when members of a collectivity [sic] feel that they have been subjected to a horrendous event that leaves indelible marks upon their group consciousness, marking their memories forever and changing their future identity in fundamental and irrevocable ways."[19] *The Haunting* could be decoded as an attempt for the characters to recover from trauma of their past. While they share a common experience of being terrorized/haunted by ghosts, each character deals with the traumatic events in different ways:

   1. When discussing *Psycho*, Leo Bersani notes that "a certain type of repetition of experience repairs inherently damaged or valueless experience. Experience may be overwhelming, practically impossible to absorb, but it is assumed ... that the work of art has the authority to master the presumed raw material of experience in a manner that uniquely gives value to, perhaps even redeems, that material."[20] Bersani's observation about repetition and art vis-à-vis unassimilated, traumatic experiences explains Steven Crain's motivation. Steven suffers from the denial of the experience but profits by making up stories to make productive meaning out the senseless tragedy and to divorce himself from any real implications, convincing himself that they are merely stories. However, as Caruth (1995) notes that even though trauma may cause one to constantly retell the story, words could not fully capture the trauma,[21] Steven's memoir of Hill House remains inaccurate;
   2. Afflicted by paranoia, Olivia fears that her children will be attacked and destroyed when they leave the house. This paranoia could be read in trauma studies as the moment of anamorphosis whereby an individual possesses a distorted interpretation of reality because malefactors destabilize the sense of security, uncovering the vulnerability of everyday life;
   3. Trauma scholar Roger Luckhurst explicates that trauma may

manifest as hypervigilance[22] as demonstrated in Shirley Crain who cannot relax and becomes an uptight control freak;
    4. Luke uses drugs to numb the trauma;
    5. Theodora avoids human contact as a form of disassociation;
    6. Nell endures a lifetime of sleep paralysis and hallucinations; and the delusional Hugh conjures the ghost of his dead wife lost in the tragedy.

The Crains clearly exhibit symptoms of trauma from living in Hill House and put up defenses just as survivors of 9/11 have.

Bringing 9/11 Trauma into Family Home Drama

Die Hard, where terrorists-turned-robbers from a country split by socialism blow up part of the commercial building named Nakatomi Plaza, could be interpreted via a Marxist, political perspective whereas in Flanagan's works, he has moved the capitalist setting to the private sphere of American home underlined by the diverse cast of *The Haunting*—Latinos, Asians, and Blacks, along with the white Crains, represent the racial fabric of American citizenry. To emphasize the concept of the American family even further, most settings in *The Haunting* and his other works occur in the confines of homes. This shift of setting does not signify that Flanagan's productions are not political but rather, the introspective movement reflects the current cultural concerns of terrorism about personal fears and anxieties being played out in the American home. The shift reflects the Bush administration's rhetoric of terrorism as exemplified by the oft-quoted statement Bush made on the fifth anniversary of 9/11: "We face an enemy determined to bring death and suffering into our homes."[23] Donald Pease argues convincingly that the creation of the Office of Homeland Security elides the public and the private because of the signifier (Homeland Security as safety for homes) and because of the Homeland Security and PATRIOT Acts that push back civil liberties such that the new symbolic arrangement "not only links the familial household to the nation but also imagines both in opposition to everything outside the geographical and conceptual borders of home."[24]

The slippage between home and Homeland creates the traumatic anxiety of potential terrorists living among Americans—as the 9/11 terrorists did for months—producing fear and suspicion in the commonplace. As a result, Colette Balmain argues that "American horror film, as ideological apparatus of the state, has reconfigured itself in the light of the shocking events of 9/11 in which the colonial invader became the invaded, as the impenetrable boundaries of America as nation-state were breached by the 'Other.'"[25] However, her generalization rings false for *The Haunting*. Hill House, we are told, has always existed and will continue to exist in America. The ghosts within Hill House are American. In many of Flanagan's productions such as *Hush*, and *Before I Woke*, the threat is as American as Raymond Andrew Joubert, the serial killer in *Gerald's Game* inspired by real-life Ed Gein who also inspired Norman Bates in *Psycho*, Leatherface in *Texas Chainsaw Massacre* and Buffalo Bill in *The Silence of the Lambs*, all very American. Although much of Flanagan's horror exhibits the official ideology that terrorists have infiltrated the heartland, causing trauma and distress to citizens, Flanagan by not differentiating the self as American and the other as foreigner and by presenting the evil presence as American implies terrorism as an immanent American problem. Therefore, unlike many blockbusters on terrorism which play "to an audience desire for revenge,"[26] killing vampires and zombies to assuage one's fears, the trauma that exists in *The Haunting* can only be resolved through an understanding of the American family.

Gender Trauma in the Haunting of the American Family

The trauma of 9/11 correlates to trauma of the shifting gender relations in the American family. Pease, in linking Homeland security with home safety, also establishes Bush as a symbol of the paternalistic figure, protecting the motherland. In the wake of 9/11, traditional masculinity, in which fair maidens and children are to be rescued, burgeoned. In an interview with NBC, then-Vice President Dick Cheney said that "weakness, vacillation … encouraged people like Osama bin Laden, as I say, to launch repeated strikes against the United States, and our people overseas and here at home, with the view that he could, in fact, do so with impunity."[27] It takes a strong American man to deter terrorism but the collapse of Twin Towers is a metaphor of American emasculation, evident in the oft-quoted proclamation by a former military officer: "The phallic symbol of America had been cut off and at its base was a large smoldering vagina, the true symbol of the American culture, for it is the western culture that represents the feminine materialistic principle, and it is at its extreme in America."[28] As Dana Heller notes:

> The trauma of 9/11 is in large part the trauma of having been abandoned by our fathers, who were unable to prevent the attacks from recurring. [...] Major television networks were quick to exploit the infantile aspects of this emotional framing of the attacks, banking on narratives of Oedipal displacement that fashioned George W. Bush as the nation's patriarchal protector.[29]

This trauma of abandonment by the father is played out in *The Haunting* where Hugh leaves the children to the care of their aunt after a traumatic incident of the possessed mother, who is analogous to a common citizen converted to terrorism, trying to murder them. As a weak father, Hugh could not hold the family together, estranges himself from them, and does nothing to prevent or help his children through their individual trauma. As a result of Hugh being a model of emasculated masculinity, Steven undergoes vasectomy, refusing to be a father, and hides the procedure from his wife who wants children.

As a final blow to masculinity, Luke is too vulnerable to face reality. In the end, however, the redemptive act of sacrificing himself reinstates Hugh's patriarchal figure and masculinity. Inheriting the position of the patriarch of the family, as seen when the ghost of Hugh explains the events solely to Steven alone and passes Hill House to him, Steven regains his virility, in contrast to the first episode where Shirley blames Steven for not protecting his siblings. As a sign of his newfound masculinity, his wife is pregnant in the end. Instead of Shirley Jackson as the author of *The Haunting of Hill House*, Steven holds the pen. This is not to say that *The Haunting* presents a sexist perspective—after all, Flanagan's other productions often feature strong women rising above their dire circumstances—but the reinstitution of traditional masculinity that the television series espouses reveals the reaction to trauma in the aftermath of 9/11.

In this return to traditional masculinity with Bush reconfigured to be the strong patriarch to lead America to the War on Terror, or putting it simply, to cope with the trauma suffered from 9/11, women are often tortured in films and media as a fantasy so that men would possess a legitimate reason to resort to violence to rescue them. However, in Flanagan's oeuvre, while women rescue themselves, they are usually dealt with in two ways. Firstly, women provide a reason for justified revenge but not before they are grotesquely hurt. In *Gerald's Game*, the female protagonist (played by Carla Gugino who also plays Olivia Crain) has to remove the skin of her hand like a glove to escape from the handcuffs, causing irreparable damage to her hand. In *Hush*, the female lead's fingers are mangled to evoke a strong reaction from the spectacle, such as one would react to Nell's bent neck in *The Haunting*.

Secondly, in post–9/11 films, women are often portrayed as villains. But Flanagan seems to take a step further to suggest that mothers are perverse. To be sure, the fear of the generative powers of women could be traced as far back as to Mary Shelley's *Frankenstein* or even further, but the trauma of 9/11 intensifies this fear. As quoted previously, the gaping hole of Twin Towers could be read as a vagina swallowing the phallus. Jean Baudrillard describes the 9/11 terrorist acts as "the absolute event, the 'mother' of all events, the pure event uniting within itself all the events that have never taken place."[30] It takes a "mother" to produce a horror that has not occurred before. Yet, even as mothers are monstrous, they are also required by the nation. As Bush is the father, America is the motherland, producing children to fight terrorism, in order to protect the American family. According to Pease, the "mother is supposed to show her love for the nation-state by sacrificing her progeny to the state for the purpose of its production."[31] Flanagan's *Absentia*, *Oculus*, *Before I Wake* and *The Haunting* reflect this contradictory stance of mothers as necessary and as villains. In *The Haunting*, Flanagan states that "Poppy ... embodied the insanity of Hill House, and she brought to it the femininity and the kind of twisted maternal instinct."[32] In turn, Olivia, the mother-terrorist of the Crains, scars and traumatizes the children for much of their adult lives even as she demonstrates her kindness and understanding qualities as a capable mother.

Conclusion

Although *The Haunting* appears to follow several tropes of post–9/11 horror, the series ultimately contributes to the terrorist discourse in a new way. Many zombie and vampire films present infections/invasions from a foreign source and depict an apocalyptic vision of the future world, mirroring the hopelessness many people feel about the 9/11 situation. However, the characters in *The Haunting* live in the aftermath of destruction and trauma. Similar to many of Flanagan's productions, the source of evil in *The Haunting* remains inexplicable. Unlike the revenge-driven zombie films, since the source is rooted in American origins, *The Haunting* suggests that destroying the source would mean self-annihilation or a complete overhaul of the American system, something that is perhaps undesirable. In placing evil as homegrown, and not a foreign invasion, Flanagan suggests that the United States needs to take partial responsibility in its creation of evil and, as follow, its own destruction. Americans could, thus, only manage their trauma, and not uproot completely the evil within.

As Flanagan brings up in many of his interviews, the characters in *The Haunting* are haunted by their trauma due to their past. Resolving this trauma would expel the haunting and the way to expel "ghosts" of trauma lies in the power of confession and veracity. Truth of the event when told by Hugh has freed the Crains from their trauma. The psychologist Theodora instructs Shirley to tell the truth about Nell's death to her children to avoid trauma, trauma that Shirley suffered as a child when Olivia could not tell the truth about the passing of the kittens. Flanagan encourages viewers to read his horror productions allegorically and the trauma and truth-telling in the television series, as this essay has argued, are often linked to 9/11: in the same group therapy with Luke, a blind soldier who fought in the War on Terror confesses his haunting by an Iraqi girl with "melted eyes" in a long monologue, seemingly disconnected from the plot of the Crain story ("The Twin Thing"). In a post-coital talk, Theodora confesses to throwing rock at a glasshouse, destroying the roof, a terrorizing act she did twice even after receiving a spanking the first time. She confides in her partner, "I thought about it for a long time, remembering the spanking, but remembering also the lovely crash" ("Silence Lay Steadily"). Destructive her act of terrorism may be, and traumatic her spanking may be, she has learnt to accept her experiences by confession. It follows that *The Haunting* implies in order to inherit the American homeland, one has to come to terms with specters of the 9/11 trauma by telling and accepting the truth, but ironically, in this case, through allegory. *The Haunting* is a ghost story and an allegory "remembering also the lovely crash."

Notes

1. Paul A. Cantor, "The Truth Is Still Out There: *The X-Files* and 9/11," in *Homer Simpson Marches on Washington: Dissent Through American Popular Culture*, ed. Timothy M. Dale and Joseph J. Foy (Lexington: University Press of Kentucky, 2010), 75, emphasis original.

2. Steffen Hantke, *American Horror Film: The Genre at the Turn of the Millennium* (Jackson: University Press of Mississippi, 2010), xxv.

3. Adam Lowenstein, *Shocking Representation: Historical Trauma, National Cinema, and the Modern Horror Film* (New York: Columbia University Press, 2005), 10.

4. Kyle Bishop, "Dead Man Still Walking: Explaining the Zombie Renaissance," *Journal of Popular Film and Television* 37, no. 1 (2009): 16.

5. Staci Layne Wilson, "Exclusive Interview with Director Mike Flanagan: *Before I Wake* and *Ouija: Origin of Evil*," *Dread Central News*, Aug. 12, 2016, accessed May 1, 2019, https://www.dreadcentral.com/news/182437/exclusive-interview-director-mike-flanagan-wake-ouija-origin-evil/

6. Cathy Caruth, *Unclaimed Experience: Trauma, Narrative, and History* (Baltimore: Johns Hopkins University Press, 1996), 4.

7. Slavoj Žižek, *Welcome to the Desert of the Real* (London: Verso, 2002), 14.

8. Christina Radish, "Mike Flanagan on 'The Haunting of Hill House' & 'The Shining' Sequel, 'Doctor Sleep,'" *Collider*, Oct. 14, 2018, accessed May 1, 2019, http://collider.com/haunting-of-hill-house-mike-flanagan-interview/#netflix.

9. Mike Bloom, "'The Haunting of Hill House' Creator Addresses the Show's Biggest Terrors and Twists," *Hollywood Reporter*. Oct. 15, 2018, accessed May 1, 2019 https://www.hollywoodreporter.com/live-feed/haunting-hill-house-finale-mike-flanagan-interview-1151590.

10. Behzad Hassani, "Trauma and Terrorism: How Do Humans Respond?" in *Modern Terrorism and Psychological Trauma*, ed. Brian Trappler (New York: Gordian Knot Books, 2007), 1.

11. Joe Murphy, "Estimating the World Trade Center Tower on September 11, 2001: A Capture-Recapture Approach," *American Journal of Public Health* 99, no. 1 (2009): 66.

12. Leonie Huddy, Nadia Khatib, and Teresa Capelos, "Trends: Reactions to the Terrorist Attacks of September 11, 2001," *The Public Opinion Quarterly* 66, no. 3 (Autumn 2002): 422.

13. Mark A. Schuster, et al, "A National Survey of Stress Reactions After the September 11, 2001, Terrorist Attacks," *The New England Journal of Medicine* 345, no. 20 (Nov. 15, 2001): 1507.

14. E. Alison Holman, "Terrorism, Acute Stress, and Cardiovascular Health: A Three Year National Study Following the September 11th Attacks," *Arch Gen Psychiatry* 65, no. 1 (Jan. 2008): 73.

15. See Arieh Shalev, "PTSD: A Disorder of Recovery?" in *Understanding Trauma: Integrating Biological, Clinical, and Cultural Perspectives*, eds. Laurence Kirmayer, Robert Lemelson, and Mark Barad (Cambridge: Cambridge University Press, 2007), 207–23; Roxane Cohen et al. "Exploring the Myths of Coping with a National Trauma: A Longitudinal Study of Responses to the September 11th Terrorist Attacks" in *The Trauma of Terrorism: Sharing Knowledge and Shared Care, an International Handbook*, ed. Yael Danieli, Danny Browm, and Joe Sills (New York: Haworth Maltreatment and Trauma Press, 2005), 129–41.

16. Judith Herman, *Trauma and Recovery* (New York: Basic Books, 1997), 33.

17. Ibid.

18. Carl Plantinga, *Moving Viewers: American Film and the Spectator's Experience* (Berkeley: University of California Press, 2009), 179.

19. Jeffrey C. Alexander, "Towards a Theory of Cultural Trauma," in *Cultural Trauma and Collective Identity*, ed Jeffrey C. Alexander, Ron Eyerman, Bernhard Giesen, Neil Smelser, and Piotr Sztompka (Berkeley: University of California Press, 2004), 1.

20. Leo Bersani, *The Culture of Redemption* (Cambridge: Harvard University Press, 1990), 1.

21. Cathy Caruth, *Trauma: Explorations in Memory* (Baltimore: Johns Hopkins University Press, 1995), 153.

22. Roger Luckhurst, *The Trauma Question* (London: Routledge, 2008), 1.

23. George Bush, "The Fifth Anniversary of September 11, 2001," U.S. *Department of State Archive*. https://2001-2009.state.gov/p/nea/rls/72057.htm.

24. Donald Pease, *The New American Exceptionalism* (Minneapolis: University of Minnesota Press, 2009), 168.

25. Colette Balmain, "The Enemy Within: The Child as Terrorist in the Contemporary American Horror Film" in *Monsters and the Monstrous: Myths and Metaphors of Enduring Evil*, ed. Niall Scott (Amsterdam: Rodopi, 2007), 134.

26. Jonathan Markovitz, "Reel Terror Post 9/11," in *Film and Television After 9/11*, ed. Wheeler Winston Dixon (Carbondale: Southern Illinois University Press, 2004), 202.

27. Tim Russert, "Interview with Dick Cheney," *NBC News: Meet the Press*, Mar. 16, 2003.

28. Elder George, *A Gender Handbook for Western Man* (New York: Mai Publishing, 2010), Chapter XIII.

29. Dana Heller, *The Selling of 9/11* (New York: Palgrave Macmillan, 2005), 15.

30. Jean Baudrillard, *The Spirit of Terrorism*, trans. Chris Turner (London: Verso, 2003), 4.

31. Pease, 197.

32. Tim Stack, "*The Haunting of Hill House* Creator Mike Flanagan on Hidden Cues, Major Scares, and a Season 2," *Entertainment Weekly*, Oct. 23, 2018, accessed May 1, 2019, https://ew.com/tv/2018/10/23/the-haunting-of-hill-house-mike-flanagan-post-mortem/.

Education, Praxis and Healing

Elizabeth Laura Yomantas

Education is the vehicle for praxis and healing in *The Haunting of Hill House*. This essay examines the ways in which Steve, Shirley, and Theo use early educational experiences as the cornerstone for healing in their adult lives. Because Steve, Shirley, and Theo encountered critically important educational experiences as children, they were able to survive and heal as they drew on formative educational experiences. Because of their young age, Nell and Luke were not afforded the same educational experiences as their older siblings. The lack of quality educational experiences suggests why Luke and Nell were ultimately unable to recover from the trauma of Hill House.

It is unclear if the Crain children attended school outside of the home while they lived in Hill House. It is seemingly unlikely that the children attended school as they are only shown on the Hill House property, and the series does not speak of friends from school, teachers, or schooling experiences. Rather, it is most likely that the children were homeschooled by Olivia. Even if the children did attend school outside the home, in this series, Olivia functions in the role of teacher. Whether her role of educator was for formal schooling, informal schooling, or perhaps both, she impresses formative knowledge on the three older children. From these early experiences, Steve, Shirley, and Theo later chose careers that require formal schooling. Formal schooling then becomes a vehicle for healing. Because Olivia dies when Nell and Luke are only six years old, they are unable to have these formative learning experiences with their mother. Because they lacked these opportunities, they are unable to draw upon educational experiences in order to heal.

Olivia's educational philosophy is rooted in whole child education.[1] Her lessons include critical thinking in academic texts, grief and loss, and social emotional learning. She teaches the children that there are multiple ways of living and experiencing life, and she prepares them for experiences they may face later in life. Freire stated that "for apart from inquiry, apart from the

86   III. The Trauma

praxis, individuals cannot be truly human. Knowledge emerges only through invention and re-invention, through the restless, impatient, continuing, hopeful inquiry human beings pursue in the world, with the world, and with each other."[2] The series is structured in a form of praxis. Each sibling's childhood and adulthood are shown in tandem in a form of praxis. The series reveals important moments from childhood, and then transitions to show how these early life events shape each character as an adult. The knowledge they gain through experience affirms their humanity and reveals each character's pursuit and struggle with the world. For the three older siblings, Olivia created learning environments which fostered praxis, the continual cycle of action and reflection, that later become embedded in the identity of each of the three older siblings.

Dewey explained that there is a connection between experience, emotions and new ideas, and conscious intent. He stated that "Experience occurs continuously, because the interaction of the live creature and the environing conditions is involved in the very process of living. Under conditions of resistance and conflict, aspects and elements of the self and the world that are implicated in this interaction qualify experience with emotions and ideas so that conscious intent emerges."[3] In this series, Olivia creates experiences in which the three older children are able to process emotions and consider new ideas. These carefully constructed learning environments establish a foundation for conscious intent to emerge later through their professional choices.

Educational philosopher Paulo Freire stressed the importance of dialogue. Moving far away from the banking model of education in which the all-knowing teacher deposits information into the students' brains, critical pedagogy calls for a radicalized form of education in which the teacher and student dialogue to co-construct knowledge, pose a problem, name the world, and act to create change. This is Olivia's primary instructional strategy; she engages with each of her children through a dialogical pedagogy. She engages with them and rather than lecturing or simply stating right from wrong, she uses dialogue to communicate and co-construct knowledge and understanding. For example, in "Touch," Olivia first addresses Theo's ability to feel through asking her a series of questions. These questions then lead to a conversation between the mother and daughter. Olivia is candid and open with Theo rather than authoritative or overly directive. Her instruction is dialogical and consequently the meaning of the gloves is co-constructed between Olivia and Theo. Olivia also applies this same instructional strategy as she teaches Shirley about the process of grief in "Open Casket." Olivia's use of dialogue to name and understand the world is an important tool for the children to learn about the world and discover strategies for how to navigate the complexities of life.

Steve is portrayed as the conscientious and thoughtful oldest child in the family. While he is later critiqued by his siblings for not seeing the same things they saw on that fateful night, as a child, Steve is presented as kind and respectful. He engages with Nell and Luke and assists his father with projects around the home. In the series, it is unclear if the children attend schooling outside of the home. In the first episode, Steve is confronted by Mrs. Dudley, who complains that in public schools, "they teach you the secular world, smother you in science. And science isn't an exact science, you know. The world is dark, young man, and the only light is the light of the Lord Jesus Christ. We need his light in the night; in the dark" ("Steven Sees a Ghost"). Steve listens politely to Mrs. Dudley; Olivia watches from the other side of the kitchen. Mrs. Dudley asks Steve, "Do you know the gospels, young man?" ("Steven Sees a Ghost"). Olivia answers Mrs. Dudley on her son's behalf and explains, "Hugh and I decided that when Steve was little, see we knew throughout his life he'd be exposed to all sorts of ideas and beliefs. That there'd be all sorts of people who'd tell him they had the answers.... So yes, he knows the Gospels. He's also familiar with the Talmud, the Tao Te Ching, the Torah, the Koran, Greek mythology, and he reads a lot of Carl Sagan, Shakespeare" ("Steven Sees a Ghost"). Based on common understanding of American school curriculum, it is unlikely that Steve learned these texts in a formal public school setting. Additionally, the way Olivia confidently and wholly responds to Mrs. Dudley suggests that she is responsible for his diverse academic reading and global understandings. This is further supported by Olivia and Steve's co-quoting of *Hamlet*. Because of Steve's age, it is likely that Olivia spent time reading and discussing these challenging texts *with* Steve. In order for an adolescent to understand the meaning of these complex texts, it is likely that Olivia read alongside Steve.

These early educational experiences with complex texts served as a springboard for Steve's career as a writer. Steve's writing is an embodiment of the *Hamlet* quote co-quoted by Olivia and Steve: "Because there are more things in Heaven and Earth, Horatio ... than are dreamt of in your philosophy" ("Steven Sees a Ghost"). The "more things" became what Steve chose to write about for his professional career. Writing serves not only as a way of connecting with the academic values his mother instilled in him at an early age, but also as a vehicle to process, sense-make, and ultimately heal from the events that took place in Hill House.

Furthermore, Steve uses his passion for writing to facilitate healing for others. In the first episode, Steve visits Mrs. Walker to see if the ghost of her husband dwells in her house. He stays overnight, sets up cameras, and listens to Mrs. Walker's story. Although Steve deems her home to be ghost-free, he offers to include her story in one of his books. He does this for two reasons: first, to validate the experiences of Mrs. Walker, and second, to honor the life of her husband because he was a fan of Steve's work. Mrs. Walker is very upset that Steve did not see a ghost in her home or believe one is there. He comforts her by redefining what a ghost is. He explains, "When I said I've never seen a ghost, that's not exactly true. I've seen a lot of ghosts, just not the way you think. A ghost can be a lot of things—a memory, a daydream, a secret, grief, anger, guilt. But in my experience, most times, they're just what we want to see.... Most times, a ghost is a wish" ("Steven Sees a Ghost"). Steve comforts Mrs. Walker with the concept of "more things" and encourages her by including her husband's story in his next book. Steve is critiqued by his siblings for writing the story of Hill House and presenting his family members in unflattering ways. However, this is Steve's personal journey toward healing and how he helps others heal. While his siblings argue his desire for wealth trumps his desire to be a successful writer, based on his early schooling experiences, utilizing his mind and ideas is the framework Olivia provided for him to understand and process the world in healthy ways.

The series portrays Steve as a writer who is focused solely on earning money and becoming a bestselling author. However, based on his actions in "Steven Sees a Ghost," perhaps his motivation is not wealth, but rather, remembering and healing. His siblings ridicule him for his absence on the most important night of their lives, so perhaps his writing is his attempt to try to remember, sense make, and tell the story. These would be qualities that Olivia fostered in him, so perhaps his journey as a writer is more about healing and less about wealth. Furthermore, because he was willing to give his siblings royalties from the book, this suggests that his motives were not solely wealth. In the same entrepreneurial spirit of his parents, Steve attempts for forge a new path and create ways to provide for his family. Despite his siblings' lack of enthusiasm for his publications, the royalties serve as the vehicle to actualize their dreams—for Shirley, this means staying in business (though she is unaware of it as it is her husband who takes the money), and for Theo, this means attending graduate school. Without Steve's publications, perhaps Shirley and Theo's healing journey would be halted or never fully actualized. Perhaps Steve is providing for the family in a way modeled by Olivia.

As a child, Shirley was both caring and nurturing. These traits are exemplified in her sincere desire to care for a litter of kittens she finds on the property of Hill House. Despite her father's reluctance to allow her to care for the kittens, Shirley convinces him that she is fit to nurture them. After she is granted permission, Shirley is seen feeding the kittens bottled milk through a small eye dropper; she feeds them with care, precision, and an ethic of responsibility. These tender acts exemplify Shirley's innate desire to care for those around her in her life. Preservation of life is her primary goal as she interacts with the kittens.

In the second episode, Shirley discovers that one of the beloved kittens is dead. She stands motionless as she watches as her father dig a grave in the yard. Olivia emerges with a small decorated box and teaches Shirley the importance of properly burying the dead. Shirley is surprised by this concept, so Olivia explains they should provide her with a proper funeral because she is "a very special cat, and she deserves a very special place to rest" ("Open Casket"). This is perhaps Shirley's earliest experience with death, so Olivia also teaches her the importance of remembering those who pass away. In age appropriate terms, Olivia explains, "You know how when you take one of your pictures you capture something forever, just the way it is? Stories do that, too ... so when we die, we turn into stories and every time someone tells one of those stories, it's like we're still here for them. We're all stories in the end" ("Open Casket"). Shirley instantaneously applies this new knowledge from her mother and provides the kitten with a proper eulogy. In this critical scene, Olivia teaches Shirley two valuable lessons that will later shape her vocation and serve as her instrumental tool for healing—to properly bury those who die and to preserve their story through preservation of the body.

Olivia's early lesson in regard to the process of grieving was a tool Shirley used to confront her mother's death. Despite her reluctance to view her mother in the casket, viewing the body initiated the grieving process and perhaps further inspired her career. As an adult, Shirley applies the concepts from her mother's early teachings about grief and loss. In fact, she selects a profession where it becomes her life's work to care for both the dead and the grieving. Shirley's decision to serve as a mortician is arguably more of a vocational call than merely a professional decision. When Shirley's husband reprimands Shirley for giving many services away for free or at cost, Shirley defends her generosity and states "we're doing more than well enough to give a little relief to families who need it most" ("Open Casket"). In the same way Olivia supported Shirley through the loss of her kittens, Shirley wholeheartedly supports others through their loss.

In "Steven Sees a Ghost," Shirley models her mother's gentle teaching about death to Max, a child who has just lost his grandmother. Shirley both empathizes with Max and also emphasizes the importance of viewing the body in the casket as means of saying goodbye. In the same way her mother explained a proper funeral to honor the life lost, she explains to Max the importance of having a final picture of his grandmother. Shirley explains, "The thing about an open casket, and I know it sounds scary, is that it's a great chance to take all of those pictures in your head ... and cover it all up with a better picture. Before she's ever even in the casket, I'm gonna fix her. That's what I do" ("Steven Sees a Ghost"). Shirley then continues to explain the embalmment process with age-appropriate information—indicating that she deeply respects the person who died. Shirley explains to Max: "I take extra special care to make sure she looks just like she's supposed to. So when I'm done, she will look just like she always did, just like you remember her, just like she's supposed to" ("Steven Sees a Ghost"). As Shirley later accompanies Max down the aisle to view his mother's casket, she proudly and yet humbly ushers him toward the grief he will need to experience as a precursor to healing.

Shirley is hell-bent on embalming Nell and preparing her for the funeral. Despite reluctance from her husband and sister, Shirley is confident that she is the one who should care for her sister's body. She states, "She's my sister. I'm hosting her funeral. That's that" ("Open Casket"). The gruesome work of preparing the body is both an act of healing and a labor of love. As she prepares the body, she sobs, grieves, and does what she does best—fixes. For Shirley, grief and healing are intertwined; pain and purpose, brutal and beautiful, sympathy and civic responsibility are brought together in this process. Her work is an embodiment of Olivia's teachings on grief, loss, and healing.

As a child, Theo is direct and protective of her younger siblings. Even though she is the middle child, she functions in the role of an older sister to Luke and Nell. Theo is careful to protect her two younger siblings, and she often serves as a defender to Luke. Despite her young age, she confidently speaks up to Mrs. Dudley to address the way she scolds Luke. In episode 3, she frankly comments: "He's playing, Mrs. Dudley. Why are you yelling at him?" ("Touch"). Additionally, when her parents dismiss Luke's version of what happened in the basement, Theo goes to great lengths to validate her brother's story. In "Touch," Luke expresses how disappointed he is with the fact that his parents do not believe his side of the story. Empathetically, Theo reaches out and places her hand on Luke's arm. She looks into his eyes and tells him, "I believe you" ("Touch"). She then puts her effort into aligning the facts to support what Luke saw. Her mother notices this, and affirms the work she did to prove that there really *was* a basement, despite what the blueprints indicated. Rather than punishing her for going down to the basement, Olivia tenderly states, "I really, really don't like that you went down there by yourself…. But I love that you're so brave" ("Touch"). In this important scene, Olivia affirms her daughter's decision to take a risk and commends her bravery. Risk taking and bravery are then instilled into Theo's identity; she will be called to draw upon these qualities again frequently in her adult life.

In Theo's childhood, there are many examples which highlight Theo's ability to feel things that others cannot feel. Early on in episode 3, Theo is seen playing with Luke. She touches the bed, and remarks, "This was a sickbed" ("Touch"). She abruptly stops playing with Luke as she is disturbed by what she felt. Theo's ability to feel is not bound by tactile limitations; she can also feel emotions that others cannot. After confronting Mrs. Dudley about the way she speaks to Luke, Theo discerns an important trait in Mrs. Dudley. Luke questions why Mrs. Dudley is "so mean," and Theo responds by explaining that she is not mean; rather, she is scared. She has the ability to perceive emotions that are undiscernible to others.

In this episode, Olivia connects with Theo in a way that forever alters her future. She acknowledges Theo's ability to feel things that others cannot feel. She uses the term "sensitive" to describe Theo's skills, perhaps inferring a lexical gap for the supernatural skills the girls in the family seem to possess, as Olivia suggests in episode 3. Rather than simply ignoring Theo's ability to feel things, Olivia calls her to a have a private conversation. She shares about her own migraines and how they allow her to see things that are not there. She positions herself as someone who has experienced similar things. Gently, she tells Theo: "We'll talk a lot more about it as you get older but, in the meantime, if you're feeling overwhelmed and think nobody will understand, you can talk to me about anything, okay?" ("Touch"). She then proceeds to present Theo with a gift—her first pair of gloves. These gloves provide Theo with an opportunity to protect herself from feeling too much too often and therefore provide her with physical protection from the world around her. Theo now has the option—she can wear the gloves for protection, or she can remove the gloves to feel what she needs to feel for each specific purpose. Olivia validated her feeling experiences and also gave her a tool for self-protection. Additionally, she did not present the concept of "sensitivity" as a problem or a negative quality. Rather, she presented it as something to be explored, understood, and unpacked as she ages. She promises to continue talking with Theo about this quality as she gets older and to support her through navigating this gift. The way Olivia treats "sensitivity" is a springboard for the ways Theo utilizes this gift in her adult life.

As an adult, Theo is seen continually taking her gloves off and on, depending on the situation and context—depending on if she needs to feel or protect, heal or preserve. Theo has chosen a profession, an act of healing, in which she uses her "sensitivity" to aid others in their own personal healing. Olivia affirmed this gift in her and her passion for defending the weak dates back to her childhood when she defends Luke and makes sure his story is validated. Theo can relate to her young clients and their needs for self-protection and self-preservation. In episode 3, Theo works with a young girl in foster care named Kelsey. After hearing about Kelsey's fears of Mr. Smiley, Theo states:

> You know, you're a lot like me, Kelsey. See, when I was little, I was afraid of a lot of things. I didn't have to be, though. They were all in my head. I just didn't know that yet. But when I was scared, I would imagine myself building a big wall, all around me, made of the strongest bricks in the whole world. And when I got scared, I'd imagine myself putting another one on, one after the other until that wall was so

thick and so strong I knew I'd be safe in there forever. And that's what you do too, right? ["Touch"].

After making personal connections with Kelsey, Theo is committed to understanding Kelsey's fear. Theo uses the traits seen in episode 3, risk taking and bravery, in order to find out what haunts Kelsey. She enters Kelsey's foster home wearing gloves, her learned way to protect herself. Upon entering the basement, Theo utilizes the gift that her mother encouraged her to use—sensitivity. She feels for what is cold, symbolizing darkness, and locates the couch where Kelsey had been sexually assaulted by her foster father. As she goes back upstairs, Theo keeps her gloves removed and reaches out to shake the foster father's hand. His cold touch serves as confirmation that he is the predator. In this moment, Theo reveals her willingness to touch darkness in order to reclaim light. She is willing to remove the gloves to feel things if it will lead to healing. This is seen again when she touches Nell's dead body in the morgue. She is willing to feel darkness if the outcome, albeit later, is light.

The younger two children, Nell and Luke, are simply not afforded the same learning experiences as the older children. The learning experiences Olivia created for the older children are what allowed them to work towards healing and restoration in their lives. However, because Olivia died when the younger children were only six years old, they did not have the same quality time with their mother. While their mother did care for them and attempt to protect them from the house, she did not have the same amount of time to pour into their identity formation through informal schooling experiences. If Olivia had lived and had more time with Luke and Nell, perhaps they would have been able to heal from the horror of Hill House. The lack of opportunity Olivia had to spend instructional time with Nell and Luke is perhaps what ultimately led to their downfall.

The traumatic events that took place in Hill House continue to impact the Crain family. Steve struggles to successfully fulfill the role of husband and father. Shirley is still haunted by the decision she made to cheat on her husband. Theo continues to build emotional walls and yet simultaneously desires to be seen and heard. Luke continues to struggle with addiction, and Nell ultimately loses her life. The things that haunted each of the children in Hill House continue to cause pain in their adult lives. However, Steve, Shirley, and Theo are able to process their trauma and continually strive for healing. For Luke, healing always seems to be just out of reach, and for Nell, the darkness won. Steve, Shirley, and Theo's continued pursuit to survive and heal were made possible because of Olivia's teachings throughout their childhood. All three of the older children were able to apply the lessons she taught them as tools for survival and healing. Olivia nurtured Steve's mind, fostered

Shirley's desire to care for others, and affirmed Theo's ability to feel. From these early lessons, Steve became a writer, Shirley became a caretaker, and Theo became a therapist. These early teachings informed and transformed the three older siblings' adult lives and professions. While they must continue on their healing journey, Olivia taught them foundational life skills from which they could draw upon. In the same way Theo removes her gloves and places them back on, the other siblings symbolically do this in their own lives. It is the skill of putting the gloves on and off that is needed for healing. Nell and Luke did not have the time with their mother to learn about their own gloves; therefore, they had limited skills to draw from in order to survive.

Another key concept in Olivia's teachings is the notion of unfinishedness. In *Pedagogy of the Oppressed*, Freire described his unfinishedness as follows:

> I hold that my own unity and identity, in regard to others and the world, constitutes my essential and irrepeatable way of experiencing the world as a cultural, historical, and unfinished being in the world, simultaneously conscious of my unfinishedness.... And here we have arrived at the point from which perhaps we have departed: the unfinishedness of our being. In fact, this unfinishedness is essential to our human condition. Whenever there is life, there is unfinishedness, though only among men and women it is possible to speak of an awareness of our unfinishedness.[4]

Once one becomes critically conscious of one's own unfinishedness, it is both freeing and empowering. This concept means that we are essentially unfinished becoming, learning, doing, and creating. The way we see and interact with the world is directly related to the notion that we are unfinished beings. Freire urged us to become aware of our own unfinishedness, and then embrace this quality as an important element of the human condition. The final episode of the series is a reminder of each character's unfinishedness—each character's continued struggle and hope to become free from the things that haunt.

Educational philosopher bell hooks wrote, "Rarely, if ever, are any of us healed in isolation. Healing is an act of communion."[5] In all three of the older siblings' paths to healings, they have brought others into their healing spaces. Steve drew readers into his words; Shirley brought dignity to families experiencing grief and loss, and Theo worked tirelessly to restore the lives and minds of children. Their continual pursuit of healing is an act of communion—an act of togetherness. Maybe the "forever house" Olivia dreamed of is not an actual place, but rather an idea that can be actualized through healing and hope. Perhaps Olivia did build her "forever house" after all. Her legacy lives on through her formative educational teachings to her three oldest children as they strive to heal and eliminate suffering in the world.

Notes

1. Nel Noddings, "What Does It Mean to Educate the Whole Child?," *Educational Leadership* 63, no. 1 (2005): 8.
2. Paulo Freire, *Pedagogy of the Oppressed* (New York: Continuum, 1972), 164.
3. John Dewey, *Art as Experience* (New York: Minton, Balch & Company, 2005).
4. Freire, *Pedagogy of the Oppressed*, 51–52.
5. bell hooks, *All About Love* (New York: William Morrow, 2018), 215.

"A House Is Like a Body"
Processes of Grief and Trauma

Dana Jeanne Keller

"As Alan Watts has speculated, this emphasis on the so-called objective may indeed be a sickness of Western man, for it enables him to retain his belief in the separateness of the ego from all that surrounds it."
—Clare Cooper, "The House as Symbol of the Self"

"We take care of the house; it takes care of us."
—Olivia Crain, "The Bent-Neck Lady"

"That house is the most dangerous place in the world for all of us."
—Hugh Crain, "Witness Marks"

"Every house needs a heart." Olivia Crain (Carla Gugino) explains this to her daughter Shirley (Lulu Wilson; Elizabeth Reaser)[1] when Shirley tells her the blueprint of their "forever home" "just looks like a lot of lines." Gesturing over the blueprint with her pencil in hand, Olivia extends the metaphor: "[A] house is like a person's body: the walls are like bones, the pipes are veins; it needs to breathe, it needs light and flow, and it all works together to keep us safe and healthy inside" ("Open Casket"). As mother and daughter converse in the foreground, an apparition moves restlessly about the room in the background—one moment against a wall, in another moment seated at the table, and then finally, gone offscreen. Hill House, its walls veined with toxic mold,[2] its rooms filled with restless, watchful ghosts, has every intention of keeping the Crain family inside, but with a different view as to what constitutes "safe and healthy."

Mike Flanagan's 2018 Netflix reimagining[3] of Shirley Jackson's 1959 novel *The Haunting of Hill House* (*HoHH*)[4] complicates the trope of a sentient, evil house by presenting the haunting as a symbiosis between human and house, and then fusing the two through form (editing, cinematography) and content (particularly character development). In other words, Hill House's haunting is shaped as much by its inhabitants as it is by the house itself. As an example, of the seven members of the Crain family—which includes a mother, father, two sons, and three daughters—six unknowingly spend time, both separately and sometimes together, in a mold-filled room (the "Red Room") that masquerades as each individual's ideal space: for one of the children, Luke (Julian Hilliard; Oliver Jackson-Cohen), the room appears as a treehouse; for another, Theo (Mckenna Grace; Kate Siegel), it is a dance studio; for Olivia, it is her reading room, but at times it also operates as a portal into the future. In "Silence Lay Steadily," Luke's twin sister Nell (Violet McGraw; Victoria Pedretti) calls the Red Room Hill House's heart, but then corrects herself upon realizing it is more like a stomach, "put[ting] on different faces so that we'd be still and quiet, while it digested." In this essay I will also compare the room to a womb, and I will argue that the three are not necessarily mutually exclusive.

How can a room, or even a house, operate simultaneously as a heart, a stomach, and a womb? All three organs work to nourish and protect, but they can also malfunction and attack. What happens when your body, your home, turns against you? By exploring the effects of architecture, grief, and intergenerational trauma on humans, and then imagining how these might be transposed on to a nonhuman "body" such as a house, we can cultivate a novel way of understanding haunted house narratives. Helpful to this approach is the work of new materialist philosopher Jane Bennett, who challenges us to reject the "quarantines of matter and life [which] encourage us to ignore the vitality *of* matter," and to instead consider "the capacity of things—edibles, commodities, storms, metals—not only to impede or block the will and designs of humans but also to act as quasi agents or forces with trajectories, propensities, or tendencies of their own."[5] Bennett's philosophy easily accommodates the sentient home, but it bears noting that new materialism's purpose isn't to illustrate how a nonhuman "thing" is like a human; rather, it seeks to dislodge humans from their perceived position at the center of the universe and give "the force of things more due."[6] Admittedly, in comparing human and house, my essay humanizes Hill House, but I have sought to do so in a way that accounts for the specific differences between the "body" of a house and that of a human being. My hope is that this will be the flint that sparks further research into the haunted house as vital matter which affects and is affected by the psychological processes—particularly the grief and trauma—of all beings (alive and dead) residing within its walls.

Although grief has long been a topic of interest in literature and medicine, it wasn't until the twentieth century that it became the focus of in-depth, systematic studies.[7] Most famously, Sigmund Freud hypothesized grief as a process which follows the loss of a "loved 'object'" (1913), and argued that "much psychiatric illness was an expression of pathological grieving" (1917).[8] In 1969, British psychologist John Bowlby further developed the idea of grief as a response to attachment, framing grief as "the by-product of a set of mechanisms which would set off the urge to search for and seek proximity with a loved one who is missing."[9]

By framing grief as a dynamic mental and physical process that arises in response to a broken attachment, such as the loss of a loved one, we can arrive at a more nuanced understanding of one aspect of the haunting of Hill House which is suggested in the opening lines of both the novel and the Netflix series:

> No live organism can continue for long to exist sanely under conditions of absolute reality; even larks and katydids are supposed, by some, to dream. Hill House, not sane, stood by itself against its hills, holding darkness within [...] and whatever walked there, walked alone.[10]

In short, Hill House is (among other things, of course) lonely.

Being alone and feeling lonely are not synonymous, but the two often go hand in hand. And while loneliness has undoubtedly produced some worthwhile works of art, the fact that prisons employ it as a mode of extreme punishment highlights just how damaging it can be. Countless studies have demonstrated the psychologically devastating effects of solitary confinement, which can even provoke "the appearance of acute mental illness in individuals who had previously been free of any such illness."[11] According to board-certified psychiatrist Stuart Grassian, the "specific psychiatric syndrome associated with solitary confinement" includes, among other things, "perceptual distortions, illusions, and hallucinations," "difficulties with thinking, concentration, and memory," and intrusive thoughts.[12] This "psychiatric syndrome" also fits as a description for Hill House's haunting—both in form and effect. Beyond the more traditional scares, Hill House expresses its loneliness in the following lines spoken by undead residents Poppy (Catherine Parker) and Olivia, respectively: "Forgive a girl for being lonely"; "I'll be alone again" ("Silence Lay Steadily"). Framing Hill House as lonely, "not sane," and chronically mourning the loss of previous inhabitants (i.e., as Olivia mourns the departure of her family) provides insight into why the house strives to ensure that those who enter its walls never leave.

Through visions, apparitions (i.e., ghosts), and "dreams," Hill House wears down its inhabitants until they leave or die. Those who die are forever stuck within its walls, "awakened" to Hill House's specific brand of reality. It relentlessly haunts Olivia until, utterly exhausted, she confides in her husband Hugh (Henry Thomas; Timothy Hutton) that while her migraines used to bring on "color storms," those storms are now only black ("Open Casket"). She explains, "I can't seem to find me ... those colors, they're all gone now ... and there's only one left. I'm scared. That's all I am. There's nothing else" ("Screaming Meemies"). Olivia's health deteriorates as her connection to the house grows—spending time in her "reading room," wandering the halls so disconnected from reality that she can no longer discern between wakefulness and sleep, stuck in "dreams that feel more real than life" (Olivia, "Screaming Meemies"). As Olivia sinks deeper into madness, the house amplifies its attack on her through the ghost of Poppy, a young mother who died in the house decades earlier, who tells Olivia about her own children and then shares with her "a way to wake [Luke and Nell] up [and] keep them safe" from the "screaming meemie" (nightmare) of reality ("Screaming Meemies"). When Poppy whispers the secret into Olivia's ear, the sound is of many voices at once, as though the entire house is speaking through Poppy's mouth. Olivia awakens from this "dream" holding a screwdriver to her husband's throat, the not-so-subtle insinuation being that the way to wake someone up from "a bad dream" is to kill them.

Hill House has a knack for turning mothers against their families, so it may come as no surprise that scholars have described the house itself as "a maternal antagonist, a diseased presence 'seeking whom it may devour.'"[13] This aspect of Hill House is particularly well represented in the Red Room, which remains stubbornly locked until the night that Olivia decides to throw her youngest children a late-night toxic tea party aimed at "waking us all up" ("Screaming Meemies").[14] Until then, the room remains protected behind a locked door, impossible to enter without special tools or, as Olivia explains, the right people ("We are the key"). Sealed to all but the right "tools," the Red Room is comparable to a uterus, a womb. But this is a sick womb, one covered in black veins of toxic mold, where children die rather than thrive. This "womb" operates like a backwards umbilical cord, sucking the life out of its inhabitants under the guise of providing nourishment by masquerading as their ideal spaces. In this way the Red Room is simultaneously the womb and stomach of the diseased, devouring mother that is Hill House.

Extending the metaphor of Hill House as a mother with a "sick womb" enables us to explore its haunting through the framework of intergenerational trauma, in which

> the residual impact of a traumatic event [...] is transmitted across generations through storytelling and behavioural and relational patterns [...] such that family members not present at the time of the violence are still substantially affected.[15]

But where does Hill House's original trauma lie? The haunted house born out of negative energy is a popular horror trope—for example, the infamous residences of *The Amityville Horror* (Rosenberg 1979), *The Shining* (Kubrick

1980), and *Poltergeist* (Hooper 1982) all sit atop ancient burial grounds. In the novel and the series, it is suggested that Hill House was simply "born bad," but a more compassionate reading might consider Hill House as a neglected, lonely, *vital* thing that feels attachment and mourns loss, for example, when a family moves out. And with all of the sickness, sadness, and death that has occurred within its walls—literally in the case of William Hill (Fedor Steer), who committed suicide by sealing himself behind a brick wall in Hill House's basement—it is possible that the house itself suffers from something comparable to pathological grief.

How does a house physically express grief? Hill House's symptoms include the supernaturally resilient toxic mold covering the walls of the Red Room and basement; the apparitions which seem to be always lurking in the house's shadows; and the way in which time and space twist and turn within Hill House, driving its inhabitants to question whether they are dreaming or awake. Translating these into the language of a human body exposes them as common symptoms of grief: the mold, which is known to cause breathing difficulties,[16] mirrors the chest heaviness and pain associated with a "broken heart"; the apparitions and twists in time and space mirror intrusive, repetitive thoughts and images, and reflect how a grieving person can feel dissociated from reality. Through its haunting Hill House not only expresses its grief, but transmits it to its inhabitants in a way that is similar to how a parent can pass down trauma to their children.

The Crain family's frightening supernatural experiences during their short stay at Hill House in 1992 climax on the traumatic final night in the house, when Olivia attempts to kill Nell and Luke, and then kills herself. In fewer than twenty-four hours the Crain children lose their home and their mother, and shortly thereafter, their father, when they are sent to live with their aunt. In his book on the nature of religion, Mircea Eliade writes, "The house is not an object, a 'machine to live in'; *it is the universe that man constructs for himself....*"[17] That final night at Hill House shatters the Crains' universe. Decades later, in the present day of the series, the family still struggles with trauma and grief. The five Crain siblings in particular have been shaped by their traumatic past, to the extent that it is possible to read them as an allegory for the five stages of grief.

The idea of grief as a series of progressive stages gained popularity in the late 1960s with Bowlby's work, however, the most commonly cited model comes from Elisabeth Kübler-Ross's 1970 book *On Death and Dying*. After observing and interviewing "dying patients in terms of coping mechanisms at the time of a terminal illness,"[18] Kübler-Ross identified five stages in a person's emotional journey from diagnosis to death: denial and isolation, anger, bargaining, depression, and acceptance. Although not specifically pertaining to the loss of a loved one, these stages have been broadly applied to various types of grief in the years since publication. While the linear presentation of the five stages of grief may suggest a distinct separation between each stage, it is important to note, as psychologist John Archer does, that

> with the possible exception of the initial reaction (shock and disbelief) the process of change through time is much more of a mixture of reactions which wax and wane in relation to outside events and may be delayed, prolonged or exaggerated according to the person's mental state and circumstances.[19]

All of *HoHH*'s characters exhibit symptoms of multiple stages of the grief process, however, individual stages feel particularly concentrated in specific Crain siblings. For this reason, in the following paragraphs I will explore the stage-sibling connection in detail. Interpreting the Crains through this lens not only enriches our understanding of how the *HoHH* television series specifically engages with popular discourse around grief and trauma, but also provides a template for decoding the human-house relationship in haunted house narratives more generally.

The first stage of grief is denial, described by Archer in the quote above as "shock and disbelief." Considering how many times he repeats the phrase "no one believes me" throughout the series, it seems appropriate that we align the first stage with Luke. In this instance it is not Luke doing the denying, but, through the people around him, he becomes associated with the language of denial (i.e., "no one believes me").[20] As an adult, Luke struggles with addiction as a way of escaping his grief. On the night of his sister Nell's death, Luke is in a rehabilitation center giving a speech in acceptance of his ninety-day sobriety chip. In his speech he describes his state of denial directly proceeding his mother's death: "I just expected her to come back." He goes on to explain, "My mom never came back but other things from when I was a kid did, and I guess that's why I started using in the first place ... to keep those things away" ("Twin Thing"). In a later scene, we witness Luke repeatedly turn his back on a tall, slender ghost from his past. Walking away from the ghost, Luke repeats to himself, "He's not real" ("Twin Thing"). For Luke, his addiction stems from his inability to face reality, his desire to remain in a constant state of denial. When Luke becomes sober, when he moves past the stage of denial, he faces the reality of Hill House and, enraged, attempts to burn it down.

Anger is a prevalent emotion in all of the Hill House siblings, but it is most often connected to Theo, described by her older brother Steven (Paxton Singleton; Michiel Huisman) as "a clenched fist with hair" ("Witness Marks"). Theo, who works as a child psychologist, relates to one of her young clients by describing her own anger as a wall:

> When I was scared I'd imagine myself building a big wall, all around me, of the strongest bricks in the world. And when I got scared, I'd imagine myself putting

another one on, one after another, until that wall was so thick and so strong I knew I'd be safe in there forever. [...] We make ourselves really safe, and no one ever gets in ["Touch"].

It may be tempting to align Theo with the denial and isolation stage, but her "wall" is designed to minimize her own emotional suffering, as opposed to rendering her blind to a harsh reality. In practice, the "wall" presents as anger and/or a cool demeanor. From a young age, Theo discovers that she can sense and feel a person's emotions through touching their skin or items they have touched. Her response to this as she grows up is to pull away from people in order to protect herself from having to deal with their grief and trauma when her own is already near-overwhelming. This is well illustrated in the episode "Two Storms," which takes place the night before Nell's funeral. Theo falls down drunk and when her family seeks to help her up she shouts at them, "Don't touch me! I have enough of my own grief. I don't need yours too."

After anger comes bargaining, whereby we convince ourselves that "maybe we can succeed in entering into some sort of an agreement which may postpone the inevitable happening...."[21] We can understand Shirley's connection to bargaining through the motifs of photographs and "fixing." As a child Shirley is often photographing her surroundings, and later, as an adult, Shirley employs photographs in her trade as a mortician in order to "fix" the dead by making them look "just like [they're] supposed to" ("Open Casket"). "Fix" has two meanings here: Shirley fixes things in the traditional sense of repairing them, but, with her photographs and painted corpses, she also fixes (freezes) things in time. Shirley's grief evolves across three key scenes: her mother Olivia's funeral, Nell's funeral, and Shirley's own funeral. At her mother's funeral a kind mortician helps a near-hysterical Shirley up to the casket. When they arrive, Shirley looks down, stops crying, and says, "You fixed her," to which the mortician replies, "Well, that's what I do." Shirley repeats, "You fixed her," and her young voice carries over as the scene transitions to present-day Shirley standing over a "fixed" Nell ("Open Casket"). Later, when the Crain family returns to Hill House to rescue a vengeful Luke, the Red Room feeds Shirley a vision of her own funeral. The same kind mortician from before guides her down the aisle, and as he does so, he describes in gory detail how he "fixed her." His soliloquy ends with, "[N]ow she is fixed and pretty, but underneath she is a horror. Yeah we pickle it and paint it but it's still death and rot and ruin" ("Silence Lay Steadily"). His final words reflect the futility of Shirley's career choice in controlling her traumatic childhood and all the loss and grief she has endured: there is no controlling death. You can disguise it but you cannot "fix" it.

The realization that nothing can be done to reverse the death of a loved one can throw mourners into a depression, the fourth stage in Kübler-Ross's theory. Because Nell struggles with depression and ends up (albeit unintentionally) hanging herself, she is closest to this stage. The series begins with Nell seeking help from each of her family members, with all except Hugh ignoring her call. A few months earlier, before dropping Luke off at rehab, Nell confides in him that she's "been having a really hard time too and nobody wants to see it," but Luke is too distracted with "getting well" (i.e., injecting a final dose of heroin) to recognize Nell's pain ("The Bent-Neck Lady"). Nell's feelings of invisibility become literal invisibility in the episode titled "Two Storms," in which the present-day Crain family gathers at Shirley's funeral home the night before Nell's funeral. The episode glides seamlessly between a storm at Hill House in 1992 and a storm outside the funeral home in present day. Nell is gone in both: in 1992 she has suddenly disappeared, and in present day she is dead; however, in both it is clear that she is there with the family but just invisible to their eyes. When young Nell finally reappears in the 1992 scenes, she tells her family, "I was screaming and shouting and none of you could see me...." The episode ends with Luke leaving the funeral home and young Nell's voiceover accompanying a spinning camera: "I was right here. I didn't go anywhere.... I was right here ... the whole time..." The camera stops spinning and lands on Nell's ghost standing beside the coffin, and the voiceover of young Nell continues, now loud and close: "Nobody could see me." Unlike a physical illness, depression can be difficult to recognize. In Nell it presents as pallid skin, greasy hair, and a messy home, but it is easy to ascribe those things to other causes. This is perhaps why Nell is associated with buttons: we "button up" to hide aspects of ourselves that we don't want others to see. Just as Nell's mental illness is invisible to those around her, so too is the broken-necked ghost she calls the "Bent-Neck Lady," Nell's "black dog" of depression that haunts her for most of her life, which she discovers too late is herself at the moment of her own death.

If one manages to overcome the depression stage, the next stage, according to Kübler-Ross, is acceptance. Of all the siblings, Steven is the one most willing to talk about their time at Hill House; significantly, he is also the only Crain who didn't experience anything explicitly supernatural there. Speaking to his father, he attributes the haunting and his mother's death to mental illness, saying "it's not the house, it's our brains" ("Witness Marks"). It angers Steven that "this family has such a hard time acknowledging mental illness"; he is so convinced that it's "in our genes," he's had a vasectomy to ensure that he won't pass it on ("Eulogy"). Steven might be the closest of the Crains to acceptance, but it's perhaps a performed acceptance. This could be because the alternative—that Hill House actually is haunted—is more difficult for Steven to accept, so instead he focuses on what his father calls an "imaginary illness" ("Witness Marks"), which, if true, also aligns Steven with the denial stage.

Here it bears repeating that grief is fluid: it is not as though one becomes immune to each stage after passing through it. As C.S. Lewis writes, "[I]n grief nothing 'stays put.' One keeps on emerging from a phase, but it always recurs. Round and round. Everything repeats. Am I going in circles, or dare I hope I am on a spiral?"[22] This aspect of repetition, of a confusion of space and time, is conspicuous not only in the dialogue of HoHH but also in its cinematography and editing, which unite to seamlessly transport the Crain family and the viewer between years and locations, encouraging the sensation that "our moments fall around us like rain" ("Silence Lay Steadily").

Episode six ("Two Storms") stands out amongst the other HoHH episodes for being edited to appear as a single, seamless shot. This formal decision encourages the viewer to regard all of the events of the episode as occurring in real time—despite jumping back and forth between 1992 in Hill House and present day in Shirley's funeral home. The first timeslip occurs shortly after Hugh arrives at the funeral home. He asks to use the washroom, and the camera follows him down the hallway as if it's a person walking behind him: it speeds up and slows down, it sways. Hugh turns a corner and suddenly he's young and back in 1992, in Hill House during a storm. The power goes out and the kids are frightened. The family gathers in Hill House's entryway, at the foot of the stairs. Most of them sit around a box of flashlights, loading them up with batteries, but Theo and Nell stand a few feet back from the group, holding hands. Echoing an earlier scene in which something crawls into bed behind Theo and holds her hand too tightly, Theo asks Nell to "let up on my hand." Flashlights loaded, Olivia shines a light towards Theo and Nell; Theo still appears to be holding Nell's hand, but Nell isn't there. Panicking, Luke wonders aloud, "What if something gets her?" Steven assures him that "She's going to be okay. […] okay? Luke… Luke… Luke—" In that moment it cuts back to present day, to Luke sitting in a chair and Steven asking him, "Luke, do you remember…" Similar cuts on sound and action occur in each episode, serving to remind us that the Crains and Hill House are forever and inextricably linked.

In "The House as Symbol of the Self" (1974), architect Clare Cooper discusses the reciprocal relationship between human and house, claiming that our living spaces affect our mental states by reflecting back to us an image of ourselves. In the case of the Crains, Hill House is a broken mirror, reflecting back to them a multiplicity of images that simultaneously frighten, comfort, and confuse. If a house is like a body, Hill House's body is a sick one, with thin, porous skin that absorbs all the joy and sadness, all the colors of emotion, from those who live within its walls, until all that's left is blackness and fear. Hill House is a diseased womb, transmitting its trauma to all who enter. With its in-depth exploration of grief and close attention to the complexities of family, Flanagan's Netflix adaptation of Jackson's novel builds on the trope of the sentient home and calls for a more nuanced, empathetic approach to haunted house narratives—one that acknowledges the "essential reality of oneness with the environment."[23]

NOTES

1. On the first mention of each character's name, regardless of whether I am referring to the young or adult version, I will name both actors who played the character, listing the young version first.
2. See Dawn Keetley's essay in this volume.
3. By Flanagan's own admission, the Netflix series is closer to fan fiction than adaptation.
4. Hereafter I've shortened the title of both novel and film to *HoHH*, but in each instance I will make it clear whether I am referring to the novel or the film.
5. Bennett, *Meeting the Universe Halfway*, vii–viii.
6. Ibid.
7. Granek, "Grief as Pathology," n.p.
8. Cited in Archer, *The Nature of Grief*, 15.
9. Ibid., 6.
10. Jackson, *The Haunting of Hill House*, 3.
11. Grassian, "Psychiatric Effects of Solitary Confinement," 333.
12. Ibid., 335–6.
13. Kahane, "The Gothic Mirror," 341.
14. She laces the tea with rat poison.
15. Carranza, "Intergenerational Trauma," n.p.
16. Brewer, Thrasher, and Hooper, "Chronic Illness Associated with Mold and Mycotoxins," n.p.
17. Eliade, *The Sacred and the Profane*, 56; italics in original.
18. Kübler-Ross, *On Death and Dying*, 31.
19. Archer, *Nature of Grief*, 23.
20. See Brandon Grafius's essay in this volume.
21. Kübler-Ross, *Death and Dying*, 71.
22. Lewis, *A Grief Observed*, 46.
23. Cooper, "The House as Symbol of the Self," 144.

IV
The Haunted

Mike Flanagan's Mold-Centric *The Haunting of Hill House*

Dawn Keetley

One of the most striking differences of Mike Flanagan's serial adaptation of *The Haunting of Hill House* (2018) is the ubiquitous presence of black mold. Mold is only mentioned in Shirley Jackson's novel (1959) when the group first ventures into the library and Eleanor stops at the door, "overwhelmed with the cold air of mold and earth which rushed at her."[1] Mold makes no appearance at all in Robert Wise's 1963 film adaptation, *The Haunting*. In the Netflix series, by contrast, Hugh Crain discovers "veins of mold" spreading over the basement walls in episode seven, and from then on mold is central to the story. The origin of the black mold is the red room, which appears to have been locked through most of the series, but which has in fact been inhabited by all the characters (except Hugh), who each experience it as a different room. The final episode of the series takes place almost entirely in the red room. And as the series concludes, the black mold spreads from the walls to the characters—signaling their death, or almost death, which may be, in fact, a different form of life.

The mold of Hill House is an earthly spreading of organic matter. The materialism that creeps in with the mold is evident in one possible reading of Flanagan's *Haunting*: what happens in Hill House is due to the toxic effects of black mold. This essay takes up this reading but then argues that what haunts the characters is mute matter more broadly—matter that they see and think they understand, matter they see and don't understand, and matter that some of them don't even see. In centering the mold, I offer a "weird reading,"[2] one that runs against the grain of the primarily psychological interpretations of *Haunting* (in all its iterations). As Mark Fisher aptly defines it, the weird is "that *which does not belong*." The weird "brings to the familiar something which ordinarily lies beyond it, and which cannot be reconciled with the 'homely.'"[3] The mold "does not belong" in Hill House: not least, it is one of the principal ways in which Flanagan's version diverges from the novel. More profoundly, though, the mold signals the nonhuman life that does not belong in what Eileen Joy calls the "psychic-cultural-historical order" that literary and film criticism is typically dedicated to exploring.[4] The mold, especially as it overruns everything, including the characters, does not belong in an anthropocentric world; it dislodges the human, showing how vulnerable we are to being consumed by matter, to becoming matter. Foregrounding the mold, my reading "ungrounds" *Haunting* from its "conventional, human-centered contexts."[5] It marks the presence of other-than human agencies. The mold ushers in the weird, orienting us to the power of the nonhuman, suggesting that "ghosts" are not emanations from either the psyche or the spirit world; they are manifestations of a material world vaster and more inscrutable than we know.

Anthropocentric Hill House

Interpretations of Jackson's *Haunting of Hill House* have been overwhelmingly psychoanalytic—not surprisingly since Jackson herself put the terrors of family at the heart of her novel.[6] Critics have predominantly argued that Eleanor projects onto the house both her desire for an ideal mother and the hatred and guilt she felt for her real (recently dead) mother.[7] From early on, Eleanor feels that the house "wanted to consume us," and she finds herself slowly disappearing into a house that, most critics agree, stands in for her loved and hated mother.[8] Indeed, toward the end, when Eleanor runs toward the library and up the perilous spiral staircase, she calls "Mother" repeatedly, and the fatal accident that concludes the novel represents a desire to come "home" that overpowers whatever there might be of the "supernatural" at Hill House.[9] Other psychoanalytic readings take up Eleanor's insecure identity formation and her repressed desire for and identification with Theo.[10] Familial and sexual politics are so central to readings of Jackson's novel that Jody Castricano has written that "it could be argued that what actually haunts Hill House is a certain interpretive model that still delimits what we can say about the 'supernatural.'"[11] This interpretive model, Brittany Roberts adds, "privileges human familial relationships and conventional domesticity" and "relies on psychoanalysis to domesticate the novel's supernatural phenomena."[12] In this interpretive model, Hill House's "ghosts" are the manifestations of Eleanor's emotions. The supernatural is subsumed by the psychological, and the unknown is rendered known.[13]

Robert Wise's adaptation of Jackson's novel similarly foregrounds Eleanor's psychology, rendering it even more questionable whether there are in fact "ghosts" at Hill House. As in the novel, Wise's Eleanor still suffers from guilt over her sense that she was negligent the night her mother died; significantly, while Jackson's Eleanor is unable to enter the library because of the smell of mold, in *The Haunting*, Eleanor stops at the door and insists, "I can't go in there.... My mother. That smell." In Wise's film, however, guilt soon gives way to sexual desire and jealousy. And while Theo is the focal point of Eleanor's ambiguous desire in the novel, Wise's Eleanor is more conventionally attracted to Dr. Markway. When Eleanor climbs the spiral staircase in the library, for instance, she is not seeking the warmth of the mother (as in Jackson's novel); instead, she sees Grace Markway, the rival who is taking Eleanor's place with the man she desires. Eleanor thinks, "I'm the one who's supposed to stay here. She's taken my place." And, a bit later, after the house has become love object rather than mother, Eleanor thinks: "The house wants me. Mrs. Markway can't satisfy it." Obsessed with Markway and profoundly unsettled by the wife she didn't know about and whom she wants to be, Eleanor repeats that Grace Markway "has my place. It isn't fair." By the end, *The Haunting* has become a conventional romantic plot: two women are vying to be Mrs. Markway and only one can succeed.

The Haunting not only centers a psychological interpretation of events at Hill House but does so in the context of a subservient nonhuman world, highlighting how thoroughly anthropocentric Wise's adaptation is. When Eleanor drives up to Hill House for the first time, for instance, she drives through woods and, in her first glimpse of the house, there are trees and vines clustered against it. The natural world is persistently relegated only to the outside of Hill House, however, and it has little place in the plot. Inside the house, we see only the occasional plant and decorative vegetal patterns on walls and drapes. Nature is a human creation with no autonomous existence (see Figure 1).

Flanagan's *Haunting*, on the other hand, overturns this vision of a controlled nature, just as it challenges anthropocentric and psychological interpretations of what happens at Hill House. When Nell dances in Hill House in episode five, "The Bent-Neck Lady," for instance, the interior of the house is festooned with vegetation—real vegetation, not the manufactured flora of Wise's *Haunting*. In this scene, the inside/outside boundary is overrun. And, of course, there is the proliferating black mold. It is significant that Jackson's novel mentions the smell of mold in the library, where Eleanor's strictly *psychological* drama comes to a climax in both the novel and Wise's film: as Eleanor climbs the spiral staircase in the library, the house fully becomes "mother" in the novel and Markway in the film. But Flanagan's mold is detached from human desire and need. Indeed, as the series unlooses nature, allowing the spread of vegetal and fungal life, it dislodges the human subject entirely, as well as the anthropocentric plots of other iterations of *Haunting*. Instead, Flanagan shapes a mold-centric narrative.

Figure 1: The etched vegetation on the walls and drapes in *The Haunting* merges with the "real" plant.

Mold-Centric Hill House

There is a compelling case to be made that the mold is what "haunts" Flanagan's Hill House. There are countervailing views, of course, including those voiced by the characters themselves. Steven expresses the most anthropocentric view, insisting that the entire Crain family is "crazy," shouting at his father that "there's something wrong with our goddamn brains" and that our "genes are rotten" ("Witness Marks"). It is certainly possible to see Olivia, Nell, and Luke as suffering from some form of mental illness, compounded, for Nell and Luke, by a barely remembered and thus all the more powerful grief surrounding their mother's death and then compounded again, for Nell, by the sudden death of her husband. One problem with Steven's reading, though, is that there is no hint of any mental illness in the Crain family until Olivia has been in the house for a while, until the mold appears. Indeed, Flanagan is careful not to offer a single detail from Olivia's or Hugh's past that predicts what will happen to them. When Hugh talks to Steven about his marriage, for example, telling him about the time he left Olivia, she is constant and loving—grounded—then and ever since ("Witness Marks"). Olivia changed, suddenly and dramatically, when she entered Hill House, which is why Hugh, who knew her best, believes that the house is responsible for what happened.

What does it mean, though, for Hugh to insist it was the house that caused both Nell's and Olivia's deaths ("Two Storms")? Jackson's novel, too, insinuates the agency of the house. As Dr. Montague says, "The evil is the house itself"; it is "a place of contained ill will." Despite his claim, Jackson's Montague is uncertain about the nature of Hill House's badness—"whether its personality was molded by the people who lived here, or the things they did, or whether it was evil from the start."[14] Montague's view that the house was "molded" by the people who once inhabited it fits with popular conceptions of haunted houses as having "an unsavory history," as Stephen King puts it, a definition that obviously shifts the focus, again, to humans and their uncanny power to form a "bad" house through their "bad" actions.[15] In this reading, the house is merely impressionable bricks and stone, stamped by what people have done within its walls: the house is inert, passive matter. My reading, though, shifts from seeing the house as "molded" to moldy—not passive but active. Instead of only human agency, nonhuman agencies emerge. What happens at Hill House, what happens in any haunting perhaps, is the result of what Jane Bennett has called the "agency of assemblages," an agency that extends beyond human bodies and subjectivities "to vital materialities and the human-nonhuman assemblages they form."[16] Assemblages, in their unfamiliar, alien distributions of agencies, in the cumulative working of many human and nonhuman actors—including humans, including mold—may well shape what happens at Hill House.

Recognizing the mold as an actor in the drama of Hill House amplifies what Dr. Montague fleetingly identifies—that "subterranean waters, or electric currents, or hallucinations caused by polluted air" may be what's wrong with Hill House.[17] Read in this light, Olivia's speech to Theo about their genetic propensity for "sensitivity" could apply to the effects of mold as well as the ability to see "ghosts" ("Touch"). Tellingly, the first thing Theo says when she walks into the house, long before the mold has been discovered, is "smells weird" ("Screaming Meemies"), resonating with expert accounts of the unmistakable smell of mold.[18] Black mold can produce poisonous compounds called mycotoxins, the symptoms of which can be both physical (fatigue, weakness, headache, blurred vision, shortness of breath, disorientation, vertigo) and psychological (depression, anxiety, brain fog, and insomnia).[19] Olivia—who enters Hill House perfectly sane but before too long begins to see "ghosts," which are what drive her to try to poison her children and then kill herself—starts to suffer from all these symptoms. She is clearly the most vulnerable to the house, a fact exacerbated by her descent into the mold-infested basement, several times, without a mask. And the camera dwells on this fact.

Mrs. Dudley might also be particularly susceptible to mold. Mr. Dudley tells Hugh that his wife's first child was stillborn after she spent much of her time—day and night—in the house; she experienced other symptoms, as well, that made her "scattered." The Dudleys believed that something about the house had caused the death of their unborn child, and so they subsequently limited their time in the house to the daylight hours, and Mrs. Dudley successfully gave birth to Abigail. While Mr. Dudley claims that the difference was staying away at night (with the suggestion that whatever was wrong was supernatural), the successful pregnancy may simply have been about Mrs. Dudley's reduced exposure to mold toxins. Even Hugh (who also holds to a supernatural explanation) directly attributes at least one strange event involving himself to the mold. After he puts his hand in the fan while working in the basement, he explains to Olivia, "I don't know if it's the mold, the chemicals, the noise down there. I just ... I—I spaced" ("Screaming Meemies").

While the effectivity of black mold should not be envisioned as a mechanical causality, it is not inconceivable that hauntings may be linked to black mold. Shane Rogers, a civil and environmental engineer at Clarkson University, has been conducting research to determine whether sightings of ghosts may be linked to specific pollutants, including mold, found in old houses. Although he says that "the connection between the fungal and the paranormal is still speculative," he also claims that the "data tells us that mold counts in places reported to be haunted are higher than those that are not."[20] Rogers cites an article by L.D. Empting that describes the research linking human exposure to molds, mycotoxins, and water-damaged buildings to "neurologic and neuropsychiatric signs and symptoms," including migraines, disorders of movement, balance, and coordination, mental confusion (or "brain fog"), and "mycotoxin and mold-induced forms of delirium and dementia," including a "nearly nonfunctional mental state that can further induce catastrophic decompensating behaviors."[21] These symptoms describe much of what afflicts Olivia, and the mental confusion or "brain fog" seems also to apply to Hugh's "spacing" and to Dudley's description of his wife's being "scattered." It is not inconceivable, in the end, that such disordered mental states, induced by black mold, could precipitate what appear to be spectral presences.

Centering the black mold and mycotoxins of Flanagan's *Haunting* is not, though, about reductively attributing a singular cause (It's the mold!) and leaving it at that. A short YouTube video about the series has asked whether the ghosts were "brought on by black mold?"[22] Not only does this question suggest there is only one answer, one cause, but it implies we know exactly how mold works and thus leads us to think, like Hugh, that all we have to do is "fix it"—spray it with chemicals and seal it off with plastic. *Haunting* shows us how futile this reaction is: Hugh sprays poison and the mold spreads. On the other hand, bringing the mold into a *spectrum* of causes for what happens at Hill House, recognizing that the microbial world is profoundly entangled with the human world, part of a human/nonhuman "assemblage," unsettles the very idea of a mechanistic cause-effect logic. In an interview, Carla Gugino (who plays Olivia) recounts that Flanagan said, "the more mold there is, the more mental disintegration is happening."[23] Flanagan is careful to refuse a straightforward causality: mold and "mental disintegration" coexist, but how? What is clear, though, is that, visually, black mold encroaches, especially

Figure 2: Olivia's tea party in the red room. Episode 9, "Screaming Meemies."

in the final two episodes and especially as the distinction between "life and death" becomes increasingly unclear. For instance, as Olivia tries to poison Luke and Nell and the mysterious Abigail (who herself is not clearly either living or "ghost" at this point), she is in fact seeking to deliver them to a safer "life." And the black mold spreads (see Figure 2).

It is telling that the YouTube video about black mold dichotomizes the fungal and the supernatural, asking "Were the ghosts real or brought on by black mold?" But what if the fungal and the supernatural are in fact synonymous? What if what we know as "ghosts" are actually physiological responses to mold and other microbial agents? What if ghosts are matter we don't know, biological causalities we can't grasp? Molds have historically played an only dimly understood causal role in human lives, and that role has frequently been confused with the supernatural. Historian Mary Kilbourne Matossian, for instance, has argued that ergot, which flourishes on rye in wet, cool climates and is the commonest form of fungal poisoning, was an underlying factor in the witchcraft persecutions that swept Europe and North America in the sixteenth and seventeenth centuries. She persuasively demonstrates how clusters of early modern witchcraft persecutions correlated with communities particularly dependent on rye, with cold winters and damp, cool springs, and, temporally, with the aftermath of harvest, when ergot is most toxic.[24] Indeed, the role of ergotism in ill health was misunderstood long after supernatural explanations of witchcraft vanished; until the nineteenth century, for instance, ergotism was "mistaken for an infectious and contagious disease."[25] The case of ergotism in particular, then, demonstrates how difficult it is to ascertain causality when it comes to fungi and molds. As microbiologist

Pat Hamilton sums it up, the "time honored concepts of cause and effect are not as simple with mycotoxins as we would wish and frequently assume."[26] The mesh connecting humans with mold, with its inscrutable causality, could well be synonymous, then, with that connecting humans with the "supernatural."

Ghosts as Nonhuman Life

If the mold is what haunts Flanagan's Hill House, it is a two-fold haunting. First, the "ghosts" could be a symptom of mold toxins, as the characters are entangled with only dimly understood microbial life forms. Second, however, the "ghosts" could themselves be even more dimly understood forms of nonhuman life. The agency of mold, in other words, points us to other "vital materialities," as Bennett puts it.[27] And who are we to say, hubristically, that we have any idea what all those materialities are? "Ghosts"—that is, post-death existence—could in fact be a continuation of "life." Rosi Braidotti has described a post-anthropocentric way of thinking that recasts death as a continuation of life—specifically of *zoe*, or "the non-human vital form of life" (as opposed to *anthropos* or *bios*, strictly human life). "Life as *zoe*," she asserts, "also encompasses what we call 'death.'"[28] In death, life goes on, "relentlessly non-human in the vital force that animates it."[29] Braidotti does not talk about "ghosts," but the "ghosts" of Flanagan's *Haunting* materialize her "life" that "goes on" through and after death. To say a house is "haunted," then, may be tantamount to saying that it is inhabited by "ghosts" that are (mostly inaccessible) forms of nonhuman life. Timothy Morton has also suggested this connection, positing that the discovery of "nonhuman beings" is akin to "something like the 'paranormal,' causalities that do not churn mechanistically underneath things, but that wrap around, flow out of, and otherwise spray and pour out of things."[30] Or, as Hugh Crain puts it when he is trying to comfort Nell after one of her recurrent dreams of the "bent-neck lady," dreams can "spill," "just like a cup of water can spill sometimes" ("Steven Sees a Ghost"). Except what is "spilling" in Nell's visions is not a dream but her own "ghost"—her own future self as the bent-neck lady after she hangs herself. Matter we can see (mold), as well as that we can neither see nor understand, spills, entangling us. This is what we call "paranormal."

Ironically, Steven—the voice of the anthropocentric, causally mechanistic, and rational explanation—articulates this understanding of a haunting as nonhuman life in the very first episode. He says that there is no such things as the "supernatural"; there is only "natural phenomena that we understand, and then there's natural phenomena that we don't." Steven says he prefers the term "'preternatural': *Natural phenomena that we don't quite understand yet*"

("Steven Sees a Ghost"; emphasis mine). Unfortunately, Steven continually returns to the strictly psychological interpretation (a "ghost is a wish"), but the truth he articulates, that hauntings constitute a natural phenomenon we don't understand, persists throughout the series, despite Steven.

In his thematic and visual emphasis on the power of mold and the idea of ghosts as nonhuman life, Flanagan evokes H.P. Lovecraft's "weird" variant of the supernatural in "The Shunned House" (1924). Flanagan has said he is "a huge Lovecraft fan," particularly of "his stories of extradimensional entities," and especially "The Shunned House." Flanagan added that Lovecraft's "depiction of the vast expanses of existence beyond the veil of our perception have [sic] influenced an awful lot of my writing."[31] "The Shunned House" is about a house that is not regarded by the townspeople "as in any real sense 'haunted,'" but in which people have tended to die and in which no child has been born alive.[32] As in Flanagan's Hill House, what characterizes the shunned house above all, its source of horror and repulsion, is the overspreading "sinister vegetation" and the "fungus-cursed cellar."[33] Lovecraft's story is replete with descriptions of the "fungus growth in the cellar," white fungous growths, "a vague, shifting deposit of mould," a "mouldy floor with its uncanny shapes and distorted, half-phosphorescent fungi," "detestable fungi," and a "cloud of fungous loathsomeness."[34] What makes the shunned house horrifying, in other words, is nonhuman microbial life.

During the course of the story, the fungi and mold (part of the known nonhuman world) merge into an unknown life. Describing his investigation of the mold-filled cellar, the narrator writes that "there seemed to me to brood," in the record of the house, "a persistent evil beyond anything in nature as I had known it." Indeed, "scientific study and reflection had taught us that the known universe of three dimensions embraces the merest fraction of the whole cosmos of substance and energy." Thus, he was not prepared to deny "the possibility of certain unfamiliar and unclassified modifications of vital force and attenuated matter"—close enough to the boundary with our own world of known matter to impinge upon it occasionally (in a "fungus cursed cellar") but alien enough to be, in "the human point of view," of "exceptional malignity," the source of tales of supernatural beings like "vampires or werewolves"—or, of course, ghosts.[35] Lovecraft's "The Shunned House" is, then, like *Haunting*, about the entanglement of mold and ghosts, of natural and supernatural worlds, of the natural *as* the supernatural. Both texts move from the ineffable causality of the fungal in human lives to the ways in which the fungal, as a nonhuman form of life, *can actually constitute the supernatural*: matter we know becomes matter we don't know; matter we don't know becomes "ghost."

Of course, like Steven when he denies the truth he utters about the "supernatural" being the "nature we don't know" (falling back instead on familiar psychological explanations), humans tend to deny the unfamiliar and the weird. The prevalence of walls in Flanagan's *Haunting* marks this propensity. The characters wall themselves up against many things, including traumatic emotions and events, but also against unknown forms of matter. Of all the characters, perhaps Theo best exemplifies the building of walls. Horrified at the vision of her dead mother she had as a child when Olivia touches her, Theo accepted the gloves her mother gave her and has, ever since, refused physical contact, only sparingly using her ability to see "ghosts," those things that others cannot. Theo explains the gloves to a woman she sleeps with by declaring she's a "germaphobe" ("Steven Sees a Ghost"), thus conflating the seemingly "supernatural" things she sees with invisible, animate microorganisms. Ultimately, though, walls fail, as illustrated by the dissolutive powers of the mold. If William Hill exemplifies the deathliness of walls by literally walling himself in the basement, the discovery of his body, behind walls covered with mold, represents the inevitable futility of building walls to stave off nonhuman life forms and processes ("Eulogy"). Mold dissolves, mold consumes, mold decomposes, producing unimaginable forms of life.

At the end of the series, Steven, Shirley, Theo, and Luke seem to have retrieved their lives from the agency of what inhabits the house, and in what to many seemed a jarring penultimate scene, they happily move on. The emotional walls these characters have built against each other have seemingly come down. But the series does not end with this happy, well-lit scene but with a final scene of Hill House, still overrun by mold and vegetation. And Hill House still contains the Dudleys, Olivia, Hugh, and Nell. "Whatever walked there," the concluding voiceover intones, "walked together"—a dramatic change from the final line of Jackson's novel, which reprises the last line of the first paragraph: "whatever walked there, walked alone."[36] The "together" in Flanagan's adaptation is important because it indicates that what persists is not singular but plural. It is the house itself and the nonhuman life with which it is overrun, the vegetation and the mold. And it is also the dead characters, whose "ghosts" are also forms of nonhuman life. The final vision of *Haunting* is one that has been there all along: humans are profoundly enmeshed with the nonhuman life, including the microbial, that we call "supernatural." Impersonal, relentless, ubiquitous, and often invisible, this "life" is an inscrutable force that unmakes the people we try to be, the conscious lives we try to lead, the bordered world we think we inhabit; it unmakes time (as it did for Nell) and it unmakes space. Most of all it unmakes what we think is the fixed and impermeable border between life and death. As Nell says in the last episode, she is not "gone" but "scattered into pieces." The life that overspreads Hill House, the swarming tentacles of barely grasped nonhuman life, the creep of black mold, poses a profound existential threat to the "human" we think we are. Mike Flanagan's *The Haunting of Hill House*, in short, suggests that what we take as a "haunting" may not be psychological but fungal, not anthropocentric but mold-centric.

Notes

1. Jackson, *Haunting*, 75.
2. This is the title of Eileen A. Joy's essay.
3. Fisher, *Weird*, 10–11.
4. Joy, "Weird," 29.
5. Ibid., 29.
6. See Lootens, "'Whose Hand,'" 152, for a discussion of how Jackson's drafts for *Haunting* reveal her movement from a relatively conventional ghost story to a story about the terrors of the nuclear family.
7. See, especially, Newman, "Shirley Jackson," and Rubenstein, "House Mothers."
8. Jackson, *Haunting*, 102, 149.
9. Ibid., 169.
10. See, for example, Lootens, "Whose Hand," 162–6, on Eleanor's desire for and identification with Theo; see also Hattenhauer, *Shirley Jackson's*, 163.
11. Castricano, "Shirley Jackson's," 89.
12. Roberts, "Helping Eleanor," 73.
13. Both Castricano and Roberts, in their readings of Jackson's novel, seek to push the meanings of what happens at Hill House beyond the preoccupation with the individual psyche, along with the social and cultural relations in which it is embedded, and even beyond the human at all. Roberts addresses Eleanor's love for the "constant nonhuman presence" of the house, as it reflects her desire to be alone, and Castricano explores the "forms of nonhuman consciousness" in the novel (such as telepathy), as well as the characters' relationships with sentient objects. See Roberts, "Helping Eleanor," 78; Castricano, "Shirley Jackson's," 89, 94.
14. Jackson, *Haunting*, 60, 51.
15. King, *Danse Macabre*, 267. For a discussion of whether Jackson's Hill House is "born" or "made" bad, see Corstorphine, "'The Girl,'" 116–7 and 124, and Downey and Jones, "King," 225–27.
16. Bennett, *Vibrant Matter*, 30.
17. Jackson, *Haunting*, 51.
18. Money, *Carpet Monsters*, 16, 18, 20.
19. Tsafrir, "Mold Toxicity."
20. Faletto, "Seeing Ghosts"; personal email dated March 19, 2019.
21. Empting, "Neurologic," 577–80.
22. Deffinition, "Haunting."
23. Schonter, "Haunting."
24. Matossian, *Poisons*, 9, 13–14.
25. Ibid., 12.
26. Hamilton, "Fallacies," 404.
27. Bennett, *Vibrant Matter*, 30.
28. Braidotti, *Posthuman*, 60, 134.
29. Ibid., 137.
30. Morton, *Dark Ecology*, 95.
31. Davis, "My Interview."
32. Lovecraft, "Shunned," 99, 103.
33. Ibid., 99, 112.
34. Ibid., 98, 100, 112, 115, 120.
35. Ibid., 113.
36. Jackson, *Haunting*, 182.

Where the Heart Is

Alex Link

"Haunted places are the only ones that people can live in..."[1]

Throughout the Netflix series *The Haunting of Hill House*, one finds a consistent emphatic return to the uncertainty of boundaries that are never quite porous enough and never quite impermeable enough, particularly with respect to family. This tension between isolation and connection as simultaneously desirable and intolerable finds theorization in Julia Kristeva's understanding of the "Abject. Something rejected from which one does not part." It "disturbs identity, system, order [and] does not respect borders, positions, rules" such as, aptly, "the killer who claims he is a savior" as Liv Crain does.[2] One finds a similar fixation in the Shirley Jackson novel, which explores the "continuity between fear of engulfment and fear of separation,"[3] and in which Eleanor longs both for a new family and for isolation, such that to walk alone in Hill House at its ending is, to some readers, a happy ending.[4] In the series, however, haunting might best be understood as absence or depthlessness made paradoxically manifest, at once too close and too far. Anxieties about physical proximity serve as a ritual and misplaced attempt to manage interpersonal emotional bonds, which defy easy material management, linear temporality, and simple explanations. In the language of the series, they mistake matters of the stomach for matters of the heart the correction of which, in counterpoint to the novel, reconstitutes the traditional nuclear family.

Temporality in *Hill House* is far from simple, even with respect to the apparently stable and ordered shift between past and present that frames the narrative. Nell, especially, focuses the narrative's meditation on time, most obviously through the projection of the Bent-Neck Lady backwards in time, such that Nell sees a ghost of her future self, and is effectively haunted by her own death. As the narrative focus of temporality, it makes sense that Nell's sleep paralysis also makes it difficult for her to distinguish between subjective and objective time, that the music playing over her courtship montage would feature the lyrics "let us go where time runs slow," and that there should be such visual emphasis on her inheritance of Hugh's pocket watch ("The Bent-Neck Lady"). This distinction between objective and subjective time is precisely the difference, in *Hill House*, between the material and the affective: the stomach and the heart. It is this distinction and the ease with which, as the red room signifies, a stomach might be mistaken for a heart ("Silence Lay Steadily"), that anchors all of *Hill House*'s tensions and hauntings.

This persistence of the past is why we rarely see any of our characters at home. We see Steven bed down in a putatively haunted house when we first meet him, and his wife Leigh calls their home "my house," not theirs ("Steven Sees a Ghost"). Nell stays in a motel and when we do see her apartment it is in a shambles, a site of grief and no longer a home ("The Bent-Neck Lady"). Luke lives in a shelter with strict rules that see him, too, unable to return to this safe space once he leaves; in a way, it is an adult version of his childhood tree house, which had its own particular rules. Theo is a guest of Shirl's, while we rarely see Shirl anywhere other than work. Effectively, the Crain children have never left Hill House, evident, too, in Shirl's refusal to recognize Leigh as family ("Steven Sees a Ghost"). The members of this nuclear unit are trapped with one another through the trauma of Liv's death and Hugh's silence, even while it is physically and emotionally scattered. Time has moved on, but the family has not. One might argue that while the narrative opens with the adult family living a painful spatial dispersal but temporal concentration, stuck in a defining moment while scattered across the country, it ends by reversing these polarities, bringing them physically together while shredding this traumatic moment and allowing it to fall around them, as Nell puts it when she exits the series, like confetti, or snow ("Silence Lay Steadily").

Other examples of unstable temporality abound, however, most simply in the very idea of haunting as time out of place. If, as Steven says to Irene when we first meet him, Carl's return as a ghost is "better than never seeing him again … [m]ost times a ghost is a wish," then ghosts demonstrate the contradiction of the ever-present absence of something or someone missed, hoped for, or mourned ("Steven Sees a Ghost"). It is the presence of absence, collapsing temporalities. Structurally, given the parallels between the events of the two storms in the episode of that name, the storms might best be understood as collapsing into a single event, and the camerawork underscores this spillage, or co-extension by having Hugh walk directly into the past, as a place, to see his former, similarly dressed self. When Hugh returns from walking through his second flashback, Luke asks "Where'd you go?" and Hugh replies "Nowhere," which, again, leaves unanswered the question of whether he has traveled to the past in mind, in fact, or whether there is even a meaningful difference ("Two Storms"). Past and future come together in the sticky persistence of the past, and its failed fears and hopes, the way the model of the forever house is an odd memento by which to remember Liv: a past iteration of future plans, remembering not a moment, but a hope or a wish for something doubly lost in that it never came to be. It inverts Nell's haunting by her own future, itself signified subtly in the ticking of the clock that slows then stops, as the camera rotates counter-clockwise above her when the Bent-Neck Lady appears floating above the couch ("Steven Sees a Ghost").

The spillage in the "Two Storms" episode begins with the moment Hugh sees his adult progeny as children, when first arriving at the funeral home, as if introducing us to the superimposition of periods, and he remarks that it has been "longer than a minute," since they last saw each other, "or a long minute." Both, it turns out, are true. Parallel events occur in each storm. The crashing chandelier, for example, recalls Nell's hanging body and anticipates her falling coffin at the episode's end. Each storm, too, is marked by Nell's present absence. The episode concludes by playing Luke's, then Nell's childhood words in voiceover while we see her adult ghost: "I was right here. I didn't go anywhere. I was right here" ("Two Storms"). This moment itself is ironic in that even Nell, when considering the Bent-Neck Lady, doesn't realize that she, too, was "right here all along" to herself. The fact resonates not only in the obvious sense that she was ignored while alive, like Jackson's Eleanor Vance, but even now. The family sits in separate rows from one another as they talk around her casket, unwilling to honor her desire that they be close and, ultimately, as the episode tends toward its climax, they stand so that everyone has their back to her casket while they fight.

The family is always together and apart, signaled most poignantly in those moments of haunting in the house when the scary creature on the other side of the door is a member of the family, rendered an analogy of interpersonal communication by the faces on the doorknobs and the seeming inability of voices to cross the door's barrier, whether it is Liv trying to get into Steven's bedroom in the first episode, the banging on the wall that comes to be associated with Luke's isolation from a family that never believes him ("Open Casket"; "Witness Marks"), or Shirl and Nell trying to get into the red room, where Theo dances, tellingly, to Janet Jackson's adaptation of Paula Abdul's "Cold Hearted" ("Silence Lay Steadily"). If one thinks of closed doors as provisional walls, the family's relationship to the door Hugh finally confesses he has been holding "closed, 'cause [he] knew here were monsters on the other side" is potentially tragic, when those monsters are family ("Witness Marks"). Against these attempts to breach divisions, the siblings also insist on new ones, with Shirl keeping her promise at Nell's wedding not to fight with Steven but immediately and secretly paying Luke to leave the premises ("Open Casket"), and Steven telling the story of Nell calling indivisibility the family's secret power before immediately launching into an attack on Hugh that culminates in his declaration that "the wrong parent died" at the climax of the storm, words that seem to cause Nell's casket to tip ("Two Storms").

The emphasis on walls in *Hill House* is obvious, from Theo's insistence on "Boundaries. Maybe a brick wall when it comes to Luke" despite her hands' insistent breach of them, to William Hill all bricked up behind a wall and then clawing to get out, to Kelsey's compartmentalization "like a brick wall" that Mr. Smiley, her molester, breaches anyway ("Steven Sees a Ghost"; "Touch"). Steven's insistence on mediation, too, establishes a kind of wall, such that our first introduction to him is a visual focus on a recording phone, Irene's narration, and a pen on a notebook, without any glimpse of his face until she stops, his further investigation of Irene's story showing him on multiple screens as he explores her dripping ceiling ("Steven Sees a Ghost"). Even he has to conclude that while he "thought that wall[s] kept us both safe ... walls don't work that way. Walls never work that way" ("Silence Lay Steadily").

The family's many walls block out pain and intimacy alike creating an imprisoning safety driven by the need to maintain a fragile sense of stability. By contrast, Nell, in a signature malapropism, remarks when she discovers the cup of stars, that "I'm not opposed to have things that are fragile" ("The Bent-Neck Lady"). While the series clearly establishes Nell as a heroine, self-sacrifice in the name of family is precisely what Jackson's novel critiques. In both the novel and the series, Hill House "reveals to its guests ... a ... vision of ... nuclear families that kill where they are supposed to nurture" and shows the toll the nuclear family takes on women, who sacrifice their identity to hold the family together.[5] In the series, it is celebrated, and Liv's suicide is treated as a betrayal, an opting out of this sacrifice, only to have it revealed that this was the ultimate purpose of her suicide, at once noble and conventional in its submission to patriarchal norms, and excessive in its attempt to consume the family and imprison them in the familial structure for which she has given her life. Nell is celebrated for her self-sacrifice, perhaps most clearly in Steven's remark that, through her death, Nell has finally succeeded in getting all the family in one place ("Two Storms"). However conventional, Nell is the one loved and resented remaining point of access for the Crains to anything like meaningful interpersonal connection.

Even simple, physical distance, however, is an imperfect barrier. Hugh reveals Nell's death to Steven over the phone from across the country, intimate news that forces the family back together in spite of distance, as he repeats her name ("Steven Sees a Ghost"). At the same moment, across the street in counterpoint, Joey kisses Luke but only as a diversion while she picks his pocket, opening a distance in spite of the intimacy of an embrace. Joey's betrayal inverts the "twin thing" of intimacy that defies distance. Perhaps this tension between physical and emotional proximity is clearest in the irony of Luke's protective invocation of sevens in the same episode, a number signaling the safety to be found in the family ring ("Twin Thing"). It plays out a ritual fantasy of emotional closeness in spite of all evidence to the contrary. As a child, Nell adopts his ritual and represents her family with buttons, each symbolically tasked with holding the collective fabric together; at the motel, before going to her death at Hill House, she arranges a semi-circle ring again, cup of stars in hand, but this time of artificial sweetener packets, Nell having become the last button to give when the ring has proven itself false ("The Bent-Neck Lady").

If physical and emotional distance have no direct bearing on one another, then physical and emotional integrity are equally disarticulated, however much one might wish the opposite were true. Shirl tries to freeze time when she "fixes" bodies, in both senses of the word, with her mortician's art, as she does with photographs. A beetle emerging from a dead kitten's throat is a literal illustration of physical decomposition, but it also suggests ways in which decomposition itself is a dissolving of the individual's integrity, and that preserving a body is no proof against the deceased's dispersal into time. We are shown its emotional correlate when the same beetle emerges from Nell's throat as Shirl reflects, in anticipation of the eventual revelation of her infidelity, her secret refusal to allow Luke to attend Nell's wedding. Here, the beetle emerges like an ugly, unacceptable, inescapable—which is to say abject—truth, which, perhaps, porosity also is ("Open Casket").

The series makes plain, in the final episode's red room nightmares, that rot can be moral as well as physical, and that the maintenance of an orderly exterior is no indication of the nature of interiority. The incompatibility of the two is apparent in Theo's visit to three separate basements in the same episode ("Touch"). All three—Kelsey's, Hill House's and Shirl's—are spaces of horror. Kelsey's is a mundane space in which she is molested. Hill House's is a concealed space of criminality, itself concealing a tomb. Bearing in mind that, traditionally, basements are spaces of the unconscious in the Gothic, it is worth noting that Hill House's cellar was assumed not to exist at all. If the red room—which, traditionally, would be the site of higher mental functions in the Gothic—is in *Hill House* the site of unthinking consumption, then perhaps the basement is its mold-poisoned, disavowed heart. Shirl's symmetrical and spotless workroom would seem to belie the fact that it is a space where, hidden, the body's boundaries are violated in the name of preserving an illusion of its integrity. It is through this inability to make physical integrity guarantee emotional integrity that one might understand Shirl's brutal remark to Steven over the phone that "I'm elbows deep in our sister's chest cavity pulling out a bag of her internal organs" ("Open Casket"), or her claim that Steven's book "raped the family" ("Steven Sees a Ghost"). The world, to Shirl, is a fixed, stable mask with a wasp's nest underneath or, as her nightmare in the red room puts it, she is "fixed and pretty. But underneath she is a horror" ("Silence Lay Steadily"). Simplicity, integrity, and the stability of walls that "continue upright" in a world where "bricks meet, floors are firm, and doors are sensibly shut" prove nothing, when the secret basement, underneath, is a horror.

Fixing bodies is like telling stories that are simpler than *Hill House*, and *Hill House* is not a simple story. It is about coming to terms with stories that are not simple, stories that speak to hearts and not stomachs. If we become stories when we die, as Liv explains to Shirl ("Open Casket"), then the lack of narrative closure around Liv's death is one way of understanding her ghost: it is a haunting in the sense that her tale remains unfinished, incompletely told by Hugh. The family remains suspended in her story lending weight to the exchange between Hugh and Liv we see in flashback at the moment of Hugh's death, with Liv saying casually "You guys go on [and play] without me," and Hugh answering, tenderly, "How could we?" ("Screaming Meemies").

Like the red room in Hill House, a simple story casts isolation—in a tree house, or a reading room, or a game room—as an easy illusion of safety. Even so, it is Nell's unflagging desire to do the difficult work of breaching that isolation that is typically treated by the rest of the family as naïve and simplistic. It could be argued that the family members avoid each other to preserve the comforting surficial simplicity of their stories that cast one another as failures. They see one another as merely the supporting players in one another's tales of personal tragedy and triumph, the way Leigh accuses Steven of having treated her throughout their marriage in his red room nightmare ("Silence Lay Steadily"). Much of the family tension focuses upon denying one another the right to tell their own story by attacking one another's credibility. Shirl calls people intoxicated when she does not like what they say ("Two Storms"), and Steven calls them mentally ill ("The Bent-Neck Lady"; "Two Storms"; "Witness Marks") as a way of silencing them, while the siblings collude in undermining Luke's believability and, in their final argument, Theo infantilizes Nell as a passive, voiceless victim ("The Bent-Neck Lady"). Steven is consistently reminded, as the siblings remind one another, that he is selfish and irresponsible; Shirl controlling and judgmental; Theo shallow and aggressive; Hugh a secretive failure; Nell flighty and weak; and Luke a simple write off.

To take this last for an example of self-serving oversimplification, Luke's lack of credibility is not a consequence of his addiction, but precisely the reverse. The relationship between the two as mirrors of one another, reflected but inverted, is evident in a dynamic of hats. William Hill, the tall man in the black hat, appears at moments of emotional distress for Luke, such as when he is abandoned by Joey, and of trauma of the sort that has been disbelieved throughout his life. The tenacious cling of his addiction, by contrast, is signaled in his cajoling Nell into purchasing him one last hit from a man, he says twice, in a white hat ("The Bent-Neck Lady"). On those few occasions when characters are given the opportunity to explain themselves, such as Hugh to Steven in front of Nell's coffin ("Two Storms"), or Theo to Shirl on the drive to save Luke ("Witness Marks"), their accusers fill the space with words so that it is difficult for them to receive the very explanation they demand, making it clear that they in fact feed upon one another as disappointments. Think, for example, of when Luke introduces Joey to Steven, as Steven actively attacks Joey's credibility and undermines Luke's confidence in his ability to succeed in rehab while, ironically, rarely appearing without a drink in his hand ("Twin Thing"). The family eats victimhood.

Like a simplistic story, *Hill House* is replete with simplified replicas, imitations, and idealizations that vainly promise order and stability. Most obvious is the House itself, with faces seeming to adorn every surface, and classically inspired statuary providing images of (mostly) still, contained bodies without interiority. Indeed, even the opening credits speak to this horror of an absence of interiority, as we are shown images of fragmenting statues with nothing beneath their surface but more surface. Depthless images are ubiquitous, from Halloween masks to Hugh's imaginary therapeutic Liv, to the anthropomorphic stains on the basement wall-within-a-wall, to the Mr. Smiley shape on Kelsey's basement ceiling. These, too, are simple stories that disavow troubling complexity, the way an embalmed corpse does. The same might be said of model houses. The one in Theo's office presents a simple, idealized doll house far removed from the experience of living in a specific home ("Touch"), just as Liv's idealized "forever house" remains forever unrealized and, as an ideal, perhaps unrealizable. It is worth noting that we first see Liv's model in Shirl's office, while Kevin is putting up a family portrait ("Steven Sees a Ghost"). This, too, is a simplification that disavows Shirl's affair, Kevin's secret acceptance of money from Steven, Hugh's absence, and so on. The inadequacy of simple stories and simple images is made plain when Shirl finds herself able to describe the physical details of Nell's death to her inquiring children, but cannot explain why she died or where she is now ("Open Casket"). Arguably, this moment is doubly surficial, in the sense that Shirl is speaking words that Theo has provided for her ("Touch"). The irony, then, is deep, when she describes Max's approach to his grandmother's open casket as the "moment of truth" ("Open Casket").

Whereas conventionally ghosts speak to the fear of an unseen world, *Hill House* speaks to the fear of an absence of one, or the fear that surfaces and simple stories are truly all there is. Much of the series is concerned precisely with the relationship between commerce and haunting, or what might be characterized as matters of the stomach and matters of the heart. Hill House is both a haunted house and a real estate investment. The haunting itself is both traumatic and a troubling source of family income, and Steven compartmentalizes the two by calling his book "just work" ("The Bent-Neck Lady"). Shirl's business, too, combines commerce and hauntings, even haunted houses, with little Max's malapropism that he does not want to see his grandmother "in the open castle," an inversion of Liv's comparison of Hill House to a body in the following scene. The former is Shirl's business, and as a child she completes Liv's description of the house, as one they will fix, with the words "to sell for a lot of money" ("Open Casket"). Now she fixes bodies for money. Irene's haunted house, too, is a question of home repair and violated boundaries, with water leaking into the house, and a stop sign gone missing identified as the culprits ("Steven Sees a Ghost"). Comparably, Luke manages his own haunting through physical, chemical means, while Theo's trysts are purely transactional, perhaps not so very different from Mr. Smiley's victimization of Kelsey in its impersonality and reliance upon compartmentalization; the two are juxtaposed, after all, when Theo places her notes regarding Kelsey's case next to Trish's phone number on her night stand. Even Theo's dawning awareness of her "sensitivity," as Liv describes it, and the discussion of it, establishes a heart's parallel to the physical process of puberty, as is often the case in stories of witchcraft: "if you're feeling overwhelmed and you think nobody will understand, you can talk to me" ("Touch").

Steven and Hugh follow parallel paths in their gradual discovery that what truly needs fixing are emotional relationships rather than physical or financial or medical material systems. After Nell's death, Hugh devotes himself to fixing relationships, not houses. After Hugh's death, Steven resolves to fix his marriage, returning not to the house, but "home" ("Silence Lay Steadily"). When searching for Luke, Hugh and Steven check with the hospital named for a model family unit as a sacred organization, "Holy Family," when this is precisely what failed to protect Luke despite his ritual arrangements of seven army men. After their experience in the red room, though, Luke is taken to a hospital the name of which invokes the language *Hill House* establishes as its real priority, "Sacred Heart" ("Witness Marks"; "Silence Lay Steadily").

In a curious reversal, then, it is the material world that is truly, traumatically haunting, while matters of the heart, as the series concludes, not rational, nevertheless are the site of sanity. These, after all, are Steven's paradoxical concluding words to the series, as he declares that love, like fear, is "the willing relinquishment of reasonable patterns" without which "we cannot continue to exist sanely" ("Silence Lay Steadily"). Joey, however untrustworthy, makes this case when Steven invokes the old saw that doing the same thing and expecting different results is insanity, by arguing that, in the case of rehabilitation, it is a persistent act of faith. Here, again, addiction is material consumption, while recovery is a function of friendships, support and love, or a matter of the heart. Consistent with the tension that runs through the series, friendships in rehab are discouraged by its management, but promoted by the inspirational posters in the dorms, and come to seem essential to recovery ("Twin Thing"). "Loud" and "hungry" are words used to describe Hill House ("Touch"), and they also describe the drudgery of material daily life when Shirl remembers her paramour, Ryan, in her red room nightmare. The resonance makes this infidelity, too, a desperate act in search of something that might exist beyond surfaces, the failure of which comes to haunt Shirl in the recurring image of Ryan raising his glass. In Steven's nightmare, he is "an eater," packaging and selling the family history, while Leigh "picked up the check for [his] dreams" ("Silence Lay Steadily"). As Mrs. Dudley points out, the house is not a shelter from time or the material world, "it's just as stupid and hungry as anything else," and not a home ("Screaming Meemies").

Ultimately, there is no safety, and so Poppy's claim that, when Hugh flees the house, he is "killing them toward disease and heartbreak and sadness and death and those teeth those teeth that'll tear and chew and eat them alive a piece at a time" ("Screaming Meemies") is simply a vivid description of temporality itself as a digestive process, against which the heart and all it stands for in *Hill House* offers some solace, as the source of time's confetti if nothing else, that makes the absent present, and ghosts comforting. The conflation of house and home, or body with person, is paralleled by that of death with absence. As Nell's ghost insists, "There's no without. I am not gone" ("Silence Lay Steadily"). One might understand "without," here, also as outside, in that the distinction between inside and outside Hill House comes to be a false one. It is all outside, an endless extension of surfaces with no apparent center, or heart, like the labyrinth that appears in the series opening credit sequence.

In a way, this focus on the material drives the divide between Hugh and the children. It is not so much a reprise of that old chestnut of the unbridled imagination of children—which is what leads Hugh to replace every paranormal event with a material, rational explanation—but of the gradual inoculation of affect as one enters adulthood. Hugh eventually seems ridiculous in his treatment of problems as practical and material, blaming pipes or responding to a secret basement with an utter lack of curiosity: "I can't expect it's up to code" is all he has to say ("Open Casket"; "Touch"). His never-ending refrain, "I can fix this," is ultimately inadequate to the complexity of repairing relationships; he is Hill House's doctor when what it needs is therapy, or exorcism. When his children are adults, the older Hugh seems to realize that what he can and must fix are not houses, whether that be Hill House, now left to rot, or the model "forever house" smashed on the floor and also rotting, but his children's relationships. True to his inheritance, then, Steven's first task upon receiving Hill House is to turn away from it, toward "home." If one rots as one ages, and if death, as Theo intuits upon touching Nell's corpse, is absolute numbness ("Witness Marks"), then aging is perhaps also a benumbing process of emotional denial and dishonesty. All one is left with, in entering adulthood, is stomach, or a "clenched fist with hair" ("Witness Marks"), or a needle in a vein as the last self-betrayal that began with accepting a "big boy hat" ("Twin Thing"), or commodified histories, or power games, in place of love. In that case, adulthood threatens to kill Liv's children after all, not by eating them, but by making them just as hungry, until Luke returns from death to remind them that "Once upon a time the world was just play" ("Silence Lay Steadily"). What is haunting the family, signified in all the house's surfaces, is an excess of surfaces, an excess of simplicity, and a dearth of play.

Perhaps the answer to the question with which Liv opens the series, "everyone alive?" isn't so simple.

Perhaps the heart dies first.

NOTES

    1. Michel de Certeau, *The Practice of Everyday Life*, trans. Steven Rendall (Berkeley: University of California Press, 1984), 108.

    2. Julia Kristeva, *Powers of Horror: An Essay on Abjection*, trans. Leon S. Roudiez (New York: Columbia University Press, 1982), 4.

    3. Judie Newman, "Shirley Jackson and the Reproduction of Mothering: *The Haunting of Hill House*," in *Shirley Jackson: Essays on the Literary Legacy*, ed. Bernice M. Murphy (Jefferson, NC: McFarland, 2005), 173.

    4. Brittany Roberts, "Helping Eleanor Come Home: A Reassessment of Shirley Jackson's *The Haunting of Hill House*," *The Irish Journal of Gothic and Horror Studies* 16 (2017): 92.

    5. Tricia Lootens, "'Whose Hand Was I Holding?': Familial and Sexual Politics in Shirley Jackson's *The Haunting of Hill House*," in *Shirley Jackson: Essays on the Literary Legacy*, ed. Bernice M. Murphy (Jefferson, NC: McFarland, 2005), 151, 166.

The Future Isn't What It Used to Be

Hauntology, Grief and Lost Futures

Melissa A. Kaufler

> One day too late, I fear me, noble lord,
> Hath clouded all thy happy days on earth:
> O, call back yesterday, bid time return...[1]
> —*The Earl of Salisbury*, Richard II [III, ii, 67–69]

In the first pages of his 1975 novel *Bid Time Return*, Richard Matheson opens his work with the quote of his novel's namesake—three lines from Shakespeare's *Richard II*. As one reads this quote on an otherwise blank and forlorn page of its own, it is difficult not to begin feeling the way the page itself looks as one reminisces of their own yesterdays—lost or otherwise. The protagonist of Matheson's work, Richard Collier, cannot live in the past and cannot make peace with his unfulfilling present that had fallen short of his expectations.

The grieving of "lost futures"—what was dreamt of and expected—is a lasting feature of our collective memory that far predates Shakespeare. This deep longing to "call back yesterday" has historically been quelled by a collective hope and faith that the best is yet to come. But what happens when the idealized future becomes the underwhelming present? What happens when society is left to grieve the lost future for which we had long hoped and dreamed? For one, we are haunted by it.

The late Mark Fisher interprets this looming haunt as a side effect of late capitalism and the adaptive neoliberal attitudes on which it is founded. Fisher premises that "globalisation, ubiquitous computerisation and the casualisation of labour" have led to a complete "transformation in the way that work and leisure [are] organized."[2] The denial of these effects has contributed to the development of an increasingly precarious working class, or precariat, tasked with serving the ever-changing demands of contemporary market society.[3] However, the demanding realities of working life cannot be separated from broader concerns for emotional wellbeing. If we are scattered and piecemealed for jobs—not stable careers—based on each skill we possess to meet the unique demands of late capitalism simply in an attempt to make ends meet, art and creativity will decline with culture suffering as a result. And it has.

Fisher summarizes Franco Berardi, an Italian Marxist, in his own work:

> [As] Berardi has argued, the intensity and precariousness of late capitalist work culture leaves people in a state where they are simultaneously exhausted and overstimulated. The combination of precarious work and digital communications leads to a besieging of attention. In this insomniac, inundated state, Berardi claims, culture becomes de-eroticised. The art of seduction takes too much time and, according to Berardi, something like Viagra answers not to a biological but to a cultural deficit: desperately short of time, energy and attention, we demand quick fixes. Like another of Berardi's examples, pornography, retro offers the quick and easy promise of a minimal variation on an already familiar satisfaction.[4]

In other words, due to the decline of job security and increase of job precariousness and the subsequent demands that neoliberalist attitudes towards late capitalism's "live to work" culture has imposed upon us, we no longer have the energy or inspiration to produce our own art and culture as we previously did. As a result, we've resorted to recycling the past. Mark Fisher suggests that "there's an increasing sense that culture has lost the ability to grasp and articulate the present. Or it could be that, in one very important sense, there is no present to grasp and articulate anymore."[5] In this struggle to survive the demands of late capitalism, we have lost the ability to create the new, and therefore, we have lost the future we thought we'd have.

Subsequently, we live in an era that is hauntological. "Hauntology," a term coined by Jacques Derrida in his work *Spectres of Marx*, is meant to describe the study of how our collective ideations of the past and future invade or "haunt" our present.[6] Whether it is through music, art, film, fashion, or whatever else, we are in a nostalgia mode. It's culture that has gone far beyond simply paying homage to the past but rather, we have reached what Mark Fisher calls a "confrontation with a cultural impasse." Now, our current culture is unavoidably "haunted"—recycled so heavy-handedly as we create monstrous mashups of what has already been done, yet we attempt to pass it off as fresh and new. In reality, we are saturated with reminders that "time is out of joint."[7] This time as "out of joint" is usually manifested by a series of anachronisms that leave us unable to conclude precisely when something is supposed to be occurring in time or from what era it hails.

We—our collective, modern society—have reached a cultural moment defined by remakes and movie sequels; an era of musicians trying to recapture the lost sounds of the sixties with manufactured record scratches carefully inserted into songs to fake authenticity: for the thirteenth consecutive year, we have witnessed the return of vinyl records en masse.[8] We are sold clothing in eighties styles that are pre-ripped and made to look well-worn but were actually just produced by child labor in Bangladesh a month before. Social media platforms feature ubiquitous photo filters that try to make us look as if we've stepped out of the seventies or starred in a '40s noir film. Lest we forget, the popular #TBT "throwback Thursday" hashtag sprawled across social media platforms each week that is literally designed to elicit a synthesized nostalgic response. We are inherently distracted by the past when we are perusing an endless internet full of articles and photos that tell the story of something that has already occurred. We are here, but not present—not really, anyway.

In his 2018 Netflix adaptation of *The Haunting of Hill House* (hereafter *Haunting*), director Mike Flanagan offers an unsettling look into our current cultural moment through the tragedy of the Crain family. To do this, Flanagan's *Haunting* utilizes hauntological concepts to demonstrate the loss of future and the expansive range of grief that goes along with it. While each surviving member of the Crain family embodies a different stage of grief, they grow and learn together in order to unitedly reach acceptance. And in the same way the Crain family lost Olivia, the creative mind behind their "forever home" and a symbol of the family's future, we as a society have lost our own version of our "forever home."

The Time Is Out of Joint

> Nell: "Everything's been out of order. Time, I mean."
> —"Silence Lay Steadily"

Derrida borrows from Shakespeare's *Hamlet* when he utilizes the phrase "time out of joint" to best describe the anachronisms which are key to hauntology. *Haunting* as a work of art is a series of anachronisms—all of which cannot be enumerated in this essay. Mark Fisher describes anachronisms as a "temporal bleed-through,"[9] or as Hugh Crain described to a young Nell about her dreams: "It's just a little spill." Fisher goes on to say that "anachronism, the slippage of discrete time periods into one another" serves as a "major symptom of time breaking down."[10] Flanagan plays with anachronisms and time in a variety of ways: through his nonlinear storytelling, temporally ambiguous aesthetics including architecture and clothing, and most importantly—through the character that is the Bent-Neck Lady. In this way, Flanagan establishes that time seems to stand still or be completely absent at Hill House. Or perhaps, even time is a fluid concept at Hill House and it refuses to abide by any rules at all.

The first narrative scene of the series—after a montage that showcases the dark, foreboding property—is labeled as "Hill House," and we see a young Steven asleep in his bed. The word "then" fades onto the screen in the bottom left corner under the text reading "Hill House." We don't know when this is supposed to take place, as there are no verbal, visual, auditory, or any other aesthetic clues that allow us to place this scene in any particular time or decade. All we know is that it is not supposed to be "now." Steven hears crying from another room and goes to investigate. He finds his youngest sister, Nell, frightened in her bed. A young Hugh Crain is just behind his eldest son.

Hill House as "then" is introduced to us just moments before Hugh and Steven arrive to comfort Nell after she has seen a particularly disturbing ghost—the curiously named Bent-Neck Lady. The audience and young Nell are blissfully unaware that this sinister ghost is actually Nell's future self, transcending time and appearing to her as her future herself when she is a child. As Hugh tucks Nell safely back into bed, he explains that sometimes our dreams will "spill" a little into real life and to not worry. This idea of a "spill" alone is very hauntological, as the Bent-Neck Lady is Nell's own self from the future/present erupting into the past. It is inherently "out of joint" and sadly, Nell doesn't realize as a child that this looming figure is actually the literal manifestation of her lost future. Hauntology is all about the spilling of things in and out of the time in which they are supposed to belong, and this is one of the first of many times that Nell is faced with her future self until she becomes her. Of ghosts, Avery Gordon writes

> that the ghost is primarily a symptom of what is missing. It gives notice not only to itself but also to what it represents. What it represents is usually a loss, sometimes of life, sometimes of a path not taken. From a certain vantage point the ghost also simultaneously represents a future possibility, a hope.[11]

The story of Nell and the Bent-Neck lady completely decimates the traditional view of ghosts and what they often represent. The Bent-Neck Lady does, in fact, represent a "future" as she appears to Nell over the years. But unlike Gordon's description of a "future possibility, a hope," the sightings of the Bent-Neck Lady are not an omen of what could happen—it's what has already happened to Nell and there is nothing she, nor anyone can do about it. This is a departure from the original function of a ghost and its intended effect of "haunting." Ghosts have typically been something that returns from the past, or as Robin Wood would categorize it: "the return of the repressed."[12] That, however, is no longer the case.

At first glance, one might be forgiven for the outdated assumption that ghosts are spectral entities of the deceased that only appear to vengefully haunt or warn the living of what perils may occur should they not heed said warning. While Charles Dickens' "Ghost of Christmas Future" is from the future as its name suggests, this ghost falls short of capturing the ghastly inevitability of fate that the Bent-Neck Lady does. Dickens' ghost appears to Scrooge to show him what *could* become of him if he fails to change his ways. In other words, Dickens' ghost is simply a warning for a possible outcome, but Scrooge is still ultimately left with the moralized choice and opportunity to change his ways before it is too late.[13] On the other hand, the Bent-Neck Lady appears to Nell—completely unprompted and with no explanation or warning—as her future self. As we learn the true identity of the Bent-Neck Lady whose boundaries are deprived of place and time, we are forced to rethink and question the role of ghosts in a cultural moment that is increasingly hauntological. The Bent-Neck Lady isn't just a ghost from the future, but one that transcends time and space while forcing us to acknowledge that the future may now not only be predetermined, but it also may have already happened. The way Franco Berardi describes the idea of a lost future, lack of choice, and its unavoidability is especially pertinent for Nell. He writes:

> the future has lost its zest and people have lost all trust in it: the future no longer appears as a choice or collective conscious action, but is a kind of unavoidable catastrophe that we cannot oppose in any way.[14]

The element of choice here is key as well as the element of hope—things that Nell Crain did not or was unable to possess. The Bent-Neck Lady *is* the future for Nell, and it is made clear that there is no alternative, even with the glimmer of hope and normalcy that her future husband symbolizes as a way out. This is precisely how Dickens' Ghost of Christmas Future functions when it appears as a warning to Ebenezer Scrooge—an old man whose morally corrupt actions have solicited this karma-driven ghost from the future—and he is offered the chance to save himself and his own future. Inversely, the Bent-Neck Lady begins appearing to Nell when she is just an innocent child at Hill House.

Worse yet, Nell is not offered any alternative to the fate with which she has unknowingly been presented. Not only is it entirely unjust and unwarranted that this fate befalls Nell, but it is rather a grim reflection of who and where we are in present-day society on a variety of fronts. These things have begun to happen to Nell not because they are deserved, but because Nell just happened to be where she was. Had she not been "there" at Hill House, someone else may very well have become the Bent-Neck Lady. Instead, Nell is simply a random casualty of Hill House. This furthers not only the idea that time is fluid and out of joint, but that the future no longer discriminates against those who are deserving and undeserving of being proverbially haunted. This idea of victim randomness, unfortunately, has been popularized in the horror genre since the 9/11 Terrorist Attacks, and Flanagan's *Haunting* is no exception.[15] As we move through late-stage capitalism, the Bent-Neck Lady serves as evidence that ghosts aren't just ghouls or plot devices meant to incite fear in the living or an attempt to influence a certain moral shift within a character before it is too late—ghosts *are* the future.

During Nell's funeral service in "Two Storms," the Bent-Neck Lady can be seen literally as a looming presence throughout Nell's funeral service. Nell as the Bent-Neck Lady causes the power to go out, leaving the family in the dark. As Hugh and his children fight over what occurred at Hill House "then," Shirley approaches Nell's casket and discovers that someone has placed buttons over each of Nell's eyes. While Shirley is horribly offended by what she believes to be a cruel joke, the buttons over Nell's eyes have been placed there symbolically by her ghost as an omen to her siblings that they must not be blinded and fractured by their grief. After Hugh and Steven continue to argue—their words and anger reaching a fever pitch—Nell's casket mysteriously falls on its own. Silence befalls the family, the power returns, and the lights flicker on again. At a loss for words, they work together to return Nell's casket to its original position. The scene cuts back to the storm at Hill House "then," and young Nell is distraught after her family couldn't see or hear her during the storm. Young Nell cries, "I was right here and I was screaming and shouting and none of you could see me. Why couldn't you see me? I waved and jumped and screamed, and you didn't even look. None of you looked" ("Two Storms"). As she says, "none of you looked," young Nell's voice fades into an echo and Flanagan cuts back to Nell's present-day funeral. Her siblings disperse and adult Luke looks over his shoulder. As he begins to leave, the audience hears the dialogue between young Luke and young Nell during the storm at Hill House "then" when Nell had disappeared. Young Luke tells Nell, "I thought that the house things had got you. I thought they took you. I'm so glad you're okay. I'll never let you go again. Never again. I promise." As adult Luke exits the funeral home, the camera pans away to reveal Nell as the Bent-Neck Lady, crying quietly on her own. Young Nell's voice continues, "I was right here. I didn't go anywhere. I was right here. I was right here ... the whole time. None of you could see me. Nobody could see me" ("Two Storms").

This is not the only time that Nell's ghost attempts to reach her divided family members. Nell appears as a different ghost—in her own form, not the Bent-Neck Lady, at the climax of the first episode. She is indeed the eponymous spirit in "Steven Sees a Ghost." At the moment of her death she is herself, her ghostly self, and the Bent-Neck Lady. Steven "sees" her but does not know what she is or what it means. (Initially he thinks it is actually her in his apartment, so real is the spirit.) Again and again, Nell is present after death in the series, observed only by the viewing audience and not her family. By failing to "see" Nell and what has happened to her, the remaining Crains risk fulfilling the predetermined futures that Hill House has laid out for each of them. She attempts to unite her grieving, quarrelsome siblings multiple times from beyond the grave before they are all drawn to the Red Room in the final episode. While this aspect of Nell, her ghost, and the Bent-Neck Lady is more traditional, Flanagan takes the audience further than the common use of ghosts as a warning.

Even after Nell has fully "become" the Bent-Neck Lady, her ghost doesn't simply disappear. Rather, the temporal fluidity of the Bent-Neck Lady and her unprecedented role as a ghost is highlighted in a rather heartbreaking manner. As Nell steps off and away from the spiral staircase, plummets down, and her neck snaps against the rope, we see that she is still conscious, her eyes are still open, and she is still sentient. Yet, we know that there is no way she survived this fall with a rope around her neck. Rather quickly, it becomes apparent that Nell herself is the Bent-Neck Lady and always has been. As she embarks on a journey that one might refer to as "timeless," the audience is then exposed—all at once—to flashbacks of every previous encounter that Nell had with the Bent-Neck Lady throughout her life before she truly became her. The only difference is that when Flanagan again shows us these appearances of the Bent-Neck Lady, they are now through the eyes of Nell who has just hung herself and fulfilled her inevitable suicide. Before this moment, the manner in which the Bent-Neck Lady had appeared to her family members at various moments in the present day was rightly in line with how ghosts have traditionally functioned. Flanagan's departure from this classic use of ghosts is worth noting—he uses Nell's perspective as the Bent-Neck Lady to further manipulate our understanding of ghosts as well as our notion of linear time as we watch the Bent-Neck Lady being dragged by a rope through the past. As we watch the Bent-Neck Lady fly across the screen with no adherence to rules of temporality, we learn along with Nell that time is not what it used to be either. Time is out of joint, and now ghosts are, too.

To further add to the "time out of joint" aspect, the transitions between scenes taking place in the present and the past are not always immediately distinguishable to the senses. In the episode "Eulogy," for example, when Hugh is discovering the extent of the mold and its damage at Hill House "then," in frustration, he pounds his fist on the wall repeatedly. The scene cuts abruptly from Hill House's basement to a shot of a white door, but the sound of Hugh's pounding fist does not end with the scene. Instead, the loud banging continues without interruption as the white door is opened from the inside by Theo, revealing Hugh in present day as he knocks on the door to Theo's backhouse. Auditory clues such as this are something repeatedly used by Flanagan in the series, but the absence or skewing of time is demarcated in other ways as well. For example, sometimes when Flanagan takes us "back" to Hill House, it will often be labeled as "then" in the lower, left hand corner of the screen. For any other flashbacks involving the Crain family that do not take place at Hill House, there is always an indication of how many years ago the flashback is taking place. In "The Twin Thing," Luke goes to visit Steven and his wife at their home. When he arrives and is informed that Steven no longer lives there, Luke stares past his sister-in-law and into the dining room where we enter a flashback of Luke and his girlfriend having dinner with Steven and his wife. In the left-hand corner of the screen, we are told this was "two months" ago. Another example similar to this can be seen in "Open Casket" when Shirley helps get Luke into a rehab facility for the first time. We flashback to Shirley and Steven sitting in the billing office at the rehab facility and the words "six years ago" fade into that bottom left corner of the screen.

In some cases, Flanagan doesn't even call upon the "then" and "now" distinction when entering a flashback. Sometimes, he simply immerses the audience without warning. This fluidity of time is demonstrated remarkably well in "Two Storms." Hugh walks away from his children gathered in the main room of Shirley's funeral home and quietly walks right back in time to Hill House. Hugh literally walks into the past and witnesses the last time the family experienced a huge storm together. The incertitude of Hill House as a "then" and "now" dynamic when shown in flashbacks wouldn't be as noteworthy had Flanagan not made this small but significant distinction that further supports the idea of time being nonexistent and relative to all events at Hill House. The concept of time is further complicated by an infinite amount of temporally ambiguous aesthetics.

Most obviously, the exterior of Hill House itself is in the style of early twentieth century English Tudor Revival; a type of architecture inspired by earlier Gothic Revival structures in the nineteenth century. Gothic lancet arches and stained-glass windows can be seen near grand, cascading staircases in many of the interior shots of the House, and the door to the infamous Red Room itself is in the shape of a Gothic lancet arch. The walls of the House are splayed in the vintage classic that is Damask floral wallpaper and the hallways themselves are lined with wainscot oak paneling, interrupted every so often by the artful placement of a half-nude Greco-Roman sculpture. Many of the bedrooms feature ornate wooden bed frames as well as Victorian fringe-lined lamps and the nineteenth century claw foot tables upon which they rest. The various sittings rooms of the House are covered in opulent rugs and furnished with velvet button-tufted Chesterfield couches which are facing a plethora of darkly colored nineteenth century oil paintings of vast landscapes in faraway places. The study—reminiscent of a scene in an old murder mystery story that offers us a spiral staircase leading to the Red Room—is bordered by walls of bookshelves that rise up and tower over all those who stand before it. The kitchen's dumbwaiter—an invention popularized in the late nineteenth century—stands just next to the 1940s stove and opposite of the sleek, black 1950s rotary phone. The anachronisms of decor in Hill House are subtle and endless as their eclectic styles help to obscure any definitive sense of time and place. In their own way, the decor and design are a haunted blending of past styles from a host of different eras. Because these objects visually and materially exist side-by-side in the House, one might observe that even Hill House itself is haunted by its anachronistic contents. Furthermore, these anachronistic objects are not simply just for show, but rather, serve a purpose.

In Episode 8, carefully named "Witness Marks," adult Steven finally begins to learn through Hugh the truth about Hill House he had always known yet never realized. According to Hugh, he never hired the specialized clocksmith needed to accurately care for the antique grandfather clock nestled into one of the House's many grand staircases. Clad in a classic flat cap, workman's overalls, and a perfectly sculpted handlebar mustache, the clock's ghostly servant is an unknowingly anachronistic specter that appeared only to Steven. Hugh confirms, "No one ever touched that clock, and certainly no one in old overalls with a handlebar mustache," ("Witness Marks"). It is no accident that Flanagan selects the temporally ambiguous clock and "out of joint" clocksmith to serve as a catalyst in the character evolution of Steven. The clock—an object that has a sole purpose of keeping time—and its clocksmith—a person whose very job it is to ensure that the clock remains keeping the time in joint—are artfully utilized by Flanagan as symbols of pure irony.

This temporal ambiguity isn't just limited to Hill House itself either. Flanagan's characters who are closely connected to Hill House are dressed in curious ways that enhance the anachronisms of the series. Mrs. Dudley, for example, is always seen in longer, more conservative dresses that cover her limbs modestly (or completely, in some cases). These dresses feature a high neckline, or a lace collar of sorts and her look is completed with a swirled, high-piled Edwardian pompadour. Even her stereotypical embodiment of the domesticated housekeeper of an old mansion is a profession of the past. Her stern demeanor and acute god-fearing tendencies make us question whether or not Mrs. Dudley herself is real or a specter. Abigail, her daughter, is similarly indistinguishable as a ghost or a real person that only Luke can see until the final night when Olivia poisons her. She's a plain, pale little girl in a blue and outdated frock. Young Luke even says to Shirley when asking to borrow her clothes for Abigail: "She's not imaginary! Abigail is real, but her clothes aren't as cool as yours! They look old," ("Screaming Meemies").

Similarly, one would be remiss to overlook Olivia's attire: a series of flowing, floor-length robes of elegant velvet paired with heeled slippers and beautiful, falling locks of hair. This regal look works in tandem with Olivia's decline in a way that evokes the image of a troubled Hollywood starlet in despair as she's seen aimlessly wandering the halls of Hill House. In a way, it's as if Olivia were assimilating to and becoming an anachronism within Hill House. It has, after all, claimed itself as her *true* "forever home."

The Crains' arrival at Hill House—a dwelling full of anachronisms, temporal ambiguity, and breakdown of time—signifies the beginning of the end for the happy family. The "cancellation of the future," as Franco Berardi describes, has begun for the Crains. With this, comes their grief.

Grief and Lost Futures

> Olivia: "You guys go on without me."
> Hugh: "How could we?"
> —"Screaming Meemies"

The other major component of hauntology that Flanagan explores extensively in *Haunting* is the grief of lost futures. By having different stages of grief acted out by the members of the Crain family who survived Hill House "then," Flanagan demonstrates to us the various stages of our collective grief—some more significant than others. By doing this, he holds up the proverbial mirror to us all, perhaps even offering us a tentative path forward.

Nell, the youngest of the Crains, embodies the depression stage of grief. As Nell attempts to live a normal life, the Bent-Neck Lady returns in full force, killing her beloved husband Arthur. But before his death, Arthur served as a guiding light for Nell: giving her hope that the Bent-Neck Lady might become something of the past. In reality, the opposite occurs.

When the Bent-Neck Lady's visits to Nell become less frequent, it becomes clear that Arthur's presence represented some semblance of salvaged future for Nell. But after the Bent-Neck Lady causes Arthur to have an aneurism that kills him, Nell's wellbeing begins to decline to a point where even her therapist cannot get through to her and the Bent-Neck Lady returns with a vengeance. After seeing the Bent-Neck Lady while buying a guilt-ridden Luke drugs before dropping him at rehab, she runs home to flush what look like prescription anti-depressants. The future is looming and it's scary—even the anti-depressants can no longer ameliorate the dread.

At the well-meaning advice of her therapist, Dr. Montague (named for the character in Jackson's original novel), Nell decides to confront her past at Hill House. On the journey back to Hill House, Nell stops in for a stay at the motel her dad drove her and her siblings to on the night Olivia died. At this point, we are unsure if we are watching what will become of Nell or what has already happened to Nell, highlighting the completely jumbled nature of time or sheer lack of it. While she's sitting in the hotel room all alone, she drifts in and out of sleep—sometimes zoning out for hours on end and completely losing track of time. But when she finally arrives to confront the House, the hauntological nature of the House exploits her and her desires. In a twisted way, Hill House presents Nell with an overly idyllic future like the one for which she had hoped where everyone she loved would be alive and happy. And in the same cruel fashion, the House strips it all away from her and convinces her that dying so she can forever remain at Hill House—a place lacking in time, space, and in future—is her only option.

Hugh represents shock and disbelief in the context of grief. As the fixer of the family, he is shocked he could not fix Olivia and how the subsequent loss of her ruined their family. Throughout the series, he remains very aloof, not discussing the loss that occurred even though he played a role and understood what happened. He's constantly stumbling over his words, unable to properly articulate himself in his grief. He also is seen regularly speaking with "Olivia" and consulting her about everything from their children to his choice of tie. Hugh's disbelief is palpable—it's as if he cannot bear the thought of having lost the mother of his children to what was supposed to be a simple house flipping project to provide for his family.

While all stages of grief are important to acknowledge, Steven's denial, its roots in capitalism, and of what it symbolizes are especially meaningful in the context of hauntology. Steven, the eldest Crain child, is a strong example of denial. Not only does he not believe his family's experience was a result of Hill House and what it represents, he actively plays into late capitalism to the very detriment of his family. Steven first decides to take the very real stories of his siblings' experiences at the House and make them his own after spending years making light of the same stories. When Nell publicly confronts Steven, she says, "Now you stand there and you talk about ghosts and spirits. And you sell tickets for the privilege. And yet you don't believe in any of it" ("The Bent-Neck Lady"). Similarly, Steven's wife, Leigh, is prominently featured in the nightmare hallucination he experiences in the Red Room that highlights some of his darkest truths and deepest insecurities. Leigh says to him:

> I mean, is anything real before you write it, Steve? The things you write about are real, those people are real, their feelings are real, their pain is real, but not to you, is it? Not until you chew it up and you digest it and you shit it out on a piece of paper. And even then, it's a pale imitation at best. You take other people's lives and love and loss and pain, and you eat it, Steve. You are an eater. You eat it and you shit it out, and then, and only then, is it real for you. Normal people's lives are flesh and blood and muscle and bone, but not yours, darling. Oh, no. Your life is plastic. You are a plastic parasite. A plastic hack, aren't you, honey? ["Silence Lay Steadily"].

By exploiting his family's tragedy for monetary gain, Steven reveals himself as an accomplice to the "cultural impasse" caused by late capitalism. Still, Steven cannot entirely be blamed for this questionable, insensitive attitude towards his family's tragedy. Steven, making money at the expense of others no matter the cost, is simply a product of late capitalism. Perhaps even he is a victim himself: the lack of new, creative production of culture can be attributed to the unrelenting demands of a capitalistic society that revolves so heavily around money—the cycle of making it and spending it—that he felt he had no choice but to use his own family to gain a profit.

Shirley Crain serves as an example of bargaining out of grief. By pursuing a career that is defined by preparing the dead to look as they did when they were alive, it is clear that Shirley is trying to hold on to what has already gone and maintain a sense of normalcy. The mysterious man at the bar with whom Shirley cheated on her husband with says: "Shirley never wants to look. But Shirley has to look" ("Silence Lay Steadily"). Similarly, we also have to look at and acknowledge the future we have lost.

According to Steven, in a line taken from the novel, "Theo's basically a clenched fist with hair" ("Screaming Meemies"). Theo Crain, the family's empath who literally can feel others' traumas by touching them, exemplifies the anger component of grief. Aside from Theo's general demeanor—constantly angry and closed off to any deep emotional connections—she bars herself from really feeling anything other than anger by wearing gloves and drinking. When Shirley asks Theo how to talk about Nell's death with her kids, Theo says she hopes the kids ask Shirley instead of her because she's "fucking angry." She continues: "Because I don't wanna have to tell them I'm fucking pissed at Auntie Nell who should have known better—better than most—what this does to a family. She fucking knew better. And she did it anyway" ("Touch"). As Theo ultimately does, we have to rise above the anger of our loss.

Grief's feelings of guilt are personified in Luke, an addict who uses drugs to escape the pain of his loss. Because of his addiction, Luke takes advantage of his family's financial and emotional resources to fuel his drug addiction, even missing Nell's wedding because of it. In "Eulogy," Luke kneels at Nell's grave during the burial and whispers to Nell how sorry he is—a reference to his addiction and behavior that he feels prevented him from being present for and potentially helping her. Nell's ghost appears to him saying "don't," almost as if to encourage him to forgive himself ("Eulogy"). In a similar way, we also must acknowledge the guilt that can come with loss and not numb ourselves as an escape.

Olivia, though she was never symbolic of grief or any of its forms, was the literal architect of the Crain family's "forever home." She is herself the lost future. Because Olivia is symbolic of the Crain's bright future and its subsequent cancellation, her character's journey is of great importance to the entire family's narrative. For the Crain family, Hill House was supposed to be the ultimate house-flipping project that would make them financially viable within society by traditional standards of capitalism. But as the Crains' housework progresses, the House begins to swallow Olivia whole and with it, the future for which the Crains had hoped. Flanagan has carefully crafted a story in which the characters must painfully confront their own series of grief and truths over the course of the show, leading them all to the same final outcome: accepting that their collective future is just not what it used to be. And although their future is not what it used to be, perhaps it does not need to be discarded entirely in the way in which Hill House attempts to convince them.

Until the end of the final episode, the Crain family was so haunted by their own individualized shortcomings as well as their collective loss of Olivia and forever home that much like the precariat—picked apart and disassembled for efficiency—the Crain family found it easier to retreat into their own forms of grief than reach out to one another. Ultimately, they did come together with Nell's help to reach the final stage of grief—acceptance—before their fractured selves destroyed what remained of their family and future.

Mark Fisher wrote extensively on hauntology in his life, and he wasn't particularly optimistic about our future either—in fact, he killed himself. I don't pretend to know if his suicide had anything to do with our lost future, but his writings on hauntology and depression are difficult to ignore in this context. Fisher didn't offer us a clear path forward to reclaim our future before he left us, and nor did he claim to have all the answers. However, he did offer us something. In his appropriately named article "How to Kill a Zombie: Strategizing the End of Neoliberalism," Fisher warns that the complete overthrow of our current system is just as dangerous as the extremes of neoliberalist attitudes that cancelled our future in the first place. On that same note, he urges that we must remain unified, organized, and ready to introduce alternatives to neoliberalist policies when the time to implement them arises:

> What's certain is that we are now in an ideological wasteland in which neoliberalism is dominant only by default. The terrain is up for grabs, and [Milton] Friedman's remark should be our inspiration: it is now our task to develop alternatives to existing policies, to keep them alive and available until the politically impossible becomes the politically inevitable.[16]

Similarly, Flanagan's *Haunting* does not provide us with an inherently happy ending or an answer to navigate the loss of our collective future, but he does give us something—a story that inspires hope. The Crain family was relentlessly haunted by the ghosts of Hill House that threatened and ultimately destroyed their future. This future was seemingly inescapable and unavoidable, especially for Nell who was haunted by her own specter from the outset of the series. As Steven, Shirley, Theo, and Luke arrived at Hill House in "Silence Lay Steadily," they each entered into their own personalized nightmare sequences that forecasted each of their respective futures: Steven as a capitalist-driven user, Shirley as an imperfect and judgmental spouse, Theo as an angry and closed-off individual, and Luke as a drug addict who dies by overdose. Nell, whose predetermined future was sadly fulfilled, was able to "wake up" her siblings so that they themselves would not fulfill the futures that Hill House had laid out for them. The fractured Crain family, like the precariat, was pulled together by a ghostly Nell in the Red Room just in time.

Perhaps our collective goal as a society can be to rally around the preservation of choice—a choice to determine our own future and not resign ourselves to the future neoliberalism has already laid out for us. While Nell Crain fought against her predetermined future and she lost, she helped her siblings reclaim a semblance of theirs, even though it didn't include Olivia and their "forever home." In that same spirit, maybe—just maybe—we can also reclaim some semblance of our own forever home.

Notes

1. Quoted in Richard Matheson, *Somewhere in Time* (New York: St. Martin's Press, 2008).
2. Mark Fisher, *Ghosts of My Life: Writings on Depression, Hauntology and Lost Futures* (Winchester, UK: Zero Books, 2014), 14–15.
3. Guy Standing, *The Precariat: The New Dangerous Class* (London: Bloomsbury, 2011), 11–12.
4. Fisher, *Ghosts of My Life*: 14–15.
5. Fisher, *Ghosts of My Life*. 8–9.
6. Jacques Derrida, *Specters of Marx: The State of the Debt, the Work of Mourning and the New International* (New York: Routledge, 1994), 10.
7. William Shakespeare, *Hamlet*, ed. Barbara Mowatt (New York: Simon & Schuster: 1992): (I, v, 188).
8. Richter, Felix. "Infographic: The Surprising Comeback of Vinyl Records." Statista: The Statistics Portal. January 15, 2019. Accessed March 08, 2019. https://www.statista.com/chart/7699/lp-sales-in-the-united-states/.
9. Fisher, *Ghosts of My Life*. 4.
10. Fisher, *Ghosts of My Life*. 5.
11. Avery F. Gordon, *Ghostly Matters: Haunting and the Sociological Imagination* (Minneapolis: University of Minnesota Press, 2011), 63–64.
12. Robin Wood, "The American Nightmare: Horror in the 70s." In *Horror: The Film Reader*. Ed. Mark Jancovich (London: Routledge, 2009). 25–32.
13. Charles Dickens, *A Christmas Carol*. The Project Gutenberg E-Book of A Christmas Carol. September 20, 2006. Accessed March 13, 2019. http://www.gutenberg.org/files/19337/19337-h/19337-h.htm. 77–93.
14. Franco Berardi, *After the Future*. Eds. Gary Genosko and Nicholas Thoburn (Oakland, CA: AK Press, 2011), 125–126.
15. Kevin J. Wetmore, *Post 9/11 Horror in America Cinema* (New York: Continuum, 2012), 82–83.
16. Fisher, Mark. *K-Punk: The Collected and Unpublished Writings of Mark Fisher (2004–2016)*. Edited by Darren Ambrose and Simon Reynolds (London: Repeater, 2018).

Ghosts of Future Past
Spatial and Temporal Intersections
Adam Daniel

A central question that emerges after the manifestation of a haunting is "what exactly is being haunted"? Is it a person? A place? Or a time? Netflix's 2018 TV series *The Haunting of Hill House* disrupts conventional approaches to cinematic and televisual ghost stories by answering this question with "all of the above." In this essay I will explore how the series dissolves some conventional boundaries in televisual representations of time and space to present this answer and I will analyze how the series' marked approach to spatiality and temporality thematizes haunting as something more than the presence of representational ghosts.

An exploration of temporality and its relation to haunting appears central to show creator Mike Flanagan's impulse to adapt the classic Shirley Jackson story into a television series. In interviews he has referred to how "playing with time was […] a major theme of the story" and that having previously worked solely in feature films, there was a definite appeal in the kind of "complex structure" allowed for in television as opposed to features.[1] The structures he and his fellow writers employ, however, are not simply the traditional "subjective narration or jumbled chronology" that Jason Mittell argues is "now almost a cliché" of complex television.[2] Instead, the show transcends this through its employment of an innovative approach which interweaves geographically distinct spatial planes and chronologically distinct moments of time to thematically represent a different kind of haunting.

The event of a haunting is commonly understood to be a form of temporal dislocation: the emergence of something from the past manifesting in the present. However, contemporary scholarship of hauntology complicates that notion by arguing that haunting also reveals the contingency of experience, in that the ghost may be that which disrupts the stability of the present by indicating that there is another narrative underneath the surface of accepted events. In his analysis of the "spectral turn" of contemporary literary theory, Jeffrey Andrew Weinstock notes that ghosts have become "a privileged poststructuralist academic trope" due to their existence as "unstable interstitial figures that problematize dichotomous thinking."[3] He notes how the phantom may operate to destabilize a linear view of history through its presence as an "entity out of place in time"—the past literally bleeding into the present—and, in doing so, draw attention to the untold narrative that its presence signifies.[4]

This understanding can be expanded to include a Derridean reading of the "specter" as paradigmatic of a deconstructive logic. In *Spectographies*, a conversation between Jacques Derrida and Bernard Stiegler, Derrida contends that the specter unveils the paradox of the invisible visible. He says of the specter, "it is the visibility of a body which is not present in flesh and blood."[5] Weinstock, in his analysis of the conversation, argues that Derrida uses this self-described "deconstructive logic" to insist on a "heteronomy"—the concept that we are influenced by an external force that rules and governs us—and that this deconstructive logic "undoes established binaries and challenges foundational, presentist, and teleological modes of thinking."[6]

However, while the figure of the ghost may function as "the paradigmatic deconstructive gesture," the presence of ghosts in film, television and literature is far more commonly engaged as a potent and versatile metaphor. As Murray Leeder asserts, the ghost can "signify the ways in which memory and history, whether traumatic, nostalgic, or both, linger on within the 'living present.'"[7] It can also be a "potent representation of and figure of resistance for those who are unseen and unacknowledged."[8] Barry Curtis further extends this approach, contending that ghosts may operate as metaphors for "themes of loss, memory, retribution and confrontation with unacknowledged and unresolved histories."[9] Many of these readings can be applied to *The Haunting of Hill House*, where the appearance of ghosts in the present day, particularly that of the Crain family matriarch Olivia Crain (Carla Gugino), represents the irresolution of the events of the fateful night depicted in the series first episode, "Steven Sees a Ghost," when the Crain family flees Hill House in the middle of the night, leaving Olivia behind. This is the ghost as a "symptom of repressed knowledge," critiquing our ability to live in a future wherein we repudiate our past.[10] Flanagan himself acknowledges that part of the show's raison d'être is an examination of how "every family is a haunted house" and "everyone is wrestling with their ghosts from their own childhood and beyond."[11]

What really occurred on that night, and the fate of Olivia, is a central mystery for the show, one that is meted out by the crystalline narrative structure of the series, which operates in two distinct timelines ("Hill House, then," and the present day, approximately twenty-five years apart) and dedicates entire episodes to understanding the world of the story primarily through an individual character's point of view on both present and past.[12] While this fractured chronology has been a focus of much of the critical attention to this show, there is value in interrogating the complex time structure beyond its narrative role in the staging and unveiling of the mystery of Olivia's fate.

Time Is Out of Joint

Time, and its operation in memory, grief, and trauma, is central to *The Haunting of Hill House*. In the show's finale, while trapped inside the Red Room, the ghost of Nell (Victoria Pedretti) makes this explicit when she tells her siblings:

> Everything's been out of order. Time, I mean. I thought for so long that time was like a line, that … that our moments were laid out like dominoes, and that they … fell, one into another and on it went, just days tipping, one into the next, into the next, in a long line between the beginning … and the end. But I was wrong. It's not like that at all. Our moments fall around us like rain. Or … snow. Or confetti.[13]

We have seen this philosophy in operation in the show long before Nell's confession. Linear narrative time, with clear distinctions between past, present and future, is constantly ruptured throughout *The Haunting of Hill House*, as moments from the past seem to transgress into the present, and vice versa. What makes the show's handling of this distinctive is that, in television, this is typically done through the operation of analepsis or prolepsis, commonly known as flashbacks and flash-forwards. Consider, for example, how the television series *Lost* interspersed the narration of the characters' lives before the crash of Oceanic Airlines Flight 815 and later, surreptitiously, their lives post-rescue, within the chronological events on the island. Mittell labels this "discourse time" and describes it as "the temporal structure and duration of the story as told within a given narrative."[14] This reorganization of story time ("the time frame of the diegesis") is often achieved in complex narratives through "flashbacks, retelling past events, repeating story events from multiple perspectives, and jumbling chronologies."[15] He notes how mystery narratives "often play with discourse time to create suspense concerning past events."[16]

The Haunting of Hill House, by contrast, presents these fractures not only through conventional analepsis, but also within the mise-en-scène, wherein characters and settings from the two distinct time periods sometimes overlap, rendering the distinctions between the two periods ambiguous. For example, in the episode "Two Storms," on elder Hugh Crain's (Timothy Hutton) arrival at the funeral home, he initially sees his children in their younger states, yet as the shot continues in a masterful single take, circling around him, the Crain siblings suddenly appear as adults. This temporal disjunction also manifests as a spatial disjunction in the same episode, as Hugh's passage through the funeral home hallway transforms during the shot into a journey through Hill House at the time of their inhabitation. Hugh literally enters into a space with his younger self, as younger Hugh (Henry Thomas) wakes after the fall of the chandelier in the foyer of the house, after which the older Hugh seems to simply dematerialize from the room and the scene.

A form of temporal liminality is also demonstrated in moments where actions seem to occur simultaneously in the two time periods: an apposite example occurs in "The Bent Neck Lady," when Nell's fearful trepidation of someone attempting to enter her motel room becomes, without a cut, the return to the motel of younger Hugh. This intermingling of the two timelines is never addressed explicitly within the narrative, and in this way, it functions as a haunting of sorts, the past always threatening to rise unbidden into the present.

An understanding of haunting as intimately connected to contraventions of linear temporality emerges in the work of scholar Bliss Cua Lim. Lim examines narratives of haunting from the perspective of nonsynchronism and noncontemporaneity, terms she draws from the work of Ernst Bloch that refer to, in the case of the former, "the differences of pace and rhythms between different social systems and institutional domains," and in the case of the latter, "the local and temporal coexistence of phenomena that are related to different historical periods or different stages of social evolution."[17] For Lim, ghost narratives have specific relevance to an exploration of these concepts because of the way the genre:

> [D]ramatizes the encounter between occluded modes of consciousness and the dominant experiential paradigms of the rational, postmodern world we know. Haunting or ghostly return insists that "prior" modes of consciousness are never completely surmounted or occluded, and that social reality depends on a fractious consensus. The spectral estranges our predisposed ways of experiencing space, time, and history and hauntingly insinuates that more worlds than one exist in the world we think we know; times other than the present contend with each other in the disputed Now.[18]

Importantly, Lim makes the observation that the ghost narrative has "a tendency to transgress the principles of narrative linearity without becoming antinarrative (as in avantgarde and experimental films)."[19] While it disrupts the linear time of conventional narrative, it does so in a manner that never completely fragments the diegesis. What it achieves in doing so is a destabilization of the presupposed boundaries of past, present and future; Lim contends that haunting "precisely refuses the idea that things are just 'left behind,' that the past is inert and the present uniform."[20]

In her analysis of "fantastic cinema," which includes films about ghosts and the supernatural, Lim argues that works such as these can "[incite] us to think in disaccustomed terms about time."[21] The ethical project of Lim's work is to suggest the fantastic as a "mode of resistance to the ascendancy of homogenous time and a starting-point for more ethical temporal imaginings." While perhaps not motivated by the same ethical imperatives, *The Haunting of Hill House* explores similar notions of the temporal phenomena of haunting for aesthetic reasons. It too wants the viewer to think in "disaccustomed terms" about the nature of time, not only to heighten suspense but also to transcend the traditional limitations of ghost stories. To paraphrase Flanagan, ghosts can become boring if they are not intimately tied to "character," "emotion" and "experience": it is this last term which is so vitally explored by the way the series approaches haunting.

The series encourages an imbrication of both the viewer and the character's experience of time, which perhaps explains the affective charge of the revelation at the conclusion of episode five, "The Bent Neck Lady." The episode focuses on Nell, both as an adult and a child, and the specter of the "Bent Neck Lady" which has haunted her since she moved to Hill House with her family as a child. The audience is first introduced to the Bent Neck Lady in episode one, when young Nell (Violet McGraw) awakens to the figure of a dark-haired woman floating over her, her face unseen. Nell appears paralyzed, unable to scream or close her eyes. As an adult, Nell visits a medical technician, Arthur (Jordan Christie), who posits a scientific explanation for what we learn is a recurring vision that has haunted Nell throughout her life: sleep paralysis, where a person passing between sleep and wakefulness is unable to move or speak.

Nell and Arthur fall in love and marry, and her knowledge of a prosaic cause for her visions appears to provide some respite from them—until one evening when, during a sleep paralysis event, Arthur suffers an aneurysm and dies, and Nell is confronted by the return of the Bent Neck Lady. Arthur's death begins a spiral for Nell that leads to her refusing to take her antidepressant medication and journeying back to Hill House.

When Nell enters the house, she remains in her adult form while her family initially appear to her in their younger forms of her childhood. She reunites with her mother Olivia, who welcomes her back and tells her she "can't be late for the reception." Returning to the foyer of the house, Nell is then greeted by her siblings as idealized versions of their adult selves, her father, and her husband Arthur, alive and just as she remembered him. These fantasies are soon revealed to be delusions provided by the house, which has lured her back to complete the act it has promised since her very first night in Hill House, when she first witnessed the disturbing visage of the dark female shape with the unnaturally crooked neck: Nell's death by hanging.

Lured to the top of the spiral staircase by the spirit of her mother, Nell finds herself with a rope around her neck and a tenuous grip on the railing. Her mother kisses her on the forehead, the slight contact sending her falling. However, while she appears to die from the first neck-breaking recoil of the rope going taut, a slow reveal of her face as she twists on the rope shows that she is still conscious of the events that follow. A second drop ensues, and the cognizant bent-necked Nell is suddenly confronted with herself from an earlier moment in the episode, recoiling near a motel vending machine. It is at this point that both Nell and the viewer simultaneously understand that *she* is the Bent Neck Lady—she has literally been haunting herself—and that now she is falling not through space but through *time*.[22] With each subsequent fall the viewer sees each of Nell's previous confrontations, only now they see them from the perspective of the dead Nell, who is tormented by her failure to acknowledge them as premonitions. It is in this scene specifically that the series stakes out a territory of liminal space that it will more fully explore in the remaining five episodes.

A "Carcass" in the Woods

In "The Bent Neck Lady," Nell's therapist Dr. Montague (Russ Tamblyn) urges her to question the rationality of her fear of the house. "How can a house, just a collection of bricks, wood and glass, have that much power over people?" he asks. Later, he describes the house as a "carcass," that is "probably littered with graffiti, dirt." In the second half of the series, the audience comes to understand just how wrong this statement is; while the house is a relic of its previous self, it is very much alive.

While the previous section has discussed how some of the temporal overlaps necessarily involve spatial intersections, such as Hugh's journey from the funeral home to the foyer of Hill House, in this section I will focus on how the series dislocates the apparent stability of space and utilizes the spatial characteristics of the house to thematize haunting as a spatial simultaneity.

In *Dark Places*, Curtis cites Shirley Jackson's description of the titular house of her novel as "chillingly wrong in all dimensions" and, in his words, a "spatial anomaly waiting to be activated by a particular encounter with a troubled subject."[23] The television series echoes this appraisal of the house, and importantly, acknowledges that it is not simply a backdrop or tableau upon which its characters wrestle with internal ghosts. The house is very much "alive" and actively transmogrifying the world around the Crain family.

The haunted house as a trope of literature, film and television is not always given this sort of agency. As Leeder notes, in both scholarly interpretations and the cinematic texts themselves, there is often a "stubborn desire to divert attention away from the capacity of houses to haunt, and toward the actions and mental states of the human beings who occupy these spectral spaces."[24] He does note, however, that a substantial proportion of American gothic fiction and film allows for the notion that "a house harbors thoughts and wishes of its own" rather than simply being "mere projections of and haunted by our darker memories and desires."[25]

Curtis contends that it is "the viewer's complex realization of the disturbing vitality of spaces and boundaries" that is the end goal of a diverse range of films that deal with "dark places." *The Haunting of Hill House* utilizes the generic components of the haunted house narrative that Curtis identifies to prompt a similar reckoning; the "apprehensive approach to the 'house' and the dawning realization that it is already occupied in a variety of disturbing ways," "the painful acquisition of necessary historical knowledge," and of course "the final confrontation with the force troubling the place."[26]

One of Curtis' central arguments is that the relationship between narrative and mise-en-scène in haunted house films (and by extension, television) is intensified. These intensifications often merge through the "unregulated and irrational spatial supplements" that haunting introduces (the example Curtis offers is the "lingering sign of a disruptive event that has left a dimensional trace").[27] In the series we see one example of this in the sudden and unexplainable mold infestation after the storm of "Two Storms," which leads to the discovery of William Hill's body and the revelation that he appeared to have bricked himself inside of the basement wall. This episode also reveals to the viewer that the existing blueprints and actual floor plans of the house are incongruous. Upon discovering this, Olivia labels the house "schizophrenic" and makes an attempt to correct the blueprint. Her new version, however, is also corrupted, this time by her repeated drawing of the footprint of the family's "forever house" over its surface—another sign of the house's sinister grip on her sanity.

This inability to chart the spatial characteristics of the house, and thus understand it, is echoed in the mystery of the Red Room, which becomes central to the narrative as the series continues. The first time the viewer sees the room's distinctive red door is in "Steven Sees a Ghost," when young Shirley (Lulu Wilson) and Nell attempt and fail to unlock it. "Something is moving," says Nell. "I saw the shadow under the door." The impenetrable room is a familiar trope in haunted house narratives, but the revelation of the Red Room's contents and purpose in the series is a master stroke. This revelation concurs with Curtis' contention that "[a]ll explorations of the haunted house involve a kind of archaeology, the uncovering of an occluded narrative that constitutes the exorcism in much the way that Freud or Marx understood the substructure as providing the key to understanding and remediation."[28]

In the series finale, the viewer learns that the occluded Red Room has been previously seen on multiple occasions, as a different room of sanctuary for each of the main characters, except Hugh: for Steve, it is a games room; for Shirley, a family room; for Theo, a dance studio; for Luke, a treehouse; for Nell, a reading room; and for Olivia, a reading room. The house, it is claimed, has created these spaces of sanctuary to keep each of the Crain family contented while it feeds on them, or as Nell describes it, "It put on different faces so that we'd be still and quiet while it digested." The "carcass," as it were, is feeding.

The "shadow under the door" that Nell witnessed in the first episode is, in the final episode, revealed to be young Theo dancing in her studio, as also shown in episode three, "Touch." Seen only from Theo's perspective within that episode, the rattle of the door handle and the loud bang on the door is somewhat menacing and unsettling. Seen from both perspectives in the final episode, the failed intrusion, now revealed to be Shirley and Nell's attempt to open the door and Shirley's frustrated slamming of a fist against it, exposes the house's ambition: to keep the Crain family members isolated as it "digests" them.

As the only family member not to enter the Red Room, Hugh Crain is anomalous, however a closer consideration of Hugh's nature and the house's effects on him explains this. When confronted with the mold problem, Hugh ascertains that it originates from a leak on the third floor but can't find the source. He tells a visiting repairman "I've checked everywhere but one room"; this room is, of course, the Red Room. When the viewer later sees the true contents of the Red Room it is indeed infested with the black mold, confirming Hugh's suspicion. However, Hugh's personal "Red Room" is not a place, but a purpose. "I can fix this" is his mantra, and rather than providing him with a room to occupy, the house uses the presence of the mold to occupy *him*.

When Curtis writes that "[h]aunting implies a temporal disruption that has a de-structuring effect on perceptions and alters the significance and often the shape of familiar spaces. The haunted house must be explored in order to trace and locate the source of the disturbance—but the exploration is an entry into other than purely spatial dimensions," he could very well be describing the spatial and temporal incongruities that are illustrated by the Red Room in *The Haunting of Hill House*.[29] Nell's explanation of the room's purpose, and the montage of the various characters spending time in their sanctuaries, allows us to understand the space as a concertina of spatial layers that exist in simultaneity. Importantly, the Red Room also appears to operate through overlapping temporalities, as demonstrated by the interruption of Theo's dancing by Shirley and Nell's attempted intrusion, two moments that were not temporally contiguous.

Returning to the rhetorical question posed in my introduction of "what exactly is being haunted," the television series *The Haunting of Hill House* offers a profound and complex response that extends beyond conventional approaches to the ghost story. Each of the main characters is indeed haunted in some way by the presence of a ghost which appears to them as a representation of a revenant. Yet, as described in this essay, haunting can be more ineffable than this—it can manifest as the haunting of time, in terms of the past transgressing into the present, or the haunting of space, as in the spatial simultaneity of the Red Room. Or, as in the case of the tragic revelation of the identity of the Bent Neck Lady, it can manifest as the destabilization of both space and time. While the series skillfully portrays the torment of the Crain family by the representational ghosts of Hill House, it is the imbrication of these supernatural elements with the non-representational "ghosts" of haunted space and time that reveals to us these more expansive dimensions of haunting.

Notes

1. Matt Edwards, "The Haunting of Hill House: Mike Flanagan Interview." Den of Geek, 12 Oct. 2018. Accessed 15 April 2019. https://www.denofgeek.com/uk/tv/the-haunting-of-hill-house/61026/the-haunting-of-hill-house-mike-flanagan-interview-my-first-response-was-that-you-couldnt-do-it; Alex Helms, "An Interview with the Haunting of Hill House Creator Mike Flanagan." *The Towerlight*, 22 Oct. 2018. Accessed 15 April 2019. http://thetowerlight.com/an-interview-with-haunting-of-hill-house-creator-mike-flanagan/
2. Jason Mittell, *Complex TV: The Poetics of Contemporary Television Storytelling* (New York: New York University Press, 2015), 2.
3. Jeffrey Andrew Weinstock, "Introduction: The Spectral Turn." In *The Spectralities Reader: Ghost and Haunting in Contemporary Cultural Theory*, edited by Maria del Pilar Blanco and Esther Peeren, 61–68 (New York: Bloomsbury, 2013), 62.
4. Weinstock, "Introduction: The Spectral Turn," 62.
5. Jacques Derrida and Bernard Stiegler, "Spectrographies." In *The Spectralities Reader: Ghost and Haunting in Contemporary Cultural Theory*, edited by Maria del Pilar Blanco and Esther Peeren (New York: Bloomsbury, 2013), 38.
6. Weinstock, "Introduction: The Spectral Turn," 33.
7. Murray Leeder, *Cinematic Ghosts: Haunting and Spectrality from Silent Cinema to the Digital Era* (New York: Bloomsbury Publishing, 2015).
8. Leeder, *Cinematic Ghosts*, 1.
9. Barry Curtis, *Dark Places* (London: Reaktion Books, 2008), 10.
10. Weinstock, "Introduction: The Spectral Turn," 64.
11. Mike Bloom, "'The Haunting of Hill House' Creator Addresses the Show's Biggest Terrors and Twists." *The Hollywood Reporter*, 15 Oct. 2018. Accessed 15 April 2019. https://www.hollywoodreporter.com/live-feed/haunting-hill-house-finale-mike-flanagan-interview-1151590
12. Steven in "Steven Sees a Ghost," Shirley in "Open Casket," Theo in "Touch," Luke in "The Twin Thing," Nell in "The Bent Neck Lady," Hugh in "Eulogy" and Olivia in "Screaming Meemies."
13. This occurs in Episode Ten, "Silence Lay Steadily."
14. Mittell, *Complex TV*, 26.
15. *Ibid.*, 26.
16. *Ibid.*, 26.

17. Bernhard Giesen, "Noncontemporaneity, Asynchronicity and Divided Memories." *Time & Society* 13, no. 1 (2004), 27.
18. Bliss Cua Lim, "Spectral Times: The Ghost Film as Historical Allegory." *Positions: East Asia Cultures Critique* 9, no. 2 (2001), 294.
19. *Ibid.*, 300.
20. *Ibid.*, 288.
21. Bliss Cua Lim, *Translating Time: Cinema, the Fantastic, and Temporal Critique* (Durham: Duke University Press, 2009), 1.
22. Barry Curtis makes the point that ghosts are often "archetypal travellers in time, caught, as is the protagonist of Groundhog Day in involuntary repetitive loops"; Curtis, *Dark Places*, 175.
23. Curtis, *Dark Places*, 12.
24. Leeder, *Cinematic Ghosts*, 143.
25. Leeder, *Ibid.*, 151.
26. Curtis, *Dark Places*, 35.
27. Curtis, *Ibid.*, 12.
28. Curtis, *Ibid.*, 34.
29. Curtis, *Ibid.*, 35.

V

Gender and Queering

Red Room, Red Womb

Phantom Feminism

Elsa M. Carruthers

When I heard the news about Netflix's adaptation of Shirley Jackson's novel, I was filled with excitement and anticipation and the show certainly did not disappoint. The show is visually stunning with an engrossing storyline. The added features and hidden ghosts in each episode make re-watching the series very satisfying. And though I enjoyed it immensely, and knew it was not an exact retelling of the novel, I was very surprised at some of the differences. If the novel was a traditional gothic ghost story, this adaption was a family drama/saga; notably because though one of the many themes of the ghost story is family tension, and explorations of the fault lines that form in relationships are built into the haunted house story structure, the series goes from that to a full-blown tale of the aftermath of their brief time at Hill House. As Rachel Syme argues in her essay, "How Netflix Made *The Haunting of Hill House* Less Scary," *The Haunting of Hill House* is a show "about generational trauma, about the silent presence of ghosts in families."[1]

This series uses the conventions and tropes of a traditional haunted house story as a springboard for the family drama, and in the process, sublimates much of the feminist critique present in Jackson's source novel. Gone is the singular point of view, the psychic/social exploration of Eleanor Vance, and the close and often biting social criticism of the novel. Also absent is the open ending that allows for many interpretive readings in favor of a story about Steven Crain and how his family relates to him. Even while we are watching the rest of the Crain family, the story ultimately revolves back to Steven's storyline and his role in the events during and after the Crain family's stay at Hill House.

In his fantastic and illuminating book *American Nightmares: The Haunted House Formula in American Popular Fiction*, Dale Bailey writes:

For most Americans, houses are infinitely more than shelters to keep off the rain. As Quintus Teal points out, houses reflect their owners—and not merely in terms of mood. In the United States, perhaps more than in any previous culture, the house is a potent symbol. Its significance is everywhere expressed, from the verse of Edgar Guest ("It takes a heap o' livin' in a house t' make it home") to statistical descriptions of the American Dream (a house, a car, 2.5 kids). The house is our primary marker of class and our central symbol of domesticity, touching upon everything from women's rights (the angel in the house, not to mention the homemaker) to the deterioration of the nuclear family (the broken home).[2]

Tension in the horror family saga, or "drama" as Sobachak coins it, "emerges from the crisis experienced by American bourgeois patriarchy since the late 1960s and is marked by the related disintegration and transfiguration of the American bourgeois family—an ideological as well as interpersonal structure characterized, as Robin Wood so frequently points out, by its cellular construction and institutionalization of capitalist and patriarchal relations and values (among them, monogamy, heterosexuality, and consumerism) and by its present state of disequilibrium and crisis."[3]

Certainly, this is the case for both the novel and Netflix's adaptation. But while the novel focused on Eleanor's struggles to come into her own as a person, how Hill House is both a shelter and an escape from Eleanor's normal life, and a means to put off taking the steps to free herself from the control and scorn her sister and brother-in-law exercise over her, the series focuses on Hill House and how it affects the Crain family, and specifically Steven and Hugh Crain. Almost immediately, we understand that this is Steven's story, even as the point of view shifts to different characters and most of the damage is inflicted on Olivia, Nell, and Luke.

As with so many haunted house stories, the Netflix series is driven by the aftermath of occupying the house, as if Hill House is an actual character with agency and sentience. Bailey posits this is because Poe and Hawthorne's *Fall of the House of Usher* and *The House of Seven Gables* have paved the way for a distinctly American version of the gothic ghost story: the haunted house story.[4] Further, later writers have adopted this very effective plot device to the point of formulization, which eventually led to canonizing the malevolent house motif. Suddenly the house itself was somehow sentient, fundamentally evil or flawed and the hapless family that inhabits it find themselves in peril, sometimes even long after they have left.

This is the case for Netflix's version, but not necessarily Jackson's novel (as mentioned above). The series has Hill House as evil, rotten through, permanently stained by Poppy's deeds. In a marked shift from the novel version, we learn that the house's evil origins start, not from it being "born bad" from the start and fueled by the possible echoes of an overbearing, evil hearted father, but from a union between two rich but mad people who met at an expensive and exclusive asylum, a "place to for the family to send their embarrassments."

Perhaps to spare Steven the details, Clara tells Steven that Poppy and her husband met in the asylum and "fell in love." There is a strong implication that the two families got together and decided to be rid of the two (perhaps Poppy's family being the more motivated, as they sent her very far away from New York City and William's later infidelity) ("Two Storms") by pairing them off and helping them set up house ("Eulogy").

Poppy is at once a tragic and odious figure. Tragic because even insanity didn't exempt her from the Cult of True Womanhood. Though mentally ill, she was still expected to marry and produce children. Not once, but twice. It was as if her family decided that she needed to keep having children until she "snapped out of it" and she settled into her rightful role ("Screaming Meemies"). Often, she gives the impression of a woman who is not mad, but so filled with rage that it spills over and taints everything she does. She has lucid and insightful outbursts, sometimes even breaking the fourth wall to speak directly to the audience. One can't help but wonder if she was committed because she was willful and that drove her to insanity, or if she was insane from the start, and the confinement first at the asylum and then at Hill House compounded her struggles. Indeed, her rage and madness have forever marked Hill House, fueling it with psychic energy to the point that the house becomes the physical manifestation of her will and soul, long after her corporal body is gone. Additionally, as Poppy recounts her reasons for "waking up her children" to Olivia, it sounds very much like she had postpartum psychosis in addition to her other disorders—a dangerous, if uncommon condition that has only recently been fully recognized. Poppy, at the very least, needed help and careful supervision. And her children deserved protection and care that the extended family failed to provide ("Screaming Meemies").

Ghost stories and haunted house stories written by women have long been understood to be social critiques. Given that the nineteenth-century "Cult of True Womanhood" structured a female world bounded by kitchen hearth and nursery,[5] it is not surprising that, in the writing of nineteenth and early twentieth-century women, the particular setting invested with the most affective energy is the space of the home.... Ghost stories, perhaps more than any other class of story, are preoccupied with these anxious spaces.[6]

From the onset it appears the Olivia, like Poppy before her, is the victim of The Cult of True Womanhood and Domesticity.[7] Obviously well-educated and upper-class, she is isolated from friends and extended family. She is a somewhat anachronistic figure, often appearing in large sunhats. In an era where it had become in vogue to show off one's summer tan—a way to signal to others that one had enough leisure time to lie about—Olivia, like the grand ladies of earlier eras, is careful to protect her porcelain complexion. She also is seen in elaborate dressing gowns between changes from her daywear to dinner wear.

Yet for all that, Olivia's character is a woman of the nineties and Third-Wave Feminism with the weight of all the impossible contradictory expectations placed on women of the era. During this time several cultural shifts fractured societal mores; it should be noted that Purity Balls, Promise Rings, Virginity Pledges, Father-Daughter dances, Abstinence Only Sex Education, and an overall obsession with female chastity and domesticity became a national preoccupation in the nineties. Domestic skills that were ditched by previous generations of women as drudgery, were back in full force. Everywhere women and girls were learning canning, embroidery, sewing and tailoring, cloth diapering, etc., all while there was much handwringing and pontificating by talk show hosts and supposed family and childhood experts over the hypothetical negative effects of childcare, single motherhood, and hook-up culture.

Olivia breaks each of The Cult Virtues or Ideals.[8] She is irreligious, impure in the sense that though she is married, she doesn't behave as though "the marriage night was the single great event of a woman's life, when she bestowed her greatest treasure upon her husband, and from that point on was completely dependent upon him, an empty vessel, without legal or emotional existence of her own,"[9] and she is not wholly submissive to Hugh. Perhaps Olivia's most grievous breach is that she is a full working partner to Hugh, even bringing the work into what should be the sanctified, strictly domestic space of the home.[10]

Of the five children, Nell is the heir apparent of Olivia's status. When she asks if Olivia found the key to the Red Room, Olivia tells her, "The secret is we *are* the key" ("Screaming Meemies"). It is Nell whom the house seeks most actively and as we learn in episode five, "The Bent-Neck Lady," Hill House was showing Nell her future as a lady of Hill House. In fact, in the same episode, Nell asks her mother about the locket she sees around her mother's neck and sweetly inquires if she may have one like it one day. Olivia promises her that once she is older, Nell may have that very locket, making it an heirloom piece. Tragically, Olivia coaxes a hallucinating Nell to suicide by tricking her into believing that the noose she is putting over her head is the locket, hers at last. And as she does this, Olivia has tears in her eyes; she has fully initiated her daughter in The Cult of True Womanhood, and the cost is death ("The Bent-Neck Lady").

Several events led up to Nell's demise. In her session with Dr. Montague, she reveals that the Bent-Neck Lady didn't visit her while she was married, until the day of Arthur's death. She did see her while Arthur spent the night before their wedding, suggesting that his status as husband kept her safe while he was alive. Sometime later, she confronts Steven during one of his readings. He is unwilling to listen to her complaints and condemnation of his exploitation and monetization of the family's tragedy, at first brushing her off, then pointing out that the time for her to speak out (legally, of course) had run out, to finally trying to silence her with insults. He belittles her by pointing out her failed coping strategies ("I've seen you through all your phases. Your religious phase, your crystals phase, your antidepressant phase...") only pull out the trump card: it is all in her head; she is manufacturing this outrage and insult. He condescendingly asks her if she is still taking her medications ("The Bent-Neck Lady").

When she tells Dr. Montague this, and how proud she is of herself for finally, for the first time in her life, standing up for herself, Dr. Montague reacts with appalled surprise. He didn't mean for her to do that and he tells her so. He meant for her admit that she should accept that the house's power is just in her head, and in an eerie echo of Steven, asks her if she is certain she is still taking her medication ("The Bent-Neck Lady").

The overall isolation she suffers as her once tight nuclear family has splintered off, some of her siblings starting nuclear families of their own (Steven's marriage still hanging on despite severe strain), compounded by Luke's near miss with Joey, drives her back to therapy. Though he is poor substitute for a loving family member or friend, at least Dr. Montague sort of listens. Nell drives back to Hill House, in large part under Dr. Montague's advice.

The year when *The Haunting of Hill House* was published (1959) was a time of tremendous social and economic change. The country was in the midst of restructure; only one year later the first sit-in protests began. By contrast, the '90s, though turbulent, was a calmer era. The Reagan boom was finished and the Persian Gulf War started. The Crain family moves into Hill House in 1992, just as the George H.W. Bush administration was ending. The U.S. was officially out of the previous year's recession, but the unemployment jobless rate was still high and not budging. Because of these things, viewers can assume that the Crains were wealthy enough to either buy outright the enormous Hill Estate, or at least secure a loan with a sizable downpayment. Additionally, they would have had another large source of capital for the numerous and extensive repairs and redesigns they had planned for the mansion, especially since they planned to have it on the market just eight weeks later, at the end of summer ("Two Storms").

All of this to say that it is striking that the couple wouldn't have brought with them caregivers and subcontractors to the house to speed things along; surely, they could have afforded it. And though Mr. Crain had Mr. Dudley for help, there are many scenes where Olivia, if not stopping her work altogether, at least pauses what she is doing to tend to one of the children.

Additionally, it is she who sleeps on the floor beside Nell ("Steven Sees a Ghost") when Nell wakes screaming from another Bent-Neck Lady nightmare.

This is significant because as the architect/designer, it would stand to reason that Olivia's workspace and time should've been prioritized, at least during the day. While Mr. Crain can see to obvious repairs and maintenance, he would have had to wait for plans from Olivia—as he does for the black mold removal ("Two Storms")—for the finer work, redesigns, and less obvious repairs.

Shortly after their arrival, it becomes evident that Olivia and Poppy have made a connection. Perhaps Poppy saw in Olivia someone like herself, that she could befriend, or someone to manipulate; her initial motivation is open for interpretation. What is clear is that Olivia was receptive to Poppy's suggestions and that Hugh wasn't paying attention. Even as Hazel Hill warns Olivia that Poppy can't be trusted ("She lies," Hazel tells her twice), Olivia continues her associations with Poppy to disastrous results. By the last episode we come to understand that Olivia, despite knowing that she murdered little Abigail and was about to murder the twins, is still under Poppy's spell.

The suggestively shaped and named Red Room of Hill House functions as a sort of traveling multipurpose room, a common addition in ghost stories. In Hill House, it serves as a honey trap, luring in the living with the promise of safety and nurturing, only to kill.

In his analysis of Madeline Yale Wynne's little-known short story, "The Little Room," Weinstock suggests that the mysterious and wandering room makes itself known only to women because it is a place of creative expression and healing in an era when there was a clear understanding that spaces were strictly either "men's space" or "women's space."[11] Perhaps by design or through a happy accident throughout their stay at Hill House, Shirley and Nell are very intent on gaining access to the little room.

> The answers, however, are not for the living because, as the story suggest, men and women are not asking the same questions. This is because their very experience of the world—the ways in which they perceive, occupy, and move through space—differs due to the ideological weight of gender. The ultimate unsettling assertion of Wynne's haunting story is that men and women occupy different-and mutually exclusive—realities.[12]

In the final episode the Red Room finally lays all bare, including the secrets each of the Crains work so hard to keep hidden, especially from themselves. First, we see Steven at home, his heavily pregnant wife supportive and helpful. He is struggling to write a sequel to *The Haunting of Hill House* and Leigh's advice and opinions are welcome. She suddenly blurts out the truth. As she so succinctly puts it, "I was never real to you." She goes on to tell him that she wrote the check for his dreams; Steven is faced with the nightmare reality that he owes much more to Leigh than he is prepared to admit ("Silence Lay Steadily").

"She lies," Hazel warned, and it is true. In the Red Room Poppy has "lied" to each of the Crain siblings, showing them a dream that quickly turns to nightmare. The Red Room is Poppy's. She is the mistress of the Red Room and it opens and shuts as she wills. It is the soul and will of the house.

Later in the same episode, we learn that Hugh has made sacrifice after sacrifice for his family, enduring scorn and contempt from his children and ultimately giving into Olivia's loneliness. He trades his life for the lives of his remaining children. While Hugh is noble in this respect, his solution takes a complex family dynamic and renders it into a simple plot point—a temporary fix for an eternal problem ("Silence Lay Steadily").

Olivia has spiraled back to the point of Poppy's influence over her parroting the manipulative and insane woman's logic. For an instant she realizes the unforgivable deed she committed in killing Abigail, and it appears that she kills herself in part because she can't ever make amends for such a sin. She tells Poppy she wants to wake up, and the audience is momentarily hopeful that Olivia will finally be free of Poppy's influence. The impression is strengthened during their fight scene, when it appears that Olivia attacks Poppy. ("Screaming Meemies"). In a final show of will, she tells Poppy to leave a sprawled and terrified Hugh alone. It rings false. We saw her stand by, acting as a lure to Luke as Poppy grabbed him from behind. In the Red Room, it is Poppy who tricks Luke and the others, just as she did Olivia before.

In the final scenes where Olivia complains to Hugh about how he took her children away, she is reduced from the vibrant, loving mother and woman, to a matron with an extreme case of Empty Nest Syndrome. She is almost petulant. Hugh does try to reason with her; "Nothing bad will happen to them," she says, and he rightly answers, "Nothing good will either." But it is too late. Olivia has her mind made up.

Hugh and Olivia's relationship is solid, according to Hugh's imagined Olivia, but compared to the Dudleys, they have a long way to go. Like many upper-class power couples, Hugh and Olivia get along, and they are kind to each other, but they don't *know* each other. This is clear when it is Mr. Dudley who suggests that though it "might not be my place," Olivia may need some help ("Eulogy"). Hugh, though riled by Mr. Dudley's pointing it out, is forced to listen. It is apparent that Hugh has romanticized their relationship over the years, smoothing over some of the holes and cracks, putting a pretty face on things ("Eulogy").

And as Mr. Dudley speaks about his wife, it is with reverence and a deep respect. He is speaking about his equal and partner, someone he loves deeply. Mr. Dudley understands and knows Clara so well that though few words are exchanged between them, he knows that she wants to be able to visit Abigail's ghost. He explains all of this to an uncomprehending Hugh, who wants to burn the house down. When he later carries a dying Clara back to Hill House to perish near their children, we understand that this is a friendship and marriage of equals; they are very devout, they make a pact to spend their eternity in the purgatory of Hill House instead of Heaven. His carrying her into the house to ensure that she die inside is a promise fulfilled ("Silence Lay Steadily"). When comparing the two relationships, it becomes easier to see how Olivia could be led astray by Poppy.

Despite these wonderful explorations, at its core, this is Steven's story, with the rest of the family as secondary characters. The entire backstory and the flashbacks that slowly reveal the details surrounding Olivia's suicide serve as the launching point for the main story and the origins of the conflict between Hugh and his children, mainly Steven. The explorative storytelling and inherent social commentary in Olivia and Poppy's points of view are shoved aside to make room for Steven's redemption tale.

Early in the series, Steven sets himself up as the perfect big brother, often volunteering to watch over his younger siblings, frequently telling Luke that he will protect him. This is fine as long as Steven sees himself as following in his father's footsteps as the patriarch and natural leader of the family. But his confidence in his father slowly erodes; we see his attitude visibly change in the car as he questions his father about leaving without Olivia. And it finally falls away entirely in the aftermath of Olivia's death.

With this comes a complete departure from the themes explored in the novel. The series turns to family saga. By adulthood, Steven has rejected his father almost entirely. Hugh has failed in his role as protector and provider; he is not the patriarch Steven thought him to be. In fact, Hugh's transformation began in Hill House and continued in the twenty years since. At first he was every bit the role model Steven wanted him to be, but Luke reminds him of how far his thinking and attitudes have changed when he recalls the time Hugh told him that "Big boys know the difference between what is real and what is imagination." The hurt is still there for Luke, but more importantly, Hugh is momentarily overwhelmed by the damage he unintentionally inflicted on his young son. Hugh is left blinking back the shock and at a loss for words ("Two Storms").

> At a time when the mythology of our dominant culture can no longer resolve the contradictions exposed by experience, the nuclear family has found itself in nuclear crisis. Rather than serving bourgeois patriarchy as a place of refuge from social upheavals of the last two decades (many of them initiated by the young and by women), the family has become the site of them—and now serves as a sign of their representation. Not only has the bourgeois distinction between family members and alien Others, between private home and public space, between personal microcosm

and sociopolitical macrocosm, been exposed as a cultural construction, as set of signifying, as well as significant, practices.[13]

In a telling confrontation, Steven blames his father for how they all turned out. He was quick to censure Hugh's near absence from their lives during Nell's funeral and then in the car while looking for Luke, and he blames Hugh for not taking care of Olivia and "getting her the help she needed." He goes on to say that Hugh didn't get Nell or Luke any help either and that he never acknowledged the mental illness in the Crain family. Throughout, Hugh quietly and quite penitently listens as Steven hurls accusation after accusation at him, never pointing out the obvious—if there were mental illness, Janet, as the aunt who raised them, would've gotten them treatment. He doesn't do this because that isn't really what the argument is about, even if Steven's understanding is opaque ("Eulogy"; "Witness Marks").

Steven is angry that Hugh no longer operates from a strictly patriarchal worldview. Worse, Hugh has abandoned it and Steven takes it upon himself to fill the void. He does so with the frenzied zeal of a newly initiated cult member who cannot stop for a moment to contemplate its religious tenets, because the truth of his situation is too terrible to accept. Steven has gone all-in, shocking his father by admitting that he married Leigh under false pretenses, knowing that she wanted children, but not telling her about his vasectomy years earlier because the time was never right ("Witness Marks").

Especially heinous is that he watched her suffer over the years, thinking that he was somehow going to be able to placate her into acceptance (I like to think that this is the case instead of the very real possibility that he simply cared so little for Leigh that what he stole from her was so insignificant, he never gave it another thought) by going through the motions of fertility treatments, all the while sitting silent as her fertility slowly diminishes. All this because he knew better anyway ("Witness Marks").

This disingenuous admission is so ridiculous that one is left to assume that he actually believes it. Steven not only robbed Leigh of biological children, but of the choice to marry someone else, or even adopt with Steven, had he been upfront with her. His excuse is that he didn't want to pass on mental illness. The reality is that he never wanted to be a father, or at least not with her, because if he did, he would've put that option to Leigh before marrying her.

As he relates to his siblings and father, he is much the same. Shrugging off their outrage and even Shirley's objections, calling it "blood money," it seems that he assuages his guilt, if he feels any, by an after the fact announcement that he is allowing the siblings a share in the royalties. Not the sizable advance on the book or movie rights, it should be noted, but just the royalties. Even so, this amount is substantial enough for him to prop himself up as the successful and magnanimous provider for the family.

The payments allow Theo to finish her post-graduate work, Luke to stay in rehab, and to her utter humiliation, Shirley to continue her funeral home business because of the undermining subterfuge between her husband and Steven. Kevin's arrangement with Steven is sanctioned by the pragmatic Theo, who points out that the book was already out there, so why not? ("Eulogy"). (Presumably, Nell gets a share as well.)

To his credit, Steven is changed by the final moments at Hill House. He has made amends with Hugh and is now the family guardian and trustee. The literal Man of the House. The estate is his to keep safe from outsiders and to pass on to the next guardian, presumably Luke, who is shown as reformed and reconciled with Steven. Off-screen he has also made amends with Leigh, and she has forgiven him ("Silence Lay Steadily"). Steven, it is understood, was not wholly responsible for his behavior and actions because he didn't possess all the facts. Now that he does, he behaves better, and the saga ends on a bittersweet note ("Silence Lay Steadily").

The result of this ending is that the Crain drama, and specifically Steven's redemption, subsumes the feminist underpinnings of the source work. The saga comes to the fore and the audience is distracted by it. What is left of the women's stories within this larger tale is filtered through Steven's interpretive lens and ultimately cast aside. Even Shirley Jackson herself is erased; the Shirley in the series is a mortician while Steven is the writer. Possibly, as Weinstock suggests, "because men and women occupy different—and mutually exclusive—realities," Steven doesn't see them at all. They are ghostly outlines and imprints of Jackson's themes; mere phantasms.

Notes

1. Rachel Syme, "How Netflix Made the Haunting of Hill House Less Scary." *The New Republic* (October 31, 2018).
2. Dale Bailey, *American Nightmares: The Haunted House Formula in American Popular Fiction* (Ohio: Bowling Green University Press, 1999), 8.
3. Vivian Sobchack, "Bringing It All Back Home: Family Economy and Generic Exchange." *The Dread of Difference: Gender and the Horror* (Texas: University of Texas Press, 1996), 144.
4. Bailey, *American Nightmares*.
5. Jeffrey Andrew Weinstock, *Scare Tactics: Supernatural Fiction by American Women* (New York: Fordham University Press, 2008), 56.
6. Ibid.
7. Bailey, 31.
8. Barbara Welter, "The Cult of True Womanhood: 1820–1860." *American Quarterly* Vol 18, No 2 Part 1 (Maryland, The Johns Hopkins University Press, Summer, 1966), pp. 151–174; Catherine Lavender, *Notes on the Cult of Domesticity and True Womanhood* (New York: The City University of New York, 1998), 2. https://csivc.csi.cuny.edu/history/files/lavender/386/truewoman.pdf.
9. Sobchak.

10. Lavender, 2.
11. Weinstock, 65.
12. Weinstock, 69.
13. Weinstock, 69.

The Horrific Feminine
Terrifying Women
CAMILLE S. ALEXANDER

Cinematic depictions of female horror characters can best be described as "limited." Either the character is crazed, reinforcing negative stereotypes about the female psyche, or a frightening, hideous monster, playing on other negative female stereotypes. While art provides an imitation of life, these stereotypical images do little to represent female roles, personalities, or behaviors in the real world. For example, Sady Doyle describes Guillermo del Toro's film *Crimson Park* (2015) as "unabashedly feminine,"[1] centering on women and their stories. In the same article, Doyle also refers to character Lucille (Jessica Chastain) as "spectacularly unhinged,"[2] noting that she is "shrieking in a gorgeous Victorian gown while wielding a meat cleaver."[3] This depiction raises questions about the exact attributes classifying a film as female-centered; how the horror genre fits into this discussion; and why there is a connection between femininity and madness in horror films. Perhaps it could be argued that because horror films and television shows entertain through escapism, there is no need to insert any level of realism. However, it could also be argued that the most effective artistic depictions are those that adequately imitate life. Therefore, horror films and television shows depicting limited female characters—those that are crazed and have a terrifying appearance—work as marginalizing factors, subliminally influencing audiences, which are largely male, while more realistic female horror characters have the opposite effect.

The Haunting of Hill House (2018), Netflix's latest contribution to the horror television series genre, takes a different approach in its depictions of female "monsters." Rather than recycling the typical female horror character tropes, such as "hideous monster" or "crazy woman," female characters are elegant and beautiful with somewhat terrifying appearances, casting them as horrific feminine characters. Barbara Creed (1993/2007) defines female horror characters as "monstrous-feminine," noting that this description refers to "what it is about woman that is shocking, terrifying, horrific, abject,"[4] further observing that the "phrase monstrous-feminine emphasizes the importance of gender in the construction of her monstrosity."[5] The female horror characters in *HoHH* are depicted as victims of Hill House, which, in its manipulation of these characters, represents a restructuring of patriarchy in the form of masculine psychic energy. Hill House is a geographic space and physical manifestation of masculine psychic energy—one that controls phantom female characters and bends them to its will—trapping these characters for eternity in the structure, and, in the process, "feeding" itself on their female energy. Hill House simultaneously functions as a sort of perpetual machine and a juggernaut; the house collects feminine energies to maintain its power through the entities' continued victimization post-mortem. As a symbolically patriarchal structure, Hill House represents the omnipotence of unchecked, male psychic energy, oppressing female entities for its pleasure and survival.

Focusing on *HoHH*'s two primary female apparitions, Olivia Crain and the Bent-Neck Lady (BNL), the apparition of Olivia's adult daughter Nell, this iteration of Shirley Jackson's novel provides a more sympathetic treatment of female "monsters," identifying them as horrific, supernatural beings who are also startlingly feminine; they are frightening but also beautiful, gentle, and sad. While Olivia and Nell are victims of Hill House, they are also concerned with protecting their family, wanting to keep it intact regardless of the personal cost. Although the horror genre is notorious for sexualizing female characters, whether victims or monsters, *HoHH* veers from this trope, addressing women's needs and hopes for their families while deemphasizing sex and sexuality. In *HoHH*, horrific female characters are portrayed as beautiful and sympathetic; they are terrifying apparitions, but undeniably feminine. Hill House, while maintaining a symbiotic relationship with the entities, also "feeds" from their feminine energy. In the series, Hill House appears not only as a site of the Crain family's torment but as a symbol of unchecked masculine energy in contrast to Nell's, Olivia's, and other female apparitions' controlled feminine energy. An examination of the female gaze directed at female horror characters in relation to the horror genre as depicted in *HoHH* reveals how this iteration of Jackson's story disrupts the traditional, female-monster trope.

Laura Mulvey (1975/2006) observes that in "a world ordered by sexual imbalance, pleasure in looking has been split between active/male and passive/female."[6] Mulvey proposes a gendered perspective to pleasurable viewing in which the female is relegated to the object of the gaze while the male possesses the "right" and privilege of viewing. Linda Williams (1983) contends that while "little boys and grown men make it a point of honor to look ... little girls and grown women cover their eyes or hide behind the shoulders of their dates."[7] Perhaps this occurs because "it has long been a dictum of the [horror] genre that women make the best victims,"[8] thus, creating an on-screen narrative of victimhood forcing female audience members to see themselves only in this manner. This observation suggests that, for girls and women viewing horror, there are some gendered, internalized expectations causing them to respond in a manner that may be contrary to their feelings about images of women onscreen.

Williams (1983), referencing Mulvey's research on the gaze, states that "a dominant male look at the woman ... leaves no place for the woman's own pleasure in seeing; she exists only to be looked at."[9] In earlier films with horrific female characters, being the object of the gaze was problematic, reframing social gender imbalances through cinematic depictions of those sociocultural issues. However, in *HoHH*, the horrific feminine characters are not at the mercy of the male gaze as the characters do not provide the blood-and-gore visuals typical of the horror genre and, while they are victimized, it is through the manipulations of a house that contains a powerful and cruel masculine energy and not by the rudimentary male character wielding a knife, axe, or chainsaw. The deaths of the horrific female characters in *HoHH* indicate a shift in the horror paradigm of psychotic, male, axe murderer and weak, simpering, female victim to a masculine psychic energy exerting its power over female victims who are neither sexualized nor fetishized. Taking this approach, de-emphasizing sexuality and avoiding the objectifying depictions of female characters in the horror genre means that there is less emphasis placed on appealing to the male gaze and more focus on character development and content.

One of the consistent complaints made about female characters in horror films, monstrous or not, is that they are often reduced to sexual objects. Sharon Smith (1972/2006) once observed that the "role of a woman in a film almost always revolves around her physical attraction and the mating games she plays with the male characters."[10] Essentially, in "their traditional exhibitionist role women are simultaneously looked at and displayed, with their appearance coded for strong visual and erotic impact so that they can be said to connote *to-be-looked-at-ness*."[11] To that end, female characters are "indispensable element[s] of spectacle in normal narrative film," but their "visual presence tends to work against the development of a story-line, to freeze the flow of action in moments of erotic contemplation."[12] When these observations were made almost fifty years ago, female roles in horror films were narrow, but female characters in this iteration of the Hill House saga indicate a marked shift from the sexual object trope. In this version of the story, female horror characters are fully developed and not objectified.

In *HoHH*, there are few references to horrific feminine characters and sexuality. Olivia and Nell, the main characters from the series who fall under the horrific feminine character rubric, are not depicted as sexualized beings. Rather, the series takes the novel approach of focusing on the loving and committed relationships both women have when they are alive. Olivia is married to Hugh, who, when discussing his relationship with her, states that Olivia always referred to herself as the kite and to him as the line: "she was a creature of the clouds, and [Hugh] was a creature of the earth" ("Witness Marks"). This statement, examining the nature of their connection, in combination with Hugh imagining that Olivia is always nearby and conversing with him long after her death, indicates a strong bond based on their twenty-year relationship, including fifteen years of marriage. The depiction of Hugh and Olivia's relationship—their commitment to each other and their family—limits the possibility of sexualizing Olivia while emphasizing her importance as a wife and a mother. When Nell begins a relationship with Arthur Vance, her sleep technologist, immediately the focus is on their romance and emotional bond. While the sexual relationship between the two is depicted, it is not central to their relationship. Instead, the scenes with Arthur's proposal on New Year's Eve and their wedding play more prominent roles in the series ("The Bent-Neck Lady"). In addition, during their relationship, Arthur cares for Nell when she suffers from episodes of sleep paralysis, which began in her childhood after first seeing the BNL ("The Bent-Neck Lady"). The only indications of the sexualization of either Olivia or Nell as the BNL are that both often appear in negligees as do other female ghosts, such as Poppy and Hazel Hill. While it would be easy to attribute their attire to the characters' sexualization, another possibility exists. Dressing these characters in negligees at certain points in the series, except for Hazel, who is the ghost of an older woman confined to her bed ("Screaming Meemies"), may be an attempt to emphasize their femininity. The negligees suggest a softness and frailty, accentuating Olivia's and Nell's femininity. The characters appear more ethereal, beautiful, and less bound to the reality of everyday life when attired in the negligees than if they were wearing more formal attire.

Another shift in the treatment of female characters in the horror genre utilized in *HoHH* is that femininity is not necessarily associated with weakness. Smith (1972/2006) notes that "[e]ven when a woman is the central character she is generally shown as confused, or helpless and in danger, or passive, or as a purely sexual being."[13] The association of female horror characters with weakness has been and continues to be a problematic trope in the genre, which is largely the purview of male filmmakers. The domination of the horror film genre by men as writers, producers, and directors is not likely to undergo a drastic shift; however, while Smith (1972/2006) called for filmmakers' minds to change,[14] Netflix's version of *HoHH* indicates that this transformation occurred. In the television series, the portrayal of female horror characters veers away from the passive or helpless towards the initially manipulated and later vindicated.

In the episode titled "Eulogy," which, like many of the episodes, vacillates between the present (2018) and the past (1992), Hugh and Horace Dudley, who is one of Hill House's caretakers, have a conversation about Olivia. During the discussion, Horace gently hints at her very noticeable emotional breakdown. Horace relates the stories of his mother and his wife Clara, who, because of Hill House, became, as he describes, "scattered" ("Eulogy"). Mentioning that he and his wife never remain in Hill House at night, Horace states, "Just superstitious at first, but here's the thing: it worked. No more nightmares. No more crying. No one acting scattered" ("Eulogy"). Like Olivia, Clara had nightmares and heard the crying of her stillborn daughter; it took the Dudleys years to conclude that there was a connection between the women's mental breakdowns and Hill House, demonstrating the house's masculine psychic energy and its pattern of victimizing female characters while simultaneously draining their energy. Horace further states to Hugh, "if you find your missus is acting scattered, then, yeah, maybe a little time away would do the trick. From the house, I mean" ("Eulogy"). In this scene, between male characters but addressing the issues troubling female characters, Horace articulates exactly what the house is doing, noting that the house directs its attacks at women and, to a lesser extent, girls as both Dudley daughters became victims of Hill House as does Nell. The use of the term "scattered" to describe the Dudley women and Olivia is less a gender-biased rhetorical device than an astute observation of Hill House's power over female characters. The house distracts and confuses female characters to engage in a pattern of feeding on their energy.

Smith (1972/2006) notes that, except for a few films prior to 1972, "women have learned to masochistically enjoy seeing women ridiculed on film"[15]—distancing themselves from these weak characters. Film genres, such as action, shifted towards the female gaze by incorporating female characters who are independent, strong, and powerful, which can be seen in the *Alien* series and in action subgenres like blaxploitation films featuring female protagonists. Horror has been slow to transform and fully address the female gaze, but its attempts at drawing the female gaze have proven groundbreaking as with *HoHH*. The series' two primary horrific feminine characters are Olivia Crain and her daughter Eleanor (Nell) Vance. These characters, while the victims of Hill House, are neither ridiculed, sexualized, nor weakened onscreen for the audiences' pleasure. Instead, this iteration of the story takes the innovative approach of depicting female victims as complex, occasionally frightening, but always loving and family centered.

Olivia Crain, the matriarch of the Crain family, is believed to have committed suicide in her thirties by throwing herself from the library balcony near the curved metal staircase. Her sudden death occurs because Hill House convinces her that her children are in imminent danger. In the episode titled "Screaming Meemies," Olivia meets the ghost of Poppy Hill, wife of William Hill, and according to Clara Dudley, Poppy "was insane. I mean clinically" ("Witness Marks"). Before her death, the beautiful, talented, loving, and soft-spoken Olivia becomes a shrieking, wild-haired, psychotic version of herself, which is a direct result of Hill House's machinations rather than a manifestation of some "hidden" personality trait. Olivia, who was, prior to her mental breakdown, the center of her family and the object of her husband's affections, becomes a terrifying madwoman—the epitome of Sandra Gilbert and Susan Gubar's (1979) mad woman in the attic as she is confined physically and emotionally to Hill House—the structural representation of a masculine energy determined to entrap her. In her love and concern for her family—particularly her children, Luke and Nell, whose futures Hill House has revealed—Olivia attempts to murder the twins as children but fails and instead murders Abigail ("Screaming Meemies"), the only living child of the Dudleys. Hugh manages to save the twins but not Abigail, and, while Olivia wakes to find the child dead on the floor of the room with the red door ("Screaming Meemies"), she is still obsessed with saving her children. When Olivia attempts to open the door to one of the rooms, Poppy appears, stating that Hugh "wants to take [the children] away" ("Screaming Meemies") from Olivia. Poppy, while clinically insane, is, at this point in the narrative, simply enacting a script dictated to her by Hill House. The house, as a structure driven by masculine psychic energy, uses Poppy, one of its many victims, to locate and trap more victims to feed its insatiable hunger. In the present, Hugh, in a conversation with his son Steven, states, "Our family is like an unfinished meal to that house" ("Witness Marks"). The house's consistent campaign to increase the number of victims who die within its walls—particularly female victims—proves the accuracy of Hugh's assessment and his observation that "That house is the most dangerous place in the world for all of us," ("Witness Marks") meaning his family, further emphasizes Hill House's power and its ability to exert power over anyone who comes into contact with it.

Antagonized by Poppy, Olivia races through the house and encounters Hazel Hill's ghost, whom she asks for help. When Hazel asks what she can do for Olivia, Olivia replies, "I need to wake up" ("Screaming Meemies"), suggesting that she is aware on some level that current events are happening in a sort of dream state—that they are, ultimately, not real or perhaps induced hallucinations. After going on a panicked rampage through the house looking for her older children, Olivia finds her husband, Hugh, begs him to return the children to Hill House to keep them safe, and pleads with him to stay with her. As Hugh drives away with the children in the car, Poppy, who Hazel claims lies ("Screaming Meemies"), is standing by the window further antagonizing Olivia by stating that Hugh "is killing them. He's driving into the dark. He's killing all of them. He's driving them toward a silver table. He's driving them toward a needle. He's driving them toward disease, heartbreak, sadness, and death" ("Screaming Meemies"). Left alone in Hill House and with her husband and children gone, Olivia returns to the room with the red door—the one room in the house that could never be opened but every member of the family had entered—she goes to Abigail's body, crying, and Abigail's ghost appears. Olivia asks the ghost, "Are you awake, now?" ("Screaming Meemies"), suggesting Olivia believes, after Hill House's manipulations, that dying in the house is the only way to save the children from the horrible visions Hill House uses to torment her. Olivia is driven to commit suicide because she views death as waking from a nightmare. In the moments leading up to Olivia's death, she repeats that she wants "to wake up" ("Screaming Meemies"), and Poppy is standing nearby telling her to wake up. While Olivia seems to fall from the balcony and committing suicide is her choice, Poppy's proximity to her and Poppy's hand reaching out to Olivia in the moments before her death could also be interpreted as a push rather than a jump or fall. Therefore, there is an implication that Poppy, under the influence of Hill House, kills Olivia, sacrificing her body so that her spirit can feed the house. Once Olivia becomes a ghost, the typical horror movie trope of the crazed female apparition with a terrifying aspect falls away, and she reverts to the soft-spoken, beautiful woman she was before Hill House manipulates her into murder and either convinces her to commit suicide or kills her. As an apparition, Olivia tries to persuade her family to join her in Hill House using logical argument: the children will be safe, and the family will remain united when they die. Yet, it is not until the final episode of the series, when the entire family is gathered in Hill House, that Hugh is able to piece together the details of Olivia's final night in the house and explain that, by taking the children away from her and Hill House, he hoped to save them ("Silence Lay Steadily").

When the events leading up to Olivia's death are depicted, they suggest a repetition of the "crazed and terrifying" horror female character trope. However, this assumption could not be further from the truth, and Olivia's appearance is subject to several underlying events. The incident that initiates the chain of events leading to the Crain family's problems involves Olivia and her love for her children. When the house has a few months to manipulate the family, Hill House convinces Olivia that her children are in danger by showing her the future—one in which Luke becomes a drug addict, Nell suffers from mental illness, and both end up dying young. However, Hill House never reveals that it is ultimately the cause of the children's issues because, unlike their older siblings Shirley, Steven, and Theodora (Theo), Luke and

Nell are very young when the family moves into Hill House. Their ages in combination with Hill House's nuanced manipulations contribute to their susceptibility; in addition, when as children Nell and Luke attempt to confide in other family members about the horrors they witness, no one believes them even when there is irrefutable evidence, such as the scratches Luke sustains when he is trapped in the dumbwaiter in the basement. While Hill House attacks each family member individually, the older children are somehow able to resist this force as they mature and become adults whereas Luke and Nell internalize the horrors they witnessed. In addition, no one ever believes Nell and Luke, who are six years old when the family lives in Hill House, so their observations are ignored, exacerbating their mental health and drug addiction issues.

As an adult, Nell, like the other characters in *HoHH*, suffers the aftereffects of living in Hill House. However, unlike her older siblings, who mask their memories by obsessively pursuing their careers, Nell is fully aware that those events were real although she spent a lifetime being told that everything she witnessed was a figment of her imagination. Nell is emotionally and psychologically tortured by Hill House, but the house's torment takes a different approach from typical horror tropes. As a child, Nell sees an apparition that she refers to as the Bent-Neck Lady (BNL). The BNL appears to Nell during the family's brief time occupying Hill House when she is a child, and this apparition often levitates over Nell's bed as she attempts to sleep in the room she shares with Luke. Eventually, when Nell is a married woman, decades later, the BNL appears in her bedroom and, within moments, her new husband, Arthur, dies of an aneurysm, leaving her widowed after only eight months of marriage ("The Bent-Neck Lady"). Nell sinks further into her depression, eventually deciding to make one last journey to Hill House after being drawn there by the house's psychic, masculine energy.

Much like her mother years before, when Nell is alive, she appears like the typical female horror character after the trauma of helplessly watching Arthur die—crazed and terrifying. To provide a contemporary take on the "mad" woman trope, Nell is depicted seeing a therapist and taking antidepressants, which are contemporary and nuanced approaches to the rest cures women were subjected to during the Victorian period. In addition, unlike the sexist trope of previous horror films in which the female character's real concerns are dismissed by only male characters, in *HoHH* Nell's concerns are ignored by almost every character, male and female, with the exception of her father, Hugh, who is the only person who truly understands exactly what Nell witnessed as a child and who believes her. However, once Nell dies in Hill House and becomes the BNL, her appearance neither gives the impression of madness nor terror. The BNL seems to be a character whose primary function in the series is foretelling—she attempts to warn child and adult

Nell about future events, but, because she is an apparition and at the mercy of Hill House's overpowering masculinist energy, she cannot simply issue warnings. As Nell was in life, the BNL has been silenced—her voice taken from her. Therefore, when she screeches, the goal is not to frighten. Instead, the BNL is attempting to verbalize—describe her own fear and torment as well as warn her loved ones about Hill House and its capabilities. This ghostly version of Nell hovers and watches as if her mere appearance will be enough to change the course of her and her family's futures. The BNL's appearance also gives an aura of something other than terror as she appears in a flowing off-white negligee, which once belonged to Olivia, her long hair streaming down her side. When the BNL appears to Nell, she seems to look at Nell with a steadiness that, after watching the entire series, is concern. Aside from her neck, which is bent at a right angle from Nell's murder by hanging, there is nothing frightening about the BNL's appearance. Nell, as the BNL, appears calmer and more at peace than she did in life, providing another disruption of the horror genre trope in which a horrific female character *should* have a terrifying appearance and behavior. In the final episode of season one, "Silence Lay Steadily," Nell saves her siblings, who are trapped in the room with the red door, from certain death in Hill House. The ghost Nell "pulls" her siblings from the dreams Hill House creates to drive them to suicide, and, once she frees them, Nell offers them some comforting words to help them better accept her death and move on with their lives. In this final act, Nell demonstrates that her goal, both in life and death, was to love and protect her family—even if it meant her own unhappiness and ultimate death.

In Netflix's television series *The Haunting of Hill House*, female horror characters are depicted more sympathetically than in the typical "crazed and frightening" manner indicative of the horror genre. These characters, who can be described as horrific feminine characters, are beautiful, gentle, sad, and victimized by Hill House, which represents a masculine psychic energy that essentially "feeds" on their souls. The series shows a marked shift in the treatment of female characters in horror. This iteration of Shirley Jackson's novel places emphasis on horrific feminine characters—female characters who are technically "monsters" but not monstrous. These characters are beautiful, gentle, and saddened because, both before death and when they became apparitions, they focused on helping their families, which is a herculean task when their opponent is Hill House. This series, which transfers horror from the big screen to the small, attempts to unfold characters in a way that a movie, with its time constraints, cannot. There is a marked effort to give horrific feminine characters a backstory to explain how and why they became ghosts and voices to articulate the events of their lives in their own way. The use of the television medium for horror means that, in a series like *The Haunting of Hill House*, there is very little reliance on the blood and gore indicative of horror films. In addition, there is little need to use women's bodies as sites of violence and torture for entertainment. With an intricate plot and horrific feminine characters, who are also given depth and complexity, *The Haunting of Hill House* demonstrates that the horror genre has changed for the better, and that this change benefits female characters, who no longer have to be victims of physical violence to provide female viewers with characters to dislike and reject or sexualized for the amusement of male audiences.

Notes

1. Sady Doyle, "Rise of Female Monsters Shows Horror Movies Are Not Afraid of Big, Bad Women," Guardian News and Media, *The Guardian*, October 29, 2015, https://www.theguardian.com/film/2015/oct/29/rise-of-female-monsters-shows-horror-movies-are-not-afraid-of-big-bad-women.
2. Doyle, "Rise of Female Monsters."
3. Doyle, "Rise of Female Monsters."
4. Barbara Creed, *The Monstrous-Feminine: Film, Feminism, Psychoanalysis* (London: Routledge, 1993/2007), 1.
5. Creed, 3.
6. Laura Mulvey, "Visual Pleasure and Narrative Cinema," in *Feminist Film Theory: A Reader*, ed. Sue Thornham (New York: New York University Press, 1999/2006), 60.
7. Linda Williams, "When the Woman Looks," in *Revision: Essays in Feminist Film Criticism*, ed. Mary Ann Doane, Patricia Mellencamp, and Linda Williams (Fredrick: University Publications of America, 1983), 561.
8. Linda Williams, "Film Bodies: Gender, Genre, and Excess." *Film Quarterly* 44, no. 4 (1991): 5.
9. Williams, 561.
10. Sharon Smith, "The Image of Women in Film: Some Suggestions for Future Research," in *Feminist Film Theory: A Reader*, ed. Sue Thornham (New York: New York University Press, 1999/2006), 14.
11. Mulvey, 62.
12. Mulvey, 63.
13. Smith, 15.
14. *Ibid.*
15. Smith, 16.

Haunted Families, Queer Temporalities and the Horrors of Normativity

Emily E. Roach

The Netflix Original Series *The Haunting of Hill House* shares similarities with Shirley Jackson's novel of the same title, exposing American anxieties around the breakdown of the family unit through the horror of the haunted house. Richard Pascal notes that Jackson brought "family monsters spawned by fears of permissiveness and authoritarianism ... arrestingly into fiction"[1] with a focus on bad parents and the child's "disruptive energies of individualism."[2] Unlike the novel the television series ostensibly finds hope in the heteronormative model of marriage and childbearing, giving striking dominance to the transcendent power of unified families and the process of maturing into adulthood. It suggests that even death cannot usurp marital vows or familial bonds between parent, child and siblings. Unlike the bleakness of Jackson's story, where the ghosts of Hill House are still consigned to "walk alone" by the novel's conclusion,[3] in the Netflix series the somewhat saccharine culmination is that the ghosts of Hill House walk "together" ("Silence Lay Steadily"). However, despite the final vignettes which see lovers setting up home together, families reunited, and marital fractures healed, the series has moments of temporal queerness that echo the dystopian energy of Jackson's novel and illuminate the horrors of the pursuit of the nuclear family. If the series is trying to position the family unit as an effective protective shield, the message is confused, challenged in particular by the short life of Eleanor (Nell) Crain, the constant troubling of time and the madness of mothers that never fully succeeds in resituating itself as an idealistic model of motherly love.

In Jackson's novel, Theodora—or Theo—is queer coded. She comes to Hill House to participate in Dr. Montague's experiment after a "violent quarrel with the friend with whom she shared an apartment"[4] and demonstrates a penchant for "softly tailored slacks."[5] Theo quickly develops a close but tumultuous relationship with Eleanor Vance which has strong sapphic undertones.[6] In the Netflix series Theo is explicitly a lesbian, translating Jackson's subtext into text. By contrast, the sapphic longing experienced by Eleanor and the desire between the Eleanor, Luke and Theo triumvirate is erased by making Theo and Nell sisters and Luke and Eleanor twins, bound by a psychic connection, the "twin thing." The core characters form nuclear family, the Crains, in contrast to the disparate group of strangers gathered together by Jackson. The textual importance of Eleanor Vance's voice in Jackson's novel takes a back seat to eldest sibling Steven, the protagonist and erstwhile narrator of the Netflix series. Steven, much like Jackson's Dr. Montague, represents the patriarchal voice of science and logic. Despite these critical differences the subversion of temporal logics by Nell and Theo are points of queer resonance. Their specific hauntings manifest through a disruption of linear time through which the family home, an aspirational marker of linear time, becomes a horrifying phantasm, a representation of middle-class American normativity that is a site of violence for queer people, and one which is literally and metaphorically broken.

Jack Halberstam defines "queer time" as "a term for those specific models of temporality that emerge within postmodernism once one leaves the temporal frames of bourgeois reproduction and family, longevity, risk/safety and inheritance."[7] Halberstam advocates for a resistance of the "paradigmatic markers of life experience—namely birth, marriage, reproduction, and death"[8] and invites us to think more queerly about time and space. *The Haunting of Hill House* reaffirms the dominance of "reproductive temporality"[9] and attempts to destabilize those temporal structures by living "out of time," resulting in madness, violence and death. Theo's hauntings occur in spaces where families hide secrets, from the basement in Hill House to the basement of a foster family's home in her adult life. She sees the specter of her decaying mother at the site of Shirley's shattered "forever house," and encounters ghosts when she is sexually active. Her hauntings are triggered by touch and they plunge her violently back in time, connected to secrecy, sexual violence and death. Nell's hauntings are the macabre vision of her own future. Queerness occurs in the violent temporal ruptures experienced by Nell and Theo in a society where normative life trajectories are idealized. For Theo it is the articulation of desexualized queer desire, the breaking down of barriers and subsequent assimilation that enables her to live, suggesting that choosing monogamy over sexual liberation is the path to queer contentment. By contrast, Nell is forced into silence reminiscent of the closet, "the defining structure for gay oppression,"[10] and she experiences the violence of linear time most acutely, resulting in an untimely death which sees her fragment like "confetti," ("Silence Lay Steadily"), a silent spectral spectator, simultaneously visible and invisible, present and absent.

Neither Nell or Theo are considered fully mature by their siblings, with Theo exhibiting adolescent qualities and Nell rendered childlike. Theo is a child psychologist who can feel the emotions of children through her psychic abilities; literally "in touch" with the psyche of the child, relating to a six-year-old girl who builds up barriers to protect herself from the horrors of the adult world ("Touch"). In her sexual practices Theo is likened to a "Frat Boy" by older sister Shirley, her sexual explorations presented as a way of avoiding true intimacy until her eventual maturation involves a capitulation to adulthood through monogamy. Nell is an example of the Gothic tradition which "infantilises many of its female protagonists,"[11] her childlike qualities emphasized by her mental instability. We first see Nell as a child with the monstrous Bent-Neck Lady looming in the background as she sleeps. As an adult when Nell calls Steven, the voice of child Nell can be heard in the background as the scene changes and the call goes unanswered. This juxtaposition of the image of adult Nell with the voice of her child self is an early indicator of the strangeness of her relationship with time, a character who experiences the temporal slippage of the "Gothic girl child," one "typically out of place or time."[12] Halberstam notes the "desired process of maturation" and "emergence of the adult from the dangerous and unruly period of adolescence"[13] are features of "straight time," explaining how such linear child-to-adult narratives do not reflect many peoples queer experience. Nell and Theo, positioned as "failed" adults in the normative sense, exhibit queerly temporal ways of living, and as a result they have the most to fear from societal expectations that seek to realign them with dominant life trajectories.

The rubric that children be "seen and not heard" comes to mind when analyzing Nell's childlike qualities in adulthood. The series is filled with moments where Nell can be seen, but she is silent, desperately trying to communicate. She suffers from sleep paralysis which leaves her unable to move or scream as she experiences the terror of immobility, under siege from her nightmares. In the first episode the viewer sees Nell making several attempts to call her elder siblings, Steven and Shirley, after attempting to contact twin brother Luke to no avail. We also learn that Nell and sister Theo are no longer speaking after a fight during their last meeting. Nell eventually contacts her father, but by that point it is too late. Nell is already at Hill House, where she is driven to her death by hanging. Steven sees Nell in his apartment and brusquely tells her she's "got everybody listening now." Steven's short-tempered indication that he is finally ready to listen to Nell has no impact. Although she opens her mouth to speak, she is unable to say anything before Steven gets a call, informing him of Nell's death. At this point Steven is confronted by Nell who opens her mouth and emits an inhuman howl. As the sound crescendos Nell's eyes become milky and her face and teeth begin to decay. Finally heard after years of being silenced, the only sound she can make is an animalistic scream of anguish, the force of which causes her to disintegrate before Steven's eyes.

Together with being silenced, Nell also experiences invisibility, one of the most powerful examples of which occurs in sixth episode "Two Storms." As a child during a storm at Hill House and as a ghost during the storm that occurs on the night of her wake, Nell screams for her family but they neither see nor hear her. When the family find child Nell she says: "I was here. I was right here. I was right here, and I was screaming and shouting and none of you could see me, why couldn't you see me?" The scene moves to Luke and Steven standing by Nell's dead body. When they leave the room, the camera reveals Nell to the viewer. She takes the form of the ghoulish specter that haunted her childhood—the Bent-Neck Lady—the terrible premonition of her future, standing beside her own open casket. The voice of child Nell is transposed over the scene, reiterating she was there the whole time, but nobody could see or hear her. This repeats the strategy of using child Nell's voice to communicate for Nell as an adult and emphasizes her moments of invisibility to poignant effect. The queerly temporal nature of Nell's life is emphasized in this episode where time bleeds in one continuous scene comprised of just five shots—a filmic device that made this episode a particularly innovative one. It feels like no accident that these unusual and ambitious filming strategies were engaged at the mid-season episode that centers on a character that most obviously destabilizes linear narratives.

Nell's ghostliness is a further disruption of linear time and a specifically queer one, as "[t]he ghost, in inhabiting both spiritual and material dimensions, also carries associations of ambiguity and contradiction, attributes that help to explain its prominence in queer theory."[14] Terry Castle's work on *The Apparitional Lesbian* points to the paradoxical nature of the ghost: "though non-existent, it nonetheless appears."[15] Castle observes how queer women have been absent from heterosexual, male-authored scholarship, erasing the lesbian from the archives of literary criticism and history. Jacques Derrida has also written about the paradox of the ghost and its relationship to identity through his notion of hauntology[16] which "attributes to the ghost a paradoxical status as neither being nor non-being that brings into view the spectrality of identity."[17] Nell's ghostly presence is reflective of the instability of her identity and creates a particular temporal paradox as the Bent-Neck Lady that haunts her as a child transpires to be the spectral image of herself after death by hanging. As Muñoz suggests, "[q]ueerness … never fully disappears; instead, it haunts the present"[18] and Nell is haunted by the ghost of herself, the mental impact of those hauntings rendering her as invisible when she is living, as she is when she is dead.

Existing outside of straight time—namely in a temporal place where others cannot see her—is indicative of Nell's inability to conform to normative temporal structures. Maria Mulvaney, writing about Elizabeth Freeman's research on queer time[19] in the context of Emma Donaghue's "Slammerkin," notes that "bodies only become socially legible through their adherence to structural norms of temporal regulation" and that those who are not in sync with such rhythms "lose their social legibility and come to exist in a queerly spectral relation to normative time and the dominant social order such temporality regulates."[20] In Jackson's novel, critics have noted that "Eleanor barely exists within a social structure at all"[21] and this feature of Eleanor Vance's life is captured through Nell's uneasy relationship with time in the Netflix series. Queerness itself has a legacy of being hidden and coded, as Muñoz writes it is "rendered illegible," becoming "lost in relation to the straight mind's mapping of time ... to a world of heterosexual imperatives, codes and laws."[22] It is a particularly queer sensation to feel lost within heteronormative temporal structures, to feel invisible, to find oneself erased from records of history or absent from stories. These moments of invisibility are emphasized by Nell's lack of control over her own story.

Positioning Steven as the narrator of a reimagining of a novel which is told predominantly through the mind of Eleanor Vance strips her narrative voice away from the Netflix series on one level, reflected within the diegesis of the show, where he also becomes the author of Nell's story. Steven is the unreliable witness, incapable of accounting for Nell's experiences because he fails to recognize them for what they are. Steven is an author who misremembers and takes liberties with his storytelling for commercial gain, and in doing so he strips the queer female characters of their agency, a failing that also extends to Theo's story, when he writes about Luke discovering the Hill House basement that was unearthed by Theo. Steven could never properly account for the stories of Theo and Nell, because he cannot see their stories accurately. Gary Needham observes that "[q]ueerness is something that is literally out-of-time in the sense of being urgent, immediate and on the outside"[23] and as such it is something that other characters fail to recognize when it is in front of them; it exists on the peripheries of straight time. Steven spends much of the series disavowing the supernatural and fails to recognize as ghostly the specters that literally stand in front of him.

In the penultimate episode Hugh, Steven's father, explains to him that the witness marks on a clock tell the story of the piece if one knows how to read it. Freeman points out that "schedules, calendars, time zones, and even wristwatches are ways to inculcate what the sociologist Evitar Zerubavel calls 'hidden rhythms,' forms of temporal experience that seem natural to those whom they privilege."[24] The clock being fixed seems normal to Steven, because he cannot read its witness marks, or see its hidden rhythms. He reads the person fixing the clock as part of the general maintenance and upkeep of Hill House, as opposed to the spectral presence his father later reveals it to be. This blindness to the specters of Hill House is caused by Steven situating himself firmly within temporal logics that afford him the privilege of economic success, his role as narrator and scribe and the one who subsequently inherits Hill House. He shares similarities with Nell's therapist who tells her she has nothing to fear from Hill House, another man of science and reason sending Nell on a quest that will ultimately lead to her death, with no comprehension of the horrors she experiences. Steven's vasectomy might indicate he has little interest in "reproductive temporality," but this is not driven by his resistance to patriarchal structures, rather his affirmation of them. He explains his decision was due to a fear of his "rotten genes," the maternal lineage of "sensitive" women and what he views as his father's indulgence of those experiences.

For Steven, there is safety in being able to retreat to the logics of linear time and he is never truly impacted by queer time. Luke is the one male sibling who noticeably feels the impact of queer temporalities because he too, as a heroin addict, does not exist within straight time. Halberstam notes that drug addicts live in "rapid bursts" and are subsequently characterized as "immature and even dangerous"[25] as a result. Luke is the also the one most psychically connected with Nell, likening his experience of her death to withdrawal. When Luke is in Hill House as an adult and in proximity to Nell, he is susceptible to drugs, underscored when Nell is positioned as enabling his addiction by taking him to a dealer before he goes into rehab. The implicit suggestion at the end of the series is that Luke may at last successfully recover from his addiction, but Nell has no such privilege or respite. Even in death she must inhabit spaces that create a temporal paradox, a queer destabilizing force that haunts and violently disrupts the linearity of the narrative. Shirley, the eldest sister, has psychic dreams, but they appear to be contained to the realm of sleep. By contrast Nell's dreams "slip" ("Steven Sees a Ghost"), her night terrors the broken image of her future death. Nell's temporal disruptions are emphasized by the frequent association between her character and clocks. When she experiences sleep paralysis as a child with the Bent-Neck Lady suspended over her prone body, the sound of the clocks ticking in the house intensifies. She is unable to free herself from the ravages of time. Moments before her death she places a pocket watch on the dashboard of the car. She talks about time leaving her fragmented when the family are gathered together in the Red Room—"Everything's out of order. Time, I mean" ("Silence Lay Steadily")—and in death she is dropped excruciatingly through history, each jerk of the rope bringing her to a moment when the Bent-Neck Lady appeared before her younger self. Passing through time literally kills her.

Writing about Jackson's novel, Ashton describes Eleanor Vance as a character who "desires above all things a kind of normalcy she has never known,"[26] something Nell pursues in the series, but even when she tries to realign herself with straight time her attempts ultimately fail. Nell's fleeting moment of respite comes when she meets sleep technician Arthur Vance. Their entire relationship is condensed into pivotal moments in time that reflect Halberstam's paradigmatic markers of life experience. Through a series of vignettes, the viewer is shown Nell's first date with Arthur, their first time having sex, the proposal, their wedding and Arthur's death. The whole span of their relationship is compressed into less than fifteen minutes of screen time. The music that plays over the montage is The Great Escape's "All You Got Is Gold"[27] which begins with the line "let us go where time runs slow." Musical references to time reappear when Nell dances with ghost Arthur before her death as Patty Griffin sings, "here's a little time we can borrow."[28] Arthur proposes during a New Year countdown, the shot focusing on the seconds ticking past. Nell's happiness can only ever be fleeting, her attempts to exist within normative temporal logics thwarted in the most violent way when the Bent-Neck Lady returns at the precise moment of Arthur's untimely death.

In Jackson's novel the narratology evokes Eleanor's uneasy relationship with time, she lives "in a complex combination of the past and the (sometimes certain, sometimes subjunctive) future, rather than in the present."[29] The series captures this temporal incoherence with Nell by making her moments of happiness compressed and fleeting, giving her horror far more screen time than her happiness. When mortician Shirley takes on the unenviable task of working with Nell's body for her open casket wake, she uses a picture of Nell on her wedding day as a reference and says, "I'm going to fix her" ("Open Casket"), implying that when Nell was a bride she was at her most beautiful, her most "normal." The fact that Shirley also does Nell's makeup on her wedding day, given her work with dead bodies, is an eerie premonition of the tragic end to Nell's life and marriage. Nell's wedding is referenced again when she returns to Hill House on the evening of her death. She puts on her mother's nightgown—reminiscent of the wedding dress in color and style—and greets ghosts of her family, all of whom are dressed as they were on her wedding day. She is allowed one final dance with Arthur, one fleeting dream, before she dies—pushed from the tower by the ghost of her mother, Olivia Crain.

Nell is constantly on the outside, and through her own experiences Theo has a certain kinship which allows her to make connections with Nell that others cannot. In "Two Storms" it is child Theo who stands with Nell outside the circle formed by the other family members, holding Nell's hand. However, unlike Nell, Theo can be pulled inside normative time and find a place within it, at which point her kinship with Nell dissolves. As the rest of the family move towards Theo, Nell slips away from her. Unlike Nell who is invisible, Theo is always seen and seeing—something she tries to resist by wearing gloves which protect against psychic abilities triggered through touch. As a child she wears thick jumpers, unlike her other siblings, adding layers to protect her from the cold lure of Hill House. The viewer learns through Hugh Crain that her mother guessed Theo's sexuality when she was eight. On several occasions Theo hides—slipping off with a bridesmaid at Nell's wedding and later with Shirley's husband, Kevin Harris. In both instances she is found almost immediately, in direct contrast to Nell who can't be found even when she never left. By virtue of being seen, Theo's queerness becomes a destabilizing temporal force in the lives of those around her, who try to protect themselves from its impact. Theo's mother gives her the gloves that she continues to wear into her adult life, and she becomes a threat to Shirley's marriage, privy to Kevin's secrets and sharing a moment of thwarted intimacy with him during the storm at Nell's wake. As such, Theo can be read as representing anxieties around the threat of queerness to the institution of marriage. These anxieties become more explicit when Theo finds the broken model of Shirley's "forever house" ("Eulogy") and the gruesome ghost of Olivia Crain who worked on her own "forever house" before her death, crawls from a grave, approaching Theo as she cowers by the ruins of Shirley's dream home.

Theo's presence in this scene, befitting of an episode called "Eulogy," places the one explicitly queer character at the site of the destruction of the dream, aspirational family home. However, a moment that could have taken queer readings much further becomes instead a pivotal turning point in Theo's life which realigns her with normative time. Theo's horror becomes her role in the breakdown of Shirley's marriage, and it is that fear and desire to right her wrongs that enables her to feel again. By extension Theo most exemplifies Jackson's preoccupation with female characters for whom "anxiety is one of their most defining characteristics."[30] In resetting her life and realigning herself with normative time, Theo disavows the void that touching Nell's dead body plunges her into, a state she describes to Shirley as like "floating in this ocean of nothing." She describes how the darkness and emptiness of Nell spread through her skin, pulling her into a similar place of bleakness that not even the touch of eventual girlfriend Trish Park could expunge. Kevin, the model of the faithful husband (he rejects Theo's advances), appears like "a light in the darkness" and causes Theo's realignment in a way that is not queer at all, but neither is the culmination of Theo's story. The feelings Theo describes when she touches Nell are most obviously a sign of mental illness, depression in particular, something Jackson frequently explored in her novels through female characters confronting "an inner emptiness."[31] However, Theo's feelings of shame, grief and fear have queer resonance and through Nell's unhappy fate she experiences the consequences of living outside of normative time first hand. She subsequently changes her life course and in doing so becomes the embodiment of queer anxiety.

These queer anxieties are particularly noticeable in the depictions of sex in the series. Nell and Theo are the only two characters whose moments of intimacy are shown onscreen. Nell and Arthur are quickly replaced by a close-up shot of Hollywood darlings Cary Grant and Grace Kelly in Hitchcock's *To Catch a Thief*, indicative of the fact that Nell's fleeting moments of happiness have a certain artificiality, situated in the realm of fantasy. By contrast, Theo's pleasure is explicitly seen and heard, with one shot capturing a moment of climax with Trish. However, for Theo sex is not liberating. In Theo's final sex scene Hill House becomes a ghoulish doppelgänger of her girlfriend Trish, who performs oral sex on her as hands creep out of the bedding and suffocate Theo. The violence entwined with Theo's experiences of sex manifest most notably when she is plunged back in time whilst investigating the case of a young foster girl who sees a monster she calls Mr. Smiley. In a disturbing scene, Theo experiences the sexual assault of her child patient, stretched out on the couch in the family basement. She discovers Mr. Smiley is more truth than fiction, the image of a smiling face etched into wood grain on the ceiling which the child patient has turned into a spectral body to cope with the trauma of sexual abuse perpetuated by her foster father. This temporal rupture is particularly jarring for the LGBT viewer, given the disproportionately high levels of sexual violence experienced by queer women. When Nell revisits the past in the last moments of her life, each drop into history is another tug of the noose, and when Theo uses her psychic ability to revisit the past, she is sexually assaulted. The site of Theo's assault, an ostensibly attractive family home, represents the threat those spaces can pose to queer people, and within it, Theo's experience of time becomes violent.

There are no women who escape the violence of the family home completely unscathed. Critics have commented on the "disturbing maternal space"[32] of Hill House in Jackson's novel and much has been written from a feminist perspective, exploring the "psychological danger Jackson perceived (not only to herself, but to all her female characters) in masculine control over women's lives"[33] and the function of madness and motherhood in the Gothic, much of which is beyond the scope of this analysis. When thinking about queer temporalities, Olivia represents an extreme example of the mother who seeks to protect their children from the harms of the world in a way that ultimately inhibits them, attempting corrective strategies that lead to violence and death. Like the specter of Hill House's original owner Poppy Hill, who met her husband in an insane asylum, Olivia's quest for family becomes horrific, her character the embodiment of the oppressions of straight time. In Nell's case her mother wants to protect her innocence by trapping in Hill House for eternity, "the daughter ... confined within a house that functions figuratively as the externalized maternal body, simultaneously seductive and threatening."[34] In a macabre attempt to keep children "safe" from the dangers of adulthood, Olivia regresses to a childlike state, becoming the host of the tea parties Nell longs for, serving rat poison in Nell's cup of stars to Abigail, the young child of Hill House caretakers Horace and Clara Dudley, and her own children Luke and Nell, culminating in Abigail's death. In Theo's case it is Olivia who provides her with gloves to protect her from the horrors of the world. When Olivia nears the end of her life the Gothic preoccupation with "familiar domestic interiors" that "transform into confining sites of mental and psychological peril"[35] are most acute, and her vision of the "forever house" becomes a dark and disturbing foreshadowing of exactly what Hill House will become for Nell, Olivia and Hugh.

Reading Nell queerly with the context of Jackson's original work makes her moments of muted invisibility even more disturbing, as the series erases any of Eleanor Vance's subtextual queer longing. Even absent heavily coded sapphic qualities to Nell however, she still reads as a queer character, always on the periphery of the family unit, one who feels the oppressions of existing outside of normative, linear time. By contrast, Theo ends the series as "happily queer"[36] but with such happiness comes assimilation through homebuilding and monogamy. It is capitulation to, as opposed to resistance of, hetero/homo-normative social constructs that enables her to cast off her gloves and start a new life with Trish. If the intention of the series is to hold up such assimilative family structures in a hopeful fashion, I'm not sure it succeeds. The Crain family are reunited through infanticide and suicide, the living Crain children saved from the murderous forces of Hill House through their father's promise to take his own life. Nell is a forever child in a forever house, consigned to fragmenting herself through time, always present but never seen. For the dead, the ghosts may walk together, but their deaths were driven by the insanity of Hill House's original owners. For the living, queerness can exist only within certain "safe," normative parameters. Flawed and dogmatic ideals of family values constructed by the people those paradigms privilege appear to be as oppressive and stifling in today's America as when Jackson explored them in the fifties.

NOTES

1. Richard Pascal, "Walking Alone Together: Family Monsters in *The Haunting of Hill House*" *Studies in the Novel*, Vol. 46, No. 4 (2014), 464.
2. Pascal, 466.
3. Shirley Jackson, *The Haunting of Hill House* (London: Penguin Classics, 1959), 246.
4. Jackson, 9.
5. Jackson, 45.
6. John G. Parks, "Chambers of Yearning: Shirley Jackson's Use of the Gothic," *Twentieth Century Literature* 30, no. 1 (1984), 25.

7. Jack Halberstam, *In a Queer Time and Place: Transgender Bodies, Subcultural Lives* (New York: New York University Press, 2005), 6.
8. Halberstam, 2.
9. Halberstam, 4.
10. Eve Kosofsky Sedgwick, *Epistemology of the Closet* (Berkeley: University of California Press, 2008), 71.
11. Lucie Armitt, "'The Gothic Girl Child'" in *Women and the Gothic: An Edinburgh Companion*, edited by Avril Horner and Sue Zlosnik (2016), 62.
12. *Ibid.*
13. Halberstam, 4.
14. Paulina Palmer, "'Queer Spectrality" In *The Queer Uncanny: New Perspectives on the Gothic* (University of Wales Press, 2012), 67.
15. Terry Castle, The Apparitional Lesbian (New York: Columbia University Press, 1993), 46.
16. Jacques Derrida, *Specters of Marx: The State of the Debt, the Work of Mourning, and the New International* (New York: Routledge, 1994).
17. Rebecca Munford, "'Spectral Femininity" in *Women and the Gothic: An Edinburgh Companion*, edited by Avril Horner and Sue Zlosnik (Edinburgh: Edinburgh University Press, 2016), 121.
18. Jose Esteban Muñoz, "Feeling Brown, Feeling Down: Latina Affect, the Performativity of Race, and the Depressive Position," *New Feminist Theories of Visual Culture*, Vol. 31, No. 3 (2006), 684.
19. Elizabeth Freeman, *Time Binds: Queer Temporalities, Queer Histories*. Duke University Press, 2010.
20. Maria Mulvany, "Spectral Histories: The Queer Temporalities of Emma Donoghue's 'Slammerkin,'" *Irish University Review*, Vol. 43, No. 1, 2013, 158.
21. Ashton 272.
22. Jose Esteban Muñoz, *Cruising Utopia: The Then and There of Queer Futurity* (New York: New York University Press, 2009), 73.
23. Needham 152.
24. Freeman, 3.
25. Halberstam, 5.
26. Hilarie Ashton, "'I'll Come Back and Break Your Spell': Narrative Freedom and Genre in the Haunting of Hill House," *Style 52*, no. 3 (2018), 269.
27. *The Great Escape*, All You Got Is Gold (2017).
28. Patty Griffin, "Heavenly Day" (2007).
29. Ashton, 275.
30. Hague, 76.
31. Hague, 74.
32. Pascal, 469.
33. Carpenter, 38.
34. Rubenstein, 317.
35. Weinstock, 56.
36. Ahmed, Sara, *The Promise of Happiness* (Durham: Duke University Press, 2010), 115–120.

VI

Comparative Hauntings

"Came Back Haunted"

International Horror Film Conventions

Thomas Britt

As a haunted house narrative, Mike Flanagan's series *The Haunting of Hill House*[1] begins as a structuralist endeavor from the ground up. The voice-over narration that frames the series quotes the source novel of the same name by Shirley Jackson, identifying the physical components from which the house is built: bricks, wood and stone among them. The speaker of this narration is Steven Crain (Michiel Huisman), an author and skeptic whose childhood experiences in the haunted house are now a framework that guides his literary composition and informs his theories of how his dysfunctional family suffers from denial of shared mental illness.

The tradition of Gothic fiction, and its clash of impenetrable settings with irrational occurrences, challenges the explainable systems by which Steven Crain lives. As a writer of haunted house narratives, within a haunted house narrative, Steven seems fated to be a victim of his own certainties from the moment the viewer meets him. He explains to a potential subject for his new book on haunted places that there is no such thing as the supernatural, merely a preternatural mode consisting of natural events not yet understood by humans. His identification with the preternatural is itself a sign that he faces doom, as historically "the inherent conceptual instability of the category of preternatural phenomena predestined it for collapse into the sturdier categories of the natural and supernatural."[2]

The central dramatic conflict that defines Flanagan's take on *The Haunting of Hill House* is that between determinism so strong that it transcends natural orders of time and space, and conjectural causality in which characters/viewers wonder if actions taken within the narrative might defeat the seemingly forgone conclusions that characters face. Complicating this conflict further are transgressions that characters commit within collisions of fate and choice. This is a narrative formula long-established within Gothic fiction, as influential writers such as Edgar Allan Poe at times explored the evasion or denial of supernatural interventions. For example, Ben P. Indick observes that "Poe's writing is of true psychological content; the grotesque behavior actually represents the normal distorted by emotion to the extreme. Even his allegorical tales follow a line of inevitability and deterministic logic. His weird stories are as rational as his detective stories, and his use of the fantastic must be understood as the ultimate extension of this logic."[3]

This essay examines *The Haunting of Hill House* as a product of a related, more recent set of influences, which are international genre films about domestic horrors, dreams, and the afterlife. I argue that in stories about homes turning horrific, in which characters vacillate between accepting a doomed existence and attempting to escape their fate, there are certain fundamental traditions and techniques that live within (and evolve throughout) the genre works that house them. I will present four international genre films spanning from the mid–1960s to 2010 as works that influence the formal execution and narrative imagination of *The Haunting of Hill House*, a series produced for Netflix: *Kwaidan*,[4] *Kairo*,[5] *El Orfanato*,[6] and *Inception*.[7] For each work, I will identify visual and narrative approaches to transgression, causality and determinism that inform a cross-cultural cinematic style and lead to several conventions present in Flanagan's series.

The first is "The Black Hair," one story of the anthology *Kwaidan*, directed by Masaki Kobayashi. Adapted from a literary source (Lafcadio Hearn's "The Reconciliation" [1900]), "The Black Hair" features "a young samurai of Kyoto" that abandons his wife for the pursuit of money and power. The domestic setting in which "The Black Hair" takes place, testifies to economic ruination and accompanying physical decay. Without money, there is no upkeep and no advancement. The samurai rejects his loyal wife's offer to work at her loom day and night to improve their situation. He rejects the remote possibility of future stability for a guarantee of instant self-advancement, marrying a new wife whose family enjoys a wealthy status. Thus, his transgression is a dual infidelity: he doesn't believe in his wife's worth and he strays from her.

The samurai's transition from his former, poor life to his new, rich one is visually punctuated by a scene of water rushing over rocks. Water imagery is ubiquitous in Japanese horror films, in part an outgrowth of the spiritual significance of water within Shintō. Though "Black Hair" is not obviously a ghost story at the point of the narrative in which the samurai marries his new wife, the rushing water portends a spiritual or supernatural reality that the samurai will later face.

In "Black Hair," the circumstances of the samurai's present wealth are intercut with the circumstances of his former poverty. For example, his selfish new wife's outing to purchase fine fabric precedes a scene of his selfless former wife's toiling away at the loom. Despite his not being faithful to her, she continues on in the activity that she pledged to do to improve their situation. The frequency with which the former wife is intercut with the present action corresponds to a narration informing the viewer that the samurai has grown to realize "how unfair and how ungrateful he had been" to his former wife. There is also a creeping feeling of uncertainty about the context for these reappearances. Are the scenes of the former wife memories of past action, information about present action, or a form of idealized characterization?

This overview of "Black Hair" consists of a few elements that appear in *The Haunting of Hill House*, especially the association of water with significant moments of transition and the intercutting between past and present. Rain and hail storms function significantly within the horrific events that take place at Hill House. And the narrative arrangement of past and present within Flanagan's series is designed to create questions about causality that build to one of the series' most satisfying and thought-provoking revelations: that of the apparent simultaneity of past, present and future. In the tenth and final episode of the first season, "Silence Lay Steadily," Steven's deceased youngest sister Nell Crain (Victoria Pedretti) speaks to her living siblings from the spirit world about realizing that time does not function as a domino-like causal chain but rather that "our moments fall around us like rain or snow or confetti."

Yet it is the final minutes of "Black Hair" that most inform the narrative trajectory of *The Haunting of Hill House*. The samurai, now a bit older, returns to Kyoto and finds the place as "silent as a cemetery." Though his dwelling remains in a state of disrepair, he discovers his wife sitting in a darkened room at her wheel. She asks, "How did you find your way to me, through all those black rooms?" His acknowledgment that she hasn't "changed a bit" should be a warning that her appearance is too good to be true. This impossibly perfect characterization persists as she blames herself for his misdeeds. At this point, the dialogue comments on a pattern that the plot has already established through temporal intercutting, when he says he wants to discuss the past, present and future with her. She responds, "I also feel as if this were a dream" before expressing her desire to keep him "forever." Their romantic nocturnal reunion turns into a sudden and inescapable horror show when the samurai awakens to find that his wife is a rotten corpse, and then a skeleton, whose black hair attacks him. In moments, he too, ages towards death.

Similarly, a few episodes of the first season of *The Haunting of Hill House* conclude with characters in the present-day returning to the abandoned house where the horrors of the past occurred. All of the Crain's present circumstances are shaped in some way by connections to these past horrors. The central traumatic scene was the fateful night that the mother Olivia Crain

(Carla Gugino) succumbed to madness/ghostly forces and poisoned to death Abigail (Olive Elise Abercrombie), the young daughter of house workers Mr. and Mrs. Dudley (Robert Longstreet and Annabeth Gish) before throwing herself from a great height in a plunge to her death.

Though none of the grown Crain children remember and/or sufficiently understand the specifics of that night, the long shadow of that night extends to all of their present afflictions. Steven's insistence on authoring and shaping the narratives of ghost stories, Nell's paralyzed panic in the night, her twin brother Luke's (Oliver Jackson-Cohen) drug addiction, their sister Theo's (Kate Siegel) overwhelming sensual perception, and sister Shirley's (Elizabeth Reaser) conflicted fixations on death and filial integrity—all of these stem from the point of no return their mother reached that night in the mysterious Red Room of Hill House. Father Hugh (Timothy Hutton) does know the truth, but has spent decades shielding his children from the horrors he witnessed.

When all of the Crain's converge at the house in present day, each of them experiences fantasies that the house and the Red Room present to them as a means of keeping them locked in, each one isolated in his or her own double-edged reverie. As is made clear in the dialogue of the series, this room is the house's stomach that digests its human contents. The reason for the family's reunion is that adult Nell met a fate similar to her mother. Nell's suicide by hanging is the catalyst that results in her siblings and her father returning against their better judgment to the site of their shared trauma. And as the older, wiser samurai of "Black Hair" returned to his bridal chamber and was greeted by his perfectly submissive, perfectly preserved wife, so too the grown Crain clan are threatened with distortions generated by the Red Room. Only through Nell's sacrifice are her siblings apparently saved. Her spirit self awakens them from their fantasies and saves them from dying and/or rotting in the Red Room, whose walls are blackened with mold.

The next film that prefigures *The Haunting of Hill House* is another Japanese film, *Kairo* (2001), directed by Kiyoshi Kurosawa. *Kairo* includes many ominous signs shared by Flanagan's series, though the apocalypse of *Kairo* is a national (and perhaps global) one, in contrast to a localized familial disintegration. *Kairo* includes two plots that are distinct for much of the film's running time before joining together. The first is the story of Michi (Kumiko Asô), who works with her friends Junko (Kurume Arisaka) and Yabe (Masatoshi Matsuo) at Sunny Plant Sales in Tokyo. Their associate, Taguchi (Kenji Mizuhashi), has gone missing while working on a computer disk, and Michi's investigation turns horrific. The parallel story is that of Kawashima (Haruhiko Katô), a lonely young man whose attempt to connect to the Internet reveals a mysterious website. His desire to know more about the site leads him to Harue (Koyuki), a post-graduate student of computer science, whose encounter with the website damns her, despite her technical knowledge.

In *Kairo*, characters' transgressions and the major theme of the film involve submitting to isolation. Here the Internet and the monitors that characters use to display Internet content, serve a function similar to that of *Haunting of Hill House*'s Red Room. The potential for connecting with others online is a specious form of socialization, and the insidious effect of using these portals is to remain isolated and subject to illusions. In truth, the users are there to be consumed by that technology. At its time of release, Kurosawa's film was prescient in its warning about machines that could dial up any fantasy. It must also be noted that the Internet of *Kairo* is not a fun place, at all. Apart from some humorous user agreement visual comedy when Kawashima is first attempting to sign on, the Internet is a desolate, isolating power that Kurosawa surrounds with an abundance of associated metaphors.

One of the key visual metaphors is a transparent curtain or veil. Whereas *The Haunting of Hill House* relies on hard structural elements such as doors, stairs, and especially brick walls to convey characters' passages and confinements, the portals and barriers of *Kairo* are often obscure. When Michi finds Taguchi in his apartment, viewers recognize the apartment from a glitch-y, spectral perspective of the interior that opened the film. Michi sees Taguchi behind a cloudy transparent curtain that hangs in his apartment. The effect of this combination of production design and blocking is twofold. First, Michi and Taguchi appear to the viewer as featureless silhouettes, shapes against light, which heralds the doomed state of *Kairo*'s disappeared citizens, who are transfigured into blackened spots on the floors and walls where they once sat or stood. Second, Michi steps through a portal that echoes the "see through" screens of the Internet in *Kairo*. On the other side of the curtain, she finds that Taguchi has hanged himself.

The visual metaphor that establishes a system of understanding for the second story is a computer program that Kawashima notices in Harue's lab. The program, which consists of pale dots against a dark backdrop, seems innocuous in its screensaver-like appearance. Harue explains that if two dots get too close together, they die, but if they get too far apart, they're drawn closer. She calls it "a miniature model of our world.... But only the grad student who designed it understands it," warning, "I wouldn't suggest staring at it for too long." To drive the point home, she later comments on the modern lack of connection among humans, saying that like these dots, individuals "all live totally separately."

Kairo's use of a computer program and computer scientist to explain such mysterious processes that govern the story-world is indicative of Japanese horror film's attitudes toward rules. As Chris Pruett has pointed out, "This is a central theme in Japanese horror; we can almost always see some sort of logical progression based on some implied set of rules that govern the way all things work.... An equally central theme is that the rules and the reasoning behind them may not be something that people can grasp, and thus one must accept that which he cannot explain."[8] Despite Kawashima's enthusiasm for life and optimism about finding Harue as a companion, Harue expresses her belief in the designs that departed spirits have for the bodies and souls of the living: "Ghosts won't kill people. Because that would just make more ghosts. Isn't that right? Instead, they'll try to make people immortal. By quietly trapping them in their own loneliness."

This dramatic scenario, of being trapped into isolation, defines mother Olivia Crain of *The Haunting of Hill House*. The house and its more deceptive spirits such as the insane Poppy (Catherine Parker) are full of deterministic persuasiveness, causing Olivia to see the horrors that await her children. As the ghost of Nell later testifies, present and future are intertwined. Olivia becomes convinced that she needs to keep her children close to her, in the house and especially out of the dark night beyond the house. The tragic irony of this wish is that the interior of Hill House is by any measure a much more dangerous place at night.

Olivia's wish goes beyond protecting her children in the short term. In "Screaming Meemies," episode nine of the first season, the viewer realizes how fully Olivia has foreseen the precise horrors that will define the lives of Nell and Luke when they grow up. Tellingly, the episode begins with Olivia cradling the young twins and expressing her desire to "freeze them—keep them just like this forever." The Red Room is the location in which Hill House traps susceptible characters in isolated circumstances. The total narrative trajectory towards that room, that figurative stomach, is heavily indebted to *Kairo*.

The mysterious website that Kawashima investigates with Harue, which is also the force that ensnared Taguchi, is called The Forbidden Room. The Internet connection exposes users to The Forbidden Room, which exhibits a series of trapped individuals existing in various isolated conditions ranging from still, to slow-moving, to suicidal. These individuals appear to be victims of the ghosts' plot that Harue articulates.

In the library, a graduate student explains to Kawashima that "the spirit, or consciousness, the soul, whatever you want to call it, it turns out the realm they inhabit has a finite capacity. Whether that capacity accommodates billions or trillions, eventually, it will run out of space. Once it's filled to the brim, it's got to overflow somehow, somewhere. But where? The souls have no choice but to ooze into another realm."

Hugh Crain offers a similar theory about how kids' dreams are "like an ocean" that spill out into waking life. He offers this explanation to convince young Nell (Violet McGraw) that her vision of a horrific Bent-Neck Lady is merely a spill, not an active threat. It is *Kairo*'s dramatization of how such oozes are announced and contained, however futilely, that completes the strong parallel between that film's events and the formal execution of *Haunting of Hill House*. Rooms associated with spirits are marked with red tape on doors and other openings. These are the other forbidden rooms of *Kairo*: The most dangerous rooms are the red rooms.

Hill House, up to and including The Red Room, suffers from the blight of black mold as a literal and figurative sign of the house's unfit condition. In the season one finale, "Silence Lay Steadily," Steven has a vision of his wife Leigh's pregnant body as black mold spreads outward from her stomach. In the same episode, Hugh is infected with the black mold more quickly and wholly than Leigh while in the hallway outside the hungry, antagonistic Red Room. Such is the fate of characters in *Kairo*, when overwhelmed by spirits and reduced to black ash against surfaces.

Kawashima, like Michi a true friend and encourager and therefore partially defended against isolation, eventually walks into a red room. There he encounters a spirit who proclaims, "Forever ... Death was eternal loneliness. Help. Help. Help. Forever. Death was eternal loneliness." Face to face with the eternal loneliness he has tried to deny, Kawashima loses the light that illuminates him. By the film's end, he and Michi have escaped to a ship on the ocean. In the last moments of *Kairo*, Michi says she has "found happiness" here with her "last friend in the world." She fails to see what the viewer sees. Kawashima is now a black spot on the wall. The final horror of *Kairo* is that Michi is trapped in an illusion from which she might not awake.

To be subject to isolation and illusion is arguably a passive transgression. Such is the apocalyptic threat of a technologically mediated existence. Other films in the grouping that influence *The Haunting of Hill House* are more hopeful, suggesting that there is a way to gain agency within a deterministic framework, even if the conclusion necessitates self-sacrifice. *El Orfanato*, a Spanish film directed by J.A. Bayona, is a classical Gothic horror film featuring many of the same narrative elements as *The Haunting of Hill House*, including a haunted house being renovated by a family, a devoted mother that poisons children, and a plot of "parallel perception" in which trauma extends beyond the natural limits of time and space.

The transgression of *El Orfanato* is ignorance, in that the central character Laura (Belén Rueda) does not initially know or understand significant information that would help her to avoid some of the horrors she experiences. Laura's unawareness contrasts with other aspects of the story over which she does appear to be in control. She is back at her childhood home, an orphanage that she is renovating with her husband Carlos (Fernando Cayo), where she intends to someday take care of "five or six" kids. She is a loving mother to adopted son Simón (Roger Príncep), who does not know he is adopted or that he is HIV positive.

Simón's illness haunts the family insofar as his time with them might consequently be limited, as well as being a part of himself about which he is unaware. In a story for which ignorance is a threat and a transgression that leads to suffering, Simón's unawareness puts him on unsteady ground. Yet writer Sergio G. Sánchez and director Bayona create a parallel current of agency for this mother and son, introducing several visual representations of changing awareness/knowledge within the first act of the film. These symbols of changing awareness are associated with the ocean and include a lighthouse, a cave, and a trail of seashells dropped for Simón's new imaginary friends to follow back to the home.

There is also within *El Orfanato* a dichotomy of real versus imaginary that separates Simón from his parents and further divides wife from husband. Specifically, Simón's new friends are ghosts who have the power to actively participate in the real world, but his parents mistake these friends as entirely imaginary. And Laura exhibits faith in unseen things, whereas Carlos is a skeptic. These conflicts, between the real and imaginary and the seen and unseen, underpin the most pivotal sequence within the narrative, which includes the appearance of Tomás (Óscar Casas), a little boy wearing a mask, and the disappearance and presumed death of Simón.

Simón may have gone missing from his parents' home, but Laura senses him in visions and dreams, which occur by and in the water. She also hears a banging sound coming from somewhere inside the house, which if understood as an effect Simón's disappearance, is a narrative event much like the banging sounds that young Theo (Mckenna Grace) and young Shirley (Lulu Wilson) experience in "Open Casket," episode two of the first season of *The Haunting of Hill House*. In "Screaming Meemies," the second to last episode of the season, Poppy shares with Olivia her troubling dream involving her disabled son banging on the walls, which seems to be a dream that has spilled over into the lives of the young Crain sisters.

Laura's quest to discover what happened to Simón is not only a journey from ignorance to knowledge, but also one of transforming the way she sees the world long after her childlike perspective is gone. A medium named Aurora (Geraldine Chaplin) encounters the spirits of children, who were Laura's friends in her youth. Their torment comes from having been poisoned by Tomás's mother decades earlier as retribution for an incident that led to his death. Aurora explains to Laura that "when something terrible happens, sometimes it leaves a trace, a wound that acts as a knot between two time lines. It's like an echo repeated over and over, waiting to be heard." Of that other time, that hidden world that now houses Simón as well, she tells Laura that she must first believe, and then she will see. This kind of actualization is a variation on the wisdom Olivia shares with young Shirley in "Open Casket": "When you're little, you learn how to see things that aren't there. And when you grow up, you learn how to make them real."

Laura's reunion with Simón involves all of these aspects of her changing awareness. Early in the film, Simón is next to Laura in bed and repeatedly asks her "Can I wake up?" as a means of waking his mother up. She responds, "You are already awake. You can get up now, darling." Later, in the third act of the film, Laura realizes that she was responsible for Simón's disappearance and death, having accidentally trapped him in a storage space from which he fell to his death in a forgotten basement. Then, in her grief, she sees his impossible awakening, which is reminiscent of the perfectly preserved abandoned wife from "Black Hair." Logically, there is no way that Simón could be in such good condition months after his disappearance. Yet Laura's fantasy of her boy finds him as if he's just woken up from sleeping. To try to keep him with her, she says "This is a fantasy, my darling, like a nightmare…. Close your eyes and keep on playing." When neither he nor she can sustain that fantasy, Laura accepts her fate. She kills herself to wake him up again, and in her death, she becomes the guardian to all of the poisoned children, the exact number of children she pledged to take care of in her renovated orphanage.

Laura of *El Orfanato* and Olivia of *The Haunting of Hill House* fulfill the same dramatic situation, which is "Self-Sacrifice for Kindred,"[9] though they differ from one another in that Laura's penitent sacrifice is a balm for suffering spirits and Olivia's is fuel for further suffering.

Olivia's growing obsession with protecting her children, fatally blinds her to how that will harm them. The distortion that allows that obsession to grow was induced by outside forces, and has everything to do with getting thoroughly disoriented about the veil between dreams and waking-life. As previously established, in *The Haunting of Hill House*, dreams are explained as threatening to children because they are oceanic in their power and can spill over. But Nell is plagued by a vision of her own fated, hanged corpse well into adulthood, and Olivia's undoing is also a burden of dreams that weighs heavily on the rest of her family for decades to come. For this reason, the final recent genre film that must be discussed is Christopher Nolan's science-fiction heist film *Inception*.

The protagonist of *Inception*, Cobb (Leonardo DiCaprio), was once a man with a unique (and technologically/chemically mediated) process for creating convincing new worlds within dream states. As a thief, this process enables him to extract corporate secrets. But his closeted transgression is that he was once so deep down into a dream state with his wife Mal (Marion Cotillard) that he implanted an idea in her head that they needed to kill themselves to wake up. This worked, insofar as they woke from dreaming to resume their lives as parents to two young children. Yet the idea he implanted corrupted Mal forever and possessed her waking state. Cobb reveals, "She was possessed by an idea … that our world wasn't real. That she needed to wake up to come back to reality. That in order to get back home we had to kill ourselves." Mal's desperate attempt to convince Cobb to die by suicide with her created conditions in which Cobb's subconscious mind is haunted by her. Also, as a result of Mal's scheme, Cobb cannot reenter the United States to see his children. *Inception* is a loud and busy film, but because nearly everything within the narrative takes place in dream worlds without consequence, the only dramatic question that truly matters is whether Cobb will succeed in another, much more complex inception/implantation scheme that if successful, will allow him to see his children again.

The Haunting of Hill House is uncannily similar to *Inception* regarding dream delusion. In "Screaming Meemies," Olivia recounts to Hugh her visions of her children as dead adults, describing them as "dreams that feel more real than life." Minutes later, the lying spirit of Poppy enacts an inception on Olivia, encouraging her to "wake" the kids from their "worst, sick, sad dreams." This implanted information, combined with the camera's increasing attention to Hugh's bottle of rat poison, sets up the fateful tea party in which Olivia nearly kills young Luke and Nell and does kill a reclusive neighbor girl, sweet Abigail.

Poppy's instruction to "wake them and keep them safe" contains the subtext of a mercy killing and implants in Olivia a subsequent vision in which little Nell and Luke recite monologues outlining their fixed future horrors as Nell asks, "what if I dream that you kill us" and "would you wake us up?" ("Screaming Meemies"). Even after Olivia realizes what she has done, faced with Abigail's poisoned dead body on the floor of the Red Room, she cannot escape the web of dreams, asking the spirits who already inhabit the house to wake her up. As was the case with Mal, that particular inception, an inversion of dreaming and waking, causes Olivia to leap to her death. Both women become subconscious projections that prevent their families from moving on.

Kwaidan's "Black Hair," *Kairo*, *El Orfanato*, and *Inception* are works in which haunted characters experience digressions from "absolute reality."[10] Caught within battles of fate and choice, the individuals within these stories embody transgressions encompassing infidelity, isolation, ignorance, and implanting deadly thoughts in the minds of others. These characters experience parallel worlds of immaterial forces that expand the causes and consequences of their actions. *The Haunting of Hill House* advances these global horror/genre conventions for Netflix, one of the largest global video services, which is itself not so unlike the Red Room. Netflix is another unreal portal that appears to offer the world to those who sit in fascination of it, individually catered to, binging and consuming, but also being ingested.

Notes

1. *The Haunting of Hill House*, directed by Mike Flanagan (2018; Los Gatos, CA: Netflix, 2018), Streaming.
2. Lorraine Daston, "Marvelous Facts and Miraculous Evidence in Early Modern Europe," *Critical Inquiry* 18, no. 1 (1991): 99.
3. Ben P. Indick, "King at the Literary Tradition of Horror and the Supernatural," in *Bloom's Modern Critical Views: Stephen King, Updated Edition*, ed. Harold Bloom (New York: Infobase Publishing, 2007), 7.
4. *Kwaidan*, directed by Masaki Kobayashi (1965; New York: The Criterion Collection, 2010), DVD.
5. *Kairo*, directed by Kiyoshi Kurosawa (2001; Hertfordshire, UK: Arrow Video, 2017), Blu-ray.
6. *El Orfanato*, directed by J. A. Bayona (2007; Burbank, CA: Warner Home Video, 2008), Blu-ray.
7. *Inception*, directed by Christopher Nolan (2010; Burbank, CA: Warner Home Video, 2010), Blu-ray.
8. Chris Pruett, "Chris' Guide to Understanding Japanese Horror," *Chris's Survival Horror Quest*, June 12, 2011, http://horror.dreamdawn.com/?p=54891.
9. Georges Polti, *The Thirty-Six Dramatic Situations* (Franklin: James Knapp Reeve, 1921), 75.
10. Shirley Jackson, *The Haunting of Hill House* (London: Penguin Group, 1987), 3.

The Beloved Haunting of Hill House

An Examination of Monstrous Motherhood

RHONDA JACKSON JOSEPH

A mother's love for her children is often portrayed as a positive expression of nurturing and caring for vulnerable offspring. This appropriately termed "mommy myth" is described by Keira V. Williams: "Women, according to this myth, were incomplete without children, and Good Mothers devoted their entire beings—body, soul, time, and mind—to their children."[1] Mothers dote on their children, lavishing them with affection and sacrifice things they need and desire in order to care for the offspring. Adrienne Rich further asserts, "Mother-love is supposed to be continuous, unconditional. Love and anger cannot coexist. Female threatens the institution of motherhood."[2] What this depiction often omits is the societal issues and circumstances that can distort these feelings and twist them into fear and acts of violence by mothers towards their children. Renee Lee Gardner affirms, "In the urgency of this moment, Morrison exposes the trauma of motherhood in a society where not all mothers can meet the criteria set by ideological constructs for that role."[3] The lived experiences and the impacts of these experiences for women who lie outside the lens of privilege that motherhood is often viewed through is largely ignored. These omissions can lead to a faulty and unwarranted assignation of monstrosity in cases where the true monsters are never named.

Olivia Crain in the Netflix original series *The Haunting of Hill House* was slowly provoked to the attempted murder of her children by societal ills such as the outright rejection of supernatural phenomenon, drug addiction, and mental illness. Compounding this pressure was the overwhelming notion of an ideal enactment of motherhood and the impossibility of living up to that ideal. An attentive mother in the beginning, Olivia grew increasingly distracted by the devastating futures her psychic abilities revealed for the two youngest of her beloved children and the physical and spiritual influences these abilities had on her own mental state. The haunting elements in her home and her sensitivity to those elements helped drive her over the edge of maternal affection and into the realm of monstrous mother.

Similarly, Toni Morrison's *Beloved* drew a haunting portrait of a mother, Sethe Suggs, who made a life altering decision to commit filicide in order to avoid the enslavement of her daughter. Desperation drove her away from loving her child in the ways prescribed by ideal motherhood to the only way she could imagine protecting the baby from the torture of slavery. When her murdered daughter, whom she named Beloved, returned as a supernatural entity (or possibly the physical manifestation of Sethe's guilt) to haunt her mother, Sethe accepted the ensuing descent into madness and the haunting as her burden to bear and punishment for having killed the girl. She sacrificed her social standing and mental stability to ensure the girl's spirit was vindicated. Sethe understood her neighbors thought her a monster—she agreed with their assessment.

Olivia and Sethe's individual descents toward monstrosity and the repercussions of that journey for both women require examination of the outside forces instigating their movement from maternal affection into what is deemed to be monstrous motherhood. Williams further explains, "It's worth pointing out the obvious here: this ideal does not describe the lives of the vast majority of mothers. Indeed, given its clear class requirements, it is wholly unavailable to most of them. So where are the voices of those millions of mothers who reject, resist, and redefine the maternal ideal?"[4] The clear parallels that can be drawn between the ways both Olivia and Sethe, within different worlds and overcoming dissimilar obstacles, fell victim to these various elements and the societal pressures placed on mothers by unrealistic boundaries of what makes a good mother create an urgency to re-examine the ways monstrosity is assigned to maternal experiences and the label's impact on re-defining the ideals of motherhood.

Domestic Foundations of Monstrous Motherhood

The portrayal of Olivia and Sethe as monstrous mothers has a foundation rooted in one of the most prolific tropes in the horror genre: the haunted house. The homes where the women's stories took place present morose representations of the women themselves. Haunted domiciles set forth a situation in which the traditionally female domestic sphere of the home symbolizes an area that should provide safety and comfort for the inhabitants, much in the way the ideal mother is expected to do. Adrienne Rich contends, "The idea of maternal power has been domesticated. In transfiguring and enslaving woman, the womb—the ultimate source of this power—has historically been turned against us and itself made into a source of powerlessness."[5] The mother in a domestic setting serves the same purpose as her womb during pregnancy: she is safety and home for her children. In haunted houses, however, the haunted structures ultimately prove to be weak protectors in the ways they can be successfully penetrated by the supernatural. The domiciles are relentlessly attacked by supernatural and other forces until they are weakened and ineffectual against the intruding forces. Eventually, the safe haven is breached, and the occupants are destroyed. This domestic breakdown is critical in the regressions of Olivia Crain and Sethe Suggs. The failure of the home to protect its inhabitants mirrors that of the flesh and blood mothers they represent, when these women also become powerless and fail to achieve maternal perfection in protecting their children.

The visage and interior of Hill House work in tandem with the viewer's impressions of Olivia Crain: regal yet whimsical, strong and fragile, and more than a little otherworldly ("Steven Sees a Ghost"). Embellished architectural details such as turrets and delicate stained-glass windows on the staircase landing create the same combination of timeless elegance and delicacy Olivia inspires. She represents an easy eccentricity that is reflected in Hill House. The fabrics of Olivia's clothing are reminiscent of the opulence of the home's woodwork and design, yet she wears the flowy, silky garments as if they are simple cotton. These intricacies and contrasts are further shown in Olivia's architectural plans for their forever home, which become more elaborate and repetitive as the plot moves along. Olivia's plans are guided by her desire to create a haven for their family to spend time together. As she explains to Shirley, "I see a family running to a dinner table, from all three directions. This dining room is the heart of the house. Everything flows in and out. Every house needs a heart, and this is ours because it's where we spend the most time together" ("Open Casket"). Olivia viewed herself as the heart of her family, where everything flowed through. Serving in this acute function, Olivia sought to shield her children from the events happening at Hill House and from unpleasantness in general. She argued with Hugh about having allowed Shirley to keep the kittens the girl found after the animals died unexpectedly. Olivia also hid the source of her migraines from them, instead allowing the true nature of the house to first be filtered through her and altered before presenting to her children ("Open Casket"). As Hill House neared success in its endeavor to break her down, Olivia recognized that if she were destroyed, her family would also be destroyed.

The first time Sethe saw her new home at 124, her experience was filtered through that of her familial positioning. She described the home as belonging to her mother in law, Baby Suggs. The house was previously filled with life, prayer and cheerfully soothing gatherings of people.[6] The welcoming environment was apparently attributed to Baby Suggs' occupancy and position in the community. The betrayal of her neighbors when Sethe's owner came to get her caused Baby Suggs to retreat into quiet contemplation, yet she still served as a maternal figure for Sethe. When the older woman died, Sethe inherited the home and the legacy to raise her children there, but she did not obtain the older woman's positive imprint on the home. Without the living maternal influence of her mother in law, Sethe and the home fell into disrepair. The house at 124 instead began to be described by the characters in the book in ways more similar to Sethe's decline towards self-castigation than the way they previously remembered the house. The house became spiteful[7] and loud.[8] The townspeople then gave the house, and its inhabitants, a wide berth, choosing to pass quickly[9] because they knew of Sethe's misdeed and that the house was haunted by her act. Their exile of her for her ultimate sin included the house. The home, as her proxy, was later described as "In any case the personal pride, the arrogant claim staked out at 124 seemed to them to have run its course."[10] Once Denver reached out to their neighbors and asked for help for her mother, Sethe was seen as having been broken by the haunting and her excommunication.

Framing Olivia and Sethe's stories within the boundaries of haunted house stories depict parallel story lines that show once beautiful and welcoming homes falling prey to supernatural parasites that the walls filled with maternal and familial love were unable to keep at bay. Concurrently, their human counterparts struggled with their own alterations from loving and caring mothers into monstrous renditions of their former selves. Olivia's efforts at protecting her children firmly positioned her as a good mother who wanted her children to be healthy and happy. Sethe's arrival at her mother in law's home with her new baby presented her as a hopeful young mother looking forward to raising her children under the wise tutelage of Baby Suggs. Neither woman was able to retain her footing on the path to positive enactments of motherhood because the parallel stories of their haunted houses and their equally haunted existences demand their destruction and transformation in remaining true to the trope of invaded femininity and by extension, the sullying of the motherhood ideal.

The Supernatural and Societal Issues as Catalysts of Monstrosity

Wanting her children to be safe and self-assured are two hallmarks of how ideal motherhood is defined. When the Crain family was first introduced to Hill House, Olivia Crain presented the question, "Everybody alive?" ("Steven Sees a Ghost"). Her words carried the simple desire of a caring mother to make sure her family had survived their trip to Hill House, where the Crain family would live while she and her husband refurbished the house to re-sell it. The utterance also provided foreshadowing to the grisly events that would befall them through the course of the story. Olivia loved her children and nurtured the individual gifts each displayed, even to the detriment of her own care. She patiently explained to her daughter, Theo, that she understood the extrasensory talents the young girl exhibited. The loving mother confided in Theo that variations of the same talent ran through three generations of women in their family. When Olivia presented Theo with her first set of gloves to help inhibit her sensitivity, Theo walked away confident in the shared knowledge of maternally inherited gifts other people likely would not understand. Olivia, however, found herself more exposed with her confession, as she verbalized the weakness through which the supernatural forces inside the house could attack and ultimately consume her ("Touch").

The attacks preyed on Olivia's desire to protect her children and facilitated circumstances that would create uncertainty and a perversion of that protection. This process led to an aspect in the depiction of monstrous motherhood in horror films that Kelsey E. Henry describes thus, "Every iteration of mommy horror tugs at the 'invisible thread' between mother and child. This is the thread of connection that supposedly exists and persists effortlessly, binding mothers to their children."[11] The thread symbolizes the umbilical cord shared between mother and child and also represents the spiritual connections mothers are expected to have with their children. When used as plot devices in horror films, those threads become severed and represent "the danger of maternal love that metastasizes, becoming violently overwrought."[12] Henry further ascertains that while loving her children is something a good mother would do, loving them too much becomes problematic. Olivia's experiences in the house created a palpable tension within her that showed itself to be irritable and fraught, creating tension on the thread that connected her to her children.

The house escalated its attack on Olivia through nightmares where she saw Nell and Luke as adults, both dead. Nell had grown from a child constantly asking for her family to simply see and listen to her into a sensitive adult plagued by sleep agoraphobia. While seeking treatment for the condition, she met the man she would marry. The sudden death of her young husband and the ensuing distance between her and her remaining family members in the aftermath exacerbated Nell's conditions ("Screaming Meemies"). During her grieving, Nell continued to suffer from depression and anxiety which were dismissed by her family in their efforts to live their own lives untainted by what they saw as a debilitating illness that Olivia passed down to Nell. Hill House called out to Nell through the same mentally weakened doors through which it had harkened to her mother and revealed Nell's ultimate fate. Luke appeared in Olivia's vision as a corpse, dead from a drug overdose. While the family lived in Hill House, the only ones who believed Luke when he said he had experienced the supernatural were Nell and Theo, the latter only because of her own preternatural abilities in knowing and experiencing such things. Hugh was skeptical and told Luke, "Big boys know the difference between what's real and what's imaginary" ("Twin Thing"). The other household members either ignored Luke's reports or, as Olivia did, remained oblivious to them.

Olivia did not ignore her youngest son out of malicious intent, though her negligence precipitated dangerous effects on his development and contributed to his later addictions. Olivia's inattention, instead, resulted from her ongoing war against the house. She experienced debilitating migraines and other physical manifestations of Hill House's attacks that not only broke her mentally but also spiritually. The escalating battle between Olivia and Hill House ensured an inability for her to allocate energy in providing the attention her children needed. Her worsening condition resulted in more time spent in bed. She also increasingly isolated herself from her family. Olivia sought this detachment, in part, to protect her family from the outbursts she began to suffer. As a result, her children felt her absence. Shirley began to take on more domestic responsibilities in the home. Theo oversaw the twins during various playtime adventures throughout the house. Steven helped Hugh with the renovations. Olivia's family was accustomed to her "spells," and the ease with which they carried on as usual while she mentally moved further away from them was evidence of their acceptance. Nell and Luke, as the youngest children, missed her the most. Nell was the typical baby of the family who tended to blend into the background as everyone else moved around her. Luke was not quite the baby, but young enough to question his invisibility within the household. He could not understand why neither his father nor his mother would protect him from the supernatural events surrounding him, and he felt abandoned. This abandonment led to his drug addiction, as he mused, "Mom never came back, but other things when I was a kid—they came back. That's why I started using in the first place. To keep those things away" ("Twin Thing"). The image of Luke that assails Olivia, him lying dead from a drug overdose, was one that showed a highly possible outcome for the life of a child assaulted by the supernatural and plagued by the absence of parental protection or explanations.

Olivia Crain understood what was happening to her in Hill House without any outside explanations, even as she was helpless in fighting the influences. As frightening as it must have been to see and feel herself spiraling downward into the soul of Hill House, Olivia remained focused on the safety of her family, specifically Nell and Luke. She knew her twins were extra sensitive and the world around them would not be kind to them. No one would understand Nell's inability to fully understand and cope with her mental conditions and Luke's powerlessness against standing up to reality and avoiding drugs. She also understood that there were no structures in place within their family or society as a whole that would provide adequate treatment to either of them that would save their lives. She became increasingly unable to understand that the safety of her children was not absolute. When the ghost of Poppy Hill appeared to her and asked her infamous question, "I'd bet you'd do anything for them, ain't that so?" ("Screaming Meemies"), Olivia was already well on her way to becoming mired in the futility of trying to keep her youngest children, Nell and Luke, safe forever. Hill House then assailed her with panic in whispered admonishments to save her children. Emily L. Stephens offers an apt conclusion, "Olivia wants to preserve her perfect, innocent children as they are now, before age and sorrow and pain and illness can sink their teeth into them."[13] Not seeing any other way out, she decided the only way to protect them was to kill them while they were young.

Where Olivia struggled in hopelessness at the thought of killing her children, Sethe succeeded in keeping one of her children safe by exercising the only agency she had to wield—that over her young daughter's life. Renee Lee Gardner indicates "Sethe's *unbeing*—her sacrifice of Beloved—is powerful precisely because her romantic, self-protective, and maternal choices are not merely personal; they are irrevocably tied to the political structures of maternity vis-à-vis the state."[14] Sethe's actions are marred by the looming reality of slavery, a life opened to few choices and completely sanctioned by the law. Sethe was a runaway slave who escaped from her owner and sought freedom for her and her children. Her husband, Halle, had gone missing during their escape attempt, but Sethe had to move forward, alone, for the sake of her babies. When the owner caught up with Sethe, she decided in the moment to kill all the children, but only succeeded in killing Beloved before she was stopped. Sethe loved her children. They had been born within a marriage to a man of her choosing and she had no reason to harbor ill will towards them. This act was not one instigated by a mother who could be named a victim of forced motherhood reacting in violence, as indicated by Adrienne Rich: "Instead of recognizing the institutional violence of patriarchal motherhood, society labels those women who finally erupt in violence as psychopathological."[15] Although Sethe did not choose violence to remedy the forced motherhood that often occurred through the rape of slave women, nor through the haze of insanity, she did make a conscious decision to utilize death as a means of safety. She mused, "Beloved, she my daughter. She mine. See. She come back to me of her own free will and I don't have to explain a thing. I didn't have time to explain before because it had to be done quick.

Quick. She had to be safe and I put her where she would be."[16] As a woman held in bondage, and with no way to escape her circumstances, Sethe chose merciful maternal violence to protect her daughter from the mandated vicious attacks the girl would have endured during a lifetime as a slave.

Sethe's choice ushered in disastrous repercussions for her remaining children. Her sons left home as soon as they could and never returned, frightened of their mother's having attempted to kill them and her successful murder of their sister.[17] Sethe and her younger daughter, Denver, lived as recluses in their town because the townspeople knew Sethe killed Beloved during her botched escape from slavery and their house was haunted with the residue of her crime. This isolation from their community created tension between Denver and Sethe, as Denver rightfully blamed her mother for their alienation. Sethe understood the exile as the price of her choices, and she seemed to accept it. She also accepted the manifestation of her guilt: the haunting of her home and her spirit by Beloved. Sethe was able to withstand her new existence, even at the cost of her relationship with Denver, because having the sovereignty to make the decision to kill her oldest daughter was worth the consequences.

As a result, Sethe was unable to continue being the loving mother to the child who stayed behind and survived whom Paul D. witnessed upon his arrival to their home: "After Paul D. finds Sethe after eighteen years of enslavement and wandering, he notes the intensity of Sethe's love for Denver, her second daughter."[18] Further, Sethe was unable to imagine herself enduring pregnancy and motherhood again under the overwhelming conditions of slavery. Paul D. asked her to have a baby with him. "Although she laughed and took his hand, it had frightened her ... but mostly she was frightened by the thought of having a baby once more. Unless carefree, motherlove was a killer."[19] Sethe seemed convinced she would never hurt Denver but she could not be sure she would not hurt another baby, especially since slavery was still legal and the baby could become enslaved.

Sethe succumbed to Beloved's haunting and extracting of her soul through torture because she felt she owed it to her older daughter for having killed her. Denver witnessed the slow death of her mother, saddened by the way, "once Sethe saw [the scar], fingered it and closed her eyes for a long time, the two of them cut Denver out of the games."[20] Where Denver once had a mother who took care of her and tried to balance her attention between the ghost of Beloved and her living daughter, she now had a mother who became enslaved by the fleshly embodiment of her dead daughter. The younger girl resorted to asking the townspeople for help with food for her and her mother as Sethe declined. The reversal of roles between mother and daughter allowed Denver to feel sympathy towards her mother as she watched her serve Beloved in ways that embarrassed Denver. She no longer blamed

Sethe for her inattention or the decision she made; however, she had turned caregiver to the mother who should have instead taken care of Denver—the monstrous mother who killed one daughter had decided to abandon the younger daughter by allowing the murdered daughter to kill her.

Redefining Monstrous Motherhood and the Ideals of Motherhood

Adrienne Rich offers valuable insights into the construction of ideal motherhood and provides a critical framework for understanding the realities of motherhood juxtaposed against those ideals; however, the extrapolation is incomplete. The context in which Rich discusses motherhood provides a privileged discourse that superficially describes the experience from the viewpoint of women with special circumstances. As stated by Emily Jeremiah, "Like Rich, then, Morrison is concerned with how individuals are interpellated by institutions in violent and oppressive ways, and with maternal murder as a desperate reaction to this interpellation."[21] Jeremiah further ascertains that Rich and Morrison do not call for absolution of these monstrous mothers, but for an understanding of the circumstances that led to their decisions to kill their children.

By extension, Jeremiah's argument allows room to include Olivia Crain as another mother with special circumstances. Although few circumstances could accurately compare in scope to being enslaved, Olivia's existence as a woman unduly affected by illnesses typically disputed or ignored by the general population is a modern form of marginalization. Olivia was psychically and physically affected by living in Hill House. Her family knew she suffered from migraines and anxiety, but they did not understand the totality of her conditions as she deteriorated. Hugh insisted she was simply stressed with the home rehabilitation, yet he did not consider her reactions might be worse than they ever were previously. By the time he realized what was happening to Olivia, it was too late to help her ("Screaming Meemies"). There were no apologies given for Olivia's actions and her family was forced to live with the truth that she killed Abigail and herself and tried to kill Nell and Luke. Olivia was fated to live in Hill House forever, as a spirit separated from the family she loved, until Nell and Hugh joined her after twenty-six years of exile.

Olivia and Sethe fell victim to the impossibilities of living up to the ideal of motherhood. Cursed with an ability to see the future but also marked by mental illness which distorted her interpretation of that future, Olivia accurately foresaw the fates of her youngest children. Although she killed Nell, she ultimately set into motion events that led to her also saving Luke's life. Had Olivia not experienced alienation due to her own struggles with mental illness and psychic abilities most people did not understand, she would not have felt hopeless at the thought of her children suffering in the same ways that would lead to their deaths in early adulthood. Sethe, under the backdrop of slavery, killed the daughter she loved to protect her. Had there been no slavery, Sethe likely would not have murdered Beloved. The two mothers were ostracized from their households and communities because of their actions. Olivia's family began the road to forgiving her for having committed suicide and the pall her mental illness draped over them only after they had the last encounter with Hill House and clearly understood what Olivia had endured while sacrificing herself to ensure they escaped the house on two separate occasions. Sethe does not present as a character who wanted or deserved to be forgiven for her deeds, but she did believe that "the return of Beloved means that she can erase some of the pain she inflicted upon herself by killing her child."[22] She sacrificed her reputation and sanity to pay restitution for filicide. Although the townspeople ultimately decided she had suffered enough and they banded together to exorcise Beloved, they allowed her to live under the negative influence of Beloved for years.

The banishment of Olivia and Sethe as monstrous mothers was unwarranted. Gardner offers an accurate summation of their experiences: "The contradictions and impossibilities of [slave] motherhood were intentionally constructed to be so. By conditioning citizens to blame mothers—despite their lack of control—for their failure to protect their children, nations establish as necessary the [racial] inequities which, ironically, caused the conditions that garnered blame in the first place."[23] Both women sought to protect their children and failed because of societal attitudes and sanctioned criminality that rendered them invisible victims throughout their suffering. No one was willing to see their need for help, therefore none was offered. The insidious cyclical pattern of blame, guilt, and expulsion for mothers when harm comes to their children ensured Olivia and Sethe would be propelled towards destruction—destined to harm their children, and then relegated to deterioration underneath the shame and sacrifice of their struggle of their sins. Can they truly be deemed monstrous if they are also sufferers?

Their experiences reflect those of numerous real-world mothers who struggle underneath the weight of unreasonable maternal perfection set against a backdrop of collective problems such as poverty, illness, racism, sexism, and ableism. These exertions and attempts to provide maternal nurturing for their children despite an infinite number of circumstances working against them binds many mothers to one another. Shirley Jackson indicates in her original novel "silence lay steadily against the wood and stone of Hill House, and whatever walked there, walked alone."[24] However, in their shared experiences, efforts, and failures, Olivia, Sethe, and other imperfect mothers should not be demonized. Rather, they are better embodied within the Jackson derived final quote from Flanagan's *The Haunting of Hill House*: And those who walked there, walked together ("Silence Lay Steadily").

NOTES

1. Keira Williams, "'Between Creation and Devouring.'" *Southern Cultures* 21 (2): 27–42: 29. doi:10.1353/scu.2015.0019: 29.
2. Adrienne Rich, *Of Woman Born: Motherhood as Experience and Institution* (New York: W.W. Norton and Company, 1976): 46.
3. Renee Lee Gardner, "Subverting Patriarchy with Vulnerability: Dismantling the Motherhood Mandate in Toni Morrison's Beloved." *Women's Studies* 45 (3): 203–14. doi:10.1080/00497878.2016.1149029: 203.
4. Williams, 29.
5. Adrienne Rich, *ibid..*: 67.
6. Toni Morrison, *Beloved* (New York: Vintage Books, 2004): 102.
7. Morrison, 3.
8. Morrison, 199.
9. Morrison, 5.
10. Morrison, 294.
11. Kelsey E. Henry, "Monstrous Motherhood," ThePointMag.com, n.d., Accessed April 1, 2019, https://thepointmag.com/2015/criticism/monstrous-motherhood: 5.
12. Henry, 2.
13. Emily L. Stephens, "The Haunting of Hill House Has the Seductive Lure of Dream Logic," www.avclub.com, October 14, 2018, Accessed April 1, 2019, https://www.avclub.com/the-haunting-of-hill-house-has-the-seductive-lure-of-dr-1829736592.
14. Gardner, 205.
15. Rich, 263.
16. Morrison, 236.
17. Morrison, 242.
18. Sandra Mayfield, "Motherhood in Toni Morrison's Beloved: A Psychological Reading." *Journal of Scientific Psychology*, January 2012. Accessed April 1, 2019, http://www.psyencelab.com/uploads/5/4/6/5/54658091/motherhood_in_toni_morrisons_beloved.pdf: 5.
19. Morrison, 155.
20. Morrison, 283.
21. Emily Jeremiah, "Murderous Mothers: Adrienne Rich's of Woman Born and Toni Morrison's Beloved," *From Motherhood to Mothering: The Legacy of Adrienne Rich's Of Woman Born* (New York: SUNY, 2004), pp. 59–71: 65.
22. Mayfield, 6.
23. Renee Lee Gardner, "Subverting Patriarchy with Vulnerability: Dismantling the Motherhood Mandate in Toni Morrison's *Beloved*." *Women's Studies* 45 (3): 203–14. doi:10.1080/00497878.2016.1149029: 210.
24. Shirley Jackson, *The Haunting of Hill House* (New York: Penguin, 2006): 1.

The Madwoman in the Parlor

Motherhood and the Ghost of Mental Disorder in Hill House and Hereditary

MARIA GIAKANIKI

In recent years, more and more horror films and TV series are distinguished by rich subtext and multiple "readings" regarding their content, constituting a new, sophisticated type of screen horror which has nearly become a subgenre. When they were first released in 2018, *The Haunting of Hill House* by Mike Flanagan and *Hereditary* by Ari Aster were thoroughly discussed and considered as significant, even controversial, samples of this new horror trend. Indeed, both of them are complex representations of the contemporary American family, in the recent tradition of many current horror films, where themes, plot and characters are multi layered and profound, reflecting social and cultural anxieties of the contemporary world. In this context of modern horror filmmaking where the primary purpose is not only to chill our bones by creating the sense of terror and awe, but also to address important social issues, *The Haunting of Hill House* and *Hereditary* employ the supernatural element as a medium to explore problematic family relationships, while also use it as a metaphor for the perpetual cycle of family trauma and (generational) mental disorder, thus constituting themselves as significant samples of modern domestic horror.

One of the prevalent themes of both *The Haunting of Hill House* and *Hereditary* is troubled motherhood and the burden of maternal responsibility towards the welfare and safety of the children, which can lead to intensely stressful emotions of fear and guilt and, in cases where metal illness may lurk, to a distorted perception of reality. In both works, an emotionally troubled and, very likely, mentally disturbed mother comes in contact with the supernatural, while she attempts to kill her own children at some point of the story, most probably in order to protect them from a vague threat. However, trying to prevent their children from suicide, drug addiction, (inherited) mental illness and death, Olivia Crain in *The Haunting of Hill House* and Annie Graham in *Hereditary* plunge into madness themselves and, instead of saving their children, they end up precipitating or even causing their destruction. In this case, the mother figure becomes a monstrous figure—challenging and/or reversing the image of the normal, sane, rational, emancipated model mother of the present-day western world.

In this respect, the purpose of this essay is to discuss and compare *The Haunting of Hill House* and *Hereditary*, in terms of the themes of troubled motherhood and mental disorder; to manifest the ways in which Olivia Crane and Annie Graham act and react towards their environment, the various stages of their growing mental instability, the nature of the danger they feel their family is threatened by, the ambivalence of the threat (whether it is real, imaginary or indeed supernatural), the consequences of the two mothers' actions and the ways that trauma, grief and mental disorder recycle within the generations.

Madness and the gothic have been very closely intertwined since the 18th century and taking into consideration the element of exaggeration that distinguishes both these notions, the theme of madness is an, inevitably, main component of gothic fiction...[1] At the same time it should be acknowledged that there have been no easy or clear definitions of "madness" in science or literature.[2] Thus, what can be considered as its depiction in art and fiction, is usually the representation of various forms of aberrational and uncontrollable behaviors that are typically considered to belong to the wide and often debatable spectrum of "mental illness." In this respect, the latter is an enduring as well as fascinating feature of gothic narratives, offering glimpses into the darkest and most unconscious parts of the human mind, in particular in cases where literary imagination makes use of medical experience.

Ambivalence of mental illness, namely in cases where the subjective experience of the, possibly, mentally disturbed protagonist may or may not respond to the real facts, has been a post–Victorian variation of the "gothic madness" trope. In particular, female characters who appear to be mentally unstable and thus unconsciously resort to psychological projection of their own inner "demons" onto the external environment, is a favorite motif in (proto)modern gothic horror: Henry James's *The Turn of the Screw* (1898) and Shirley Jackson's *The Haunting of Hill House* (1959) are among the most prominent and finest examples of this recurrent trope. Also, a legendary horror film of the '60s, Roman Polanski's *Rosemary's Baby* (1968), features a psychically troubled pregnant woman who has to deal with certain sinister supernatural incidents which may or may not be products of her (possibly) unbalanced mind. Other more recent examples of troubled motherhood dealing with the supernatural are Alejandro Amenábar's *The Others* (2001) and Jennifer Kent's *Babadook* (2014); in the latter the element of the supernatural is also inextricably linked with family trauma, and serves as a medium in order to portray intense emotional experiences and psychic discomfort associated with the disruption of family normality.

In this context and following the long tradition of supernatural ambiguity and complicated, mentally unstable heroines, Mike Flanagan's Netflix series *The Haunting of Hill House* introduced an intriguing, complex female character, that of Olivia Crain (played by Carla Gugino), the mother of the Crain family. Throughout the series, Olivia balances between (apparent) peace of mind and emotional turmoil, wisdom and irrationality, reality and imagination, while she is "haunted" by deeply rooted maternal anxieties, which will lead her to commit the hideous crime of infanticide, thus becoming "monstrous."

Olivia's character is depicted in a contradictory manner throughout the series. She appears to be alternately strong and frail, wise and unbalanced, loving and hostile—but above all human and tragic. The signs of her growing mental instability make their appearance gradually in the first episodes and they come out fully blown towards the end. From start to finish of the story, Olivia's eldest son, Steven, refers repeatedly to his mother's mental illness, her committing suicide and his fear that this disease is "hereditary," while his father, Hugh, insisted that Hill House's sinister energies got a hold of his wife weak nerves and constitution.

Olivia's appearance in the first episode's flashbacks reveals that she is very caring towards her family, an open minded, cultivated woman and a free spirit who does not intend to entrap her children's minds ("Steven Sees a Ghost"). Nevertheless, she also has a strong sense of familial and especially maternal bonds, which is verbally expressed in such cases as in Shirley's traumatic experience with the dead kittens when Olivia tries to stress to her the symbiotic connection between the kittens and their mother and the ways that death transforms loving relationships. Moreover, Olivia, being an architect herself, designs the family's dream "forever house" (in an interesting almost uncanny analogy with Annie in *Hereditary*, who has made a miniature house of the family's real one)—an "ideal" version of Hill House. Despite Olivia's affectionate nature, which is manifested during the first episodes through flashbacks of the family's summer sojourn in Hill House, there are also distinct signs of her fragile nervous system as well as her possible susceptibility to the invisible world: she has severe migraines on a regular basis while at some points she is "feeling" cold spots in the house—which suggests a special connection with spirits and hauntings. Olivia admits to her daughter

Theo that this trait is inherited from her grandmother and that they share that special characteristic, while she also tells Nelly during the storm scene in a later episode that *she* sees strange (meaning "dead") people too—hinting to what could be a special ability but also a symptom of schizophrenia in the family ("Touch"; "Two Storms"). The boundaries between mental illness and connection with the invisible world are blurry and indistinct throughout the series; what could be considered as a "gift," can also be a disease, ending up working as a curse.

In the fifth episode, which is a dramatic climax for the series, we start seeing Olivia under a more "disconcerting" light. In her locket she has photos of the twins which she shows Nelly, thus expressing her special preference for the little ones, her youngest children ("The Bent-Neck Lady"). In the same episode Olivia becomes very upset with her youngest daughter, because she believes she wrote on the wall of Hill House, while at the same time she has a fit of migraine. She claims that they have to take care of the house as it does with them—as if it was a live organism—alluding to an identification of the family with Hill House ("The Bent-Neck Lady"). Furthermore, this is a stereotypical conflicting maternal image: love but also strictness. The sentence "come home Nell" that was found on the wall when the latter was a child, will be morbidly realized as Nell will indeed go back to Hill House as an adult, all alone, in order to confront the past and her own nightmarish visions of the "bent-neck lady." Back in Hill House, Nell imagines her mother giving her the very same locket of her childhood, a token of unconditional love, which the depressed but now also deranged young woman feels like a noose around her neck—indeed maternal love and parental protection can be suffocating and strangling. Nell sees her mother pushing her to the gap and then she hangs herself. Nell *is* the bent-neck lady and in this vision where she has totally lost contact with reality—this is also indicated by the camera's switch between the objective point of view and Nell's subjective point of view—Olivia was the one who "urged" her to kill herself, and this is obviously connected with Nell's traumatic memories of her mother ("The Bent-Neck Lady"). From this point on, both Olivia and Nell will alternately appear as spirits to the rest of the family, as they have sort of "merged"; they are strongly connected to each other due to their having committed suicide inside Hill House. After her physical death Olivia haunts, literally or figuratively, all her children, inevitably reminding them of their orphaned, traumatized childhood.

In the remaining episodes, Olivia's symptoms of mental illness presented in the flash backs, either these interact with the house's haunting past or not, escalate. While searching for Nelly during the storm scene, Olivia has a proper "encounter" with the ghosts of the previous residents, while her husband sees her wandering like a madwoman ("Two Storms"). Another sign of Olivia's rapidly deteriorating mental state, are her designs of the new house which do not make any sense and then her unconscious attempt to injure or even murder her husband by holding a knife on his throat while he is sleeping (echoing Annie Graham's attempt in *Hereditary* to set her children on fire during the night). This scene probably expresses the breach in the couple's relationship: nothing is as perfect as it seems and Olivia might indeed feel an unconscious hostility towards Hugh, who had at some point early in their marriage left her or because, in reality, they are so different personalities. Olivia drew the "forever house" again and again, which mirrored her own psyche or the Crain family itself: dark, chaotic, full of psychological horrors and secret corners. The emotional torments of Olivia culminate when the little twins trigger (in what she thinks is a dream from which she must wake) her sense of maternal guilt, asking her whether she would save them from "the dark." At that point, her deeply buried maternal angst comes to the surface.

In a state of paranoia and disconnection, Olivia lets the "spirits of the house"—the ghost of Poppy Hill, the clinically insane flapper which appears as Olivia's dark, inner voice—warn her against her husband and urge her to commit something unspeakable: poison the twins so as to protect them from a worse misery—as she believed. Undoubtedly, this is not something that she did consciously. The tragedy in *The Haunting of Hill House* takes place in the form of a self-fulfilled prophecy. Olivia, either due to her special insight or her maternal concern exacerbated by her pathology, has previously "seen" the horrible future of her grown-up twin children, Nelly and Luke, by having either a vision or a hallucination: Nell has committed suicide while Luke has become a drug addict. Thus, she will try to spare them this terrible fate by killing them while they are still very young and untouched by the great miseries of life. As Mrs. Dudley tells her, a mother should follow her instinct regarding the protection of her children from the outer world, and this is what desperate Olivia attempts to do, transforming to a monstrous abject mother[3] who will not let her children grow up, echoing what she herself had said about the inextricable bond between kittens and their mother. But what if this traumatic experience itself is what eventually pushed the adult twins to self-destruction in the first place: the horrible memory of a dark family secret (an attempt of murder towards them by their own insane mother), the sorrow of losing her and then their father, wouldn't those be enough reasons for their becoming depressed, psychotic and self-destructive, in particular if these experiences are combined with a hereditary vulnerability towards mental illness? According to the latest developments in psychiatry, most mental disorders are a combination of genetic and environmental factors since the latter can interact with genetic predisposition to affect brain chemistry and thus transform the mental condition of an individual.[4] In this respect, the twins' destiny was rather portentous from the start, having very likely inherited their mother's inclination towards mental instability, while she herself, with her involuntary yet utterly disturbing actions, created the appropriate conditions for the prosperity of this tendency. Thus, by trying to save her children, Olivia only precipitated their fall, most possibly provoking a trauma-related disorder.

Olivia probably unconsciously knows that the problem is rooted in her own situation and not the outer world; perhaps she is afraid her children might become somehow like her, unbalanced, depressed, stigmatized—little Nell already sees the bent neck lady and Luke talks about an imaginary friend; or she might worry they will grow up without her as she will be in no condition to take care of them. Thus, the real danger comes from within the core of the family itself and not the external world.

So who is Olivia after all—a madwoman, a tormented soul, a caring mother or a perverse wife or all of these together? Regarding this intriguing yet tragic maternal figure, there are no distinct boundaries between insanity and second sight, mental instability and clairvoyance. Olivia seems to have a psychotic break but at the same time she might also have foreseen the future (ironically the one she created). Thus, what or who Olivia is really afraid of remains undefined. Above all, Olivia is afraid of her own illogical, isolated, "monstrous" and, sadly stigmatized, self.

Finally, what actually may have triggered Olivia's psychic disorder or aggravated her symptoms in the first place are the practical difficulties of everyday life and the multiple roles which are socially imposed on women. Pressures created by maternal duties and expectations from others even in a seemingly "ideal" family can lead to feelings of guilt and inadequacy and create the proper conditions so that mental illness grows—especially if there is some sort of genetic predisposition, while at the same time the signs of mental illness themselves further disrupt domestic normality.[5] In this respect, Olivia is also a woman who cannot live up to the expectations of the multiple roles related to her gender—to be the perfect mother of five children, wife but also have her own profession—thus she collapses under the weight of these responsibilities to the extent that her latent mental disorder comes to the surface. Overall, despite the ambivalence of the supernatural element throughout the series and hints to Olivia's special abilities, her symptoms and actions point towards severe mental pathology, since she actually decided to murder her children.

The figure of a modern mother who crosses the "threshold" of insanity, trying unsuccessfully to protect her children from an unknown threat, while becoming monstrous herself, also features prominently in Ari Aster's horror film *Hereditary*. In this rather controversial cinematic work the supernatural serves, as in *The Haunting of Hill House*, as a metaphor for family trauma, which mainly consists of loss, death, and the fear of mental illness.

Hereditary starts with a minute copy of the middle-class household itself being presented as one of the works that Annie, a miniature artist (played by Toni Colette), the central character of the film, creates. Through her art, it is as if Annie "immortalizes" the disturbing story of her own family or indeed as if her own possibly unstable mind (re)constructs the whole tale; while on the other hand, Olivia's drawings of the Crain's dream house, reflect her own psychosis as well as the psychic disturbance that develops in the core of her family. But Annie's case is slightly different: she makes miniatures of all her distressing memories and experiences—but in particular those that had to do with her mother, Ellen. It is rather clear that Annie had been haunted and obsessed with her mother, well before the old woman's death, which has just occurred when the film begins. Moreover, Annie sees Ellen's ghastly specter in her house right after the funeral, while she seems to be very perplexed and somehow guilty by her own emotional detachment towards this recent family loss.

Apart from Annie herself, both her children, Peter and Charlie also seem to be haunted by something indefinable as they look nervous and agitated at home or at school. Charlie, in particular, seems to be a deeply troubled child—incessantly drawing strange, grotesque figures, always clicking her tongue, and seeming isolated from the rest of her family. Annie confesses relatively early in the film that her own family were all mentally ill: her mother suffered from dissociative identity disorder (multiple personality disorder) as well as dementia, her father from psychotic depression and her brother from schizophrenia; the latter committed suicide at the age of sixteen. This unsettling past of family mental illness is a key to the story as well as what the title of the film implies: *Hereditary* is what Annie fears her family's pathology might be. This ominous scenario, the possibility that her children and herself already are or are destined to become, due to the laws of heredity, mentally unstable, is something she never confesses or fully realizes; instead, this deeply concealed anxiety, inflamed by a family tragedy—the unexpected death of Charlie—takes the form of a supernatural threat which symbolizes the growing mental instability within the family. Throughout the film there is a complex web of incidents which are presented as supernatural manifestations and signs of an uncanny conspiracy against the Grahams—yet the subtext is rather clear: the demon Paimon, whom Annie's mother and her secret sect were supposed to be worshipping, is no more than an external manifestation of inner demons, those of mental illness and mourning—in a similar manner in which the supernatural elements in *The Haunting of Hill House* are symbols of childhood trauma and self-haunting.

In the support group's meeting, which takes place early in the film, apart from her traumatic family past of severe mental illness, Annie also confesses that she feels an indefinable sense of guilt. Later in the story, in a dream within a dream, or rather a nightmare, she tells her son she never wanted to have him since she didn't feel like a "mother," but she also tells him she now loves him—revealing an inner conflict. Annie believes or, rather, she knows she cannot be a model mother—one reason for that is that she is herself disturbed by her ill-boding family past. Furthermore, we also learn that at some point she had entered her children's room while sleepwalking and attempted to set them on fire—reminding Olivia's holding a knife on her husband's neck while he was sleeping or even her murderous attempt towards her youngest children. This horrifying experience—and maybe more similar to this one—might as well have contributed to Peter and Charlie's being psychically disturbed. Moreover, with her erratic behavior Annie might have unwillingly activated their (inherited) inclination towards mental instability, since environmental reasons can play a definitive role regarding the development of mental disorder.

The family tragedy that ensues after the grandmother's death—the accidental death of Charlie after a party—will bring even more maternal guilt to Annie and will start unleashing the madness that lurked within the family from the start. Annie, in an unconscious process of emotional displacement and in order to cope with the loss of her daughter, will ascribe everything that happened to supernatural agency. In a similar vein, her son Peter, also starts "seeing" the ghost of Charlie in his room just like his mother saw the apparition of his grandmother—the dead members of the family haunt the living ones, in ways similar to *The Haunting of Hill House*. Since Annie feels guilty and extremely distressed about Charlie's horrible death and the image of her decapitated body, she acts more and more like a madwoman; she makes a morbid miniature of the accident with her dead daughter's head, while she talks with Charlie's voice during the séance they have at home. By bringing Charlie "back" through spiritualist practices, it is as if the distraught, neurotic mother is absolved for the death of her own daughter.

Furthermore, Annie believes that Charlie's notebook with her bizarre sketches is a supernatural weapon against the family; yet, it is also a reminder of guilt and sorrow for the girl's demise, thus it cannot be destroyed. After her husband's horrific death due to the notebook, Annie becomes demonic, just like Peter at school in a previous scene, during which he had a horrible fit: according to the supernatural interpretation of the story, both mother and son are possessed by evil forces, yet at the same time the total change of facial expressions might well refer to a serious mental disorder like dissociation, with which the grandmother of the family had been diagnosed. Annie's sinister side is unleashed and her insanity fully manifested: in the final scenes of the film, she will persecute Peter and then he will witness her decapitating herself. All three females in the family end up beheaded—like a family curse that cannot be prevented, similarly to the story of the Crains where both

Olivia and Nell committed suicide by falling from the same spot—in a culmination of feminine abjection. At that point of the film, reality and illusion are altogether mixed in a delirium where Peter seems to have lost total contact with the environment, "seeing" his grandmother's religious sect offering his body to a demon to host it. Moreover, he is internally transformed into that demon—what would be a more eloquent allegory for mental illness where a person "becomes" somebody else?

Olivia Crain and Annie Graham have some major things in common: their mental state is deteriorating while their stories evolve to reach a horrible climax—Olivia attempting to poison her twin children and then committing suicide and Annie attacking her son right after her husband's death and then decapitating herself.

Furthermore, both Olivia and Annie spot "enemies" within their families: Olivia becomes convinced that her husband will take the children away from her (another instance of self-fulfilled prophecy), while Annie believes that her own mother planned to offer her children to a demon—after all it is rather common for mentally disordered or even just severely stressed people to feel hostility towards members of their own family, as well as project onto them their profoundest fears, reaching the point of delusionary thinking.

Moreover, apart from troubled motherhood and latent insanity, the two women share another trait which is of considerable significance regarding their stories: they are both artists who work on spatial creation, and focus on reconceiving/reconstructing the domestic space. Olivia attempts to design an ideal home which cannot be realized as it takes the shape of her inner turmoil, and Annie's model art much consists of emblematic family scenes associated with haunting emotional traumas. While art and creativity are often sided with mental instability, in the case of Olivia and Annie, who work and practice their art at their homes, motherhood is also related to a domestic sort of creative art; due to closeness with their children and the homely environment, the art of the two women is inevitably inspired by and diffused in the domestic space. Furthermore, the artist-mother is more imaginative and creative than the "average" mother, but also more prone to mental imbalance. Thus, Olivia and Annie are presented both as unstable, caring mothers and as unstable, talented artists, who, through their artistic representations, render their homes a field of emotional intensity and psychological terror.

Regarding the supernatural element, in both cases it is never fully resolved whether such an influence actually interferes with the, most possibly, unbalanced minds of the protagonists, thus it makes more sense to consider the supernatural manifestations as a symbolic representation of inner hauntings—those of death, loss and unfathomable grief.

On the surface, Olivia fears her children are threatened by the external world, while Annie convinces herself the menace comes from a supernatural agency; of course, behind both the rationality and the irrationality of these possibilities, lie other, hidden, anxieties—those of the dissolution of the maternal bond as well as the passing of mental illness.

What these women really dread, apart from everything else, is their own selves. Plagued by maternal guilt, they are worried they are inadequate mothers. Olivia is afraid she will not be able to protect her twins from derangement, self-destruction and death or, worse, that she will push them to that direction herself due to her declining mental health. In this respect, she might also unconsciously harbor the archetypal maternal desire of not letting her children grow up and leave the parental home, not only in fear of external danger but also unconsciously worrying about family disunion, since familial life is of utmost significance for her. Annie, on the other hand, worries deeply about the effect of the family's past of severe mental illness on the next generation and the possibility she might harm her children herself due to her latent insanity; after her daughter's death, she is plagued even more by self-blame and grief which obviously make her mind susceptible to irrational thinking. Therefore, although for each of the two heroines the menace takes different forms and they might attribute it to real people or the supernatural, above everything else, it resides deeply inside their tormented psyche. After all, the weight of maternal responsibility and guilt, as it is already mentioned, is sometimes so heavy that it may lead to various degrees of distorted perception of reality, in particular when combined with a frail nervous system and a genetic inclination towards some type of mental illness.

In this respect, both *The Haunting of Hill House* and *Hereditary* destabilize established notions regarding the normal, balanced, rational, modern mother figure, by creating dark and disruptive female characters with contradictory traits: Olivia is, at first sight, closer to that ideal model, therefore, the fact that she attempts to poison her children comes as even more shocking, revealing a very disquieting side of her, while Annie's attitude is more ambivalent in the first place: she is often hostile towards her son even before his sister's death, while she also projects to him her own feelings of guilt. Moreover, both women are in contrast with their rational, apparently sane husbands. Olivia and Annie are more susceptible and open to the supernatural world than their male counterparts and of course more prone to insanity—regarding this, they seem to be modern descendants of the Victorian prototype of female lunacy. Besides, female madness and monstrosity is a prominent motif in both *The Haunting of Hill House* and *Hereditary*; a motif which comes strongly visual, though it takes somehow different forms: in the end, Olivia appears as an unsettling, macabre female figure, while Annie becomes demonic and animalistic. The familiar figure of the sane, caring, protective mother has become utterly uncanny and threatening, compromising all sense of normality, safety and balance within the family core. Thus, naturally, mental instability recycles within the generations not (only) because of the power of genes, but also—and perhaps mostly—due to traumatic experiences to which the youngest members are often submitted as a result of the behavior of their mentally unstable parents.

In conclusion, the motif of mentally disordered characters dealing with the supernatural, continues to be a very powerful device of the Gothic horror tradition in order to explore the dim-lit corridors of the human mind through psychological projection and ambivalence. Moreover, the theme of emotionally troubled/psychically disturbed motherhood, which is also a very prominent motif of uncanny literature and cinema in general, is thoroughly examined and imaginatively enriched in *The Haunting of Hill House* and *Hereditary* providing with fresh perspectives regarding the representation of modern motherhood as well as the complex connection between mental disorder and family trauma. In this respect, those two much debated and, as many claim, breakthrough horror screen productions, which boldly deal with difficult and disconcerting social issues—thus following the latest tendencies of the horror genre on screen—can very well be considered as contemporary horror classics.

NOTES

1. Scott Brewster, "Seeing Things: Gothic and the Madness of Interpretation." *A New Companion to the Gothic*, edited by David Punter (Malden, MA: Wiley-Blackwell, 2015), 482.
2. *Ibid.*, 482.
3. Julia Kristeva. *Powers of Horror: An Essay on Abjection*, trans. Leon S. Roudiez (New York: Columbia University Press, 1982), cited in Barbara Creed, *The Monstrous Feminine: Film, Feminism, Psychoanalysis* (London: Routledge, 1993) 11.
4. Charles W. Schmidt. "Environmental Connections: A Deeper Look into Mental Illness," *Environ Health Perspect*, 2007, 115(8): A404–A410. https://www.ncbi.nlm.nih.gov/pmc/articles/PMC1940091.
5. *Marisley Vilas Boas Soares*, Ana Maria Pimenta Carvalho. "Women with Mental Disorders and Motherhood," *Rev. Latino-Am. Enfermagem* vol. 17, no. 5, Ribeirão Preto, Sept./Oct. 2009. http://www.scielo.br/scielo.php?script=sci_arttext&pid=S0104-11692009000500006.

Family Remains
Family Bonds Against the Paranormal in The Haunting of Hill House and Supernatural

MELANIA PASZEK

In October 2018, the streaming platform Netflix released their rendition of *The Haunting of Hill House*. The story of the Crain clan has taken the platform and the internet by storm, gathering dazzling reviews and viewers' approval. Over a decade earlier, in 2005, the CW television network began to air a dark fantasy/horror series revolving around two peripatetic brothers—Sam and Dean—hunting supernatural creatures all over North America: *Supernatural*. With its eleventh season, it became the longest-running American live-action fantasy TV series, gathering a vast fanbase. Its fifteenth and final season premiered in October 2019.

At first glance, the mentioned series have little in common—both include paranormal elements, but *The Haunting of Hill House* is rooted in drama and presents a rather murky, serious and disturbing story, whereas *Supernatural* relies on a mixture of drama and humor and is often referred to as a fantasy soap opera. However, upon taking a closer look, one can recognize a crucial theme in both productions—namely, the particular depiction of family. What makes *The Haunting of Hill House* and *Supernatural* unique is that the protagonists of both shows have experienced paranormal occurrences almost on a daily basis, and both series are built around surviving the supernatural. These shared experiences simultaneously divide the characters and give them a common purpose—either comprehending or fighting the paranormal. I will investigate this motif by comparing the two productions in terms of the illustration of sibling dynamics and parental figures, but I will also focus on the matter of the paranormal prevailing in the two shows—my main interest being the effect of the uncanny events on the protagonists and their family ties.

"The Twin Thing" and the Struggles of Parenthood

Both *The Haunting of Hill House* and *Supernatural*'s main protagonists are families. However, the plots of the shows focus mostly on siblings, respectively: the five Crain children (Steven, Shirley, Theodora, Luke and Nell) and the Winchester brothers (Sam and Dean). The setting of *The Haunting of Hill House* might initially seem as a wholesome, tender environment. The patriarch, Hugh, is a dedicated, loving father and husband; his spouse Olivia is portrayed as an artistic, free spirit and a warm, affectionate mother of their five children.

The main challenge that Hugh and Olivia have to face is not only raising and keeping all their children safe, but also doing so in an environment that is increasingly disturbing and threatening. The more time the family spends within the walls of the manor, the more their mental state deteriorates, especially in Olivia's case.

One of the most popular interpretations of *The Haunting of Hill House*—which has started off as a fan theory, yet ended up being confirmed by the show's creators[1]—is that the Crain siblings can be perceived as an embodiment of the five stages of grief. Consequently, Steven might be recognized as the incarnation of denial, Shirley is anger, Theo is bargaining, Luke embodies depression and Nell is the personification of acceptance. Such approach underlines the aftermath of the suffering the Crain clan has experienced, causing the siblings and their father to drift apart.

Steven, being the author of books about hauntings and yet an avid skeptic, refusing to accept the existence of the supernatural, is certainly a brilliant personification of denial. "I've seen a lot of ghosts. Just not the way you think. A ghost can be a lot of things. A memory, a daydream, a secret. Grief, anger, guilt. But, in my experience, most times they're just what we want to see. Most times, a ghost is a wish," he emphatically states ("Steven Sees a Ghost"). Shirley's anger is also rather obvious throughout the series: from scorning Steven for releasing his revealing book, Luke for his addiction and refusal to treat it, Theo for her apparent rejection of maturity and even Nell, after her death. Theodora spends her days trying to cope with her issues by living an eventful, yet unfulfilling existence, constantly trying to negotiate with her past. Luke, on the other hand, stifles his demons with alcohol and drugs and succumbs to depression. Nell, though, overcame her past by accepting her fate and eventually, becoming a part of Hill House. At the end of the series, as a ghost talking to her brothers and sisters, she states that she has come to a moment of clarity and reflects upon coming to terms with her own death. She explains to Luke: "I am not gone. I'm scattered into so many pieces, sprinkled on your life like new snow" ("Silence Lay Steadily").

The mixture of the siblings' personalities, temperaments and the transformations they undergo by the time of the series' finale is definitely crucial in *The Haunting of Hill House*. The constant clashing and banter between the Crain children is often explained through flashbacks that illuminate the relationships between the individual siblings, but their clan as a whole, too. The culmination of their conflicts occur in the series finale—in the Red Room, the Crains embrace all the mentioned stages of grief, but most importantly, let go of their remorse and, in consequence, of the past. The presence of Nell's spirit in that scene is a moment of forgiveness and a true reconciliation between the siblings as well as coming to terms with their mother's and sister's passing; ultimately, they reunite to fight Hill House and its demons. After returning to their old home by the end of the series, each of the protagonists has to battle their greatest weakness ("Screaming Meemies"; "Silence Lay Steadily"). Steven finally accepts his childhood suffering (or some might say, allows his blocked-out memories to resurface and finally receives an explanation, however irrational it may be), admitting the reality of a lifetime of the supernatural. Shirley expresses her anger on several occasions, one of the most notable ones being her behavior at Nell's wake. Ultimately, however, she must let go of her anger at the insufficiencies of others and admit to her own infidelity and weakness. Theodora comes to terms with her hurt and ceases bargaining with an emotional monologue she delivers to her sister on the way to Hill House, which serve as both an explanation for Shirley (who caught her husband and Theo in an ambiguous situation at Nell's wake), but also a cathartic speech that sums up Theo's experiences after Nell and Olivia's deaths:

> And I felt ... nothing. Just nothing. And it spread, it spread everywhere in me, this nothing, until I couldn't feel anything anymore. I was just this dark, empty black hole. And I tried to fill it up, I tried to fill me back up, (...) and I felt nothing. And then I tried to mourn at the wake and I felt nothing, and so I drank and I drank and nothing worked. I couldn't feel anything, Shirley. (...) And I'm just.... I'm just floating in this ocean of nothing and I wonder if this is it, if this is what death is, just out there in the darkness, just darkness and numbness and alone, and I wondered if that's what [Nell] felt and that's what mom feels and it's just numb and nothing and alone. What if that's what it is for all of us when the time comes? (...) I started feeling things again and I felt.... I felt shame, and I felt grief, and I felt ... scared. (...) That thorough, fucking shame was so much better than that horrible, empty nothing ["Witness Marks"].

In this scene Theo is completely honest about what she was going through. The monologue is a turning point for her; it serves as a sort of confession that she makes not only in front of Shirley, but also herself.

Luke's combat with depression and addiction culminates once he decides to return to Hill House, the first sibling to do so since Nell's death. He attempts to burn the mansion down, demolishing it once and for all, but the house defends itself, almost as if it was a living being and its ghosts were protecting it from being destroyed. Luke finds himself in the Red Room—the most mysterious part of Hill House—on the verge of death. On one hand, he is eager to finally give in and end his suffering by staying in the Red Room forever and being able to reunite with his deceased twin and mother. On the other, he is aware that this choice might have a catastrophic result, not only for him, but also for the rest of his (living) family—it simply means he has to die.

Nell has embraced the past as well as her mother's enigmatic death by breaking the unwritten pact the Crain family had: being enticed by Hill House at the beginning of the series, and in a certain way, becoming a part of it, giving in to its apparitions and secrets. Her ghost, however, is the transforming force that mitigates the power of Hill House—she does not allow the house to take new prisoners and she is the one who helps her siblings break out of the vision in which they are stuck in the series finale, saving their lives. Before disappearing, she states that her family members have loved each other completely ("Silence Lay Steadily").

These breakthroughs, aside from Nell and Olivia's deaths, are the main trigger for the Crains' actual reunion. Instead of basking in the traumatic past (that cannot be either changed or erased) and mourning the deaths of their close ones, they finally find comfort and manage to destroy Hill House once and for all before it finds fresh victims.

Supernatural, on the other hand, portrays the two main sibling protagonists as opposing forces: most of the time Dean being the righteous sibling, "chosen by God," and Sam being the conflicted one, cooperating with a demon and eventually revealed to be a descendant of Lucifer himself. This dynamic shifts in the tenth season of the series when Dean is turned into a demon. That portrayal deeply influences the bond between the Winchester brothers, turning them into an incarnation of psychomachy, the eternal fight for the human soul between virtue and evil. As one can notice throughout the series (and in flashbacks or mentions of the characters' childhoods), Dean has taken the role of the protector of his younger brother, Sam. Since Dean was the older sibling, he was the first to be trained by his father—John—in monster-hunting and taking care of Sam. This model, however, is reversed in the show on a variety of occasions, putting Sam in the role of the savior. It is commented upon for example in the exchange occurring in the second season of the show:

SAM: I don't want you to get yourself hurt.
DEAN: Oh, you protect me?
SAM: Yeah!
DEAN: Oh, that's hilarious.[2]

This dialogue wittingly stresses the dynamics between the Winchester siblings; it has always been Dean who took care of the younger sibling, Sam. Hence, whenever this situation is reversed, Dean finds it unnatural, in that case even amusing. Perhaps it derives from his hero complex, his doubt in Sam's independence, more so his ability to become the guardian between the two of them. He has always perceived him as his fragile baby brother, a notion his father imprinted onto him and something he stuck to even long after John's death. Still, Dean admits that he always has and always will care about Sam deeply and will do whatever it takes to stay by his side:

DEAN: Sammy, all I'm saying is, you're my weak spot. You are. And I'm yours.
SAM: You don't mean that. We're ... we're family.
DEAN: I know. And those evil sons of bitches know it too. I mean what we'll do for each other, you know, how far we will go.... They're using that against us.
SAM: So what, we just stop looking out for each other?
DEAN: No. We stop being martyrs. (...) And if we go down ... then we go down swinging.[3]

Through this scene the viewer can notice the unshakable devotion between the Winchester brothers; even on the verge of disaster, Sam and Dean refuse to go without a fight and reject the idea of being separated, even by death.

In "Mystery Spot," the brothers encounter a trickster they believed they have killed some time before; at the end of the episode, the being is revealed to be Gabriel, one of God's archangels. The entire episode is based upon Gabriel imprisoning the Winchesters in a time loop on a Tuesday, which causes Dean to die repetitively in a multitude of ways. Every time the older Winchester is killed, the cycle restarts, forcing Sam to live through a huge number of identical Tuesdays, reliving his brother's death in each one, the only altered detail being the cause of Dean's death. With the apocalypse hanging over the world and Dean's death being one of its imminent elements, with this prank Gabriel attempted to make Sam realize that this time he could not cheat fate or death (something the Winchesters actually manage to execute in the series repeatedly) in order to rescue his brother. When Sam finally uncovers the solution to this mysterious predicament, breaking out of the time warp, forcing the archangel to bring Dean back to life, he has already experienced torturous, bleak months without Dean by his side.

In "What Is and What Should Never Be," Dean is held captive by a djinn who put the Winchesters in a fairy-tale alternate reality. In this version of his life, his beloved mother, Mary, is still alive (whereas John is deceased; this switch reveals much about Dean's attitude towards his father) and so is Sam's girlfriend, Jess (who in reality died at the beginning of the series, in the same way as Mary). Dean not only has the opportunity to return to his childhood home in Kansas; it also turns out he, as well as Sam and John, never hunted. On the other hand, he learns that in this alternate universe he barely stays in touch with his brother, since they had numerous disagreements. The older Winchester also comes to another terrifying conclusion—since his family never got into hunting supernatural creatures, all of the paranormal-related tragedies that he and Sam (or their father) managed to prevent, actually transpired and took multiple lives.

Even though in this dream-like parallel world the bond between the protagonists has changed significantly, once Dean investigates and tries to break out of the djinn's spell, his brother still accompanies him. When asked by Dean why Sam is helping him (considering their fallouts and not believing in the supernatural), the younger Winchester simply replies: "Because you're still my brother." The episode finishes with a switch in the usual dynamic—it is Sam who manages to rescue Dean, instead of the older Winchester playing the role of the defender. This change is not only one of the rare opportunities in which Sam becomes the caretaker, but it also underlines that Dean's strong and seemingly unshakable façade has its weak spots as well. He manages to control it solely due to his mission of being his brother's guardian. Therefore, once Sam takes over in this role, Dean learns that there is nothing weak or humiliating in being the protected one or asking for help.

The two mentioned episodes are the best examples of *Supernatural* that impeccably illustrate the resilient bond between the protagonists. Even though Dean has witnessed his brother's death on multiple occasions (and brought him back to life through various, often perilous means), in "Mystery Spot" it is underlined that Sam's greatest fear is not being able to protect or save his sibling. It is ironically a reflection of Dean's obsession about protecting his younger brother. The older Winchester is so focused on being the hero that most times he is unaware that his brother actually has the same attitude towards him. After their mother's death in their youth and failing to rescue their father, the Winchesters desperately strive to protect one another, as well as friends who are not their blood relatives (characters such as their father figure Bobby Singer, the angel Castiel, their friends Jo, Charlie or Kevin etc.). Unfortunately, often due to circumstances out of their control, they frequently fail at saving the ones they love, witnessing their premature, gruesome demise. The brothers face a dilemma throughout most of their journey in the series: they can either save one another (or the people they care about) or they can stop a major disaster that would prove catastrophic for far more individuals or even the whole world. Often, they simply cannot do both.

Even though the show focuses primarily on the interaction between Sam and Dean, it also addresses parenthood, especially John's struggle to raise his sons after his wife's passing. *Supernatural* illustrates fatherhood mostly through various flashbacks, however most of the facts the viewer has about John Winchester are delivered through the perspective of his sons (usually Dean). On one hand, the series portrays John as a dedicated father and hunter, who would do anything to avenge his wife's brutal death and to protect his children from a similar fate; on the other, John is a strict, mostly absent father figure that focuses more on his unusual calling than on helping his sons to adjust not just to hunting, but also everyday life. Sam and Dean have frequently changed schools, spent most of their lives in motels, and never really had the chance to form any stronger bonds with their peers. Hunting has become their way of life and they got used to the fact that their existence will never be a mundane, rational one.

One of the main mottos of *Supernatural*, within a sea of catchphrases and quotes, is "saving people, hunting things—the family business," coined by Dean in the first season.[4] This phrase certainly reflects the premise of the show, which is an elaborate, emotional story of troubled brothers. However, this slogan also brilliantly underlines the ineffable link between family representation and the supernatural in the series. In Sam's and Dean's case, it is connected to defeating the supernatural; in the case of the Crain family this element is tackled in a slightly different manner.

Spirits, Haunted Mansions and Salt Circles

The paranormal is undeniably one of the main pillars of both *The Haunting of Hill House* and *Supernatural*; whereas the former relies mostly on the motif of ghosts and a haunted mansion, the latter explores a plethora of supernatural creatures, lore and myths, with almost every episode uncovering a new story and beast.

As Steven J. Mariconda points out in his chapter "The Haunted House," included in *Icons of Horror and the Supernatural. An Encyclopedia of Our Worst Nightmares. Vol.1*:

> A house provides a sense of containment, of enclosure, warmth, protection from the elements, a sense of intimacy and nurture. As such, it is an extension of the Mother archetype. Home is the center of one's existence and one's security. A profound affect inevitably accrues to one's house over time; few can leave their childhood homes without regret or feel a deep complex of emotions upon seeing it again after a space of years. Given that we have such a significant investment in the physical and emotional aspects of our house, it is not surprising that the notion of it being violated by something threatening—worse, something unnatural—feels so fearful.[5]

This observation is deeply connected to the story of the Crain family in *The Haunting of Hill House*. The series revolves predominantly around the family's reunion after Nell's death, the reinvention of their mutual trust and facing the demons of the past, in that case, predominantly the home they inhabited decades prior. Hill House is almost a separate protagonist in the show—the source of outlandish, evil, horrifying experiences the Crain clan has suffered from. The space, which was meant to be a warm hearth, a place where the family could make memories and find shelter, even if only for a while, has turned out to be a ravenous beast, awoken from a deep sleep by the Crains' arrival. The mansion not only provides fuel for the children's nightmares, but it also seems to feed on the parents' energy, eventually driving Olivia into lunacy and suicide.

The paranormal elements in *The Haunting of Hill House* are usually tackled by the Crains threefold: by denial, rationalizing, or a form of acknowledgment. The first strategy is definitely most visible in Steven's case: he utterly rejects the idea of the existence of the otherworldly for most of the series, at the same time writing books about hauntings or other supernatural phenomena. One might say such behavior is his way of coping with what he has experienced as a child; it is much easier to push out the trauma instead of attempting to understand and embrace it.

Both Hugh and Olivia tend to rationalize any eerie occurrences in Hill House, reported by their children. In "The Twin Thing," Hugh patiently explains to Luke that "It's normal for kids to have imaginary friends and nightmares," after his son repeatedly claims he saw a terrifying man while being trapped in the basement. Olivia, however, is much more open-minded and susceptible to the supernatural; her approach is slightly diverse from her husband's. After realizing that Theo might possess a special ability, Olivia discloses that "being sensitive" is a somewhat hereditary trait, earlier possessed by Theo's grandmother ("Touch"). This conversation is one of the scenes that put Olivia's approach on the fringe between justifying the inexplicable (in certain moments of the series) and learning how to coexist with it. Her giving the gloves to Theo emphasizes the fact that Olivia was not only aware of the supernatural (in that case, her daughter's unusual skill) but she tried to devise ways to not necessarily evade it, yet to strike a balance, some solution that would help coping with it.

Even though each of the Crain children was somehow affected by the supernatural, Theo, Luke and Nell are connected to it the most, yet each of them copes with it differently. Theo is aware of her bizarre talent, often using it while working as a children's psychologist to protect youngsters in problematic family situations. Simultaneously, however, she rejects true intimacy in her life, among other factors due to feeling like her skills are a burden. Luke self-medicates in any way possible (which eventually brings him to heavy depression and various attempts of rehab) and Nell suffers from sleep paralysis and anxiety. Ultimately, the entire trio comes to terms with the existence of the supernatural in their lives.

One of the most prominent and skin-crawling apparitions in *The Haunting of Hill House* is the Bent-Neck Lady. In "The Bent-Neck Lady," when the circumstances of Nell's death are explicitly shown, as she is driven by Hill House to hanging herself, she sees herself fall and travel through the past revealing that she herself is the Bent-Neck Lady haunting her younger self and becoming a ghost of the house. This idea is certainly an interesting take on the paranormal, ghosts in particular—that our future self haunts our past selves. The Bent-Neck Lady starts off as one of the most disturbing components of the show, but ends up to be, in a way, a humanization or at least a means that evokes sympathy and understanding for supernatural beings in the viewer, a shift that occurs after we learn Nell is the Bent-Neck Lady (see "Two Storms" for her presence being less threatening and more empathetic).

Years after the family flees the house, Steven is the only member that revisits this dark era of his life by writing a book inspired by what transpired in Hill House. His siblings interpret it as a form of betrayal, madness, and an immensely insensitive way of exploiting their distress in order to earn profits from it. Being the eldest of the Crain children, Steven was routinely nominated responsible for his sibling's safety by his parents, Hugh in particular. It seems that he never fully accepted that duty and often felt inadequate in the role of a "big brother," since he was not able to protect Nell from killing herself. Interestingly, a quite similar motif prevails in *Supernatural*—once Dean fails at protecting Sam, he is tormented and blames himself for any harm that his younger brother might experience.

In *Supernatural*, the paranormal has a multitude of forms—from demons, vampires, werewolves and poltergeists up to creatures that are less frequently depicted in culture (or at least television), often connected to specific folklore and myths, such as shōjōs, banshees or rugarus. The Winchesters' main purpose is to hunt these beasts down and eradicate them or at least make sure they will no longer do anyone harm. Contrary to the Crains, who are generally more passive and helpless against the supernatural, the protagonists of the CW series not only actively and ruthlessly fight the monsters, but actually conduct research and move around instead of simply waiting in one place until a paranormal occurrence transpires. The otherworldly phenomena have become almost a routine; the siblings are equipped and trained to fight almost any beast that they come across, making saving the innocent their main priority. Their dedication often results in critical danger not only for them or their close ones, but repeatedly—entire towns or humanity as a whole.

After all, the brothers realize that the most terrifying notion in their lives is not the otherworldly creatures they hunt down, but the perspective of losing one another and the only speck of family they have left.

Family Remains

In the initial pitches for *Supernatural*, disclosed by its creator—Eric Kripke—on Twitter in February 2019 (as part of the celebration of the 300th episode of the show), it is highlighted:

> Every episode of *Supernatural* will contain three points of our tonal triangle: scary as shit. Popcorn fun—with lots of humor. And real, involving characters—because this is a story about brothers, and our issues are always rooted in family.... And in every episode, we'll tell an emotional b-story about Sam and/or Dean, in which we'll reveal new dimensions of our leads. Their rivalries, their history, their royalty.[6]

The exact same premise can be distinguished in *The Haunting of Hill House*. The series might seem as simply another adaptation of Shirley Jackson's prose, a murky, gothic drama exploring the story of a bizarre haunted manor, however upon deeper inspection it tackles, first and foremost, family: sibling relationships and parenthood in particular. The Netflix production presents a complex, multilayered image of a slightly dysfunctional family that in the end struggles to stay together after the harrowing incidents in their earlier years.

Taking into account the plots of both of *The Haunting of Hill House* and *Supernatural*, one might bring forward an episode title of the latter series, namely "Family Remains." This ambiguous expression immaculately represents the Crains' and Winchesters' hardships. The bizarre occurrences shown in both productions have both reinforced the protagonists' bonds as families (in that case one might interpret *remains* as a verb) or quite the contrary— it all had a harmful influence on family ties, straining or even breaking them and triggering numerous tragedies (*remains* as a noun). The horror and fantasy genre tends to rely on gore, especially the presence of blood as the trigger for disgust, or more importantly—fear. However, once we shed more light on *The Haunting of Hill House* and *Supernatural*, it is not the image of blood understood literally that causes the viewer to feel uneasy, but *blood* in a metaphorical sense—as *bloodline*. The traumatic and paranormal events that have touched the Crains and the Winchesters have irreversibly transformed them not only as individuals, but also as families. Both series certainly show that family is not defined by last names or blood, but the undying love, support and never giving up on one another even in the toughest and most surreal circumstances.

Notes

1. Meaghan Darwish, "'The Haunting of Hill House': How the Crain Siblings Represent the 5 Stages of Grief." TVInsider.com. Last modified November 2, 2018, accessed June 8, 2019, https://www.tvinsider.com/728507/haunting-of-hill-house-stages-of-grief-siblings/.
2. Eric Kripke, dir., "What Is and What Should Never Be," *Supernatural* (Warner Bros. Television, May 3, 2007).
3. Kim Manners, dir., "No Rest for the Wicked," *Supernatural* (Warner Bros. Television, May 15, 2008).
4. David Nutter, dir., "Wendigo," *Supernatural* (Warner Bros. Television, September 20, 2005).
5. Steven J. Mariconda, "The Haunted House," *Icons of Horror and the Supernatural. an Encyclopedia of Our Worst Nightmares. Vol. 1.* S.T. Joshi, ed. (Westport, CT: Greenwood Press, 2007), 268.
6. Eric Kripke. Twitter Post. Posted on February 7, 2019, 9:17 a.m., accessed April 12, 2019. https://twitter.com/therealKripke/status/1093559472507674624/.

"They Never Believe Me"
Discourses of Belief in Hill House and #MeToo

BRANDON R. GRAFIUS

As evidenced by the range of essays included in this volume, Mike Flanagan's *The Haunting of Hill House* is many things: a haunted house narrative, a family melodrama, a meditation on the past, and a reflection on the effects of trauma.[1] One particular thread of traditional ghost narratives that Flanagan pulls on consistently through the series is the question of belief. As in most ghost stories, the haunting does not reveal itself to all of the characters at once. It's a gradual process, with characters coming to grips with the reality of the house's presences in different ways, at different times, as they have unique encounters with the many ghosts of the house.

Hill House arrives at a time when we have been grappling with similar questions as a nation, in the form of the #MeToo movement. The stories of sexual assault that have poured out in the last several years have confronted us with several questions, among them the question of how a story can be judged as credible. This is intricately connected to the question of who is allowed to play this role of judge in the first place; too often in the past, the gatekeepers have been the same class of people (if not the very same individuals) who have created the structures and conditions that have allowed these violations to occur in the first place.

Michel Foucault discussed societal "discourses," in which the way we talk about things is determined by our culture; rather than being value-neutral, the language we are supplied with as individuals carries with it the judgments of our society.[2] As F.W. Bateson describes this phenomenon, discourses "supply a set of concepts which can be used to analyze the object, to delimit what can and cannot be said about it, and to demarcate who can say it" (Bateson, 64). Within any given discourse, Foucault discusses the existence of "subjugated knowledges," which he defines as "a whole series of knowledges that have been disqualified as nonconceptual knowledges, as insufficiently elaborated knowledges: naïve knowledges that are below the required level of erudition or scientificity."[3] The dominant discourse determines the experiences which are allowed to constitute as knowledge, and which experiences can be safely dismissed. In Foucault's terminology, the dominant discourse establishes the boundaries for who is to be believed.

We see this discourse of belief operate in horror movies most frequently when the family patriarch (or a societal equivalent, such as a police officer or scientist) is established as the arbiter of whose story is considered credible. However, in order for this patriarchal figure to survive, he must expand his understanding of what constitutes a believable narrative. The essay will also explore how a similar discourse runs through the #MeToo movement, as one of its foundational assertions is that our idea of what constitutes a "credible" story is far too narrow to account for the experiences of the many survivors who have come forward.

Flanagan's *Hill House* foregrounds this discourse of belief in a way that suggests the influence of the #MeToo movement. Both *Hill House* and #MeToo ask similar questions: what determines whether a story is credible? Who gets to make those determinations? And how does the experience of not being believed affect an individual? Both *Hill House* and the #MeToo movement suggest similar answers to these questions: societal rules for determining how credibility is measured, and who is allowed to measure it, have been the domain of dominant patriarchal powers, usually to the exclusion of other voices. And the effects of these decisions can be devastating, both for society as a whole and for the individual.

The #MeToo Movement

Soon after Harvey Weinstein found himself on the front pages of newspapers across the country, facing a wide variety of horrifying claims from a number of women who had worked for him, the hashtag #MeToo was born. Rosalind Gill and Shani Orgad suggest that the #MeToo movement marks a shift away from discussions which focus on "'fixing' women's psyches," and instead is "fundamentally concerned with the intersection of sex and power and has framed its concerns in terms of justice."[4] While the early voices of the movement were primarily women with at least some degree of professional privilege, the conversation quickly expanded to the experiences of working class women, many of whom have stories of unwanted advances or touching in the workplace.[5] It is too early to predict the long term effects of the movement, but it has already made its mark in popular culture through the number of powerful men who have been called to account for their behavior, as well as the number of women who feel able to speak out about their experiences.

A watershed moment for the nascent movement came during the struggle over Judge Brett Kavanagh's appointment to the Supreme Court. The highly qualified, socially conservative justice seemed to be on a smooth path to Senate confirmation, until rumors surfaced of an accusation of sexual assault from Kavanaugh's past. At first, the accusation was anonymous; after a few days of speculation, Dr. Christine Blasey Ford identified herself as the accuser. Ford's testimony was powerful and riveting. While she couldn't remember all of the details of the event in question, for those who have studied cases of sexual assault this only made her testimony more believable.[6] The fact that she was a professor of psychology and could succinctly explain how the brain reacts to trauma served to make her an even more impressive witness. It's hard to imagine a witness more credible than Dr. Ford.

For decades, however, men accused of sexual assault have understood that attacking the credibility of their accuser is their best chance of escaping any negative consequences. We saw this clearly in Clarence Thomas's confirmation hearings, over two decades ago, when one of Thomas's former staff members accused him of inappropriate sexual behavior within the workplace. Anita Hill was subject to relentless attacks on her character, intended to make her seem "a little bit nutty, and a little bit slutty," in the words of David Brock.[7] If the accuser's character can be discredited, the specifics of her claims are no longer of any concern. And as we have seen again and again, Anita Hill's gender made many observers predisposed to view her credibility as suspect.[8]

#MeToo has pushed back on this framework in several ways. First of all, the movement encourages strength in numbers. Whereas one woman's story might be dismissed, it becomes more difficult to dismiss a number of women making similar claims against the same man. The Senate Judiciary Committee understood this dynamic well, both in the 1990s and in 2018, and took steps to ensure that multiple witnesses were not allowed to present testimony. In the hearings for both Clarence Thomas and Brett Kavanaugh, the Committee restricted the accusations to a single witness, declining to hear from other women with similar stories to share. With this simple move, the senators were able to construct an artificial "he said/she said" scenario, rather than a more damning chorus of accusations in which the judges were confronted by multiple accusers. For Clarence Thomas, this created a dynamic in which a slim majority of senators felt comfortable ignoring Anita Hill's accusations. In a similar manner, Brett Kavanaugh was confirmed by the narrowest of margins. One of the last undecided senators, Arizona's Jeff Flake, stated that he wasn't sure who to believe. Nevertheless, he decided to vote to confirm

Kavanaugh to the Supreme Court. While Flake might have felt that both witnesses were "compelling," or "persuasive," he made the decision to give more weight to Kavanaugh's testimony.[9] While we can never know his reasons for sure, it seems likely that he viewed "believe the man" to be the default setting, to which he fell back in his uncertainty.

Believing in Ghosts

The question of belief looms large over many horror subgenres. The events of horror films are out of the ordinary, extreme, and surprising, so characters are often slow to understand the gravity of their situation. Frequently, once the film's protagonists understand the threat they are facing, their next challenge is to convince the authorities. This model plays out clearly in many 1950s teen horror films, perhaps most famously in *The Blob*. While the teenagers, led by Steve McQueen, have seen the blob in all its violent and gooey glory, the police view them as delinquent kids playing a prank. They're not credible.

In narratives involving the supernatural, often it's not society's authorities who need convincing; it's other members of the family. Frequently, it is the vulnerable members of the family who are more attuned to the supernatural presence—the women and children. In many narratives, this also includes racial and ethnic minorities, such as Halloran in *The Shining*. The patriarch positions himself as the rational member of the family, able to rise above the hysteria of his wife and their children. We've seen this recently in films such as *The Conjuring*, in which Roger resists believing his wife and five daughters when they try to convince him they are experiencing supernatural hauntings. In this case, the voices of six women are (barely) enough to counteract the skepticism of one man. The Sam Raimi film *Drag Me to Hell* features a similar scene, in which Christine, deeply unsettled after a workplace attack, wants to see a fortune teller. Her psychologist professor boyfriend is condescendingly dismissive of the fortune teller, making clear he views the man as a con artist. This is often true even when the men have special abilities that grant them access to the supernatural, such as in *Insidious* or Nicholas Roëg's earlier film *Don't Look Now*; these men still don't believe. Consistently, the patriarchal male is placed on the side of reason, over against the irrationality of the women.

By the end of the film, the male figure is convinced of the presence of the supernatural, and understands that his rationality is not sufficient for the situation.[10] Frequently, he comes to this realization too late, either to save himself (*Don't Look Now*) or his wife (*The Orphanage*). These protagonists make the mistake of assuming that their rationality provides them mastery over the world; often, they are unable to adapt when their rationality proves inadequate for the situation they are facing. Their worldview does not encompass the supernatural; the question in the film is whether they will change fast enough. In many horror films, the plot is structured around the growth of these male characters, with tension arising from whether they will learn to adapt fast enough to save themselves and their family. In the framing of Robin Roberts, this is the story arc of the male characters "learning to understand feminine knowledge."[11]

The Haunting of Hill House takes a different approach by foregrounding the experience of the children, who have a deep understanding of the house's haunting, but are not believed by their parents. Part of this is the extended length and episodic structure, which allows *Hill House* to spend more time with the experiences of a greater number of characters, rather than privileging the perspective of only one. *Hill House* doesn't neglect the narrative of the patriarch being forced to "unlearn" his rationality. But it also gives significant weight to the narratives of those who are harmed by the assertion of rationality as the privileged form of knowing.

Belief in The Haunting of Hill House

In a departure from traditional haunted house narratives, the Netflix series spends more time with the Crain siblings as adults. They escaped from the house when they were children but still find themselves haunted by it metaphorically (through the continued effects of the traumatic experiences on their adult psyches) and, in the case of Nell, literally (through the recurring presence of the "bent neck lady"). The children have all grown into damaged adults who struggle to form and maintain healthy relationships. But the effects of their traumatic childhood seem to be felt most acutely by Luke, who will spend most of his adult life struggling with drug addiction, and the ever-haunted Nell, who wrestles with sleep paralysis and depression before finally taking her own life. The series details how their trauma has been heightened by both the experiences themselves and the lack of belief on the part of their family members—their parents when they were children, and their siblings in adulthood.

These are also the two Crain siblings who experienced the most direct and pervasive hauntings in their childhood. In the series' third episode, "Touch," young Luke is playing around with the dumbwaiter and is trapped in the cellar, where a ghostly figure crawls out and attacks him, ripping his shirt. When he first tells his story, his parents do not believe him; they are skeptical of the presence of a cellar in the house (it doesn't show up on any of the house's blueprints), and even more of the presence of a malevolent attacker. After Theodora is able to locate the cellar's hidden entrance, their parents continue to insist that Luke is imagining the attack. Even the corroborating evidence of the previously unknown cellar is not enough to convince them of the truth of the rest of Luke's story. The episode shows the impact this experience has had on Theodora's life by juxtaposing this event with Theodora's adult profession as a child therapist. When one of her patients tells Theodora the story of a recurring nightmare, involving a monster rising from the floor to attack her, Theodora takes the story seriously enough to uncover the abuse the child is suffering at the hands of her stepfather.

The effect of their parents' disbelief on Luke is explored in the next episode, "The Twin Thing." This episode opens with young Luke, sitting in the idyllic spring lawn, recounting the story of his attack to his "imaginary" friend. "He even ripped my shirt," Luke says, "and they still didn't believe me. They never believe me." When Luke produces a drawing of his assailant, his father (Hugh) responds with a dismissive smile. "It's normal," he says, "for kids to have imaginary friends, nightmares." Luke protests that he is not describing an imaginary experience, and Hugh says to him, "Go ahead, I'm listening." But Hugh does not respond when his son tries to tell him that the house is "bad," instead allowing his wife to interrupt the conversation. A "bad" house is not one of the realities that Hugh is willing to accept. While Hugh does not view his son as a liar, acknowledging that Luke probably believes the story he is telling, Hugh is unwilling to consider his son's narrative as anything other than a childhood fantasy run amuck. As father, Hugh knows best.

We see the same response to Nell's claim of a haunted visitor. After Nell sees the "bent neck lady," her father is quick to tell her that this is just a nightmare, and her mother suggests that perhaps it was Theodora playing a joke. Nell's visions persist for multiple nights. Her parents try to comfort her, with her mother going as far as to sleep in a different room with Nell, but believing her is not a consideration. In the eyes of her parents, Nell is a child, undergoing the sort of night terror experiences that many children undergo. In a similar manner to their response to Luke, Nell's parents offer sympathy and kindness, but not belief. Luke does not express how deeply this disbelief hurt him as an adult; this sentiment is left for Nell to reveal.

Nell continues to be haunted by visions of the bent neck lady into adulthood, and she continues to struggle with her family's refusal to believe her accounts of her experiences. As an adult, this mantle of the disbelieving patriarch is passed to her oldest brother, Steven. Steven has become a celebrity from his tell-all book about his experience growing up in a haunted house, but has never believed himself. Instead, Steven chalks their experiences up to mental illness, which is then exacerbated by a sort of shared panic among the family. Nell confronts him at a public reading. "You tell our stories," Nell says, "my stories, the same stories you told me were just dreams, delusions." As Nell starts to cry, she says, "You were supposed to protect me. But you said the meanest things to me when I tried to tell you." This outburst reinforces that Nell's trauma does not stem only from the persistent hauntings of the bent neck lady. Nell has also been deeply wounded by the disavowal of her experiences by her family members.

Like many horror narratives, *Hill House* engages with the question of belief, and the resistance the rational (usually associated with the male) mind has to the idea of the supernatural. On one hand, this reflects the age-old dichotomy, in which women (and other marginalized groups) are in tune with the spiritual and the emotional, while the European males are connected to the rational and the intellectual.[12] But frequently, horror challenges this dichotomy; the rationality of the male is insufficient to handle the threat they are facing, and the protagonists' only hope of salvation is through the insights offered by the non-dominant voices. The family patriarchs have created the rules of the game: rationality rules. But the horrific forces they are confronting are not beholden to these boundaries, and are determined to play a different game.

While most haunted house films present this kind of challenge to the rational mindset, *Hill House* goes a step further. Not only does it provide the critique of rationality as being insufficient to encompass the narratives supernatural occurrences, but *Hill House* shifts the emphasis of its narrative to decentralize the family patriarchs (in this case, Hugh and Steven), and focus more about the experiences of the people who are not believed.

Hill House *and the Kavanaugh Hearings*

This plot device of the unbelieving patriarch has taken on an increasing amount of relevance when read in conjunction with recent struggles over what, precisely, it means to listen to women and men who have been the victims of sexual violence. The dominant voice of patriarchal reason has told us, for years, that experiences of sexual abuse and harassment should be swept under the rug except in the most extreme cases. (And even then, American culture has been very good at latching onto any hint of ambiguity to allow us to disregard potentially damning evidence.) It's not only that power means the ability to adjudicate an individual case. Power means the ability to determine what is or is not worthy of being heard in the first place. In Foucault's parlance, power establishes the discourse. In a similar manner to Hugh Crain's refusal to consider his son's story, regardless of the evidence that was produced for its validity, power provides the ability to determine which stories can be heard, even before the stories are evaluated on their merits.

As the #MeToo movement has gained visibility, it has become painfully obvious that American culture has operated out of a highly constrained discourse around sexual harassment and abuse for far too long, one which tightly controls the script around cases of inappropriate sexual behavior to the advantage of powerful men. We recently had an example of how pervasive this discourse can be, even in the face of the #MeToo movement's growing strength.

The Supreme Court has the power to decide cases; they also have the power to refuse to hear an argument. Similarly, when a political party is in control of the House of Representatives or the Senate, they not only round up the votes for bills, they determine which bills are brought to the floor for debate and voting at all. This political power also extends to committee hearings, and the rules by which these committee hearings will function. Normally, this kind of work is done out of sight of the public; it is one of the discourses that we accept with little thought. But in high profile cases, such as the Kavanaugh hearing, the mechanisms of this system become extremely visible.

The judiciary committee felt enough public pressure that they scheduled a hearing to consider Blasey Ford's allegations, but then circumscribed it so tightly as to preclude any actual evidence from emerging. The hearing was set up to enable senators to feel like they had done their due diligence before voting to confirm Kavanaugh, not to further investigate the allegations brought against him. There was an arbitrary single-day time limit, along with an unhelpful 5-minute questioning format; even more problematically, the committee refused to call additional witnesses, ensuring that this hearing would become nothing more than a "he-said/she-said" argument, which could not be adjudicated with any degree of certainty. In case we were unsure as to whether the outcome had been pre-determined, the Senate scheduled a vote for Kavanaugh's confirmation before the hearing had even taken place. The same is true of the FBI background check that followed this hearing. The White House determined in advanced who would and who would not be listened to by the FBI, in effect crafting the narrative they wanted to create. Kavanaugh's history of alcohol abuse as a young adult, as described by a number of witnesses who were not allowed to speak to the FBI, was considered outside of the narrative. As such, the possible (likely) untruths that Kavanaugh told about his drinking as a young adult during his hearing were also determined to be out of bounds. The result is an investigation that supported the pre-determined narrative. When you know the results you want to find, it's easy to set up the rules of the game so that you can achieve those results. This is a perfect example of how Foucault's idea of "discourse" works in society. We have decided that accomplished, educated men like Kavanaugh do not commit sexual assault, and construct systems that protect them and confirm this preconceived notion. The societal discourse of sexual assault served as the most powerful referee for the Kavanaugh hearings, and it was a referee that had set up the rules so that the winner was inevitable.

In *The Haunting of Hill House*, this job of referee is served first by family patriarch Hugh Crain. While his wife is certain there are ghostly presences in the house, Hugh will only consider that she is overly stressed, and needs some time away from the house. Similarly, the children who are experiencing terrifying supernatural visitors (primarily Luke and Nell) are dismissed as not knowing the boundaries between dreams and reality, as letting their anxieties run amuck. In short, they are accused of being unreliable witnesses. By establishing the rules in advance for what experiences are believable and what experiences are not and determining to seriously consider only those experiences that were determined to be within these acceptable bounds, the Crain family was unable to hear the actual stories of trauma that were being experienced by their members. As a society, we're wrestling with the same question; the rules we have established over what stories are acceptable are no longer working. (And actually never did, though our society pretended otherwise.)

Hill House not only understands how these discourses work to privilege some belief systems over others—Cartesian rationality over the acceptance of supernatural powers—but it also understands the damage this discourse can do. When people are not believed, particularly by those they trust most, the result can be lasting damage. In the case of Luke and Nell, these effects prove to be devastating.

Horror has long understood the perils faced by the patriarch who refuses to listen; twenty-first century America is just now getting the same message. Horror films, particularly those in the supernatural subgenre, have served as an arena to explore these contested questions of knowledge and belief, exploring the dangers of a discourse that is centered exclusively on Enlightenment ideas of rationality. If the male representation of this discourse is unable to adapt quickly enough, the consequences are dire. *Hill House* continues this trend of exposing the limitations of the discourse of rationality but pushes further in the direction of questioning our bases for believing, while also forcing us to face the consequences for the characters who are not believed. As the #MeToo movement continues to reshape our societal discourse around issues of sexual assault and belief, horror films can play an important role in continuing to ask questions about how we believe each other.

Notes

1. Of course, this combination is not new; the ghost story has a long history of addressing these concerns. Michael Walker, in his monograph *Modern Ghost Melodramas: What Lies Beneath* (Amsterdam: Amsterdam University Press, 2017), argues for a particular trajectory of ghost stories in which the ghost is more sympathetic than monstrous; Flanagan's *Hill House* would fit comfortably within this discussion. A solid introduction to the haunted

house genre is Curtis, *Dark Places: The Haunted House in Film* (London: Reaktion Books, 2008).

2. Much of Foucault's work is devoted to this concept and the various ways it expresses itself in culture; see, in particular, *The Archaeology of Knowledge* (trans. A.M. Sheridan Smith; New York: Vintage, 2010), 1–76, for an introduction to Foucault's understanding of the ways in which power is used to construct and circumscribe discourses. The edition of this work cited contains, as an appendix, Foucault's lecture "The Discourse on Language," which attempts to summarize these thoughts.

3. Foucault, *"Society Must Be Defended": Lectures at the Collège de France 1975–1976* (trans. David Macey; New York: Picador, 2003), 7. The Jaunary 7, 1976, lecture included in this volume provides a lengthy discussion on the idea of "subjugated knowledges."

4. Rosalind Gill and Shani Orgad, "The Shifting Terrain of Sex and Power: From the 'Sexualization of Culture' to #MeToo," *Sexualities* 21, no. 8 (2018): 131–1324, quote from 1318. A personal account of the cultural and structural realities from which the #MeToo movement arose can be found in Di Leonardo, "#MeToo Is Nowhere Near Enough," *HAU: Journal of Ethnographic Theory* 8, no. 3 (2018): 420–42. Jessica Valenti's *Sex Object: A Memoir* (New York: Dey St., 2016), provides a powerful account of the pervasiveness of sexual harassment and unwanted touching in modern American culture.

5. Judith Levine, "Beyond #MeToo," *New Labor Forum* 27, no. 3 (2018): 20–25, focuses on the high frequency with which women in service professions experience inappropriate sexual behavior in the workplace, both from supervisors and customers.

6. Brian Resnick, "Donald Trump's Attack on Christine Blasey Ford's Memory Is Cruel—and Wrong," *Vox*, October 3, 2018. Accessed March 8, 2019. https://www.vox.com/science-and-health/2018/9/20/17879768/brett0kavanaugh0christine-blasey-ford-trump-memory-psychology.

7. Brock has apologized for his part in the treatment of Anita Hill in his memoir *Blinded by the Right: The Conscience of an Ex-Conservative* (New York: Crown Publishers, 2002), 92–120. The quotation is found on page 98, originally from the March 1992 issue of *American Spectator*.

8. While predating the #MeToo movement, an important essay on the difficulty women have being taken seriously is Rebecca Solnit's *Men Explain Things to Me* (Updated Edition. Chicago: Haymarket Books, 2014). It was from the discussion surrounding this essay that the term "mansplain" was born.

9. Flake discussed his decision process on ABC's morning show *The View*, October 25, 2018.

10. Leo Braudy, *Haunted: On Ghosts, Witches, Vampires, Zombies, and Other Monsters of the Natural and Supernatural Worlds* (New Haven, CT: Yale University Press, 2016), 141–178, discusses the prevalence of the "detective" theme, in which the (predominantly male) characters must use their rational faculties to solve problems which, in the end, will elude their rationality.

11. Robin Roberts, *Subversive Spirits: The Female Ghost in British and American Popular Culture* (Jackson: University of Mississippi Press, 2018), 77; discussing *Supernatural*, Season 2, Episode 9: "La Llorona."

12. This tradition has a long history in Western thought. A history of the idea can be found in Steven Horigan, *Nature and Culture in Western Discourses* (New York: Routledge, 1988). Much of the current discussion stems from Susan Griffin's 1977 monograph *Women and Nature: The Roaring Inside Her [1977]* (3rd edition. Berkeley: Counterpoint, 2016). For recent essays discussing the binary connections between man/culture and woman/nature, see the essays in Douglas Vakoch and Sam Mickey, eds., *Women and Nature?: Beyond Dualism in Gender, Body, and Environment* (New York: Routledge, 2017).

VII

Horror Makers on *The Haunting of Hill House*

A Ghost Is a Wish Your Heart Makes

CHRISTA CARMEN

"I've seen a lot of ghosts. Just not the way you think. A ghost can be a lot of things. A memory, a daydream, a secret. Grief, anger, guilt. But, in my experience, most times they're just what we want to see. Most times, a ghost is a wish."

These words are spoken by Steven Crain in the first episode of Netflix's *The Haunting of Hill House*, to a woman who is desperate for validation that her deceased husband is communicating with her from beyond the grave. Upon watching all ten episodes of the show a second time, I realized that these possibilities of what a ghost can be, as described by Steven, foreshadow each of the ways the seven members of the Crain family have been, or come to be, haunted.

Steven, the first lens through which the story of the Crain family is viewed, appears to be the least haunted, the least affected by the events that took place at Hill House, despite having grown up to become a writer of ghost stories and a chronicler of "haunted" places. But Steven has turned the ghosts of his past into an elaborate daydream, one in which he saw nothing that fateful night as he was carried by his father down Hill House's red-swathed stairs, and that any apparition he, his mother, or his siblings have seen over the ensuing twenty-six years is nothing more than a hallucination, the product of "not getting one's shit together" combined with a sickness in the Crain genes.

Luke, on the other hand, has nightmarishly vivid memories of his time at Hill House, enough to fuel a lifetime of drug and alcohol use in exceedingly ineffective attempts to escape them. Bowler-hat wearing, cane-wielding William Hill stalks Luke, mocks him, even—facing backwards into a past from whence Luke has come and yet always materializing too close for comfort to the youngest Crain sibling, despite Luke's earnest protection incantation (*one-two-three-four-five-six-seven*)—as if to point out just how little distance Luke has managed to amass between himself and that haunted childhood.

Like Steven, Theodora spends the two-and-a-half decades post–Hill House convincing herself that whatever supernatural phenomenon walked there, walked in her mother's and younger siblings' imaginations. One phenomenon that she could not attribute to fantasy, however, could not explain away with a Ph.D. in Psychology or dull with a parade of one-night stands, is her ability to receive telepathic information through the conduit of her hands, and she contends with this reality by keeping it a secret from everyone in her life.

Though she's adopted several of the coping mechanisms of her siblings—the daydreamy denial of Steven (as a mortician, Shirley relegates the dead to the material world, not the spiritual one) and the malignant secrecy of Theo—the ghosts of Hill House manifest themselves most strongly to Shirley as frustration, anxiety, and a simmering anger that bubbles continuously beneath the surface, poised to overflow. Shirley directs this anger at her family members indiscriminately: at Luke for his addiction, at Stephen for his book, for "propagating delusions" and for taking Nell's and Olivia's "paranoia and craziness" and mass marketing it to jumpstart his writing career, at Nell for her neediness, and Theo for her standoffishness. But as becomes clear in Episode 7, "Eulogy," a great deal of Shirley's anger is reserved for her father.

Hugh maintains throughout the series that everything he did, he did to protect his children, but he is wracked by guilt, and by the fear that he did not make decisions that resulted in the best outcome for his family. Maybe he shouldn't have left Olivia alone in Hill House that final night. Maybe he should have been more honest with his children about what really happened, and about the promise he made. And maybe he should have spoken to one of his children in particular about the *not sane* conditions of Hill House, on the chance that Nell's visions of the Bent-Neck Lady might have ended differently.

Nell is tortured by both the past and the future, by a grief she cannot understand until she has fulfilled her fate to become the very thing that's terrified her since she was a little girl. In addition to the Bent-Neck Lady, however, Nell becomes so many pieces of confetti, sprinkled over her siblings' lives to be thought of while they stand in the rain. She saw "Come home, Nell," written on the wall, and heeded the house's message so that her siblings could go on living.

And if it was Nell's fate to be digested by Hill House, it was Olivia's ghosts who coaxed her into a position where she could be swallowed up. Olivia's greatest wish was to have her children near and safe, locked away in a forever home more perfect than any she could have drafted up. Stephen,

Shirley, Theo, and Luke were able to transcend that wish, to leave behind their anger, secrets, daydreams, and memories, and walk away from Hill House for the last time. But they'd felt the pull of the Red Room, and knew how justifiable their mother's ghosts, their mother's wishes, were.

Who hasn't wished for the past to have played out differently than it had? Who among us hasn't sought to escape their troubles, to extend a happy present forever into the future, or to keep those they love close, free from harm, and from the darkness of the world? Who hasn't pressed their eyes closed tighter rather than lose the thread of a delicious daydream, or attempted to erect impossible barriers around a loved one to save them from themselves?

Ghosts can indeed be a lot of things. Memories, daydreams, secrets, grief, anger, guilt. They are these things to all of us, in different measures, at different times. But, if *The Haunting of Hill House* series taught me anything, it is that the ghosts that are wishes are the strongest ghosts of all. They are the ghosts that are projected from your heart. The chains that they rattle are the chains you have forged with your love.

The Screaming Meemies Resurrected

ANGIE MARTIN

Like a lot of children, I used to be afraid of the dark. Mine was more from overexposure to horror novels and movies than a normal phobia that nips at the heels of innocence, but the fear was there, waiting for me to turn out the lights and close my eyes. Hands clenching a blanket to my chest as a shield, wrinkles of someone eight times my age around my eyes from squeezing them so tightly shut. They couldn't open. If they did, they would see something horrific, that *thing* surely leaning over the bed, breathing its evil intentions on me, waiting to devour me and consume my soul.

As I grew older, I realized that those are the best moments of horror: the after party, when you're all alone, in your bed, lights out, windows and doors locked—you think. The knowing that something might be lurking, watching, biding its time. The irrational, erratic, hysterical fear, the panic of wondering when "it" will come to get you. The screaming meemies (as redefined by *Hill House*) visiting night after sleepless night, bringing delicious terror with them.

That same overexposure to horror, however, results in the desensitization to the world of frights, and the screaming meemies soon forget you exist. They move on to easier targets, more innocent ones, those who aren't so skeptical and can't predict what happens next. Those who haven't lost their ability to scream, who don't rationalize every bump in the night. And, I didn't realize how much I missed them until *The Haunting of Hill House* entered my life.

There is so much to be said about the show that brought true horror back to Netflix in October 2018. Two days after it hit the popular streaming service, I binged all ten episodes in one sitting, then again two weeks later. It's easy to focus on the depth that creator Mike Flanagan brought to his version of the Shirley Jackson horror novel—the symbolism and ghosts, guilt and family, addiction and mental illness, death and all that follows. The conversation points are endless, as Flanagan instilled such fluid beauty into each moment of the show. The entire thing is devastating, emotionally disturbing, heart-shattering, and downright traumatic.

But, after four, five, ten binge-viewings of *The Haunting of Hill House*, it makes no difference how much profound wisdom can be harvested from every moment, or how deep I can dig into the various meanings each time I consume the show. I can't help but think of one thing: those darn screaming meemies. That show scares the hell out of me. Every single time.

Doesn't matter if I know where the jump scare is coming from. I know that one ghost has been hiding in the same location in the fourth episode. William Hill will still frighten me with that bowler hat and tapping cane as he did the first five times I watched it. Crazy Poppy Hill will continue to freak me out with her creepy poetry and fast-talking mannerisms, discussing death as if it were just another Sunday afternoon tea party.

I will still shake from fear—no, absolute dread and terror. That's what Flanagan does to me, a self-proclaimed desensitized horror-junkie, and not just with *Hill House*, but with all his little gifts to the world of horror. He turns me into a mass of jelly, quivering on my bed, under the covers, with the lights out, at night, all alone, save my seven-pound dog who I hope will rescue me. Because through all its meaning and morals and grief and guilt, *The Haunting of Hill House* is brilliant in its ability to scare—just as all Flanagan productions are (*Oculus* always manages to make me jump and shiver, even after dozens of viewings).

Perhaps the most memorable of all ghosts, possibly the most talked-about, and the one that petrifies me even writing this is the Bent-Neck Lady. Making her debut in the first episode and remaining with the viewer through most of the series, the Bent-Neck Lady haunts Nell from the first night the Crain family moves into Hill House and through her adulthood. She is an impressive specter that overshadows all others, and rightfully so. There is nothing typical or normal about her. From her name to her appearance and especially when the viewer finally learns her origin, the Bent-Neck Lady continues to scare and surprise us in the best of ways.

Though the Bent-Neck Lady origin comes halfway through the series in Episode 5, it is considered a spoiler, so now's the time to stop reading if you haven't yet watched. The amazing intelligence behind her origin is that if her existence and how she came to be were not there, the entire show would have changed direction. It would not be as beautiful. Then again, once you learn about her, you can't take it back. It floats around in your brain whenever you see her, gnawing on you, digesting you like the Red Room digests the residents of Hill House. You will forever know that Nell is the Bent-Neck

Lady and vice versa—and then, the quantum physic questions begin, and if you're anything like me, that's a whole new level of fright.

Yet, despite knowing all about the Bent-Neck Lady, even learning all the secrets of Hill House after the series ends in Episode 10, I can go back and watch it over and over. The revelations enhance the show even more, and the Bent-Neck Lady never fails to scare me. In fact, knowing she *is* Nell terrifies me even more.

Because of that, I will always look to Flanagan's *The Haunting of Hill House* as one of the greatest horror creations in not only my lifetime, but in the history of horror. And, I will lie in bed, binging on it again and again, clenching my blanket to my chest as a shield, all the lights out at night, the Bent-Neck Lady breathing her evil intentions on me, and the screaming meemies nibbling on my nerves.

What Really Walks There?

Tim Waggoner

Ghost stories function like mysteries, with the living investigating the cause of a haunting in order to discover how to lay a troubled spirit to rest. But in Mike Flanagan's *The Haunting of Hill House* we learn almost nothing about the unearthly entities inhabiting the titular structure. That's because the ghosts that *truly* haunt the Crain family aren't supernatural at all.

The forces that plague the Crains are all too real: trauma, disconnectedness, inability to deal with or express emotion, and above all, difficulty reconciling the past with the present. Hence the series' narrative structure: fragments of the past interspliced with scenes of the present. The ghosts in the series are a metaphor for a struggle to come to terms with the past, or, if you like, an excuse for it to take place. Really, you could remove the ghosts from the story and replace them with natural traumatic events, and the Crains' family dynamic would play out much the same. You see, it's not houses that are haunted in the word Flanagan has created. It's people.

Houses—the places where we live, love, grow, and should feel safe—hold our memories, and not all of them are good. Sometimes, as in the case of the young girl that Theodora helps, almost none of them are. The ghosts in Hill House are symbolic of these memories, and of the fears we have as children, parents, and lovers. This is why the spirits in Hill House are, for all intents and purposes, nameless, faceless forces. The Crains succeed in the end only by overcoming their pain and repairing the broken bonds between them. They don't exorcise the spirits from the house because we don't exorcise our memories and our pain. We learn to live with them, to not give them any power, to keep them in the past where they belong, to focus on the present and look to the future.

I have a confession to make, and this might seem odd coming from a writer of horror fiction, but as a rule, I *hate* ghost stories. They usually bore me to tears. By their very nature, ghosts reassure us that death is not the end, that life continues beyond the grave. So what's the worst they can do? Kill us and make us ghosts, too? (The movie *Shallow Ground* has a wonderful answer to this question.) And usually ghosts are bound to one specific place—I'd argue that they're ultimately extensions of the Bad Place horror trope—so all the living need to do in order to thwart them is stay the hell away from their lairs. (Which is why in *Poltergeist*, the parents can't flee their haunted house—they must remain to save their young daughter who is held captive by spirits somewhere inside it.) And when hauntings are depicted in stories, they're usually little more than the special effects equivalent of someone jumping out from the shadows in a Halloween mask and shouting "Boo!" (*Beetlejuice* wonderfully lampoons the banal nature of hauntings with the Maitlands' clumsy attempts to scare off the new owners of their house.)

But I love *The Haunting of Hill House,* and it's because Flanagan knows that the best horror stories aren't about monsters. They're about the effect monsters have on people. Hill House and its spectral occupants aren't the story. The *Crains* are. Yes, the family's experiences in the house shape them and come close to destroying them, but it's their individual and collective response to those experiences that is the real story. And that's what makes Flanagan's series so damn excellent. *The Haunting of Hill House* is what horror can be when it's created by someone who understands that the best stories are ultimately about people—about *us*.

But I have to admit, the ghosts Flanagan created were pretty damn creepy, too.

Spirits and Mediums
Adapting Jackson

Kevin J. Wetmore, Jr.

Since its publication in 1959, Jackson's novel has been adapted for other mediums at least seven times: two films, a Netflix series, a radio abridgement, and three stage versions. Robert Wise adapted the first film version in 1963, with an ensuing adaptation in 1999 directed by Jon de Bont, both under the title *The Haunting*, although the films rarely resemble each other. Wise's film is often singled out for praise as not just a great horror film but a great film. The 1999 version was a critical and popular flop. F. Andrew Leslie adapted the book for the stage in 1964. Subsequently, Paul Edwards adapted and directed *The Haunting of Hill House* for City Lit Theatre in Chicago in 2014, and Anthony Neilson wrote a new stage adaptation produced at the Liverpool Playhouse in 2015. The book has also been abridged by Alison Joseph to be read by Emma Fielding for eight fifteen-minute episodes for BBC Radio 4.[1] In 2018, Mike Flanagan's adaptation into a ten-episode series for Netflix is the most recent reworking of Jackson's narrative into another medium.

Adaptation from one medium to another involves choices of what to keep, what to add, what to change, and what to cut. For example, Mrs. Montague and her companion Arthur Parker from the novel are virtually the same in the 1964 play. They are cut from the 1999 film altogether. They are transformed in the 1963 film to just Mrs. Montague, who is a skeptic who then has a transformative experience with the supernatural (radically different from the character and fate of the Jacksonian original). Mrs. Markway insists on sleeping in the nursery, the most haunted room, not because she believes and wants to be where the action is but precisely because she does not believe. Her driver/assistant is cut entirely from the film. Lastly, the Netflix series reimagines Arthur as Nell's sleep therapist and eventual husband, who leaves her a young widow (although his name is Arthur Vance, not Parker, which is how she becomes Eleanor Vance, the name from Jackson's novel). We might note, the Wise film, praised for adhering to the novel, removed a key character (Arthur) and transformed another one (Mrs. Montague) into something different. Flanagan does virtually the same thing, just on a much larger scale for a much longer duration.

The key issues in adaptation of Jackson's novel are rooted in the target medium itself—is the form visual, aural, live, film or television series? The primary question is what do you do with the ghosts? Jackson is ambiguous, as I noted in the introduction—even the title might be misleading. Wise's film is also ambiguous. No ghosts are ever seen and Eleanor could be subjectively experiencing the bulk of the haunting and objectively creating the effects for the others in Hill House. De Bont's Hill House is obviously really haunted; whereas Flanagan's Hill House is obviously really haunted and yet also metaphorically so. The stage versions remain ambiguous, but I must confess this is where my chief interest lies.

F. Andrew Leslie's adaptation for the stage was written the year after Wise's film was released.[2] Leslie stays very close to the book's plot and characters, beginning the play with chapter two of the novel, but for the purposes of keeping production easy reduces the entire book down to two locations: the parlor of Hill House and Eleanor's bedroom. All action is either transferred to one of these two locations or reported about in them. As in the novel, no ghosts are seen, but writing mysteriously appears, noises are heard, and we witness Eleanor's breakdown directly in front of us, live.

Which brings us to the challenge of ghosts on stage. When staging a disembodied spirit in a live show, the production is challenged in attempting to make the uncanny and the disembodied present. An actor is a corporeal body, which in plays such as *Hamlet*, *Macbeth* and *A Christmas Carol*, plays an ostensibly disincorporate spirit in costume and makeup to suggest a ghost. Missing is any sense of the uncanny—how does a body present the disembodied?

Theater also faces competition from film, in the sense that the audience has most likely seen special effect spectaculars that feature effective presentation of disembodied spirits (or not, as in the case of the 1999 version). Whereas theater in the nineteenth century would use Pepper's Ghost (an elaborate optical illusion using light and glass, best known by contemporary audiences through its use in the Haunted Mansion at Disney parks), experiments have been carried out in the twentieth century at creating an uncanny effect for stage ghosts in intimate theaters, rendering the theatrical haunting more effective and uncanny. Stephen Mallatratt's two-hander stage adaptation of Susan Hill's *The Woman in Black*, for example, does so through deceit with the audience. The program announces only two actors, but a secret third playing the eponymous woman lurks throughout the theater (not just on stage), appearing only in the shadows. Rather than attempt to compete with film in terms of realism, Mallatratt takes a meta approach, with Arthur Kipps (the protagonist) hiring an actor to play all the other characters in Kipps' dramatization of what happened to him. The two characters (Kipps and Actor) are unaware of the actual Woman in Black. Thus through playing with both the conventions of theater going (the actor playing the Woman in Black, for example, is not credited in the cast in the program but in the Special Thanks) and audience expectation, combined with keeping a silent characters in the shadows, never fully visible and breaking the fourth wall, Mallatratt is able to create an uncanny stage ghost.

The potential to be less interesting to contemporary audiences is present in Leslie's script, but the tools and techniques of the medium allow this adaptation of Jackson to be effective. The benefit of theater is that it is live—actors and audience are in the same space. We experience Eleanor's nightmare in her bedroom with her. She makes eye contact with us in the auditorium. Theater also benefits from its unique use of lighting, sound and presence (as seen in *The Woman in Black*). In 2012 the Aux Dog Theatre of Albuquerque presented Leslie's play for Halloween. One local review noted, "It's a more genteel, refined, old-fashioned kind of scary, not like today's gory, slash-a-minute horror movies."[3] That same reviewer observed, "the stars of this production are sound designer John Hull, lighting designer John Aspholm, props designer Claudia Mathes, sound and light operator Sean Donovan, and the backstage crew..."[4] Through sound design, especially placing noises throughout the space, and the use of lighting (or lack thereof), the audience is present in the haunted space. When the theater is unable to use the power of liveness and suggestion, the production fails to raise the level of fear for the audience, to wit the productions at City Lit Theatre, Chicago, which "never gets the atmosphere at the Hill House eerie enough to get us to believe that poltergeists are inhabiting the place," and Liverpool Playhouse, which despite being co-produced by Hammer was perceived to be a ghost of what it could have been.[5]

Wise and Flanagan both succeed in doing something none of the stage versions do—maintain Jackson's unique voice. Jackson's novel begins:

> No live organism can continue for long to exist sanely under conditions of absolute reality; even larks and katydids are supposed, by some, to dream. Hill House, not sane, stood by itself against its hills, holding darkness within; it had stood for eighty years and might stand for eighty more. Within, walls continued upright, bricks met neatly, floors were firm, and doors were sensibly shut; silence lay steadily against the wood and stone of Hill House, and whatever walked there, walked alone.[6]

Because it is not dialogue, these words would not show up in an adaptation. They are missing in the stage versions, for example. Wise's film remixes some of the language from various points in the novel, but opens with a voiceover from the renamed Montague, who is now Dr. Markway:

VII. Horror Makers on *The Haunting of Hill House*

> An evil old house, the kind some people call haunted, is like an undiscovered country waiting to be explored. Hill House had stood for ninety years and may have stood for ninety more. Silence lay steadily against the wood and stone of Hill House. And whatever walked there, walked alone.

The credits then follow, followed by more of Markway's voice over, stating the house had been "born bad." In other words, through the use of voice over, Wise was able to give voice to Jackson's poetic descriptions of the home. Not to be outdone, Flanagan simply has Steven Crain read the entire first paragraph, as recorded above, and the notes it is the opening of his book, *The Haunting of Hill House*.

Whereas Markway's voice over is to an anonymous, general audience, Steven Crain is reading to a group of fans and potential buyers of his books. This marks a key difference between how the two use the opening pages to establish the world. Crain reads to an external group (within the narrative itself). Markway's voice over is used by Wise to approximate the interiority of Jackson's novel, repeated later in the film by Eleanor. Even when being terrified in the night with Theo, even up to the moment of her death, Eleanor's inmost thoughts are available to the audience, just as if reading the novel. The voiceover allows us inside the characters in a way that the visual medium of film does not. Flanagan darts towards the text by having Steven read it, but then denies the audience access to his character's interior lives, which may be appropriate in the case of Steven, as he is a ghost writer who does not believe in ghosts. His entire opening paragraph (Jackson's, actually) is to set a mood, a tone, an atmosphere, in order to sell books. His interior reality is kept away from his writing.

In *Danse Macabre*, Stephen King observes of Robert Wise's version, "The film and the book do not differ greatly in terms of plot, but they differ significantly, I think, in terms of thrust, point of view, and final effect."[7] I think it fair to say that those who like Wise's adaptation and dislike Flanagan's ignore the many similarities in approach, technique and overall relationship to the source material that both Wise and Flanagan carry out. Perhaps the challenge is in adapting Jackson herself. Perhaps, like Ray Bradbury, her work challenges adapters in that it works better as literature than performed or adapted via visual storytelling.

Several adaptations of "The Lottery" were produced for television: as an episode of *Fireside Theatre* in 1951 and an episode of *The Robert Herridge Theater* in 1960; short films were made in 1969, 2007 and 2008, and a feature-length made-for-television movie in 1996. The last starred a pre–*Felicity* Keri Russell and Dan Cortese, best known to that point for his work on *Melrose Place*. Adapted by Anthony Spinner, the ninety-minute adaptation greatly expands and updates Jackson's narrative to the present, with the eponymous lottery continuing into the nineties. Cortese's character remembers the death of his mother in the small town he and his father left when he was a child and he returns to investigate why there is always a death on the same day every year in the town. The critical consensus is that it is at best a run-of-the-mill television movie that does not do Jackson justice.

Similarly, as of this writing, a film version of *We Have Always Lived in the Castle* entered limited release to cinemas. It has also not been reviewed well. "It's no small feat to make Shirley Jackson's eerie prose portraits of cloistered eccentrics in hostile surroundings feel like the forced whimsy of Tim Burton in sleepwalk mode," wrote Robert Abele in the *Los Angeles Times*, "but that's how Stacie Passon's 'We Have Always Lived in the Castle' regrettably plays."[8] It would seem Jackson, brilliant in literary form, is doomed to haunt any adaptation in a new medium.

NOTES

1. See https://www.bbc.co.uk/programmes/b00b9888.
2. F. Andrew Leslie. *The Haunting of Hill House* (New York: Dramatists Play Service, 1964).
3. Dean Yannias, "Regional Reviews: Albuquerque/Santa Fe: The Haunting of Hill House." *Talkin' Broadway*. N.D. https://www.talkinbroadway.com/page/regional/alb/alb118.html. Accessed October 22, 2018.
4. *Ibid.*
5. Tom Williams, "The Haunting of Hill House," *Chicago Critic.com* (March 31, 2014). https://chicagocritic.com/haunting-hill-house/. Accessed October 22, 2018; Susannah Clapp, "The Haunting of Hill House Review—a Spectre in Search of a Feast." *The Guardian* (December 20, 2015) https:www.theguardian.com/stage/2015/dec/20/haunting-of-hill-house-liverpool-playhouse-observer-review. Accessed October 22, 2018.
6. Shirley Jackson, *The Haunting of Hill House* (New York: Penguin, 1984), 1.
7. Stephen King, *Danse Macabre* (New York: Berkeley Books, 1982), 111.
8. Robert Abele, "Family Mystery Is Strangely Clueless," *Los Angeles Times* (May 17, 2019): E9.

Gothic Storytelling

John Palisano

For the past three centuries, Gothic storytelling has morphed and adapted to current cultures, all the while maintaining many of the elements traditionally thought of as characterizing the gothic. This holds true from gothic storytelling beginnings in poetry and literature in works such as Horace Walpole's *The Castle of Otranto* (1786) and Ann Radcliffe's *The Mysteries of Udolpho* (1784) and on through current modernized incarnations such as Mike Flanagan's series adaptation/expansion of Shirley Jackson's *The Haunting of Hill House*.[1]

Haunted Structures and Houses

Since the earliest incarnations of gothic storytelling, structures have been represented as being much more than stone, brick, and wood, constructions engineered by people: they're shown to have souls of their own, independent of their builders. Often, the current inhabitants live inside a structure with history and style far older than that of their current generation's taste.

From the ancient castle in Walpole's *The Castle of Otranto* to the Spanish churches setting Matthew Lewis's *The Monk*, to the halls and secret rooms of Shirley Jackson's 1959 novel *The Haunting of Hill House*, sentient supernatural locations are a key element in defining gothic storytelling.[2]

The castles, churches, and houses are alive. And they mean us harm.

From the very first moments of the series, we are placed square in the heart of Hill House. The Victorian architecture and design play an integral role in setting the mood and feel of the series.[3] Going back to early gothic storytelling in works such as what is widely considered the first true gothic novel—Walpole's *The Castle of Otranto*—large, dark castles represented a walled environment that seemed to be an omniscient force, ready to steer its inhabitants through many measures of supernatural and weird goings-on. Originally constructed as strongholds for safety against outside antagonists, castles became places that could also be seen as imprisoning their occupants. Gothic storytelling used castles as oppressive, jail-like encampments. People's lives rarely extended past the castle moats. Characters' lives were spent reliving their past outside glories through reminiscences spoke in drawing rooms and dining tables. People became ghosts of themselves, whittled down to reliving a portion of their lives over and over.

Over time, the castles absorbed the stories just as it absorbed the supposed souls and energy of those who lived and died inside their walls. Their stories were passed down, generation to generation, until every creak and rustle was attributed to a past inhabitant, trapped in the purgatory of the castle's walls. As in life, the dead could not scale the walls or slip outside the gates.

A structure became infused with the supernatural energy of the dead, a repository and guardian or the souls. The castle itself seemed to have a life of its own, charged from the many souls entrapped within. Likely, the original source of the supernatural energy were horrific events such as murders and suicides.

From Walpole's *The Castle of Otranto*, many Gothic stories continued to be set inside an old, intimidating castle. Many stories told of far off lands and epic destinations, as seen in the travelogues of Ann Radcliffe's works such as *The Italian* and *The Mysteries of Udolpho*, whereas Italian castles loomed and lured their unfortunate visitors into their svelte, womb-like majesties, only to trap and drive them to madness.[4]

Castles were swapped for houses in the late nineteenth century, as Gothic stories found root in mansions and even haunted inns, such as was the setting for Daphne Du Maurier's *Jamaica Inn*.[5] These structures were smaller and much more personal than the medieval castles. Stories more reflected the times and environments, bringing haunted places into the realm of believability for many readers. A great modern example would be the Brampton apartment building central to Ira Levin's *Rosemary's Baby*.[6] The Brampton is believed to be based upon the infamous gothic architectural revivalist mansion/apartment building The Dakota in New York City, last home of John Lennon, and the scene of his horrific murder. His spirit is said to infuse the property. In modern and postmodern gothic storytelling, the most common haunted dwellings are suburban houses instead of the castles and mansions of history.

These mansions also were large enough to have their own secrets: hidden passageways, old, refined decorative and architectural features from earlier time periods, lots of empty space to find oneself lost, and oftentimes, where the supernatural to lie in wait.

Gothic fiction is filled with examples of haunted castles and mansions. The structures themselves often act as a repository and record of past sins. Where better for ghosts to hide than in dark corners of structures that have plenty of room?

Even in gothic stories without traditional supernatural elements, ghosts can appear in the form of remnants and remembrances of people and events long passed. In another Shirley Jackson novel, *We Have Always Lived in the Castle*, a father's influence remains ever present, as his study has been preserved, along with many of his rules and sayings, right down to the stub of a cigar.[7] His presence in the story, and the effect it has on the inhabitants of the house, acts very much like a ghost would in a traditional supernatural gothic story.

There are many echoes of similar situations in Mike Flanagan's *The Haunting of Hill House*.

Of course, Hill House itself is haunted, but why what, or whom, we don't realize until the end of the series.

Shirley's mortuary is haunted, as well, even being seen as directly connected to the house at the end of the series, when Hugh literally heads away from the viewing area, down a hall, and finds himself back within the maze-like womb of Hill House, complete with visions of his family from both their time there, and in their present forms and age.

Hidden Passages and Rooms

We cannot talk about *The Haunting of Hill House* and gothic storytelling without visiting the infamous room behind the red door. Throughout gothic stories, people have had to navigate dark subterranean passages, dungeons, and rooms. Going as far back as *The Castle of Otranto*, Ann Radcliffe's *The Italian* and Matthew Lewis's *The Monk*, secret passages and hidden areas have played a large role. Often used to hide character's movements, they've also hidden liaisons, tortures, and many a poor soul who has crossed the main proprietor of a home or castle.

These hidden places can also act as a metaphor, mirroring undercover thoughts and feelings.

Most importantly? These are more often than not the areas inhabited with the most supernatural, haunted happenings.

The Haunting of Hill House novel has several such sequences as Eleanor finds herself experiencing ever more paranormal and upsetting supernatural occurrences, and we are never entirely certain if they are truly happening, or just her own heightened imaginings and visions.

In the Flanagan *Haunting of Hill House* story, we have many prime occurrences. The door behind the red room, once opened, seems to be the house's heart or brain. From within, it is a place that causes those inside to go mad. It is there that we see Olivia serve the poisonous tea to the children. When Hugh and the others finally open the door ... basically opening the lock and revealing the riddle at the center of *Hill House*, we see just how manipulative and evil the soul of the house can be.

In Jackson's *We Have Always Lived in the Castle*, the father's room in the house is preserved, down to his last cigar. It is as though he is still there. The study acts as many hidden, unspoken, forbidden rooms in gothic fiction where they seem to connect the living to the dead, as well as a place where the dead have been preserved somehow. This also applies to Shirley's work area under the mortuary where she receives and preserves the dead for their final showings.

Secrets and Tragedies

A hallmark of gothic storytelling is its use of highly emotional characters and situations. Often, characters are deeply enmeshed in a romance that cannot be, or a lover who is either far away or who has passed away.

We have so many examples in *The Haunting of Hill House*. Lost love. Grief. Hugh's loss of his beloved wife Olivia. The loss of Luke to drugs. Theo losing herself in sex, yet unable to truly connect with anyone due to her extrasensory empathic affliction. Shirley as a Dr. Frankenstein, trying to understand and beat back death, if only for a service. (The irony being, she only restores the appearance of life to something that is truly dead—much like a ghost.)

The fractured Crain family processes their mother's suicide in different ways.

Steven Crain, the eldest sibling, becomes a bestselling author with his memoir *The Haunting of Hill House*, using the notoriety of his childhood at the house to launch his career. Even as he is accused of profiteering off the family notoriety, his other siblings also make career choices directly impacted by the events they experienced in Hill House. Theo loses herself in her lifestyle. Shirley becomes a workaholic in her mortuary, where it can be argued she works with the dead every day, maintaining their bodies, making them look like they did when they were alive through the proper clothing and through specialized makeup skills. There is a metaphor for her dressing the dead to make them appear as they did in life. A theatrical presentation studied and used to impart a kind of genuine truth as a final chapter and last impression. The stress ultimately leads her to an affair, which has haunted her since. The two youngest Crains, who were individually haunted by specific spirits, are the most broken. An adult Luke numbs the pain with drugs. His visions haunt him so badly, his curse is felt so profoundly, he finds himself continually seeking outbursts of self-medication. He is close to his twin sister Nell, who seems to process her own haunted memories through depression and anxiety, her marriage cut tragically short, leaving her alone and vulnerable to the house.

These secrets and tragedies define each family member. Their father seems to be knocked off normal, his communicative skills hampered and damaged, talking more to his absent wife than his living children. It's clear he loves those children more than anything, yet, he is so damaged from trying to build a life for them through flipping Hill House with tragic results, that he has never been able to fully participate in their lives. He has never moved on.

These are classic gothic storytelling character motivations and types. In stories such as *The Castle of Otranto* and *The Monk*, characters process loss and tragedy in a similar fashion. They often turn to self-loathing and turn their actions inward. This is true in *The Haunting of Hill House*, as well. Most of the characters cannot escape the events haunting their innermost psyches and emotions.

This is no more apparent than with the revelation of Nell and the Bent-Neck Lady. The phantom figure seems to follow her, appearing just as she seems to be turning positive corners, to pull her back into the depths of *The Haunting of Hill House*'s horrors.

Unusual Parental Relationships

The relationships between parents and their children are often abnormal, strange, and borderline uncomfortable. To cite a close cousin of Hill House, in Shirley Jackson's *We Have Always Lived in the Castle*, dysfunctional parental relationships seem to be the norm. In many cases in modern gothic storytelling, the children appear to be the ones doing the parenting. Their mothers and fathers come off as almost irredeemably broken—haunted. In the Netflix *Haunting of Hill House*, their father Hugh is constantly taken to task for choices he made as their father. In the house Olivia seems distant, and finally abandons her children through her mysterious death. To further convolute the situation, some of the children have taken on the role of a parent between themselves. Shirley seems to believe it her duty to serve as a mother-figure to her younger siblings. At one point, it seems Steven, Nell and Shirley act as surrogate parents to a drug-addled Luke. Near the end, though, the brothers take on the caretaker roles for Nell, although with spectacularly tragic results.

Aristocratic Decay

A defining theme in Gothic Storytelling centers around the concept of Aristocratic Decay. Defined, this often portrays a previously well-to-do family unit who have lost their fortunes, or that such fortunes have greatly diminished. Of those who remain rich, most have decayed in other manners. In most cases, there is a breakdown of social norms. Families become reclusive and cut off from the normal routines of civilized lives.

In an early example of aristocratic decay, in Ann Radcliff's *The Mysteries of Udolpho*, a father brings his daughter on a long journey to a faraway castle, using the last of their wealth. He does so without telling her until it is too late. All the while, he indulges in the lifestyle they always have, convinced the money will return. It is his daughter who ends up finding new avenues of prosperity, even as his life turns tragic.

This is also a theme in Shirley Jackson's work, and very present in her final novel, *We Have Always Lived in the Castle*, where a family continues their strange lifestyle, even as their house crumbles around them. Even after a portion burns down, they camp out and rebuild what they can, refusing to leave.

In *The Haunting of Hill House*, the series shows us a family who are doing well for themselves as successful house rehabilitators. Once the renovation on Hill House is complete, they will be fiscally secure enough to move into their "forever house." After they move into Hill House, their fortunes take a turn for the worse. The formerly tight and comfortable family unit splinters. We find some of the characters, such as Hugh and Luke, who are borderline destitute. Other siblings—especially Shirley—rebuild their lives but are still deeply scarred from the dissolution and damage of their childhood familial unit.

Supernatural Elements

In early gothic stories, supernatural happenings were standard and expected elements. As the Romantic period began, and later, as the realist movements of the 1940s gained in popularity, gothic fiction changed this element so that many of the ghosts of past stories evolved into people being haunted more by their psychoses and memories than actual phantoms and monsters. In Shirley Jackson's late period novel *We Have Always Lived in the Castle* there are no obvious supernatural elements to be found, yet, there is a definite feeling of dread, isolation, and sadness.

In both novel and Netflix reimagining *The Haunting of Hill House*, the story first leads us to believe the characters may just be spooking themselves out. By the halfway mark in each, we are certain there are definitely external supernatural forces at play. Ghosts prey upon the living, both metaphorical and physical. The house itself is like a psychic resting spot for the afflicted and purgatory.

Shirley's work in her mortuary also reflects another classic gothic story: Mary Shelley's *Frankenstein*.[8] Our protagonist is another misunderstood, yet well-meaning young person interested in bringing life ... or some semblance of life ... back from the dead. Shirley employs make-up and stents in place of electricity and stitches. The intent is the same, though: to pull back death's curtain for a brief encore before returning once again into the darkness.

As a child, Shirley finds and adopts a litter of small kittens. They die, and it affects her deeply, as she feels she was unable to care for them or "fix" them before they passed. When she sees her mother in her coffin, instead of becoming totally freaked out, Shirley becomes fascinated with how a mortician could fix a dead person to look as they did when they were alive.

In *The Haunting of Hill House*, Nell seems to be reanimated from the attention and the electricity of her family gathering for her viewing. "She's here with us," Theo says at one point. Can there be something manifest between the family's invisible chemistry and "electricity" enough to bring back Nell, even as a phantom, glimpsed before fleeing, similar to Victor Frankenstein's use of electricity? After it is revealed who the Bent-Neck Lady is, she is finally able to rest in peace. Although symbolic, this is mirrored in *Frankenstein*, as in the original gothic novel, the creature is last seen paddling away into the icy, winter darkness of the Arctic ocean. Both characters die a second time, and both dramatic and tragic.

In gothic storytelling, supernatural elements are often used to represent and illustrate situations that were never truly given closure. Lost loved ones appear as ghosts to the living. Their appearance alone can send the viewer into a state of melancholy, fear, or terror. Rarely are the apparitions comforting. Instead, they reopen wounds and force those seeing them to confront their feelings. To make matters worse, these ghosts usually present themselves as they were at the moment of their deaths, making them horrific. In *The Haunting of Hill House*, we learn the Bent-Neck Lady is actually Nell at the moment she'd hung herself. Olivia returns to Hugh at key moments to speak and advise him.

Sometimes the ghosts are not literal ghosts but incidents and memories that haunt people. The entire Crain family are haunted by the memories of their mother's slow decline. They, and we, get to view her prior to her breakdown. We are left wondering if her mental state is due to a biological predilection toward depression, a reaction to mold spores set free from the construction work, the discovery of William Hill's body, walled up in the basement, or some other nefarious, supernatural entity working its way on the house's inhabitants.

Gothic storytelling offers another possibility: the ghosts, the structures, the castles, and houses, are themselves antagonistic, dark entities, somehow infused with evil. Sometimes the supernatural can be explained by an act so heinous it infuses its surroundings with its evil. Other times? It's just a case of the place being born and made that way, and to be avoided, or else.

In *The Haunting of Hill House*, we are shown one of the home's original owners, his body trapped behind a wall, long deceased. Was his death the seed of the haunting? Or was there something before his arrival? The Crains also see countless phantoms of past inhabitants gather in the main proscenium of Hill House in one of the last episodes. The house seems to be acting as a kind of soul trap, or purgatory.

Conclusion

Mike Flanagan's addition to the lore of *The Haunting of Hill House* hits all the hallmarks of the tradition of Gothic storytelling going back to the late 1700s while bringing the mythology into modern sensibilities. The story employs so many defining elements of gothic storytelling from a haunted dwelling with hidden rooms and passages, to characters witnessing ghosts and supernatural phenomena, from family secrets to the deterioration of both house and household, *The Haunting of Hill House* is a tragic, dark story about the decay of a family from the madness that was bestowed upon them, and the reverberations it caused the Crain family over generations. In a last commonly held theme of gothic storytelling that ties *The Haunting of Hill House* back to the very beginnings of the genre, the tale ends on a positive note—one where the future holds promise of living, healing, and perhaps prospering after making it through the heartbreaking and threatening curses, and to look ahead to lives centered around hope, having learned the darkness is only a few lonesome corridors away, lurking, waiting, and watching.

Notes

1. Horace Walpole, *The Castle of Ortranto* (London: Penguin Classics, 2001); Ann Radcliffe, *The Mysteries of Udolpho* (London: Penguin Classics, 2001). See also Jennifer Laredo's essay in this volume.
2. Matthew Lewis, *The Monk* (London: Penguin Classics, 1998); Shirley Jackson, *The Haunting of Hill House* (London: Penguin Classics, 2006).
3. For a fascinating explanation as to why Victorian mansions have become the defacto gothic structure in the United States, see Coleman Lowndes' video essay "Why the Victorian Mansion Is a Horror Icon" https://www.vox.com/videos/2018/11/13/18092400/victorian-mansion-horror-icon (November 13, 2018).
4. Ann Radcliffe, *The Italian* (London: Penguin Classics, 2001).
5. Daphne Du Maurier, *Jamaica Inn* (New York: Harper Collins, 2016).

6. *Rosemary's Baby* (Polanski, Roman, William Castle, Mia Farrow, John Cassavetes, Ruth Gordon, Sidney Blackmer, Maurice Evans, et al. 2006. *Rosemary's Baby*. Hollywood, Calif: Paramount Pictures).
7. Shirley Jackson, *We Have Always Lived in the Castle* (London: Penguin Classics, 2006).
8. Mary Shelley, *Frankenstein, or the Modern Prometheus* (London: Penguin, 2007).

About the Contributors

Camille S. **Alexander** is an assistant professor of English literature. She completed her Ph.D. in English at the University of Kent. Her research interests include Caribbean studies and literature; African, African American, and Black British literature; American film; and third-wave feminism. She is researching manifestations of Indian culture in Indo-Trinidadian literature and symbols of the divine feminine in Trinidadian culture.

Matt **Bernico** is an assistant professor of communication and media studies at Greenville University. He published a collection of essays on the digital humanities called *Ontic Flows: From Digital Humanities to Posthumanities*. His primary interests are media studies, media archeology, and popular culture.

Thomas **Britt** is an associate professor in the Film and Video Studies Program at George Mason University. He is the head of the screenwriting concentration and teaches Ethics of Film and Video and Global Horror Film. His essays have appeared in several journals and edited collections. He is a staff writer and columnist for *PopMatters*.

Christa **Carmen**'s work has been featured in myriad anthologies, ezines, and podcasts, including *Fireside Fiction*, *Year's Best Hardcore Horror*, *Outpost 28*, and *Tales to Terrify*. Her debut collection, *Something Borrowed, Something Blood-Soaked*, won the 2018 Indie Horror Book Award for Best Debut Collection. You can find her online at www.christacarmen.com.

Elsa M. **Carruthers** is a speculative fiction writer, academic, and poet. She earned an MFA in creative writing and English from Seton Hill University. Her work has been published in several anthologies and magazines, and she has presented papers at ICFA, IVFAF, and AnnRadCon. She is an active member of HWA and regularly attends writing and academic conventions. She is editing a collection of essays on *Westworld*.

Adam **Daniel** is a member of the Writing and Society Research Centre at Western Sydney University. His research investigates the evolution of horror film, with a focus on the intersection of embodied spectatorship and new media technologies. He is the vice-president of the Sydney Screen Studies Network, and the author of

Affective Intensities and Evolving Horror Forms, scheduled for 2020 publication from Edinburgh University Press.

Maria **Giakaniki** is an independent scholar and co-owner/editor in chief of Ars Nocturna, a small publishing house in Athens that focuses on Gothic fiction. She is the coeditor of *Bending to Earth: Strange Stories by Irish Women* (Swan River Press, 2019), as well as the uncanny woman in film. Her research interests center around gothic and supernatural fiction by Victorian and first half of the 20th century women writers. You can reach her at mariayiakaniki@yahoo.gr.

Brandon R. **Grafius** is an assistant professor of biblical studies at Ecumenical Theological Seminary in Detroit. His first book, *Reading Phinehas, Watching Slashers*, was published by Lexington Books/Fortress Academic in 2018, and his second book, *Reading the Bible with Horror*, is forthcoming from the same publisher.

Aaron K.H. **Ho** has taught at universities in New York, China, and Singapore; and contributed on gender and sexuality in various journals and books. Although most of his publications focus on media studies, he has also worked on the Victorian period and Asian Anglophone literature. He is editing a book about witches in twenty-first century television.

Rhonda Jackson **Joseph** is a Texan writer/professor and a life-long horror fan and writer. She mostly enjoys writing creatively and academically about the intersections of race and gender in the horror genre.

Melissa A. **Kaufler** writes about Gothic pop culture, hauntology, and the many iterations of *Frankenstein* in film and literature through a feminist-Marxist lens. She earned an MA in Gothic culture from St. Mary's University in London and has deferred pursuit of a Ph.D. in cultural studies in order to work for the California Legislature.

Dawn **Keetley** is a professor of English and film at Lehigh University. She is editor of two collections on *The Walking Dead* (McFarland, 2014, 2018), coeditor of *Plant Horror* (Palgrave, 2016) and *The Ecogothic in Nineteenth-Century American Literature* (Routledge, 2017), and author of *Making a Monster: Jesse Pomeroy, the Boy Murderer of 1870s Boston* (University of Massachusetts Press, 2017). She is working on a collection on Jordan Peele's *Get Out* and a book on folk horror.

Dana Jeanne **Keller** completed her MA in film studies at the University of British Columbia, where she specialized in documentary-style horror and digital folklore (with her thesis on *Marble Hornets*, the Slender Man, and the emergence of folk horror in online communities). She works as a fiction editor in Berlin, Germany, and is independently researching occult and horror narratives across literary, cinematic, and post-cinematic media.

Jeanette A. **Laredo** (@monsterscholar) is a scholar of all things awful, including 18th-century British Gothic literature and Victorian horror. She is interested in trauma, literary and cinematic monsters, horror films, and how digital tools can help us understand the dark specters of our past.

Alex **Link** is an associate professor and the associate vice president of Academic Affairs at the Alberta University of the Arts. He is co-author, with Riley Rossmo,

About the Contributors 269

of the horror comics *Rebel Blood* and *Drumhellar*, has published articles in *The Journal of Popular Culture*, *Contemporary Literature*, and *Gothic Studies*, and has published chapters in books such as *Animal Comics* (Blackwell) and the forthcoming *Violence in Comics: Volume 1* (Routledge).

Steve **Marsden** is a professor of American literature at Stephen F. Austin State University in Nacogdoches, Texas. He has published on the racialized use of ghost stories by Thomas Nelson Page and Paul Dunbar, and written and presented on the ghost stories of Ambrose Bierce. He teaches (among other things) American Gothic literature and film adaptation.

Angie **Martin** is a multi-award-winning author who relies on her Kansas upbringing to add a certain Midwest, small-town creepiness to her work. She has released several novels and short stories in thriller and horror genres, some with a unique paranormal or supernatural edge. She resides in Calimesa, California, where she is working hard and losing sleep over her latest nightmarish novel.

Fernando Gabriel **Pagnoni Berns** (Ph.D. student) works as a professor at the Universidad de Buenos Aires (UBA)–Facultad de Filosofía y Letras (Argentina). He teaches courses on international horror film and has published chapters in the books *To See the Saw Movies*, edited by John Wallis, *Critical Insights*, edited by Douglas Cunningham, *Gender and Environment in Science Fiction*, edited by Christy Tidwell, among others. He is working on a book about the Spanish horror TV series *Historias para no Dormir*.

John **Palisano** is the author of *Dust of the Dead*, *Ghost Heart*, *Nerves*, *Night of 1000 Beasts*, *Starlight Drive: Four Halloween Tales*, and his first short fiction collection, *All That Withers*. He won the Bram Stoker Award in short fiction in 2016 for "Happy Joe's Rest Stop." His nonfiction is serving as the president of the Horror Writers Association and can be reached at: www.johnpalisano.com.

Melania **Paszek** is pursuing a Master's degree in English and American studies at the University of Graz, Austria. Her MA thesis is titled, "Hawkins versus the Upside Down: Conveying Intertextuality and the Retro Aesthetic in *Stranger Things*." Her research interests include cinema and television, contemporary literature (predominantly American) and popular culture in general.

Emily E. **Roach** is a doctoral candidate in the Department of English and Related Literature at the University of York in England. She researches transgender performance poetry on YouTube, contemporary LGBT American poetry and fiction, queering popular culture and large internet fandoms. She has published on Harry Potter, *Stranger Things* and pop music and has forthcoming articles on *Supernatural*.

Zachary **Sheldon** is a doctoral student in the Department of Communication at Texas A&M University. His research interests include digital media and religion, religious cinema, philosophy of cinema, and popular culture.

Tim **Waggoner** has published close to fifty novels and seven collections of short stories. He writes original dark fantasy and horror, as well as media tie-ins, and his articles on writing have appeared in numerous publications. He has won the Bram

Stoker Award and been a finalist for the Shirley Jackson Award, the Scribe Award, and the Splatterpunk Award. He's also a full-time tenured professor who teaches creative writing and composition at Sinclair Community College in Dayton, Ohio.

Kevin J. **Wetmore**, Jr., is the Bram Stoker Award–nominated editor of *Uncovering Stranger Things* and a dozen other volumes, as well as the author of such books as *Post-9/11 Horror in American Cinema*, *Back from the Dead: Reading Remakes of Romero's Zombie Films as Markers of Their Times*, and *The Theology of Battlestar Galactica*. He is also the author of over five dozen book chapters on topics from Godzilla to ghosts to exorcism films to Catholic horror to Lovecraft and the stage. He is a professor at Loyola Marymount University.

Elizabeth Laura **Yomantas** is an assistant professor in the Department of Humanities and Teacher Education at Pepperdine University in Malibu, California. She teaches in the teacher preparation program and thoroughly enjoys her work with pre-service educators. Her research interests include teacher education, indigenous Fijian education, culturally responsive curricula, and critical pedagogy.

Index

Absentia 82
Altman, Robert 76
The Amityville Horror 31, 98
Aster, Ari 8, 211, 216
Aux Dog Theatre 255

Bachelard, Gaston 39, 40, 51, 53, 54; *Poetics of Space* 40, 51, 53
Before I Wake 30, 76, 80, 82
Bennett, Jane 96
Bent-Neck Lady 6, 7, 9, 10, 35, 67, 69, 70, 81, 102, 114, 118, 120, 121, 134–137, 145, 146, 147, 150, 158, 160, 167, 173, 174, 178, 179, 181, 182, 194, 214, 216, 230, 237, 238, 239, 246, 249, 250, 262, 264
Bisham Manor 41
The Blob 236
The Boogey Man 31
Borley Rectory 16
Bowler Hat Man 9, 56, 68, 249
Bush, George W. 75, 76, 79, 80, 81, 159

The Chilling Adventures of Sabrina (television series) 28
Chomsky, Noam 74
City Lit Theatre 253, 255
The Conjuring 236
Cooper, Claire 103
Crichton, Michael 28; *Westworld* 28
Crimson Peak 166

De Bont, Jan 2, 15, 19, 21, 23, 253–254
Deleuze, Gilles 5, 39, 42, 43–48
Del Toro, Guillermo 166
Derrida, Jacques 65, 74, 129, 130, 143, 179; *Spectographies* 143; *Spectres of Marx* 129
Die Hard 5, 76, 79
Disney's Haunted Mansion 254
Don't Look Now 236
Drag Me to Hell 236

Eddings, Nelson 18
Eliade, Mircea 99

Flanagan, Mike 2–10, 15, 23, 24, 27–28, 29, 30–31, 34, 35, 36, 41, 42, 51, 55, 56, 57, 58, 71–72, 75, 76–82, 95, 103, 104, 107, 108, 109, 110, 112, 114, 115, 116, 130, 131, 133, 134, 135, 136, 137, 140, 142, 143, 146, 189, 190, 191, 192, 210, 211, 213, 233, 234, 241, 248, 249, 250, 251, 252, 253, 254, 256, 258, 260, 265
Fodor, Nandor 18
Ford, Christine Blasey 8, 235
Foucault, Michel 29, 233, 240
Franklin, Ruth 11, 16, 18, 24
Freire, Paulo 86, 93; *Pedagogy of the Oppressed* 93
Freud, Sigmund 66, 76, 97, 148

Gerald's Game (film) 2, 30, 76, 80, 81, 196
"The Ghosts of Loiret" 16; *The Haunting of Hill House* (novel) 1, 2, 3, 29, 31, 41, 63, 72, 81, 95, 107, 108; *The Lottery* 256–257; *We Have Always Lived in the Castle* 257, 260, 261, 263
Glamis Castle 16
Goodrich-Freer, Amy 16, 19, 20, 24; *The Alleged Haunting of B— House* 16, 17, 24,
The Gothic 3, 5, 9, 16, 18, 29, 42, 63–65, 72, 122, 135, 148, 155, 156, 178, 184, 185, 189–190, 195, 212, 221, 231, 258–265
Guattari, Félix 5, 39, 42–48

Håfström, Mikael 22
The Haunting (film) 2, 15, 19, 22, 41, 42, 109
The Haunting of Hill House (1999 film) 2, 253, 15, 19, 41, 42
The Haunting of Hill House (stage play) 253, 254, 255
The Haunting of Hill House (television series) 2–3, 5, 6, 7, 8, 15, 22, 27, 28, 29, 32–35, 41, 47, 48, 50, 51, 53, 60, 63, 64
hauntology 6, 35, 128, 129, 130–131, 138, 140, 142, 179
Hawthorne, Nathaniel 156; *The House of Seven Gables* 156

Index

Hereditary 8, 211, 212, 215–221
Hill, Anita 8, 235, 242
Hill, Susan 254; *The Woman in Black* 254
hooks, bell 93
Hush 2, 80, 81

Inception 8, 190, 197–198
Insidious 64

Jackson, Shirley 1, 2, 3
James, M.R. 16

Kairo 8, 190, 192–195, 198
Kavanaugh, Brett 235, 236, 239–241
King, Stephen 1, 2, 3, 22, 51, 111, 256; *Danse Macabre* 256; *1408* 22, 23
Kübler-Ross, Elisabeth 99, 102; *On Death and Dying* 99
Kwaidan 8, 190–192, 198

Leslie, F. Andrew 253
Levin, Ira 259; *Rosemary's Baby* 259
Lewis, Matthew 258, 260; *The Monk* 259, 260, 262
Liverpool Playwright 253, 255
Lost (television series) 144
Lovecraft, Howard Phillips 115; "The Shunned House" 115

Mailer, Norman 76
Mallatrat, Stephen 254–255
Marx, Karl 44
Matheson, Richard 128; *Bid Time Return* 128
McQueen, Steve 236
Milgram, Stanley 20
Mirror, Mirror 31
Morrison, Toni 8, 200–210; *Beloved* 8, 201–210

Netflix 2, 4, 5, 7, 8, 9, 10, 24, 28, 30, 51, 63, 64, 95, 97, 103, 104, 107, 118, 130, 142, 155, 156, 166, 169, 174, 176, 177, 180, 190, 198, 200, 213, 222, 231, 237, 245, 248, 253, 262, 263
9/11 5, 74–83, 133

Oculus 2, 5, 27–35, 76, 82, 249
Oculus, Chapter 3: The Man with the Plan 30
El Orfanato 8, 190, 195–197, 198, 236
Ouija: Origin of Evil 2, 76

The Passage 76
Pepper's Ghost 254
phenomenology 39, 51–54
Poe, Edgar Allan 41, 156; "The Cast of Amontillado" 41; "Fall of the House of Usher" 156
Poltergeist 99
Psycho 78

Radcliffe, Ann 258, 260, 263; *The Italian* 260; *The Mysteries of Udolpho* 258, 260, 263
Raimi, Sam 236
Roëg, Nicholas 236

Sagan, Carl 87
St. Aubyn, Astrid 22; *Ghostly Encounters* 22
Saw 76
Shakespeare, William 6, 87, 128, 130; *Hamlet* 87; *Richard II* 128
Shelley, Mary 81, 264; *Frankenstein* 81, 261, 264
The Shining 98, 236
The Silence of the Lambs 80
Sontag, Susan 74
Stanford Prison Experiment 20
Supernatural (television series) 8, 222–231

terrorism 75, 76, 77, 79, 80, 81, 82, 83
Texas Chainsaw Massacre 80
To Catch a Thief 184
Thomas, Clarence 235
"torture porn" 76
trauma 4, 5, 6, 8, 24, 30, 32, 39, 47, 48, 63–72, 74–83, 92, 96, 98, 99, 101, 103, 119, 124, 173, 184, 195, 200, 211, 217, 229, 235, 237, 239, 241

Walpole, Horace 64, 258, 259; *The Castle of Otranto* 64, 258, 259, 260, 262
Weinstein, Harvey 8, 234
Winchester Mystery House 22
Wise, Robert 2, 15, 18, 24, 107, 108–109, 253–256

X-Files 21

Zimbardo, Philip 20
Zombies 75, 82

www.ingramcontent.com/pod-product-compliance
Lightning Source LLC
Chambersburg PA
CBHW032034300426
44117CB00009B/1050